中国传统教育文化研译

理念与箴言

严明　俞越　著

東華大學出版社·上海

图书在版编目（CIP）数据

中国传统教育文化研译：理念与箴言 / 严明，俞越著. —上海：东华大学出版社，2024.2

ISBN 978-7-5669-2325-7

I. ①中… II. ①严… ②俞… III. ①教育学—文化学—研究—中国 IV. ① G40-055

中国国家版本馆 CIP 数据核字（2024）第 036092 号

中国传统教育文化研译：理念与箴言

严　明　俞　越　著

责任编辑：周慧慧
封面设计：冯林晔　Tina

出版发行：东华大学出版社
社　　址：上海市延安西路 1882 号，200051
出版社官网：http://dhupress.dhu.edu.cn/
天猫旗舰店：http://dhdx.tmall.com
发行电话：021-62373056
营销中心：021-62193056　62373056　62379558

印　　刷：上海龙腾印务有限公司
开　　本：787 mm×1092 mm　1/16
印　　张：19
字　　数：489 千字
版　　次：2024 年 2 月第 1 版　2024 年 2 月第 1 次印刷

ISBN 978-7-5669-2325-7
定价：78.00 元

序

多年来，我一直推崇柏拉图助产婆式的教育理念，也一直践行这一理念，而对操练式、填鸭式的教育方式，很不以为然。在课堂上、在聊天时我常把这类操练式、填鸭式的教育定义为“反教育”。近年来我致力于经史子集的英译，也常接触古人的教育思想。当拿到严明教授发给我的《中国传统教育文化研译：理念与箴言》书稿，便感到从宏阔的历史中吹来了教育的智慧之风。因此，能为这本书撰写序言，我深感荣幸。

这本书是严明教授和俞越校长共同努力的结晶。她们以深厚的学识和敏锐的洞察力，对中国传统教育文化进行了深入研究和精彩解读，完成了这部助益当下外语教育与教育文化传播的杰作。我所认识的严明是语言教育的专家，但我更看重的，是她作为诗人的情怀，而其诗中又多有禅意。有了这样的心境，她自然能够领悟到教育的本质。

这本书分为上下两篇，相互补益、相互印证。上篇“传统观念识悟”，从中国文化的基本要略，到中国教育的文化基础，再到中国学府的文化性格，以及中国教育的文化览胜，深入浅出地揭示了中国传统教育文化的精髓。下篇“教育箴言赏析”，则从学派思想选读，到经典名言拾味，再到名人家训举隅，以及大学校训简览，生动展现了中国传统教育文化的多维空间和丰富内涵。在全球化的今天，中国传统教育文化的价值和意义愈发凸显。它不仅是中外读者理解中国历史和社会的重要途径，也是我们构建和谐社会，推动社会进步的重要资源。这本书正是在这样的背景下应运而生，它旨在通过深入研究及解读外译，让更多的人了解和理解中国传统教育文化，从而更好地传承、发扬和传播这一宝贵的文化遗产。

严明教授和俞越校长精心甄别，为我们勾勒了中国传统教育文化的精髓和内涵。她们的研究不仅深入，而且全面；不仅有理论，而且有实践；不仅传承历史，而且面对现实，展望未来，为我们理解和欣赏中国传统教育文化提供了一个全新的视角。这本书是一部研究中国传统教育文化的重要著作，也是一部传播中国传统教育文化的重要工具。我相信，无论是对中国传统教育文化感兴趣的读者，还是从事相关研究的学者，都会从这本书中获益良多。

在此，我们要感谢严明教授和俞越校长的辛勤努力，她们的研究及翻译为读者打开了一扇通向中国传统教育文化深邃世界的大门。我们也要感谢所有参与出版本书的人，他们的工作使得这本书能够顺利面世。我期待这本书能够引起广大读者的关注和热议，能够摆到学者的案头，能够走进课堂，由此推动中国传统教育文化的研究和传播。

最后，我再一次真诚地向所有热爱中国人文精神和教育文化的读者推荐这本书。我相信，无论你是对中国传统教育文化有浓厚兴趣的读者，还是从事相关研究的学者，都会从这本书中获得深深的启发和丰富的收获。让我们一起，通过研读这本书，深入理解和欣赏中国传统教育文化的魅力，共同传承和发扬这一宝贵的文化遗产。

2023 年 6 月 22 日于美兰湖

前言

在教育竞争国际化的今天，人文学科中的“跨文化传播力”在中国文化“走出去”的背景下逐渐成为关键词。从文化圈“文化认同是最深层次的认同”的共识，到翻译界“文化转向”的觉醒，再到外语界“语言结合教育”的教育语言学学科发展，都使得“中国人文精神”与“文化传播”成为当代并驾齐驱的热点。然迄今为止“微观量化实验”和“语言学本位”的主流研究所导致的人文学科自然科学化，深刻揭示了教育界“道之情怀”让位于“器之工具”的倾向；同时由于我国跨文化教育目标刚刚从“了解世界文化的国际视野”转向“弘扬中国文化的国际价值”，故而本土教育文化“自上而下的课题研究”仍多于“自下而上的解析推广”，求新的跟风西方模仿犹热于传统的本土挖掘传承。因此，中国传统教育文化的质性研究及其跨文化跨学科的传播亟待加强与深化。

了解一方文明的最好途径是解读其传统教育文化之精髓。作为融合教育语言学理念与文化外译的探索研究，也作为高校课程思政与民办教育实践的合作成果，本书着眼于中国传统教育文化的传承与研译，将中国传统教育的千年沉淀与万里风物通过植根于华夏大地的文化理念与教育箴言以双语形式系统呈现给中外读者。上篇“传统理念识悟”由“中国文化的基本要略”“中国教育的文化基础”“中国学府的文化性格”“中国教育的文化览胜”四章组成；下篇“教育箴言赏析”由“学派思想选读”“经典名言拾味”“名人家训举隅”“大学校训简览”四章组成。全书模块设计基于中国传统教育文化的高频话题、著名人物、经典著作与传世文献，虽无法面面俱到、涵盖所有，但力图博观约取、彰显精华，有理念也有实例，有反思更有弘扬。整体采用教育学、文化学、语言学的跨学科视角，通过文献梳理、归纳思辨及翻译实践，采用以点带面、点面结合的方式，以顺应文化汇通时代之呼声与传统人文习得之市场需求。在向中外读者展析传统教育文化精髓画卷的同时，着重凝练四大特色：理念与箴言的双向融合、语言与文化的双科视角、学术与通识的双重定位、外语与教育的双效实践。因此撰著的基本原则是：

1. 以历史为线索，还原中国文化的传统足迹。
2. 以经典为核心，凝练中国教育的千年精华。

3. 以双语为载体，呈现本土教育的多彩元素。

4. 以科学为依据，梳理权威文献的重要主题。

千年华夏，物类万千；真知灼见，层出不穷；政通人和，教化无尽。文化共荣方兴未艾，侪辈幸逢盛世，始得放眼塞北，览景江南，前游细数，旧史重温。观中国教育文化历史长河之深幽洞远，如俯瞰苍茫悠旷之中华大地，缀以无数睿智心灵与绚丽华章，遂悟红尘无常而学海有恒。拙笔虽如雪泥鸿爪，却愿力绘教育风貌于一斑，孜求折射出本土人文的一抹亮色。行文至此，心生感慨，抬眸远眺，云淡风轻。付梓在即，思绪万千，谨以拙句几笔表达此时此刻的所思所见，寄语杏坛同仁的不倦耕心：

览景案前

碧芽入盏暗香闻，一笔心泉涌未休。

谁隔寒窗催皓鬓，春来依旧笑枝头。

多谢著名学者兼翻译家上海大学赵彦春教授的拨冗赠序与悉心指点，每次交流我们都能感受到他诗意教育的启迪，从中领悟文化外译的力量；也感谢东华大学出版社编辑老师们的辛勤付出；更感恩在拙著成型过程中所有给予帮助支持的善缘，是你们在此信息爆炸、技术潮涌、竞争激烈、物质丰盈的时代，与无数普通教育工作者一起，依然呵护着传统文化中无法量化的人文情怀，共同传承着中国教育中美德与诗意的内涵。拙著虽无奢望成为华夏人文精神家园中的参天一木，但期能衬作摇曳其间的苇草一叶，陪伴中西读者穿越时空对话贤哲，静心体悟教育本真，继而共同仰望神州大地上文教星空的无限璀璨。

学海无涯，文不厌改，水平有限，疏漏难免，诚以广大读者不吝指正为感。

著者 2023.06

于上海奉贤海湾大学城

目　录

上篇　传统理念识悟

下篇　教育箴言赏析

上篇

传统理念识悟

第一章　中国文化的基本要略

中国文化是世界上最古老的文化之一，至少有五千年的历史。中国文化所涵盖的地理范围主要在东亚地区，其传统与习俗在各省市和城镇之间都不尽相同，其饶有特色的文化元素包括陶瓷、建筑、文学、武术、烹饪、戏曲、哲学及宗教。中国文化的发展脉络离不开地缘环境、民族历史和社会传统的影响，同时这些元素反过来也深深影响着中国传统教育文化的形成。

第一节　环境与文化初态

任何文化都有其发源地和文化初态，文化发源地的最初特征往往决定了特定文化的成型。文化的本质是自然的人化，华夏地区的地理环境与生存格局形成了中国传统文化的丰富性、独特性和连续性。本节主要从大河文明与宗族制度两个方面阐述中国传统文化的自然与社会特征。

一、大河文明

考古学证实，中华文明的起源是在黄河的中下游地区，尤其是在今天的陕西、河南一带，因此黄河也被称为中华民族的母亲河。但同时，中华文化是多元发生的，是多民族和多向度融合产生的，文化多元发生的自然基础是土地辽阔、地貌多元所形成的河流纵横、南北各异的地理环境。大江大河对中华农耕文明的产生起到了决定作用：黄河流域的仰韶文化、大汶口文化、龙山文化、二里头文化；长江流域的河姆渡文化、三星堆文化；还有辽河流域的红山文化，都是大江大河孕育出中华农耕文明初态的印证。[1]

轴心时代形成的世界诸古文明，多已消弭在历史长河之中，唯有中华文明于起伏跌宕间传承不辍，其重要原因之一是中国领域广阔、地理形势错综复杂，存在平行互补的两个大河文化：雄浑的黄河文化、清奇的长江文化，所谓“北峻南婕，北肃南舒，北强南秀，北僿南华”。当黄河流域因垦殖过度、气候干冷、胡马南征等缘故而导致文明衰落之际，长江流域后来居上，焕发其优越的自然禀赋，成为粮食财富的主要供应区和人文胜地。又因黄河流域邻近游牧区，一旦长城被游牧人群突破，“长江天堑”便成为一道天然防线，拥有巨大经济、文化潜力的长江流域为华夏文明提供退守、复兴的基地。经由长江文化对黄河文化的承接与创造性发挥，中华文化之精义得以保持

[1] 严明．中西文化风物志 [M]．上海：上海交通大学出版社，2018，2-6。

与光大，两条大河的滋养与回护是中华文明数千年间延绵伸展、从未终绝的原因之一。

中国独特的大河文明为农耕经济提供了天然的平台，因此长期以来农业是中国文化发展的基础，也是华夏社会最早出现的产业。中国伴随着大河文明的农耕经济是随着社会分工的发展而发展的，社会大分工的深化将农业进一步细分为种植业和畜牧业，又分化为多系统、多层次的产业结构，这也深深影响着民族文化的发展。在如此幅员辽阔的疆土上，传统的中国文化在每一片区域通常又分成不同的亚文化群，且都有不同的传统文化器物与象征，因而有句话称“十里不同风，百里不同俗”。

二、宗族制度

宗族是理解中国社会的一个重要视角。宗族是指有血缘关系的人聚族而居，并有组织地参加祭祀活动的一个社会共同体。一般情况下，族长管理祭祀活动，作为祭祀场所的祠堂发挥着核心作用。随着中国古代封建社会的发展，族权与中央王权势力的此消彼长，特别是族长所代表的阶级利益及阶层利益的转变，使宗族制度在不同历史时期呈现出不同的特质。[1]

构成宗族的基本要素有四：一是父系血缘关系系统的人员关系；二是以家庭为基本单位；三是聚族而居或有相对稳定的居住区；四是有组织原则、组织机构和领导人进行管理。有血缘关系的人相互之间可称为族人，但是否成为一个宗族，要看其是否有组织。这一组织就体现在要有一个共同祭祀祖先的场所：祠堂。从周朝至清朝，根据族长身份的变化可将中国宗族发展史大致划分为先秦、汉唐、宋元及明清四个阶段。

中国自古以来绵延的宗族制度文化与其和谐、稳定、传承与团结的社会理想密不可分。这种族长制的宗族制度与家族伦理成为中国古代长久的最具特色的文化特质。在中国古代，宗族制度曾在秦朝遭到革除，但是在汉朝的上层家族中又重新出现并在唐朝的普通家庭中演化盛行。人们普遍相信这种崇尚等级性的宗族制度在提升社会中人们的信任与合作上起到了辅助作用。宗族规约可以使人们自觉地参与集体行为并同时影响统治阶层的决策。从这个意义上来说，中国宗族制度是稳定与延续两千年封建政治统治的有利因素。

第二节　历史与民族特征

中国历史源远流长，就像一条奔腾的大河，同时也在大河两岸孕育出多彩的风景。而中国历史上的民族发展有其鲜明的特点，中华文明被历史证实具有某种特殊的凝聚力并得以延续千年，这与这个民族的精神结构和思维方式有密切关系。本节将从华夏文明的历史轨迹和民族性格两方面进行述略。

[1] 谢爽．中国古代宗族制发展趋势述论［J］．黑河学院学报，2014(3):97-99。

一、历史轨迹

总体而言，中国文化作为独立的文明发展体系有着清晰的演进轨迹，它呈现出以中原地区为核心，经过多元的发展而成为具有渗透性与包容性的文化。[1] 正如上文所述，被大河文明滋养的华夏祖先伴随着农业经济的发展从古代农耕群体进入了一个新的文明时代，宗族族长们也转型成了以各种权利为中心的统治阶层。这种家族裙带与管理体系渐渐融入了潜在的社会机构中，形成了人际关系，群体生活和权力集中的一股向心之力。

依靠着进步的生产力、生产模式以及团结精神，中国古代创造了以四大发明为标识的灿烂文明，在相当长的时期里引领着世界。夏商周时期代表着中国早期国家与青铜器文明时期。春秋战国时期则见证了中国大地上的诸侯争霸与各种社会变革。到了秦汉时期，华夏出现了统一的大国。在魏晋南北朝时期，中国经历了政权分裂与民族大融合。隋唐时期，中国历史上迎来了最繁荣与开放的时代。宋元是一个多元文化碰撞和社会经济大发展的特殊时期。进入明清之后，中国既延续了农耕文明的繁荣又遭遇了鸦片战争与现代变革前的危机。鸦片战争打破了中国独自发展的走向，中国遭到西方列强的凌辱与侵略，被迫签订了一系列不平等条约并割地赔款，从此逐步成为半殖民地半封建社会。鸦片战争后，近一个世纪的反帝反封建反官僚资本主义的斗争，中国继续发展着民族产业与文化。孙中山领导的推翻清政府的辛亥革命使得民主共和的理念深入人心。而后无产阶级领导的新民主革命，彻底完成革命的任务，并及时实现由新民主主义向社会主义的过渡。

一九四九年的十月一日，中华人民共和国成立了，从此开创了中国走向社会主义现代化的新纪元。在经历了曲折探索之后，中国走上了加强民主法治建设、建立社会主义市场经济、积极参与国际竞争与合作的具有中国特色的改革开放之路，正力图努力建设一个可持续发展的富强、民主、有文化的和谐社会。[2]

二、民族性格

民族性格是一个民族共同的精神结构和思行方式。中华民族在几千年的发展过程中形成了其独特的民族性格。这种性格特征的形成受到了上古神话、儒家思想，以及地缘文化的多元影响。可以说，这三者是中华民族性格形成的内在基因，时过千年却割不断它们之间延续、发展的关系。

2.1 上古神话

首先，在中国人的传统性格里存在着敬神之心。先民创造的诸神神话在鼓舞敬畏自然，激发知恩图报、锲而不舍的民族性格方面起到了显著的作用。上古神话中还给我

[1] 史澎涛．中原文化的内涵与特征略论［J］．芒种，2015(2):105-106。
[2] 曹大为，孙燕京．中国历史［M］．北京：五洲传播出版社，2010:197-210。

们塑造了许多具有高尚道德的神。他们历尽艰险，救万民于水火之中，没有丝毫个人的私心。比如炼石补天的女娲、教民农作遍尝百草的神农、为开天地而身死的盘古、具有强烈反抗精神的刑天，都体现了先民在强大自然面前吃苦耐劳、勤恳无私的不屈性格。[1]

2.2 儒家思想

其次，儒家思想对中华民族性格影响深远。体察人类最普遍的伦理道德是儒家思想中的主要部分，而这种伦理道德是建立在等级制度基础之上的，表现在仁、义、礼、智、信几个方面。一方面，受这种思想的影响，华夏民族学会了克己复礼、忍辱负重、内敛自省。在形成重义轻利、刚正不阿的性格的同时，也习惯于安贫乐道与中庸谨慎，诚服于社会规约及官本位的等级思想；另一方面，儒家很关心社会现实，忧国忧民，把人生价值同国家、民族的兴衰联系在一起，这使得中国知识分子具有较强的历史使命感和社会责任感。

2.3 地缘文化

再次，受地缘文化的影响，中华民族形成了以南方为代表的农耕文化以及以北方为代表的游牧文化，南牛和北马则是二者文化的象征符号。[2] 中国历史上的南北民族与牛马关系密切，“南牛北马”的比喻所蕴含的是中华民族的性格写真。中国从春秋开始有了牛拉犁的技术，在以农业为主要生产方式的南方，牛是人们生计的主要帮手，受到善待和尊崇。在农耕民族看来，牛如同自己的衣食父母 ，牛的品格就是农民的品格。中国人常以牛自喻自励，儒家的修身术的实质，也是以牛为范，如孔子的弟子冉耕，字子牛。在近代，中国人也还是把牛作为人的精神楷模。鲁迅有“俯首甘为孺子牛”之句。在北方，马是游牧民族生活内容的核心。蒙古族、藏族和前期的满族都是游牧文化的代表，自古就有祭马的风俗。对马的崇拜还存在于包括汉族在内的许多民族在内的理念和民间活动中。各种散见于神话和俗语中的马都有着特殊的象征意义，包括神圣、辟邪、权威、天君、灵魂使者、祭物和吉祥等多方面。“龙马精神”这一习语足见“马”的地位可与民族图腾相提并论。总之，中国南北民族的文化个性，无不具有牛与马吃苦耐劳和勇往直前的精神和性格，牛和马也成了中华民族魂的象征。

由此可见，中国各民族在长期的交往融合过程中，受上古神话、儒家思想和地缘文化的影响，互相补充、互相促进，形成了中华民族的多元互补的总体性格：知恩图报、敬畏自然而又坚强不屈；温良恭顺、克己复礼而又胸怀大志；吃苦耐劳勤劳、朴实而又勇往直前。

[1] 付海艳．从上古神话看中华民族性格之形成 [J]．西安文理学院学报，2011(4):28-30。
[2] 刘永红．南牛北马——中国民族性格的象征 [J]．语文学刊，2009(6):128-132。

第三节 传统与社会体系

一个地区的文化发展离不开它根深蒂固的传统观念和社会体系，也具体反映在社会各群体成员的生活态度与方式之中。中国“家国同构”的社会传统，成为主流文化理念的政治基础，也构成了传统中国社会以伦理为核心的社会价值体系。这种文化理念强调中心主义与和谐为上，而这种社会体系则由血缘关系与良知体系构成。

一、中心主义与和谐为上

中心主义与和谐为上的理念共同构成了中国社会的传统结构和发展模式。历朝历代的更替发展与奋斗理想都围绕着这样的传统体系建构并轮回着，这一传统理念也影响着历代的教育思想。

1.1 中心主义

回溯中国文化传统，可以发现中国的“中心主义”文化源远流长。早在中华民族刚刚进步到文明的边沿，就形成了“一个祖先，一个权力，一个核心”的传统。“中心主义”文化认为“多中心”是祸乱的根源。荀子说：“隆一而治，二而乱。自古及今，未有二隆争重而能长久者。”中国传统社会从未设想过多元横向的权力关系和结构，他们的共同倾向是把权力关系完全纵向化，最终权力都集中于君主一人手中，从而使权力结构和运行方式单向化。在纵向上，从“中心主义”权力原点出发形成的权力结构是单向放射型的，在下者绝对服从在上者，“无从下之政上，必从上之政下”。[1] 中国传统社会的“中心主义”文化塑造了中国人重“中心”的思维传统，也引发了中国人求“中心”、重“集中”的价值取向，事物总要有一个中心才能符合中国人的传统习惯，连国家也冠以“中国”之名。宋人石介[2]的《中国论》说：“居天地之中者曰中国。”“中国”“中华”，即天下之中之意。中国人在自然与社会生活中也有着深刻的“中心主义”文化痕迹。自然界中的“天”、寰宇中的“日”、方位中的“中”、万物中的“金”、家庭中的“父”、百兽中的“龙”、五脏之中的“心”、五音之中的“宫”、数字中的“九”，这都是中国“中心主义”的价值取向和思维方式的反映。[3]

1.2 和谐为上

回顾我国社会传统，不难发现以德礼治天下的和谐理念深入人心。最典型的是《周易》把自然完美的和谐叫作“太和”。儒家传统继承发扬了这一理念，认为“太和”观念包含着普遍和谐的意义。王夫之曾说，“太和，和之至也”“未有形器之先，本无不和，

[1] 方松华．中国模式与中国文明 [J]. 社会科学，2011(12):12-18。
[2] 石介，字守道。北宋初学者、思想家，宋理学先驱。
[3] 金太军．中国传统政治文化新论 [M]. 北京：社会科学文献出版社，2006:35-72。

既有形器之后，其和不失，故曰太和”。两千多年过去了，这种传统已经渗入中国人的血脉之中，训诫引导着我们的言行，使得中国文化传统的核心渐渐聚焦于培育秩序，弘扬和谐，推崇和为贵。近百年前，曾经把《易经》翻译成德文的著名德国汉学家卫礼贤在谈及欧美文化与中国文化的区别时，突出强调欧美文化的扩张性和中国文化的包容性。他指出，中国文化是柔性文化，具有极强的韧性和包容性。中国文化能够发扬光大，并保持强大生命力，最主要原因是中国人相信“对立的力量最终将会达到和谐”。由此可见，中国文化传统在本质上是建立在和谐基础之上的传统，它处在宇宙和社会组织的理性之中。[1]

二、血缘关系与良知体系

血缘关系与良知体系在维持与稳定中国社会秩序方面发挥了深远的作用，成为中国漫长历史中的定海神针和传统教育文化中的重要前提，也体现了中国式思维的显著特征。

2.1 血缘关系

受地缘和经济因素的影响，中国传统社会形态在演进中是以血缘关系为纽带的。作为农业国，中国社会早期建立了稳固的血缘群落。另外，由于地缘环境比较封闭，基本没有遭遇过外族文化的入侵，因此中国是以一种循序渐进的方式告别原始社会的，在这个过程中，中国社会很难摆脱血缘社会关系的主导地位。直到西周，中国还在实行以血缘关系为纽带的宗族制体系，因此，中国社会从其最初就表现为“熟人”式特征。从静态和微观的层面看，中国社会可以称为熟人社会，其构成主体就是千千万万个小家庭、大家庭。在社会中，父母子女之间便是最亲密最熟悉的社会关系主体。可以说，这种模式是社会人员主体构成得以扩展的基础。由此，首先决定人与人亲密程度的是血缘关系的远近，血缘越近越亲密。整个社会于是以“家”为中心，逐步往外扩展，最终形成了一个以“熟人”为基础的社会。很显然，这是一个“家”与“国”高度统一的社会建构模式。与此相关，各种社会关系、社会事务皆以此为根基并可以从中得到一定阐释。[2] 同样，中国自西周确立封建政治制度以来，社会体系就基本定型了，这种模式由于位高权重者主要是皇帝一人，依次是各个层次的官员，由高到低人数也越来越多，处于最底层的人数最多的是平民百姓，因此，中国这种经久不衰的社会体系被称为“金字塔”模式。从结构上看，这种模式呈现出较为封闭的特征，与血缘或亲缘密不可分，社会按照血缘的亲疏划分为严密的社会等级，整个国家的管理系统也都被纳入血缘关系极为浓厚的宗法关系之中。

---

[1] 何兰芳．乐天与忧时——中国文化特质再探 [J]. 北方论丛，2022(6):56-67。
[2] 贺毅．中西文化比较 [M]. 北京：冶金工业出版社，2007:10-33。

2.2 良知体系

在这种血缘关系的基础上，中国社会的整个体系实际上也是属于人治而不是法治的传统模式，依靠的是教化和良知体系，而且历史相当悠久。“尊长”“师长”“长官”等词汇和概念，也都是血缘式人治与良知教化体系的映射，同时贴切地反映出中国传统哲学的特征与伦理内核：良知为重与道德主导。因为中国社会传统的精神，不在宗教，而是生命的体验，是教人安身立命与修身养性的教化哲学。[1] 中国社会的良知体系也得到了儒家思想的传承与弘扬。它界定和维护了中国社会中君子和小人的分野，但同时又主张君子与小人的分野不按传统的以家庭出身贵贱来划分，而以个人的德才来划分。在这样的社会体系中，中国人的“身行”是必须由“心性”去照顾。因此，在中国人的文化行为里，屈服人的最佳办法就是“攻心为上”，中国人的“良知”与“人情”是不可分割的。孟子说“仁者无敌”，的确是触及了“良知体系”之根本。[2] 反观中国社会的良知体系与教化传统，注重人文知识与厚德载物的特征尤其显著。孔子要求弟子“博学于文”“文行忠信”，“礼”和“仁”为核心，以“孝”为基本的道德教育贯穿中国人全部的思想体系，这是与中国传统强调“天人合一”与“万物和谐”的文化传统及努力保持“和合”的民族思维相辅相成的。

[1] 冯友兰．中国哲学简史 [M]．北京：外语教学与研究出版社，2015:2-30。
[2] 孙隆基．中国文化的深层结构 [M]．北京：中信出版社，2016:15-85。

第二章　中国教育的文化基础

在教育视域中，中国不仅仅指地缘意义上的中国，更多指文化意义上的中国。中华民族在这块土地上繁衍生息，薪火相传，孕育了绚丽多彩、别具一格的传统文化与哲思，在历史的长河中不断渗透在本民族的物质文化、行为文化、制度文化和精神文化中，这是中国教育发展的基础。

第一节　优秀传统对教育的影响

一直以来，中国教育文化所提倡的许多要求和规范，都可以在中华优秀传统文化中找到其历史渊源。在几千年的历史发展中，中国这些传统文化通过其独有的生命哲学、语言魅力及文化标识为本土教育文化提供了无数精神和物质的范例，保持着极为强大的生命力，也积累了极为珍贵的财富。

一、生命的哲学

中国传统的哲学是“生命”的哲学。[1] 在这种价值观引领下，宇宙是所有生灵的源头。如《易经》所言，不断繁衍的生命是变化的，天地的厚德在于创造生命。孟子言：“老吾老，以及人之老，幼吾幼，以及人之幼。”中国历代文人学者不断传承“万物生于天地间”的理念，笃守着“仁爱无疆”的信条。因而在中国教育界“与人为善”“君子怀德”的思想比比皆是，人们相信人与万物平等共生。清代著名书画家郑板桥的家书中就曾表达了他对世间万物包括蝼蚁的情感，他相信这是天地之愿，人当悟之。与这种哲思相关的是中国传统文化的生态美学，中国古代哲人把自然当作包含人类在内的生命的整体。天地间万物皆有自己的生命与存在状态，因此人们在对自然的欣赏敬畏中能够汲取精神的愉悦。明清时期的儒家文人尤其崇尚洞悉自然，格物致知。兼爱万物，崇尚自然的理念在中国古代的文学艺术作品中屡见不鲜。明末书画大家董其昌曾言，画者多长寿，缘于观察揽取生灵万物。中国画家从不绘无生气之物，花鸟鱼虫在他们笔下生趣盎然。中国古代文学有着同样的视角。在唐宋诗词中，中国的诗歌艺术达到了巅峰，花鸟被描写得具有了人性与情感。在蒲松龄的《聊斋志异》中，其他生灵被描写成能与人类共通，许多故事就是关于人类与幻化的动植物之间的爱情。

---

[1] 叶朗，朱良志．中国文化读本 [M]．北京：外语教学与研究出版社，2008:3-13。

二、语言的魅力

近年来，全球汉语学习者的人数在增加。广泛的研究解释了汉语较其他语言的优势。汉字的书写是基于系列表意符号的，从一个简单的汉字人们就能读到其丰富的隐含信息，其包含的历史踪迹。这就是为何历史学家有可能破译刻在甲骨上残缺的古代汉字，而这对于其他拉丁语系的语言是绝无可能的。表达同一思想，汉语在简洁、精确、高效方面是首屈一指的。

从狭义的视角来看，汉字因被称为情感符号而令人叹为观止。[1] 许多汉字中的象形符号深切表达出了人们对世界的观察与体验。这就是一些欧洲诗人觉得汉字激发了他们的想象力的原因。这种诗意的典故是不无道理的。以汉字“旦”为例，上半部分代表太阳，而下半部分代表地平线。换言之，这个汉字展示了太阳从地平线升起的含义。上海知名高校复旦大学正式立名于汉字“复”和“旦”，意为“日复一日，太阳从地平线上升起”。一系列的包含“旦”字的汉字都与太阳的起落有关联因素。比如，汉字“東”的繁体结构看上去就如同太阳从林中升起。汉字“暮”的最初写法是“莫”，模拟了太阳隐落于林中。汉字“明”的左边部分最初是“窗”的符号，右边部分代表了月亮，因此“明”字就描绘出了月光盈窗的场景。这难道不是一种诗意的设想吗？汉字“丽”的最初复杂结构是“麗”，描摹了成双的鹿奔跑在山岗上，好一番美丽的场面。

从广义视阈而言，汉语有着悠久的历史和特别的影响力。中国远古历史以甲骨文的形式刻在动物的甲骨之上已有五千年之久。还有一项重要的中国书写文字记录叫“竹书纪年”，可以追溯到公元前 296 年，这是一部记载在竹片上的历史记录，记载了关于中国古代发展的历史，以时间顺序展示了史实与事件。[2] 当活字印刷术经活字黏土改良之后，木版印刷的粗糙弱点被克服了。这种印刷技术因大大降低了书籍印刷的成本和时间而帮助提高了古代汉语的阅读和教育水平。1924 年，现代化维新派说服了政府选择规范的北京话作为标准普通话，以汉字记载了规范的语法和词汇。届时普通话成为中国的官方语言。到了 20 世纪 50 年代，中华人民共和国中央人民政府通过两种途径规范了汉字。首先，把标准化汉字总数精简到七千个通用汉字；其次，将汉字结构进行简化，简体中文就此诞生。普通话的教育语言和简化的读写汉字形成了现代标准中文，顾名思义是“通用语言”。这种语言现在已经成为全球至少五分之一人口教育与文化交流的媒介与载体，同时也是人类历史上一门重要的语言。

---

[1] 赵武宏．新说文解字 [M]．北京：大众文艺出版社，2010:1-10。
[2] 张文涛．史学史视野下的《竹书纪年》辨析 [J]．郑州大学学报，2016(6):118-122。

三、文化的标识

略过典型的文化标识来谈论中国文化都是不生动不完整的。这里我们将枚举一些典型的中国文化标识，帮助读者形成对中国传统艺术和文化遗产的总体印象，这些典型标识在中国漫长的历史上都有着深刻和典型的蕴含。

3.1 长城

长城是中国最典型的文化标识。从公元前七世纪到公元十六世纪的两千多年，中国的 19 个王朝陆续为它添砖加瓦，形成了两万多千米的长城。长城一路断壁缺口不少，如今保存最好的是北京的慕田峪长城城墙。长城在规模构造、建造质量和施工难度上是世上无可比拟的，它被认为是渴望和平的中国文化标识。由于长期遭受战争的毁灭性破坏，华夏人民发现建造起保护生灵的城墙远胜于埋葬战壕中的尸骨。长城的建造艰苦无比，有时甚至意味着付出生命的代价。但是与战争相比，修建长城可以保护更多的生命。因此，筑造长城的初衷是保卫和平。长城代表着华夏民族对和平的渴望，它在历史中的确起到了至关重要的作用。长城文化价值包括作为客观物所凝结的华夏儿女保卫和平的劳动与智慧、人的生命力与本质；也包括作为文化符号存在于华夏儿女集体记忆中的身份认同、中华民族的不屈精神与中华文明崇尚和合的特质。[1] 时至今日，长城的存在依然是中国人和中国教育者爱好和平的标识。

3.2 天坛

天坛位于永定门内大街，是世界上最大的祭天建筑群，由三道坛墙、五组建筑、九重坛门形成南方北圆的宏大格局，具有“苍璧礼天”的庄严气势，它是中国传统文化的另一个标识。[2] 天坛的两个主体建筑圜丘坛和祈谷殿是向心结构。此类建筑给人一种拾级而上的感觉。当你走上天坛，无论从东南西北哪一方向，都会感觉在走向中心。登顶之时，你会看到一方圆石置于中心，人称“天心石”。当帝王在冬至节气祭祀时，这代表天堂的石碑会被虔诚供上。中国古人相信天人合一，天与人可以沟通，而天坛的建造则正是为此。圜丘坛的回音和皇穹宇正是中国人及其祖先相信自己处于世界中心并与天地对话的印证。

3.3 瓷器

“瓷器”在英语中与中国同名，这说明中国人与瓷器的渊源举世闻名。换言之，瓷器被视作中国文化的名片，在中国文明进程中的地位举足轻重。瓷器是我国先民在长期从事陶器生产的基础上所发明的，中国是世界上最早制作和使用陶器的国家之一，瓷器则是中国独享的一项重大发明。考古发掘所获得的资料证明，早在约两万年以前，我们的祖先就已经开始有意识、有目的地制作和使用陶器。借助于现代科学技术手段

[1] 彭健，石雨诺．长城国家文化公园文化价值阐释与传播研究［J］．河北学刊，2023(1):210-214。
[2] 陈传康，牛宇宏．天坛文化及其旅游开发［J］．旅游论，1994(2):31-33.

进行检测后，文物博物馆界和科技界的专家将瓷器发明的时间确定在东汉。[1] 中国瓷器以其清朗的色彩，纯净的原料，优雅的设计和精致的制作而备受世代工艺匠人的青睐。这张文化名片代表了中国文化的结晶及中国式审美的化身。中国人喜欢碎纹瓷器因为他们欣赏天然神功。瓷器虽是人造艺术，但是它最忌讳的是雕琢痕迹。中国瓷器追求的是朴实的效果。瓷器绘画包含了山水和花鸟。中国人相信大美必然简朴而自然，任何过度雕琢或靓丽的事物往往与这个理念背道而驰。代表中国瓷器精髓的青花瓷就展现了一个简明优雅、淳朴、端庄的艺术世界。大多数中国青花瓷都融汇了儒家的审美哲学。在不断追求柔和精致的瓷器艺术中，人们可以通过中国瓷器工艺含蓄高冷的艺术风格，洞察到儒家思想的保守本性与审美倾向。

第二节　教育哲学中的文化渊源

教育哲学是涵盖哲学观点和方法研究教育基本问题的学科，是以形成应然和理想的人为目的对教育规律和教育实然、实际、实践的研究，也是时代教育精神的教化与形塑，因此教育哲学对教育的导向与发展有重要作用。[2] 本节将从中国传统的哲学与伦理及基本价值观这几个视角来呈现中国教育哲学的文化渊源。

一、哲学与伦理

哲学在中国文化教育中的地位，历来可以和宗教在其他文化中的地位相比拟。在中国，哲学是每一个受过教育的人都关切的领域。在中国古代，一个人如果受教育，首先就是受哲学方面的启蒙教育。儿童入学，首先要读的就是《论语》《孟子》《大学》《中庸》。这“四书”也是宋以后，道学认为最重要的文献。孩子刚学认字，通常用《三字经》作启蒙教材，每三个字为一组，每六个字成一句，偶句押韵，朗读时容易上口，也便于记忆。事实上，这本书乃是中国儿童的识字课本。《三字经》的第一句“人之初，性本善”，便是儒家教育哲学的基本思想。[3]

部分人认为儒、佛、道是中国的三种宗教。其实，儒家并不是一种宗教。道家和道教是不同的两回事，道家是一种哲学，道教才是宗教。它们的内涵不仅不同，甚至是互相矛盾的:道家哲学教导人顺乎自然,道教却教导人逆乎自然。举例来说,按老庄思想,万物有生必有死，人对于死，顺应自然，完全不必介意，而道教的宗旨却是教导长生术，这不是反乎自然吗? 道教含有一种征服自然的科学精神。如果有人对中国科学史有兴趣，《道藏》里许多道士的著作倒是可以提供不少资料。至于佛教，佛学和佛教也是

[1] 吕成龙．中国瓷器：文明使者［J］．中国政协，2020(13):76-77。
[2] 郝文武．教育学与哲学都需要教育哲学强化本质联系［J］．当代教育与文化，2023(4):1-9。
[3] 冯友兰．中国哲学简史［M］．北京：外语教学与研究出版社，2015:70-90。

有区别的。对中国知识分子来说，佛学比佛教有趣得多。在中国传统的丧事仪式中，僧人和道士同时参加，并不令人感到奇怪。中国人对待文化的态度，也是充满哲学意味的。中国人比其他民族更加重视伦理，这是中国教育文化中的一个核心理念。中国人被认为宗教意识不浓，是因为他们的哲学意识太浓了。他们在哲学里找到了超越现实世界的那个存在，也在哲学里表达和欣赏那个超越伦理道德的价值；在哲学生活中，他们体验了这些超越伦理道德的价值。根据中国教育哲学的传统，哲学的功能不仅是为了增进正面的知识（对客观事物的信息），还为了提高人的心灵，超越现实世界，体验高于道德的价值。《道德经》第四十八章说："为学日益，为道日损。"这句话表明了中国哲学传统对于"学"和"道"是有所区别的。"学" 就是增长正面知识，"道" 则是心灵的提高。哲学是在后一个范畴之中的。

中国哲学的主要精神既是入世的，又是出世的。它的使命正是要在这种两极对立中寻求它们的综合。能够不仅在理论上，而且在行动中实现这种综合的，就是圣人。这种品格可以用"内圣外王"四个字来刻画：内圣，是说他的内心致力于心灵的修养；外王，是说他在社会活动中好似君王。这不是说他必须是一国的政府首脑，而是有积极的作用。中国教育哲学的使命就是使人得以发展这样的品格，其中伦理起着相当大的作用。

二、基本价值观

中华文明史从上古三代夏商周一直到清代，传统儒佛道思想无疑占据中国文化的主导地位，从先秦百家争鸣到秦始皇统一罢黜百家、独尊儒术的思想大一统局面开始，直到近代，儒佛道三家从思想上主导中国文化思想局面的大局基本定型。中国精英思想文化人士游弋于入世、出世、弃世之间，儒家治世、佛法治心兼道家治身，获得一种超级稳定的平衡状态，从而使得华夏文明命脉随同其价值观一起一直延续。[1]

2.1 儒家

儒家思想是孔子所创立，是先秦时期众多学派之一，后渐渐发展成了有独立体系的儒学。之后儒学在中国古代哲学领域独树一帜，它所强调的仁义礼智信及思想行为的仁爱、孝道与和谐都是中华优秀传统文化的思想典范，对中国、东南亚甚至世界都产生了巨大的影响，儒学还为我们留下了以"四书五经"为代表的丰富的人文遗产。在中国封建社会中，这些儒家经典成为教育领域及政府各级官员选拔考试的基本要求，这种选拔方式长达六个世纪。儒家思想的道德原则是发现人类社会关系最高品德并为当时的社会矛盾提供解决方法。儒学思想的中心就是"仁"。对仁的翻译有善良、仁慈、人道、与人为善，等等。总之，"仁"意味着情感与关爱。孔子因被尊为"万世师表"而备受敬仰。从文明之初到辛亥革命，孔子对中国人的生活和思想的影响如此深远，以至于他被当作中国人精神与性格的铸造者。他的思想和教学被当作中国传统文化与

[1] 黄芹．从传统儒佛道思想看中国法治建构的缺位 [J]. 渤海大学学报，2015(1):51-55。

国家精神的标识。正如孙中山所言，孔子的思想可以总结如下：忠孝、仁爱、正直、和谐。

2.2 佛家

佛教徒慈悲平和的生活方式与智慧在古代印度与今天的教育界同样意义重大。佛陀解释说我们的困苦都来自内心的消极与困顿而所有的快乐与幸运都来自平和积极的心态。佛家思想认为人死后灵魂将进入中间状态，即藏传佛教所说的“中阴界”，在这个状态中人们看到了各种被激发的业力所致的幻觉。佛家相信人们的所作所为都留下了痕迹或潜能，在灵魂中每种业力都有果报。灵魂如同一片土地，人们的所作所为犹如播撒种子，善行则播下将来的殊胜，作恶则为将来种下孽缘。这种善则有善报，恶自有恶报的确定关系叫因果报应。了悟因果报应是佛法修行的基础。佛教的传入对中国文化的发展进程以及佛教本身都意义重大。经过长时期的吸收同化，佛教在中国形成了一种重要的思想，丰富着中国德行向善的宗教文化，并深远地影响着中国人的心性与教育。

2.3 道家

以中国著名本土思想家老子为代表的道家思想与儒家文化一样对中国人的思想及政治经济与文化生活产生了重大影响。道家思想与儒家思想在很多方面都相辅相成，就像并列而行的两大河流奔腾在中国后世教育的文学与思想领域中。道家奉老子为至尊，以《道德经》为经典，尊创立者张道陵为本派天师。从立派到盛行，道家很长时期属于上层的文化，被中国传统的上层社会所追捧，因而许多掌门道士受到朝廷的器重。老子认为世间万物是相互依存关联的。是与非、难与易、长与短等皆是一对对的矛盾之统一。 同时也阐述了两者之间能此消彼长相互转换的。由于对混战不断，生活艰苦的社会现实的不满，老子提出了小国寡民、闭关锁国的主张。他的许多观点与生活准则，如以柔克刚、返璞归真、清心寡欲、顺其自然、急流勇退、无我谦逊等都极大影响了中国人的思维与教育，并被运用到了政治、经济、军事、文化、商业与社会交往中。

表 1　儒佛道传统教育思想比较

教育文化 / 比较视角	儒家	佛家	道家
文化主旨	进取文化	奉献文化	规律文化
做人标准	仁、义、礼、智、信	诸恶莫作、众善奉行	修道养德、隐世出尘
人生观	积极进取、建功立业	慈爱众生、无私奉献	顺其自然、自我完善
世界观	世界是展现才华的舞台	世界是自己心中的善恶	世界是天人合一的境界
价值观	在创造中实现自我价值	在奉献中净化心灵，印证因果	以完善的自我与天地和谐
哲学倾向	入世哲学	以出世之心，为入世之事	出世哲学

儒佛道思想是中华文明的根基和命脉，是人类文明交流互鉴的基础叙事。儒释道思想的国际传播是推动中华文化更好地走向世界的新时代文化战略。[1] 儒佛道传统教育思想的比较可用表 1 概括，可以看出，儒释道传统思想虽有不同侧重，但所蕴含的仁爱和谐、积极向善、天下大同、和而不同以及天人合一等观点，同样体现了中华民族的价值追求和精神境界，彰显了鲜明的中国底色和中国智慧。[2]

第三节　中国教育的演变与特征

根据中国教育周期的统计，中国古代教育高潮迭起，一浪高过一浪，绵延不绝，最终在清末表现出向近代教育转型的趋势；唐宋时期两峰耸峙，是中国古代教育的高峰[3]。但进入近代之后，中国教育更多的是受西方现代教育制度和教育思想的影响。

一、历史的踪迹

中国教育的历史踪迹其实也是中国文化发展在漫长历史长河中的浓缩画卷。教育文化的形成总是一定时代和历史的产物，只有被置于当时的历史时空中才能被真正了解。

1.1　总体脉络

在先秦时期的中国，孔子和孟子奠定了儒学教育的基础；与此同时，百家争鸣，以儒学教育为主导，其他教育为补充的格局基本形成。战国后期，荀子全面总结了儒家教育思想并且吸收了法家的理性主义成分，他的传经活动为儒学在西汉的复兴做好了准备。在董仲舒等人的推动下，西汉制定了儒学独尊的文教政策。从此，儒学教育的统治地位一直保持到清末。由于理学家的推动，儒学教育在宋代达到顶峰。魏晋玄学融合儒道，其重视个性的自然主义教育倾向影响了南北朝和隋唐知识分子和教育思想家的心态，在一定程度上改变了儒学独尊的地位，使隋唐时期的教育呈现出百花齐放的局面。佛教在东汉传入中国后，逐渐被知识界接受，佛学教育在隋唐达到高峰。佛道两家的思想经隋唐教育思想家的传播，其追求形而上意义的思想方法被宋明理学家所吸收，不着痕迹地融入儒家教育思想中。随着西学东渐的出现，一部分海纳百川的大儒自觉调整心态，从容应对，从社会需要出发，高扬学以致用的儒学传统，提出了实学教育的思想，为中国古代教育向近代教育转型作了准备。同时，强调伦理本位的理学家仍保持着强大的势力，中国教育的近代化步履维艰。事实上，中国教育进入全面近代化的时间比西方整整晚了一个世纪。1840 年第一次鸦片战争爆发，1862 年京师同文馆的创办被认为是中国近代教育开始的标志。中国第一所近代学校到 1862 年才

[1] 陈先红．“走进去”与“走出去”：儒释道思想国际传播战略研究［J］．人民论坛学术前沿，2023(2):58-72。
[2] 肖洁．人类命运共同体理念中的中国传统文化智慧［J］．文学教育，2023(5):126-128。
[3] 姜国钧．断裂与绵延：中西教育周期比较［J］．比较教育研究，2003(6):25-30。

开始建立，新学制的创建到 20 世纪初才开始。以教授自然科学和社会科学为主的学校教育的普及是 1922 年新学制以后的事情，因为此后中国教育近代化的各种因素逐渐显现出来。不同于西方教育近代化的循序渐进，中国教育的近代化是在急速变化中匆匆完成的。

1.2 重要阶段

中国教育的发展大致经历了几个重要阶段。[1] 一是远古原始形态的教育，我国原始社会的教育是和人们的劳动联系在一起的。我国古籍中还有图腾崇拜、宗教祭祀等活动的记载，这些活动都是通过教育一代一代传下来的。至氏族社会末期，“家学”的学校教育形式开始萌芽，但是这种学校是由氏族显贵垄断着的。二是文字的出现与学校的产生和发展。我国最早发现的文字是甲骨文，后来又刻在青铜器皿上，称为金文。也有文字刻在竹简、木简和布帛上。东汉纸和 11 世纪印刷术的发明和应用对学校教育的发展起了巨大作用。根据古籍记载，我国最早的学校有“庠”“序”“校”等名称，我国的学校大约出现在氏族社会后期，奴隶社会早期。三是孔子首开私学之风。孔子在鲁国曲阜设学授徒，以诗书礼乐教授弟子。他还带着学生周游列国，是春秋末期最大的私人讲学团体。经战国、秦汉、魏晋后，私学又有了新发展。除了世俗性的私学外，还有佛教、道教的宗教教育的私学。唐宋之后，私学的名目更是丰富多元，私学在我国教育发展史上有着重要的地位。需要注意的是，中国教育虽然也随着朝代的更迭而有所变化，但“独尊儒术”的文教政策自西汉确立以来并没有本质的改变，只是到近代才受到较大的冲击。四是科举制度的产生，这是选才与教育的结合。科举制度始于隋唐，它一方面使庶人子弟有机会通过考试而进入仕途，极大地调动了庶民读书的积极性，形成了中国人重视教育的传统；另一方面，它强化了脱离实际的经院主义学习，使学校教育更加僵化。五是洋务运动和维新运动的冲击。鸦片战争打开中国的门户后，统治阶级内部逐渐认识到中国军事、经济、教育均落后于西方列强，便开始倡导“中学为体，西学为用”的洋务运动。中国第一次办起以外国语学校、工业学校和军事学校为主的洋学堂，派出了第一批留学生。维新运动是 19 世纪末一批具有资产阶级改良主义思想的知识分子发起的。他们要求废除科举考试，改革传统的教育模式，学习西方的科学技术，培养实用人才。废科举、兴学堂就是这两次运动的结果。1905 年，在中国存在了约 1300 年的科举考试终于被废除，西方的教育制度和科学教育内容才得以在中国建立和传播。六是五四运动的冲击。五四运动提出的科学与民主的口号，沉重地打击了封建主义教育传统。学校采用白话文进行教学，使学校教育接近大众的生活实际，为教育的普及创造了条件；教育界开展了平民教育运动，提倡男女受教育权利的平等；提倡科学的教育内容和方法，等等。这一切都使中国教育的传统发生了质的变化。中华人民共和国成立以后，我国教育经过多次改革，特别是 1978 年改革开放以来，中国教育的改革和发展进入了一个新阶段，具有中国特色的教育传统正在形成。

---

[1] 顾明远．中国教育的文化基础 [M]．太原：山西教育出版社，2004:1-3。

在中国教育发展进程中，传统教育哲学带着特有的大教育观、德智统一观和内在观经过不断创造和革新并以变化了的形式存在于现代教育之中，对中国教育的发展及特征产生了巨大而深刻的影响。[1]

二、传统的特征

中国教育家自古所重视的是培养亲和力的和谐教育，对培养创造力的创造教育重视不够。因此，教育思想往往能互相包容，教育制度大都能前后相继，教育高潮一浪高过一浪，绵延不绝；同时，教育结构存在缺陷，周期性复制多，发展创新少，以至于教育转型与改革步履艰难。与中国文化传统一样，从纵向的中国发展的历史来看，中国教育传统在发展中发生了质的变化；从横向与别国的教育相比，中国教育传统又有中华民族的特点，是前后有着继承关系的，归纳起来大致有以下几个方面[2]：

第一，中国教育有政教合一的传统。政教合一最明显的特征是教育与选拔人才相结合，具体表现在科举制度上。科举制度是一种人才选拔制度，经过逐级统一考试，按成绩选录人才，授以相应的官职。政教合一的传统在我国革命根据地表现得也很充分。当时教育以干部教育为主，学校里的学生，既是学员又是干部，享受国家公务员的待遇。第二，中国教育有重伦理道德的传统。中国文化是伦理型文化，中国教育也可以说是伦理型教育，重视人的道德修养。“修身，齐家，治国，平天下”长期是中国教育的最高理想，这种传统具有较高的人文精神，强调教书育人的社会化功能。第三，中国教育有重经典轻技术的传统。这个特点与重伦理是有关系的。中国历来的学校教育只是教给学生统治政权的本领，很少教给学生生产的技能。这种思想直接影响到我国科学技术的发展，而且至今仍在影响着我国职业技术教育的发展。第四，中国教育传统重视基本知识的传授，而方法是经验主义的。中国教育历来重视背诵记忆的内在体悟，俗话说：“熟读唐诗几百首，不会写诗也会吟。”这种方法有利于巩固基本知识，却不利于培养学生独立思考的能力和创新精神。第五，中国教育有尊师重教、师道尊严的传统。因为重视教育，所以尊重老师。在中国有“一日为师，终身为父”的传统，把教师放到与父母同等的地位。韩愈的《师说》把教师的任务归纳为“传道、授业、解惑”，也强调师道尊严。这种传统一直流传到今天，不得不说这与中国人的教育价值观有关。总之，中国教育传统有着政教结合，非宗教性、注重德育、传承经典、尊师重教等特征，也存在脱离生产、轻视技术创造及古板灌输等值得反思的一面。[3]

文化是民族精神的载体，教育是民族进步的动力。了解中国教育文化传统的特征有利于在教育全球化竞争的背景下培养会通的教育文化借鉴意识，不断反思和进取并产生出教育文化发展的新动力。

---

[1] 禹芳琴．中国传统教育哲学的历程与现代影响［J］．求索，2005(9):132-134。
[2] 梁瑜华．从文化视角比较中西教育思想差异［J］．传承，2008(1):90-93。
[2] 葛金国．论中国教育的历史传统［J］．安徽师大学学报，1992(4):465-470。

第三章　中国学府的文化性格

自20世纪末以来，中国学术界开始了有关学府文化的研究。在这里，学府大多指学术教育机构，以大学为主。与此同时，“中国学府的文化性格”这一命题涉及中国文化、教育历史、大学精神、办学理念等越来越多的概念，取得了丰硕的成果，对深入了解中国教育文化的历史和现状提供了丰富的视角。

第一节　中国学府的基本格局

中国学府的基本格局在此主要指社会体系中的学校教育。从战国时的大学堂之稷下学宫到现代社会的各类基础教育学校及高等学府，中国学府的基本格局所反映的不仅是中国社会的教育制度，还有教育文化中的思想变迁。

一、教育制度与中国学府

中国历史上的教育制度有几次重大转变。封建社会初期统治者为了培养自己的助手开始办学，包含着选士、取士的目的。到了汉代，选士的选举制度从学校分离出来，与学校制度并行。从隋唐开始，科举制度逐步替代选举制度，学府成了科举的附庸。宋代以后，由于学府越来越有名无实，于是私人办学之风逐渐盛行，产生了与朝廷学府同时存在的书院制度。书院制度是我国特有的一种文化教育组织，是读书人围绕着书，开展包括藏书、校书 、修书、著书 、刻书、读书 、教书等活动 ，进行文化积累、研究以及创造传播。书院是中国传统从事教学活动的场所，还有研究机构性质。传统书院组织形式既是高等教育和基础教育、应试教育和素质教育相结合的产物，又是官学和私学相结合的产物。书院自唐至清末存在了一千多年，成为士子读书治学活动集中的地方。书院创办的目的在于培育士子，移风易俗，教化乡里，敦睦社会，具有强烈的社会教化功能。[1]

中国历史上，学府和教育制度是上层建筑，是一定历史时代的产物。中国传统社会的整合机制（国家 / 民间精英 / 社会）在近代失去效力之后，作为传统的农业国，中国教育制度的近代化进程就一直处在一个被分割的零散化格局中，缓慢地 、局部地脱离传统形态步入近代世界，中国学府也是如此。中国近代为富国强兵而兴办的学府到当代大学的发展总体上经历了一个立足古代教育传统，辅助性地引入西方大学文化，到

[1] 崔树芝，林坚．中国传统书院的社会教化功能［J］．文化学刊，2014(6):151-158。

较全面、系统地与国际接轨的过程。诚如季羡林先生所言：中国的学统应该从太学起，中经国子监，一直到大学堂，最后转为现代意义的大学。可以说中国学府的教育传统是一脉相承，没有中断的。从中国大学的发展历程来看，中国大学从一开始就是在中国文化强大的包容性与同化力中得以成型，至今仍深受中国文化的影响。因此，不仅是中国文化生成中国大学，而且中国大学本身就是中国文化的实体存在。[1]

二、中国学府的教育文化

中国学府文化的形成与中国文化中的“大学观”不无关系。所谓“大学观”即指中国文化中有关高等教育的基本思想与观念，是中国古典高等教育文化的灵魂所在。中国古代高等教育思想很大程度上源于孔子的教育思想。首先，中国学府的教育文化起点是“学以为己”，以“人”为逻辑起点。此“人”严格意义上即指“己”亦可称“自”，即“我”。这个自我有别于西方的个人主义。相反却是为了达到一种极度无私的境界：“至善”，所谓修身齐家而后治国平天下，即是此理。“学以为己”在于以学为本，以学为本在于以德修人。同时，以德修人要以为社会服务为己任。换言之，个人的学术与道德成就就是教育的基本目的，但道德成就也必须实现其社会功能，才能产生效果，这是传统中国教育思想中的一个核心概念，始于孔子，后长期影响中国学府的文化。在南宋时，因为朱熹的提倡，它变成了广泛的信念。其次，中国传统学府的教育文化出路是“学而优则仕”，是为政府或社会培植人才的教育。如果说《论语》中的“学以为己”是注重学习本身的快乐与个人内心的高尚，体现着一种教育或读书的“艺术美”，那么“学而优则仕”则是一门非常现实的“实用性技术”，是读书人学以为己的根本出路。诚然自孔子后，读书人积极入仕已蔚然成风，然真正将读书人牢牢固定在政治仕途上，将学而优则仕思想制度化的则是科举制以及相应的传统学府。[2] 再次，中国传统学府文化的最高理想是“大学之道明明德，在新民，止于至善。”涂又光在《中国高等教育史论》中，将上述大学之道概括为中国古代高等教育的总规律。称之为规律，是说中国高等教育在遵循它，此种文化理想贯穿中国高等教育历史全过程，就是总规律。近代以来中国大学既立，以《大学》解中国大学者不乏其人，并且聚焦于“明明德”与“新民”以强调现代大学道德教育与社会服务职能。[3] 综上，中国传统学府的教育文化以“为己之学”为出发点，大学观伦理性尽显；以“学而优则仕”为出路，大学观实用性尽显；以“明明德、新民、止于至善”为理想，大学观超越性尽显。因此，中国传统学府的教育文化以尚德、尚实、尚善为基础。当然，传统学府有失“物”学且以文治天下、有失科技、有失制度构建的副作用也是存在的。

[1] 贾佳，王建华．中国大学的文化性格 [M]．福州：福建教育出版社，2017:38-42。
[2] 李弘祺．学以为己：传统中国的教育 [M]．香港：香港中文大学出版社，2012:45-70。
[3] 涂又光．中国高等教育史论 [M]．武汉：湖北教育出版社，2002:1-20。

第二节 当代大学的文化变迁

从中国传统学府的教育制度与文化可以看出，从古至今，对中国大学文化性格与传统精神的形成影响最大的是儒家思想与文化。同时，近代社会文化的变迁也对中国大学文化精神产生了重大的影响。

一、儒家文化的精神坐标

在追求世界一流的过程中，中国学府并不想为了追求“共性”而失去“个性”，从而迷失自己的文化根基。因而儒家文化成了当代中国大学文化变迁中守护文化身份的精神坐标。

1.1 核心地位

国际化与本土化是大学在现代社会不断前进过程中天平的两端。国际化，是大学前进的加速器，本土化是大学前进的方向盘。世界一流大学理念反映了当前占据世界主导地位的研究型院校尤其是那些美国和西欧重要大学的规范和价值观。今天中国大学的人才观与孔子提倡的“鸿儒”具有同构性，大学文化常常向传统文化中的儒家文明寻找智慧之光。当代“通识教育”既是大学的一种理念，也是一种人才培养模式，其目标是培养具备远大眼光、通融识见、博雅精神和优美情感的完整的人。它的精神坐标即是儒家思想的同心圆结构，在“修身、齐家 、治国、平天下”的延伸过程中，因其包含着自我实现和社会责任的双重含义而至今被奉为经典。[1] 当代大学生常被要求读的两本书是《老子》与《论语》，可以看出儒家思想在今天仍然具有十分重要的意义。前文章节提到的儒家思想中的“普遍和谐”观念不仅对高等学府的人才培养有深远影响还会对人类社会的和平与发展做出特殊的贡献。作为一个完整意义的观念，它至少包含四个层面：“自然的和谐” “人和自然的和谐”“人与人的和谐” “人自我身心内外的和谐”。这四个“和谐”也仍然是今天通识教育和社会生活的要义所在。

1.2 文化要义

儒家文明为代表的传统文化，在中国大学人文教育中从来没有缺位。儒家不但注重自身修养，更强调“化民成俗，其必由学”。显然，儒家教育首先的任务是教以人文文化。在教育全球化的大潮背景下，无论是工具理性和人文性在大学文化的博弈中，还是在育人还是制器的抉择中，儒家文化无疑为人的全面发展提供了精神坐标。[2] 此外，传统儒家思想是中国学府文化的源头，对人格要求、价值体现和实践这种价值的方法，都体现为一种稳定的“道”元素，这种元素通过“仁义礼智信”的信条表述出来，成

[1] 陈向明．对通识教育有关概念的辨析 [J]. 高等教育研究，2006(3):64-68。
[2] 黄成亮．儒家文化：中国大学的精神坐标 [J]. 教育学术月刊，2009(2):90-92.

为中国知识分子和大学精神世代传承的内在基因。这种文化要求知识分子在学习时不仅仅要提高自己，同时还要有一种广阔的胸襟，积极传播大学文化，教化自己周围的人。正所谓“士志于道”“明道济世”，这表明大学精神不应该是封闭、私利的，应该是开放、达济的。这既是中国几千年以来传统的士人思想，也为中国历朝历代学府精神的塑造起了重要的作用，成为当代中国大学精神的本根。许多大学都从儒家传统文化中提炼精神的养分，形成了各具特色的大学精神。这种以“道”为中心，以“仁义礼智信”为信条的儒家传统的精神坐标如图 1 所示。

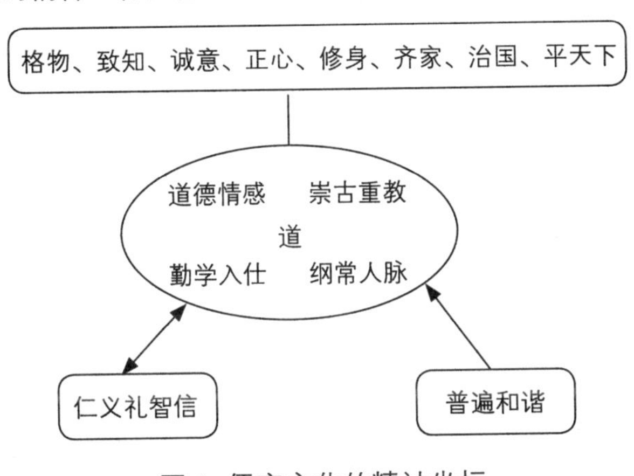

图 1 儒家文化的精神坐标

二、大学精神的内涵演变

中国大学精神的内涵演变离不开本土教育文化的发展。在国家政权的兴衰的过程中，传统儒家精英的社会责任感得以激发，在近现代中国环境下，不难发现融合西方文化的大学精神也能在中华优秀传统文化中找到源头。

2.1 主要内涵

现代意义上的大学起源于中世纪欧洲，但纵向考察我国的古代教育会发现，虽然中国古代社会没有现代意义上的大学之形，但确实存在有现代意义上的大学之实。战国时期齐国的稷下学宫、汉代的太学及后来的国子监、唐朝开始建立的书院等都是中国古代的大学，它们都担负着中华优秀传统文化的传承与发展。两千多年来，它们已经具有了现代意义上的大学精神。中国的传统文化教育一直更注重社会伦理关系，中国古代大学对“节操”的要求也影响到现代意义上的大学。鸦片战争后，中西文化开始了大规模的交流与冲突，而“以天下为己任”的传统精神无疑是饱受外侮的近现代环境下，中国大学精神的丰富源泉，这也正合了孟子所说的“生于忧患”。在“中学为体，西学为用”思想的指引下，我国高等教育开始了向西方国家全面的学习与模仿，中国大学也在中西文化的交流与融合的过程中，逐步形成了具有中国特色的大学精神。从上文的阐述可以看出，儒家文化是中国古代大学的精神。中国大学教育的主要精神内涵与演变体现在“德至上”“自治精神”“自由兼容”“民族精神”和“民主科学”。[1]

2.2 演变历程

受儒家文化的影响，我国古代大学教育与各类书院教育的根本目的在于“明人伦”，即让学生懂得并遵守封建社会中人与人之间的各种伦理准则。[2] 近代的中国大学在积极吸收西方教育思想、借鉴西方办学经验的同时，仍始终把德育放在重要的位置。自治精神是现代大学的主要精神之一，起源于西方中世纪大学。[3] 其实，自治精神在中国古代大学早已有之。萌芽于唐代末期，形成于五代，强盛于宋代的书院大多是由民间创办的，经济与管理是相对独立的。书院的院长、山长、讲师都是由公众担任，注重真才实学，并有“不称职则易”“按季更换”的规定，有显著的自制精神。我国现代大学制度建立初期，清华大学自 1925 年设立大学部后只用了十年时间成为世界知名大学的最重要原因是大学独立和教授治校，这是现代大学的命脉。大学的自由兼容精神是现代高等教育发展的必要条件。在我国，这种精神最早体现于战国时期齐国的稷下学宫。这是中国教育史上最早的实行自由讲学、自主办学的高等教育机构。后来的私学和书院秉承自由和兼容精神的优良传统，践行“门户开放”理念，崇尚自由讲学。在近代北京大学的改革中，这种精神体现得最为突出。以爱国主义为核心的民族精神是中华民族的优秀文化传统。孟子所言的“富贵不能淫，贫贱不能移，威武不能屈”也是古代学府所遵循的价值原则。 中国古代书院在传承中华文化的同时，也具有强烈的民族精神。培育了民族英雄文天祥的白鹭洲书院的主要特点是追崇先贤、培育气节。明朝东林书院的“风声雨声读书声声声入耳，家事国事天下事事事关心”的训导至今尤为世人传诵。近代中国大学的民族精神是伴随着中国的救亡图存的爱国运动而形成的，主要表现为由强烈的社会责任感、使命感而产生的社会忧患意识和社会参与意识。北大、清华和中山大学的命运在近现代一直与民族的兴衰紧紧地联系在一起，是中国大学民族精神的例证。科学与民主的概念都是中国近代从西方引进的观念。因此，中国大学的科学与民主精神也是伴随着中国近代历史发展的进程而逐步形成并发展起来的。在清末“西学东渐”以后，西方的民主与科学的观念开始进入我国。维新运动的领袖康有为、梁启超、谭嗣同等都曾介绍、宣传过西方的民主与科学的思想。思想家、翻译家严复作为系统介绍西方思想的第一人，在宣传民主与科学的过程中成绩最为显著，他为五四新文化运动奠定了基础。五四新文化运动以民主与科学为两面旗帜，对前人既有继承又有很大程度的超越。1906 年，时任北洋大学校长的赵天麟，提出了“实事求是”的校训，这也是追求科学精神的最直接的体现。

中国近代大学已经在继承中华民族优良的文化传统和古代办学经验的基础上，吸收

[1] 李文山．中国大学精神的内涵及演变 [J]．河南大学学报，2006(6):153-157。
[2] 班高杰．人伦与规范：传统蒙书中的道德养成 [J]．江西社会科学，2020(7):22-28。
[3] 伯顿·克拉克．高等教育系统——学术组织的跨国研究 [M]．杭州：杭州大学出版社，1994:1-20。

和融合了西方文化和办学理念而逐步发展。可同时，近代中国大学是处于列强侵略、社会动荡、政权更迭、社会变革的环境之下，因此，在经历了百年以美国高等教育模式为参照、对苏联模式的全面照搬以及参照各国大学经验，构建中国特色学府精神的三次转型后，[1] 处理好继承与创新、大学自治与国家意志、本土化与国际化等诸多方面的关系显得尤为重要。

第三节 著名学府与文化理念

一个地区的著名学府所承载的不仅仅是培养人才的重任，还代表着一方水土的文化理念，引领着未来教育的走向。著名学府往往通过大师来呈现它的文化价值，并通过特定的文化符号来传承自身的教育特色与理想。本节将简要回顾中国一些知名校长的历史足迹及一些名校的代表性文化符号。

一、知名校长足迹

著名大学大都与众多闪亮的校长名字联系在一起。外国如此，中国也同理。蔡元培之于北京大学，梅贻琦之于清华大学，竺可桢之于浙江大学，郭秉文之于东南大学，都犹如夜空中的明星，指引着后人前行。在他们的努力倡导下，我国的高等教育从思想到实践都发生了很大的变化。他们勇于创新、开拓进取，为中国高等教育的发展留下了浓厚的文化色彩和丰富的实践经验。

1.1 蔡元培

蔡元培曾经这样说过："大学者，'囊括大典，网罗众家'之学府也。……各国大学，哲学之唯心论与唯物论，文学、美术之理想派与写实派，计学之干涉论与放任论，伦理学之动机论与功利论，宇宙论之乐天观与厌世观，常樊然并峙于其中，此思想自由之通则，而大学之所以为大也。"他担任北京大学校长时，聘用教师的标准是：学识为主，唯才是用。只要教师有较高的学术水平，其他的条件都不重要。他有六个"不论"：不论派别、不论年龄、不论学历、不论资历、不论国籍、不论政见。在他的努力下，当时的北大汇聚了一批全国一流的学者。[2-3] 文科方面，由陈独秀任文科学长，还有李大钊、鲁迅、胡适、钱玄同、刘半农、沈尹默等人。理科方面，有夏元、李四光、颜任光、任鸿隽、李书华等。

1.2 梅贻琦

梅贻琦任清华校长时宣布办大学应有两种目的：一是研究学问，一是造就人才。他

[1] 孟中媛．百年来中国大学的三次转型发展的历史回顾［J］．黑龙江高教研究，2008(5):11-13。
[2] 高平叔．蔡元培教育文选［M］．北京：人民教育出版社，1980:1-30。
[3] 高天明．名校长与近代中国大学精神［J］．深圳大学学报，2003(11):114-118。

相信“所谓大学者，非谓有大楼之谓也，有大师之谓也。”他身体力行地对教师们予以尊重，深得教授好评。梅贻琦在清华大学期间和领导西南联大时，都千方百计广招人才，提高教授待遇，使清华园内人才济济。[1] 其中有陈寅恪、赵元任、朱自清、闻一多、钱锺书这些国学大师，也有冯友兰、金岳霖、吴晗、李达、张岱年等社会科学领域的大家，还有熊庆来、马大遒、华罗庚、钱伟长、钱学森、周培源、梁思成这样的数学、自然科学、工程科学的奠基者。

1.3 郭秉文

郭秉文在东南大学时主张办学要力求四方面平衡，其中人文与科学的平衡即包含了平等对待各种学术思想，提倡学术自由之意。当时的南京尚处于北洋军阀统治时期，但在南京高等师范学校、东南大学，教授们却可以公开介绍各种新的思潮和理论，既可宣传社会主义、马克思主义，也可宣传三民主义、国家主义、改良主义，形成百家并存、自由争鸣的局面。同时他发展并完善了江谦的“以诚为训”“三育并举”的人才培养方针，主张通过训育、智育和体育三者并举而使学生的才能、体魄、精神、道德和学术诸方面都得以相当的发展，特别是他主张以养成学生的思想和应用能力为标准，使学生拥有普通知识又有专门技能，达到通才与专才的平衡。

1.4 蒋梦麟

蒋梦麟继任北大校长后依然坚持学术自由的原则。他提出大学为研究高等学术而设，故“当以思想自由为标准”。在任校长后，特别是著名的“科玄之争”更证明了他维持学术自由的思想。他要求在校长之下设评议会、行政会、教务处、总务处等各种事务委员会。他的核心就是继续坚持教授治校的原则，辅以健全的组织。他主持制定的《大学组织法》，依然重申了教授治校、民主管理的方针。

1.5 竺可桢

竺可桢在浙江大学时，对于古今中外的教育制度和教育理想都颇有研究，他主张学生全面发展，既重视德育，又重视智育和体育，他提出要把学生培养成为有崇高信仰、奉公守法、体格健全的通才。他一贯主张通才教育，认为大学教育不仅仅给予学生全面的知识，更重要的是培养学生的各种能力。[2]

二、名校文化符号

中国高等学府自诞生起就在当时教育宗旨令所规定的“注重道德教育、以实利教育、军国民教育辅之、更以美感教育完成其道德”的影响下发展。《大学令》中的“大学以教授高深学术、养成硕学闳才、应国家需要为宗旨”基本规定了中国大学的基本文化方向。近代开始发展起来的传统名校的文化符号被认为体现在办学理念、校园风物

[1] 李硕豪．梅贻琦的高等教育思想和办学实践［J］．高等教育研究，1998(4):91-94。
[2] 高天明．名校长与近代中国大学精神［J］．深圳大学学报，2003(11):114-118。

及学子情怀上。[1] 以北京大学、清华大学、西南联大为例。

2.1 北京大学

北京大学的前身是晚清的京师大学堂，1912 年更名为国立北京大学，严复出任校长，后蔡元培接管。五四时期北大作为新文化重镇而名扬四海，百年以来见证历史变迁，历经辉煌。北大传统的办学理念是“砥砺德行、参政爱国、网罗众家”。经过一代代北大学子的践行，北大的理念通过“天下为公、厚德载物”的文化性格得到进一步发展与诠释。从校园风物来看，北大素来被称作“紧挨着皇宫的大学”。从红楼、沙滩到图书馆，“老北大”的建筑古色古香，散发着独特的古典文化气质。即使后来迁入燕园，不变的仍然还是其独具风味的皇家建筑园的风韵。“云里帝城双凤阙，雨中春树万人家”的景致也许就是北大独特的文化符号。北大的校园风格是自由散漫的中国传统书院和 19 世纪末高度学术化的德国大学的混合。从 20 世纪初，北大第一栋与其他建筑风格相异的拥有现代化卫生设备并供应热水的宿舍楼到学子的校园生活中学生的制服服装到长袍的回归，都可以感受到他们身上的开放包容的士人精神和根植中国文化的情怀。[2]

2.2 清华大学

清华大学的前身是作为留美预备学校的清华学堂。因受美国退还的庚子赔款资助建成。从最初的仿照美国的文化性格到增加中国文化成分，到在曹云祥、罗家伦等的努力下确立了中西文化融合过程中的立足中国文化根基的方向，最终使办学理念中的两大核心得以突显：重体育尊大师；中西融合。寻迹清华大学的文化符号，就如同其校歌所遵循的一方面“东西融汇、古今贯通”，另一方面“立德立言、无问东西”。其校园文化蕴含着中国传统的融合东西的大同精神、行健不息的自强精神以及格物致知的治学精神。校园风物中的纪念碑颇具特色，如“三一八断碑”和“王国维纪念碑”。在清华北山之麓的“三一八断碑”为白色大理石残柱改制而成，为纪念在爱国示威游行中牺牲的韦杰三所建，其临终遗言是“我心甚安，但中国快要强起来呀！”清华以此般爱国学子为荣。王国维纪念碑位于清华园后山之麓，碑文由陈寅恪教授所写。清华大学为这位晚清遗臣国学大师立碑显示了其校园文化中的尊崇大师，以及保持独立精神和自由思想的个性。清华学子的校园生活中有鲜明的体育与律己特色。学生规则是校园生活的必备内容，凡是有关学生的起居、上课、学行、赏罚等均需在管理条例范围内，淘汰率高。清华校园虽然没有古代书院的自由气氛，却彰显了传统科举制度层层选拔的严格精神。

[1] 贾佳、王建华．中国大学的文化性格 [M]．福州：福建教育出版社，2017:120-125。

[2] 叶文心．民国时期大学校园文化 [M]．北京：中国人民大学出版社，2012:1-30。

2.3 西南联大

西南联大是一所与中国抗日战争共始共终的大学。七七事变后，国立北京大学、清华大学和私立南开大学先后迁往长沙和昆明，更名为“国立西南联合大学”，是一所有独立精神气质与文化品格的大学，直到1946年解体。西南联大的办学理念体现在以中国文化为根基，寻求中西融合的“中体西用”之上。此外，重大学之道，行通识教育是西南大学对“厚德载物、兼容并包”文化性格的具体阐释。西南联大的校园风物往往和三校分离之际冯友兰所撰的“国立西南联合大学纪念碑”联系在一起。碑文内容写的是校史，赞的是联大精神，追溯的是中国文化的传统意义。碑文中对中国文化的肯定明显可见，将抗日战争的胜利归溯于中国历史之悠久，将联大兼容并蓄的精神归因于中国文化之民主真谛。从校园风物来看，师生从游现象是联大校园的又一文化符号。赵瑞蕻曾这样谈论从游现象：“师生之间可以随意接触谈心，可以相互帮助和争论；在春秋假日中，师生结伴漫游或喝茶下棋，促膝聊天，海阔天空，无所不谈。”[1] 周末的联大宿舍常常有学生“拜谒、请益”，络绎不绝，形成了独特的风景线。而“泡茶馆”也成了联大学生特有的交流语言。借茶馆读书、论学、谈天下事，既有“天下事事事关心”的书院学子身影，又有身处喧嚣“心远地自偏”的修士境界，反映了西南联大学子的独特情怀。后来许多的科学文学家都称深深怀念联大的“泡茶馆”经历，可见这一校园文化符号的独特魅力。

---

[1] 王喜旺：学术与教育互动：西南联大历史时空中的观照 [M]. 山西：山西教育出版社，2008:127。

第四章 中国教育的文化览胜

千年华夏，物类万千，政通人和，教化无尽。观中国教育文化历史长河之深幽洞远，如俯瞰苍茫悠旷之中华大地，无数睿智的心灵与绚丽华章，虽言语无常却理想有恒，虽雪泥鸿爪却足窥教育风貌于一斑，折射出本土文化的永恒光芒。

第一节 比较视野中的文化风景

国内外学者在比较东西方文化特征时，有人认为中国传统文化是一种调节“人我”关系的“内学”，西方传统文化是一种调节“物我”关系的“外学”，因而中国传统教育文化被认为是一种崇尚道德的“德性”文化，西方传统教育文化是一种崇尚理性的“智性”文化。东西方教育文化在价值取向上确实各有侧重，同时也反映在教育目的上。在比较的视野中，五千年的中国传统教育的根本特征更加凸显：立德树人、以文化人。

一、传统理念的对比

文化的任何果实都离不开承载着文化理念的土壤，中西教育理念的差异直接影响了教育文化的特征及其文化环境中人的教育及发展。[1] 了解中西教育各自的基本理念有助于揭示中西教育文化差异的根源。

1.1 中国教育理念

在中国教育思想史上，有以儒佛道三家为代表的众多的学术文化流派。儒家、佛家和道家的教育价值取向，构成了我国主要传统教育价值观念独特的形态，也产生了重大而持久的影响。儒家文化作为封建政治构架的符号化表征，其教育价值取向带有明显的“工具论”色彩。儒家十分重视教育的作用，几乎都是从国家和社会这个视角，来审视教育的价值。[2] 当然，古代的教育家们也并未忽略教育与人的关系问题，但他们大都是从抽象的人性出发来阐述教育对人的作用的。从孔子的性相近说到孟子、荀子的“性善论”“性恶论”之争，再到后世的性混合说、性三品说，尽管他们对人性的认识是大相径庭的，但对教育作用的认识却是一致的，即都认为通过教育使人性完善，以达到稳定社会秩序的目的。这样，教育的政治价值、道德伦理价值便是教育实践的出发点，满足社会需要便是教育的落脚点。儒家教育观念对我国封建社会教育影响至深，

[1] 严明．教育语言学语境观及其战略启示 [R]. 上海：首届教育语言学国际论坛主旨报告，2022 年 7 月。
[2] 陈浩．中西古代教育理念比较 [J]. 贵州民族学院学报，2008(3):174-177。

接受教育是为了将来在社会上施展才华、实现抱负，这成为名门显贵与平民百姓的共识。科举取士制度确立后，“学而优则仕”的教育价值取向，便牢固地印在了中国人的思想深处。

与儒家不同，佛家与道家的教育价值取向和产生的影响并没有与中国封建社会的官方教育接轨，其教育价值观的影响主要体现在个人修行中。虽然在不同历史阶段和地区有不同侧重，道家教育思想的核心是“道”。虽说“不可道、不可观”只能用自然的方式去感受去体悟，但道家追求合乎人性与天性的自然状态的理念却是人们对道家顺应万物规律的共识。道法自然的价值取向与万物一体的物我观念在中国传统的教育历程中也有着不小的影响力。于智育，道家主张“大智若愚、明道若昧”，这有助于受教育者淡化功利的追求，尊重自我意识。于德育，老子提出的“圣人天地不仁”并区分上德与下德，是反对形式主义的虚伪仁义。于美育，道家所说的“大音希声、大象无形”体现的都是见素抱朴的至纯艺术精神。[1]

虽然儒、佛、道三家各有其妙。各有侧重，却也有共通之处。其一是无一例外地重视德育：儒家仁政的“为政以德”“民德归厚”；道家圣人的“常善救人”“常善救物”；释家宗旨之“诸恶莫作、众善奉行”都是典型的道德中心教育。其二是对关注生命的共同认知：释家的“修己安人”“自强不息”的理念；道家的“天人一体”“贵己重生”的思想；佛家的“慈心悲愿”“普度众生”的情怀都是对中国传统教育中敬重生命的诠释。南怀瑾先生曾说中国文化的儒、佛、道三家，孔子开的是粮食店，没有粮食店，光吃面包牛排是吃不饱的，会吃出毛病的。道家开的是药店，不病就不需要药店，一旦生病非要去药店不可。佛家开的是百货公司，吃饱饭没病，有空就去逛逛百货公司，这都是生存的必要。这三家店的比喻是对中国传统教育风格和社会思想缩影的高度概括，映射了一方水土的传统教育理念。

1.2 西方教育理念

与中国的文化传统一样，西方的文化传统也是其教育文化传统形成和生长的土壤。西方教育传统，尤其是欧美的教育传统的发展进程显示了以下特点：神学化、人本学化和心理学化。这些特征可以从西方五大教育名著的巨大影响中窥见一斑。它们分别是柏拉图的《理想国》、夸美纽斯的《大教育学》、卢梭的《爱弥儿》、赫尔巴特的《普通教育学》和杜威的《民主主义与教育》。[2]

在《理想国》中，柏拉图提出了通过教育培养最高统治者的标准，试图使之能成为超越一切利己欲望的超人，即具有神性的人。使人具有理性、接近神性，是柏拉图的教育思想的核心。柏拉图把人的心灵看作由低到高“欲望”“精神”和“理性”三个部分组成的复杂的整体。“理性”包括公正、智慧和德行三个要素。在柏拉图看来，

[1] 胡碧洋，朱珠．道家教育思想的基本论述与思考［J］．文学教育，2019(7)：140-141。
[2] 张法琨．神学化·人本学化·心理学化［J］．华东师范大学学报，1984(2)：83-90。

对人类的天性加以训导，使之富于智慧，节制情欲，以接近上帝是教育的基本功能。以后的罗马时期，新柏拉图主义结合了东方的神秘主义和基督教科学观，认为真正的认知来自信仰。后来阿奎那确立了经院哲学的神学体系，使基督教主义与柏拉图主义进一步结合，使理性与信仰更趋一致。到了文艺复兴运动兴起之后的夸美纽斯时代，人道主义思想体系开始出现。夸美纽斯在《大教育学》中宣称“人是造物中最崇高完善和美好的。”夸美纽斯把“神道”和“人道”结合在一起，创立了既推崇神性又提倡人性，既坚持皈依上帝又强调遵循自然的教育理论体系。在教育实施上，夸美纽斯注重自然作用与人为训练之间的平衡，重视人的自然本性的和谐发展。之后 18 世纪的卢梭，接受了自然主义教育的思想，写下了不朽篇章《爱弥儿》，开辟了教育科学发展的人本学化道路。卢梭在《爱弥儿》中指出，教育事业是一切人类的事业中首要的一件，进而他呼吁教育方法，必须“适合于人，适应人心”。卢梭大大发展了文艺复兴运动以来夸美纽斯的自然教育思想。夸美纽斯所谓“自然”是指“客观的自然”，卢梭的“自然”则指人所具有的自然天性。 西方教育发展真正进入心理学化的时期是从赫尔巴特开始的，他生活在德国哲学大革命的年代，毕生在教育实践中运用哲学。赫尔巴特把人的全部心理活动都看作各种观念的活动，把观念及其相互联合和斗争视为心理活动的基础。20 世纪初，赫尔巴特《普通教育学》成了教育中的统治力量。在赫尔巴特学说盛行的同时，杜威学说也开始产生。同时代，杜威的《民主主义与教育》问世，批判继承了古希腊以来几乎全部教育家的理论，提出了许多有价值的见解。杜威把机能主义、工具主义和社会有机论三者凝练在一起，系统论述了教育性质、过程和价值等各个方面问题，而其中最注重的是人的“兴趣、沉思、经验、认知”等方面的心理发展。

二、教育思想的差异

从上述中西传统教育理念可以看出，虽然有相通之处，在教育思想上却有各自的侧重点与特征。从形式层面而言中国教育重同一性，西方教育重多样性；中国教育重持久稳定，西方教育重变革创新；中国教育重权威，西方教育重平等。[1] 从内容层面而言，中国教育重视人文主线，西方教育强调科学主线。[2]

2.1 中西教育形式差异

首先，中国是一个以群体文化为主要文化特征的国家。国人的群体意识来源于以农耕为主的小农经济生产方式。这种生产方式使得中国人习惯于集体作业，这种约定俗成的典型情境，造就了中国人的群体文化心理。在群体文化中，群体的整体利益是个体利益的唯一参照物，是个体利益的出发点和归宿。中国人关心的是“别人怎么看”，

[1] 杨春苑．从文化视角看中西方教育思想的差异 [J]. 教学与管理，2007(4):10-11。
[2] 王峰．中西人文教育和科学教育的历史嬗变及启示 [J]. 合肥工业大学学报，2007(4):135-138。

会用普遍认可的道德行为规范自觉约束自己的言行，来获得群体的认同。儒家的“和而不同”“求同存异”即具体的表述。“大一统”是中国教育的主旋律，即用统一的内容、同样的方法、单一的评价机制进行教育活动。中国古代的科举制度以及当代的高考制度在一定程度上反映了这一种教育思想。西方文化的基本特征是个体主义。因而在教育思想上也强调个人的价值与尊严，个体的特征与差异，提倡新颖，鼓励独特风格。这种思想助长了西方人对多样性的追求，造就了以多样性为特征、多元化思想共存的西方教育。“多样性”在西方教育制度方面得到了充分体现。西方学校的教学氛围自然灵活，教师的教和学生的学都没有太多必须遵守的强制规范。特别是文艺复兴之后的人本化教育使得为儿童教育选择有用和有益于人们幸福的知识成为共识，20世纪后的杜威教育思想更是强调了在活动中了解文化，使个人成为掌握自身经验构建的主体的理念。其次，中国几千年的农耕经济催生了传统文化中根深蒂固的“求久”观念。反映在教育上，就是经世济用的教育观和学术价值观。由于要“求久、求稳”，中国教育特别强调基础知识的重要性，所谓“万丈高楼平地起”，强调基础知识本身与经典学术传统的重要性是中国教育的基本思想。相反，西方教育文化鼓励独特、注重多元的思想使他们并不强调基础知识与前人经典而寻求独辟蹊径、标新立异，欣赏新奇且富于创新和冒险精神。再次，以儒家思想为核心的中国传统文化，历来主张尊卑有别、长幼有序的等级观念，这体现在教育思想上即传统的“师道尊严”，教师承担起传道、授业、解惑的责任，具有一定的威严。这有助于文明有序的求学环境，却对独立性与批判性的培养有一定阻碍。在西方“平等主义”的教育思想影响下，教师在教育过程中扮演学生的向导和平等交往的伙伴的角色。因而学习者对知识与智能的追求，超越了对社会等级秩序的遵从，从而变得更具挑战性与独立性。

2.2 中西教育内容差异

以人文为主线的中国教育内容源于中国传统文化对天人关系的关注。对天人关系的不同思考和定位，形成了对教育与人、教育与自然的关系，以及对自然知识和人文知识价值的不同认识，从而在中国传统教育史上出现了长期重视人文教育而忽视科学教育的局面。这具体反映了中国传统教育的“主德”特征，一般文化知识服从于道德教育的需要。如“子以四教：文行忠信”“弟子入则孝，出则悌，谨而信，泛爱众，而亲仁，行有余力，则以学文”。在儒家教育体系中，德育始终放在首位。在其影响下，中国传统教育在目的论、课程观和方法论等方面都体现出浓厚的伦理色彩与价值色彩，崇圣尊经、重道轻艺反映了人文知识体系的经学教育为本思想，理工医农等处于辅助的地位。到了近代以后，伴随西方科学主义思潮的传入，人们在分析思考军事上失利的过程中才产生了对科学技术知识的青睐和敬仰。西方教育强调科学主线源于他们特别强调人与自然的区别。西方教育在主张以人为中心的同时，还重视人与自然关系及重视科学知识在人的健康成长和社会发展中的作用，因而提倡科学教育。这体现在西方传统教育的“主智”特征，自古强调智慧的重要性。苏格拉底认为“美德就是知识”“美德是灵魂的一种属性"。柏拉图、亚里士多德也十分重视"理性"教育，在他们看来，学生的身体、情感和理智诸方面的发展都是必要的，而最要紧的是使理性(智)得到发展。因此西方古代教育内容就比较广博，涉及许多自然科学的知识。[1]

2.3 中西差异的文化渊源

中西教育传统思想的差异除了政治、经济、军事、民族、风俗等社会因素的不同影响外，还因中西教育家本身的政治观、哲学观、人才观所决定。

中国儒学教育家强调人与社会的关系，把人才培养与政治需要结合起来，主张培养"明人伦"的治术之才。这种人才必须是通过自我修养以达到社会道德要求的人。鉴于这种主"善"的观点，在教育上就形成了以道德教育为轴心的体系。教育就是教人如何"做人"，强调对自身的肯定，通过"修己"以达到圣人的境界。这种自我修养以自身的伦理道德为主导，表现在教育内容上可以排除天命鬼神的思想，使宗教与神学在中国教育传统中屈于皇权与圣贤之下。但是，这种把伦理道德教育当作人类生活决定性因素的观点，限制了实证科学的发展。儒学教育家主张内省，而不主张向外探求宇宙规律，反映在教育内容上就是教育与自然科学脱节，教育内容排斥了科技知识。从某种意义上说，由于过分强调道德方面的作用，从而使自然科学的发展受到了限制。而古希腊的教育家也强调人与自然的关系，主张培养有智慧的心灵、和谐完美的人。基于这种主"真"的观点，在教育内容上就要求对受教育者施行德智体美诸方面的教育，其中必须以智育为主，只有具有广博的知识，才能发展理性灵魂，所以教育内容比较全面。这种主张对后世有积极影响，特别是对欧洲文化科学的发展为文艺复兴时期一些意识形态的产生奠定了基础。同时，由于重视教育与人的自然发展相适应，因此确定教育内容时考虑到了不同年龄阶段学生的特点，这也为近现代学制的建立提供了依据。但是，古代西方教育家把教育目的看成是为了使人达到"理念世界"，发展所谓的"理智灵魂"，在他们看来，衡量一个人是否完善，要看他是否达到了"神"的境界。这反映在中世纪直至启蒙时期相当长阶段的教育内容上就带有许多神秘的唯心主义观念，直到人本主义与科学主义进入西方教育的主流思潮。

由此我们可以看出中西教育价值取向差异渊源是：中国重调和社会和自我、重知识的应用价值、重教育的世俗性；西方则注重个性自由和主体意识、重知识的内在价值、重教育的宗教性。[2]

三、文化名人的对话

中西文化名人虽然天各一方，却在各自的文化家园上都留下了宝贵的财富，产生了不朽的影响力。本节选取相似时期中西方代表性文化名人进行比较，通过他们风格与

[1] 白瑾．中西教育传统差异对教育观念现代化的启示 [J]．内蒙古师范大学学报，2010(2):14-17。
[2] 蔡中宏．中西教育价值取向嬗变的考察与思考 [J]．科学·经济·社会，2005(3):74-77。

思想的碰撞展现出中西教育文化的别样风情。

3.1 孔子与苏格拉底的精神风范

作为文化轴心时代的领衔者，苏格拉底与孔子对各自的轴心文化与教育的建构产生了核心影响。他们都以救世主的心态积极介入历史的场域。苏格拉底曾把自己比喻为希腊民族的牛虻，自己的存在就是对民族奋进的鞭策。孔子也是踌躇满志，曾曰“凤鸟不至，河不出图，吾已矣夫”。后世见证了两者都以毕生的努力扮演着各自民族的“伦理学之父”的角色。虽然两者都述而不作，但是两者都倾力于教育事业，对后学大力培育，且在教学中都用启发式教学。

虽然二者有诸多的相似之处，但两者的教育文化风格却迥然不同。首先两人的政治取向不同。两人虽都有深切的救世情怀，但苏格拉底仅将自己的理想定格在精神领域，不曾有过做官的打算。在对古希腊文化进行深刻反思和总结之后，他提出“认识你自己”的口号，得出“美德即知识”的结论，实现了古希腊伟大的“伦理学转向”。虽然他关注和思考的是人间事，是实践理性哲学，但对政治实践不甚钟情。与苏格拉底不同的是，孔子对政治实践热情很高，而且周游列国，主动寻找入仕机会。孔子曾说如果有人用他，东周礼崩乐坏的局面将会得到彻底的挽救，一年可产生明显的治理效果，三年可实现稳定繁荣。后终不得见用，遂用心于《诗》《书》《礼》《易》《春秋》五经，以此寄托深厚的仕情。孔子与苏格拉底政治取向的差异，导致了东西文化旨趣上的分野。首先，儒家具有强烈的入世与功名观念，而西方的文化却相对超脱，为真理而真理，更趋向于自由独立的人格取向。其次，在思维方式上，苏格拉底是共时性思维，而孔子则是历时性思维。历时性思维较之共时性思维更接近历史主义和保守主义，希望能在历史中寻求解决问题的答案，孔子就是典型的“未尝离事而言理”的上古史学叙事风格。于此，章学诚评价道：“事有实据，而理无定形。故夫子之述五经，皆取先王典章，未尝离事而著理。”这就呈现了孔子“祖述尧舜，宪章文武”，善于在历史中挖掘说教范例。共时性思维由于自由活泼，立体感和创新性强，是一种本质主义的思维。罗素认为，苏格拉底式的探索方式会受知识之限，在逻辑领域较适用。就其实质而言，因为苏格拉底的方式包含了归纳和综合思维手段，所以对于知识没有排挤的嫌疑。再次，两者在教育方式上都善于运用启发式教学，但实质上却存在很大的差异。他很强调定义（即本质）在探讨中的前提地位，或曰，探讨的最终归宿便是本质。这就决定了苏格拉底的话语是一种求真的思维过程。这种过程也是一种形式上的智慧游戏，在其中能让谈话者感受到智慧的愉悦，尽管很多时候这种探讨并没有一个确定的结果。苏格拉底虽自比于希腊民族的牛虻，但在探索真理的过程中却相当低调。他首先承认自己对拟探讨的东西一无所知，然后提出问题让对方回答。其谈话的目的和核心即真理。他们是在玩追逐真理的游戏，苏格拉底的这种言说方式也真切地体现了辩证精神。反之，由于孔子的思维方式是历时性的，具有强烈的情景倾向，因此他在教学中通过范例来达到伦理教育的目的。而历史的范例是既成事实，会让更多的人产生信服与模仿，印证了历史在教育中有很重要的作用也体现了注入式教学过程，《论语》充分表现了一种话语权威与师道尊严，无需辩驳，也无需探讨以寻求更深一层的答案，这也是儒家君子人格的风范。[1]

作为文化轴心时代的精神领袖，这两种截然不同的思维方式、政治取向和教学模式，熏陶和铸造了两种大异其趣的民族文化精神，这种差异和影响表现在很多方面，其影响源远流长。

3.2 孟子与亚里士多德的教师理念

作为轴心时代的另外两位大师：孟子与亚里士多德所代表的教师形象反映出了中西教育发展的差异。作为东方中国传统文化代表的孟子注重培养经世致用的人才，要求教师德才兼备，做好学生的引路人，形成尊师重道的良好氛围。而古希腊西方文化教育者代表亚里士多德则注重培养全面发展的人才，要求教师具备专精化的知识，形成自由平等的师生关系。[2]

关于教师地位，孟子将教师与国君并列，通过称教师“天佑下民，作之君 ，作之师”而把教师的地位抬到较高的高度，反映了战国“士”阶层地位重要和参政的愿望。孟子说：“大匠诲人，必以规矩；学者亦以于规矩”即是高明的工匠教人一定要遵循原则，学的人也一定要遵循原则才行。这表明教师在教学中应为学生树立一定的原则标准才行。当然，孟子也指出“能与人规矩，不能使人巧”，“君子引而不发，跃如也。中道而立，能者从之”，[3] 教师恰到好处地做出样子，有能力的人就会学习他。这也表明孟子认为教师只是教学中的引路人，关键在于学生自身修养的提高和磨炼。亚里士多德将教育看作是构建人才、治理城邦的重要手段，他说“城邦应该是许多个体的集合，唯有教育才能使它成为团体而达成统一”。同时认为人的心灵就像一块蜡块或白纸，任何事物都孕育着发展的可能性，要使人的潜能变成现实，需要依靠教育和教师，重视教师的指导作用。学生要向智者学习，才能获得知识技能，可见教师在教育过程中起着主导的作用。关于教师素质，孟子对教师提出的条件可归为三点：一是良好的道德品质。孟子提出教育的内容就是封建宗法五伦道德，以明人伦为中心，所以提倡“存心寡欲，反求诸己，知耻改过，养浩然之气 ，磨炼意志”，以此要求教师本身的道德应高尚。二是广博且专精的知识。孟子说：“博学而详说之，将以反说约也”，即教师应当有渊博的学识，并能详细地解说，在融会贯通以后，再概括出简要的大意，因此学识深广是教师必备的基本素质。三是教师修养。孟子要求教师要热爱教育事业，忠于职守以及为人师表。孟子不仅以“得天下之英才而教育之，三乐也”的言辞表明自己对教育事业的热爱，而且也借用对公子丑说的话“教者必以正”要求教师要以身作则，

[1] 向达．孔子、苏格拉底思想比较研究 [J]. 攀登，2010(5):63-68。
[2] 王建梁，帅晓静．德性与智性文化下的教师形象 [J]. 当代教师教育，2011(2):70-74。
[3] 金沛霖．孟子语录 [M]. 北京：中国文联出版社，2006:98。

为学生作表率。而亚里士多德对教师提出的条件可归为两点：一是专精化知识的要求。亚里士多德将知识或教育的内容划分为两类：一类是适合自由人学习的；一类是不适合自由人学习的。而适合自由人学习的自由学科的知识传授都需要教师拥有艰深专门的知识。二是热爱教育事业的品质。在亚历山大统治的强盛时期，亚里士多德并没有流连其中，而是在所创办的学园中从事教学和科学研究活动长达十多年，其间几乎很少过问政治，可见亚里士多德对教育的热爱。关于师生关系，孟子在师生关系中更强调要尊师重道，即学生对教师的尊重。孟子说“徐行后长者谓之弟，疾行先长者谓之不弟。”即慢一点走，谦让长者叫作尊敬长者；快一点走，抢在长者之前叫不尊敬长者。孟子期待的是整个社会能形成学生尊重老师的良好氛围。亚里士多德在师生关系中更强调教学相长，他爱戴自己的老师柏拉图，然而他也提出“更爱真理”的格言，他不是盲目信从而是不为贤者讳，能毫不客气地提出不同的观点。亚里士多德的教学形式多是与学生在林间散步游玩，共同探讨知识，这也使后人将他及其追随者称为“逍遥学派”，体现了注重师生间自由平等的理念。

作为文化轴心时代的大师，孟子与亚里士多德各自的教师理念反映出了中西教育文化的异同。中国教师文化的核心价值是“德”，高尚的师德、较高的修养是我们对教师的首要要求，尊师的文化传统以其特有的形式得以传承。西方文化的核心价值是“智”，追求的是知识与真理，教师的知识水平与专门化是其重要要求。

3.3 庄子与卢梭教育思想

庄子和卢梭都是教育的高人，他们都发现了人类文明进程中的二律背反问题，并提出了有关“自然”的理想观念，他们的教育观分别代表着中西方自然教育的高峰。二人虽然生活在不同的时代和地域，但是对他们自然教育观异同的比较是学界热衷的话题。[1]

共同点是他们都对压抑人性的教育及其内容提出批判和质疑，主张教育要顺应大自然的规律与人的天性，而且对科技都持有否定态度。在庄子看来，人类社会的发展就是不断地人为破坏自然，这种做法无异于“落马首，穿牛鼻”。关于知识，庄子认为知识能使人乱性，也能使人引起争夺，易为奸人所假借。因此，庄子认为解决的办法只能是“绝圣弃智”。庄子对儒家所提倡的教育思想是持批评态度的，认为是违反人的本性的。因而庄子在《养生主》中提出“缘督以为经”，主张凡事都要顺着自然的路径而行，教育也不例外。庄子《至乐》篇提出只有顺应教育对象的个性，才能引发兴趣，充分发挥潜能，从而达到“自化”目的。庄子认为技术的使用使自然的本性受到摧残，他说：“有机械者必有机事，有机事者必有机心。机心存于胸中，则纯白不备；纯白不备，则神生不定；神生不定者，道之所不载也。”同样，卢梭认为在封建制度下“我们的种种智慧都是奴隶的偏见，我们的一切习惯都在奴役、折磨和遏制我们，文明人

[1] 王文礼．庄子和卢梭的自然教育观之比较 [J]. 内蒙古师范大学学报，2006(12):25-28。

在奴隶状态中从生到死无处不受到教育和制度的束缚”。他认为传统的古典主义教育只注重学习神学和人文课程，这些知识内容不仅枯燥，而且狭窄，只发展儿童的某一方面。卢梭在如何实施自然教育上，主张教育应遵循儿童的天性，按照自然运行的规律。他主张对儿童实施“消极教育”，采用自然后果教育原则，防止儿童的思想产生谬误。卢梭在《论科学和艺术的复兴是否有助于敦风化俗》中还明确指出，科学和艺术败坏了人类之善，无异于是道德的毒素。

庄子与卢梭的教育观也存在不同点：首先他们理论指向的对象不同。庄子的教育是修成圣人，“圣人”是指达到绝对自由境界的贤者：圣人者，原天地之美而达万物之理。而卢梭的自然教育是培养“公民”。卢梭在《爱弥儿》中把理想的公民形象描写成当时贵族和资产阶级优点的结合，是富有知识和文化、身心健康、具有独立思想的人，即现代意义上的“公民”。其次，是对教育年龄分期的认识不同。庄子对自然教育的论述是从一个整体的人的角度，没有把教育对象分成儿童和成人，更不存在把人的成长过程分成几个时期进行教育。而卢梭把儿童的教育划分为四个阶段，主张根据儿童的不同发展阶段来实施相应的教育。最后，是教育理论依据的哲学基础大相径庭。庄子依据的是“道”，他在《知北游》中明确指出：“有先天地生者物邪？物物者非物。”对于这种非物质，庄子认为是最根本的“道”。卢梭依据的是感觉经验，他认为：由于进入人类心灵的知识以感觉为门户，所以人类最初的理性，来自感觉经验。最后是对教育作用的认识不同。庄子主张“不言之教”“绝圣弃智”“无为之教”，否认教育的积极作用。而卢梭则一方面否定那些违背儿童天性的教育，另一方面充分肯定了教育的作用，认为正是教育导致人与人之间的差别。他在《爱弥儿》中阐述了“我们成长所需要的东西，要由教育赐给我们”。[1]

就人与自然的关系而言，虽然庄子与卢梭都强调人与自然的和谐统一，但在哲学基础上又存在着一元论与二元论的差异；就社会理想而言，虽然他们都表达了对自由、平等的向往和追求，但在实现途径上又表现为至德之世与契约社会的差异；就审美态度而言，虽然他们都提倡素朴本真、拒斥异化的一种生存，但在内容指向上又体现出以“道”观物与以“善”观物的差异。庄子“顺应自然”的虚无主义与卢梭“回归自然”的理想主义虽然从历史上看并非前沿或主流，但因其都共同呼唤人性与社会的返璞归真，[2] 对于现代教育而言意义显著。

[1] 李沛蓉．浅谈爱弥儿中的教育思想 [J]．新丝路，2020(6):196-197。

[2] 董晔．虚无主义与理想主义：庄子与卢梭的自然观念异同及价值批判 [J]．中国社会科学院研究生院学报，2012(6):21-25。

第二节 教育世界里的精神核心

众所周知，历朝历代中国传统教育的核心是人的观念教化。在中国教育精神中，无论是皇家还是庶民，不分朝代和学派，培养子弟形成理想的符合要求的世界观、人生观和价值观是观念教化的主要任务，这也时刻渗透在现实社会和教育文化的各种内容中，形成了中华民族特有的精神哲学。

一、世界观的缩影

“天人合一”的世界观是从先秦至明清时期大部分哲学家们对于中国传统哲学秉持的一个基本观念，使得中国文化从一开始就在一个广大和谐的环境下产生、成长。对于“天”的释义可从三方面理解，其一是物质之天，与地相对，也可以认为就是当代所认为的自然；其二是精神之天，对人的命运和世间万物具有主宰作用；其三是义理方面，是世间万物所必须要遵从和认可的至高真理。教育史上诸多的先贤和学者对于天的释义存在大同小异的分歧，却不约而同地认为“天人合一”思想所表达的就是一种人与自然的内在统一关系。这样的世界观除了彰显在文人著述和教育理念中，还生动地表现在中国人的时空概念、民间传说和人情社会中。

1.1 时空中的美学

在农耕文明的背景下，中国教育中人与自然的关系元素常常是一道美丽的风景。在朝堂、学府和庶民之间互相传授和品悟。无论是节气还是节日都反映出人们对一方水土的细腻情感。

二十四节气是中国人通过观察太阳周年运动，认知一年中时令、气候、物候等方面变化规律所形成的知识体系和社会实践。中国古人将太阳周年运动轨迹划分为二十四等份，每一等份为一个节气，统称二十四节气。具体包括立春、雨水、惊蛰、春分、清明、谷雨、立夏、小满、芒种、夏至、小暑、大暑、立秋、处暑、白露、秋分、寒露、霜降、立冬、小雪、大雪、冬至、小寒、大寒。二十四节气指导着传统农业生产和日常生活，是中国传统历法体系及其相关实践活动的重要组成部分。在国际气象界，这一时间认知体系被誉为“中国的第五大发明”。从常见的优秀传统诗词中人们就能潜移默化地体会到节气给中国人思想与生活的影响。如：

晚春

元稹[1]

昼静帘疏燕语频，双双斗雀动阶尘。

柴扉日暮随风掩，落尽闲花不见人。

---

[1] 元稹（779—831年），字微之，别字威明，河南洛阳人。唐朝大臣、文学家。有《元氏长庆集》传世，收录诗赋等共100卷。现存诗830余首。

山中立夏用坐客韵

文天祥[1]

归来泉石国，日月共溪翁。
夏气重渊底，春光万象中。
穷吟到云黑，淡饮胜裙红。
一阵弦声好，人间解愠风。

秋词

刘禹锡[2]

自古逢秋悲寂寥，我言秋日胜春朝。
晴空一鹤排云上，便引诗情到碧霄。

邯郸冬至夜思家

白居易[3]

邯郸驿里逢冬至，抱膝灯前影伴身。
想得家中夜深坐，还应说着远行人。

诗人们没有刻意强调生态和谐和节气文化，但古诗词中却尽是人与自然、心与时光，以及情与万物的交融。在品读这些传统诗词时读者体会到的不仅仅是诗人称羡的自然与时光带来的美感，也有中国文人向往的遵循自然的生活状态和超尘拔俗的人生理想，更有一种心有灵犀的民族文化认同感。这种来自文学的审美超越时空，传播在中国人的生活环境与教育领域中，不仅丰富了精神的内涵，还增强了民族凝聚力。

在民间谚语中同样可以看到反映中华民族特有的生活方式与文明理念的节气文化元素。这些节气民谚形式多样，意象生动，流传甚广，蕴含着鲜明的习俗和深厚的积淀，成为民间文化的重要组成部分。如：

立春晴一日，耕田不费力。惊蛰到春风，秧田要管勤。
霜降到交冬，翻地冻虫虫。生产要丰收，秋收是关头。
清明不冷食，冰雹下满地。吃了夏至面，一天短一线。

节气谚语来源于历代中国农耕劳动者生产生活实践经验的总结，世代相传，反复

[1] 文天祥（1236—1283年），字宋瑞，又字履善。江西庐陵县人，南宋末年政治家、文学家，著有《文山先生全集》。
[2] 刘禹锡（772—842年），字梦得，江苏徐州人，唐代中期诗人、哲学家。政治上主张革新，是王叔文派政治革新活动的中心人物之一。
[3] 白居易（772—846年），唐代著名现实主义诗人，字乐天，号香山居士，山西太原人，主张新乐府运动，有近三千首优秀作品留世。

检验，闪耀着智慧的光芒。二十四节气反映了农耕生活的古老文化，在现代社会中依然反映中国人时空审美与家国情怀。各种节气不仅继续引导着人们的农业生产，影响着相关的饮食习俗，并且在一代又一代的教育思行中不断丰富和传承着。近现代以来，各地农民根据气温、降水、物候的变化，不断修改和完善与节气相关的农谚，将二十四节气本地化。比如以前的农谚说“清明断雪，谷雨断霜”，表示谷雨之后，寒冷的天气基本上结束了；如今在一些地方改成“谷雨雪断霜未断，杂粮播种莫延迟”，成为农民安排农事的新依据。除了实用价值外，二十四节气在今天继续传承，更因它蕴含着中华民族鲜活的文化基因。它在不知不觉中干预我们对缤纷世界的认知，在潜移默化中影响我们对大千气象的体验。比如清明原本是一个提示农民抓紧春耕的节气，在后来的发展中，逐渐融入寒食节的习俗，形成了祭拜扫墓、踏青出游两大代表性节俗，应时而变，又有了慎终追远、追思先贤、缅怀先烈等内容。“清明”承载着中华民族特有的生命意识，直到今天依然指导着人们的行为，具有重要的教育意义。

什么节气做什么，什么天候预示什么，已经浸润到华夏民族的血脉中，使得中国人的精神与物质生活极具韵律之美。二十四节气反映了尊重自然、顺天应时的智慧。总之，二十四节气是“中国人用大自然给生活加上的标点”，是华夏民族集体世界观里的一套“天人感应装置”，穿越古今，历久弥新，始终焕发着光彩和活力。

1.2 神话中的精神

中国世界观文化中的神性观念体现在神话和民间传说中，不仅题材多样，语言也独特优美，是中华优秀传统文化中非常重要的分支。从中国古代文化来看，中国人很早就有了鬼神的概念，神话也是中国人认知世界的开端，是民族精神的体现，是文学艺术和民族信仰产生的土壤。

中国人的祖先认为，天与神不可分。中国创世神话提供了天神一体的认识基础。首先，他们认为自己的祖先是人兽同体的神，其次，“天神一体”的“帝”拥有呼风唤雨凌驾于万物之上的力量。殷商之际，宗教观念由“尊神”向“尊礼”转换，是后世孔子文化思想的历史体现。传统上，天作为神的化身，是超乎自然之上的一种无法捉摸的力量，随着人类社会的发展，人们开始认识到人固有本质的伟大之处，因此“人文性”开始得到张扬，宗教也因此转化为一种“人文性的宗教”或“道德的宗教”。自从孔子把天神相分，中国文化也从“神人之间”走向“天人合一”，反映在天命论上即是将天命与道德联系起来，“天”通过“命”的方式，自下而上成为了人性与人道的形而上的来源。地上的人通过鬼神以及祖先相交以趋吉避凶，或者获得王朝统治的合法性；地上的人王代表的不仅是整个王朝，而且是所有治下之民。因此，“天命”也必然属于集体的性质。[1]“天人合一”意味着以人合天，是人在现实层面上通过不断修为，最终达到超越的人性。这种超越是中华民族的精神所在，反映在《山海经》《淮南子》

[1] 余英时．论天人之际 [M]．北京：联经出版公司，1970:9。

等收录的众多神话故事和人物文本中。如鲧面对滔天洪水，敢于承担起治水重任，拯救苍生。他用尽一切办法治理洪水，后身死生禹，超越个体肉体，使治水工作后继有人。最后，大禹青出于蓝，因势利导，用人与自然和谐相处的方法成功治理了洪水；盘古的“死后化生”也以天人合一的方式体现了个体超越。盘古的伟大不但在于他开天辟地，又日复一日、年复一年辛劳地顶天立地，更在于他在即将倒下之际还不忘孕育天下万物，他以献身的方式向先民们阐释了顶天立地的创世神的形象，也体现了中国古代“天人合一”的哲学思想。这都是个体超越的例子。女娲面对天崩地裂，她到昆仑山采炼五彩石，“断鳌足以立四极，杀黑龙以济冀州，积芦灰以止淫水”，每一壮举都是惊天动地，这个故事与后羿射日、精卫填海神话一样，反映了先民们在恶劣的灾害面前改造自然的努力与勇气，是超越自然的例子。共工是一个敢于抗争天帝的英雄，他超越困境，在受挫折以后，继续反抗，打破了旧社会的格局，虽败犹胜；牛郎织女神话超越凡人婚配方式，超越普通婚姻经营模式，虽远隔银河，却也要长久相守，这些是社会超越的例子。刑天反抗天帝被斩首后“以乳为目，以脐为口”继续舞动干戈进行反抗；哪吒割肉还母、剔骨还父后，“碧藕为骨、荷叶为衣”的再生体现了脱胎换骨的坚持，这是精神超越的例子。中国神话的天人合一所体现的除了超越精神外还有尚德的神性，集中表现为舍身和奉献精神，这一精神由创世神话传承而来。传说中英雄人物几乎都是圣贤的化身，他们庄重和善、心存济世救民之心，他们不存私欲，奉献精神是他们共有的美德。如神农不忍看人民得病，于是亲自尝遍世间百草，最后中毒而亡；大禹为了不让百姓再遭受洪涝之害，将所有的精力都放在了治水之上，三过家门而不入。中国传说中的天神是远离人间，不食烟火的，他们大多都是无欲无求，没有七情六欲的，不仅是至高无上的权力化身，而且是美德全知全能的化身。这种神性所代表的是人们对完美人格向往的典范，这种尚德的神性加之天道观念逐步形成了中国教育文化中最初的对无比高尚人格的追寻和对人性的鞭策。[1]

总之，中国神话蕴含着民族思想的开端，阐释了初民们在顺应自然中的抗争意识和超越精神。这种精神影响了一代又一代华夏子孙，展现了中华民族思想文化从“尊天事神”的依附性到“天人合一”的超越性，进而超越个体、超越自然、超越社会，最后超越精神，从外向超越到内向超越，最终到达“天人合一”的至高境界。中国神话故事中的精神不但表达了先民征服自然、变革社会的愿望，更演绎了中华民族百折不挠、自强不息的精神品质，也是中华民族初始信仰的精华和“天人合一”世界观的生动写照。

1.3 阴阳中的世界

四时、阴阳和五行是极具中国特色的文化观念。如果说二十四节气是在传统的“四时八节”基础上形成的完整历法，那么阴阳五行学说则与四时观念在血缘上有着一种亲和性。中国先民在解释天地运行、四季交替之时，引入了阴阳二气、五行的概念。

[1] 鄢予晨.《山海经》和《淮南子》中共工形象探究［J］. 文教资料，2017(31):3-5。

老子可以说是第一位站在哲学的高度对阴阳观念进行阐发之人。《老子・四十二章》云："万物负阴而抱阳，冲气以为和。"阴阳五行与四时观念各有渊源，各自独立，各自发展，春秋战国时期逐渐相互影响、相互渗透，出现合流的趋势。在战国中后期由阴阳家完成了融合统一，形成阴阳五行学说，成为中国人认识和思考宇宙人生的理论工具和思维模式。[1] 至此，中国文化在许多领域的萌芽、产生、发展、定型中无不蕴含着阴阳五行学说的观念，强调阴阳二气交感变化，化育出宇宙万物。

阴阳五行学说源于我国古代劳动人民对于自身、自然和社会的敏锐洞察与深刻认识。阴阳本质上是指事物的矛盾统一性和动态平衡性，而对立统一与动态平衡正是一切事物最基本的运行质态选择。五行思想实际上就是对事物内部各要素以及事物之间关系的深刻理解与规律把握。五行最早见于《尚书》，五行之"五"甲骨文写作"X"，寓意天地万物的交汇与融合；五行之"行"甲骨文写作"[illegible]"，就像四通八达的十字路口。五行其实代表了五种事物的元素、功能及其相生相克的基本序列与规律，犹如一种简化的世界模型，不断地汲取诸如儒家、道家、法家、农家等学说的精神元素，经由箕子、管子、邹衍、董仲舒、刘向等人的总结而发展与完善，具有古代朴素唯物论与辩证法特质。阴阳五行学说将阴阳视为事物最基本的表现形态，将矛盾统一视为一切事物变化发展的原始动力，认为宇宙万物皆由金木水火土等五种元素构成，都遵循相生与相克两大客观规律，将阴阳彼此消长五行轮换转移视为宇宙观的理论基础。五行学说的基本含义在于事物内部各要素以及事物之间所存在的相生相克的次序与联系运行不息，而五行的特性是分析事物属性和事物之间联系的基本法则。举例来说：凡是剧烈运动的、外向的、上升的、高处的、温热的、明亮的都属于阳；凡是相对静止的、内守的、下降的、低处的、寒冷的、晦暗的都属于阴。[2] 此外，木具有生长、生发的特性，火具有温热、繁茂的特性，土具有生化、承载的特性，金具有变革、收敛的特性，而水具有润泽、向下的特性。阴阳五行学说依据五行的特性推演出五行之间的生克乘侮。五行相生以木生火、火生土、土生金、金生水、水生木为次序，循环往复、生生不息。五行相克以木克土、土克水、水克火、火克金、金克木为次序，如此循环，生生不息。而五行相乘是指五行中的某一行对被克的一行克制太过而引起的一系列的异常反应，五行相侮实为五行中的某一行过于虚弱，对被原来所克的一行进行反侮。阴阳五行学说的核心思想是整体关联、和谐平衡、相互连结、动态发展、遵循规律、师法自然。集中体现为统一性、完整性与自我调适性，一旦出现了某一行过强或过弱就会引起五行运行的异常反应，事物将失去动态平衡性，从而影响事物的和谐发展。

阴阳五行学说根植于太极图，来源于生活实践，是一种科学的和谐化了的辩证法。阴阳是对客观事物既对立又统一的两个方面或两种基本属性的抽象概括，而五行乃是

---

[1] 孙玲．论二十四节气的哲学意蕴［J］．苏州科技大学学报，2019(5)：18-22。
[2] 陈德述．略论阴阳五行学说的起源与形成［J］．西华大学学报，2014(2)：1-5。

阴阳二气周期性相对变化的五个不同的阶段。阴阳五行学说在中医学领域和传统教育思维中已经得到了广泛的应用并有着深远影响，可以说这个思维方式反映了中国传统文化和民间生活中的世界观，体现着人们对万物协商性共生合作关系的重视，对现代教育依然有着显著的启示。[1]

二、人生观的映射

所谓人生观在中国文化中被视为“为人之道”或“处世之方”，指的是如何看待人生、度过人生和安排人生的问题，换言之，就是关于从人的生存与生活到生命的意义与归属的关切问题。总之，人生观的核心是人生理想和终极关切，了解一种文化的传统人生观，不但能够认识这一文化的社会历史精华，还能够从中体验到特定教育文化背后的人文精神与目标。中国传统文化中所包含的儒、佛、道三家之人生观，不仅是中华民族文化自信的映射，也对中国历代的教育宗旨与文化特征有着巨大的影响。[2]

2.1 儒家

儒家在中国传统文化中一直占主导地位，儒家的人生哲学是讲道德、重进取的现实主义人生观。其生命意识主要表现在对人性的理解和理想生命的探寻上，特别重视对人生价值的积极追求和对生命意义的道德完善。[3]

儒家是道德型人生观，要求为人“入则孝，出则悌，谨而信，泛爱众而亲仁”(《论语・学而》)。儒家的核心概念仁义礼智信，温良恭俭让，恭宽信敏惠等，都是做人的基本规范和信条，也就是儒家为人处世的道德标准。凡在自己的生命活动中能够坚持以上操节，并以之为安身立命者，就是儒家所称誉的“圣贤”“志士仁人”，他们能够做到“杀身成仁，舍生取义”，为践行儒家规定的道德规范而奉献生命。儒家人生哲学的另一个突出特点是求进取，讲现实。儒家都是现实主义者，追求现实的道德的永恒价值和现实生活中的理想人格。孔子一生罕言性、命，不谈鬼神，总是教导弟子们在现实生活中学习、进取、奋斗。孔子曾言：“其为人也(指他自己)，发愤忘食，乐以忘忧，不知老之将至云尔。”他经常教导弟子为人要做到“学而不厌，诲人不倦”“三人行，必有我师焉；择其善者而从之，其不善者而改之”(《论语・述而》)。孔子总是教导人们有意义地度过自己的一生，对人生采取积极有为的态度。他曾语重心长地劝导说：“饱食终日，无所用心，难矣哉！”(《论语・阳货》)，他还用流水一去不复返激励人们要爱惜时光，做有意义的事情。“子在川上曰：‘逝者如斯夫，不舍昼夜’。”(《论语・子罕》)根据孔子的教导，曾子论述了人生“任重而道远”的积极思想，他说：“士不可以不弘毅，任重而道远。仁以为己任，不亦重乎？死而后已，不亦远乎？”(《论语・泰

[1] 尹达．古代阴阳五行学说及其现代教育价值［J］．临沂大学学报，2020(1):62-67。
[2] 李向平．楷模伦理与完美心态：以儒释道共有之伦理特质为例［J］．社会科学，2022(12):141-151。
[3] 杨士连，于则元．儒道传统生命观与现代生命理论教育构建［J］．福建论坛，2010(8):83-84。

伯》）儒家认为义重于利，强调要“见利思义”“义以为质”“义然后取”“先义后利”。儒家还十分推崇重视精神境界的理想人格，孟子说：“居天下之广居，立天下之正位，行天下之大道。得志，与民由之，不得志，独行其道。富贵不能淫，贫贱不能移，威武不能屈，此之谓大丈夫”。（《孟子·滕文公》）我国历代爱国志士和民族英雄的出现，以及“文明古国”和“礼仪之邦”的美称，都与儒家思想的影响密切相关。[1]

总之，儒家人生观的宗旨是“兼善天下”“济世利他”。儒家总是强调国家、民族利益的重要性，要求个人服从整体，强调人际关系的和谐、国家统一、社会太平。儒家人生哲学的核心就是重视精神境界，认为人的精神需要高于物质需要。这一思想充分体现于人生理想、人生态度和人生修养之中，对于塑造“志士仁人”“大丈夫”这样的理想人格，对于陶冶民族性格，提升精神文明，在历史上起着巨大的进步作用。[2]

2.2 道家

与儒家不同，道家的人生哲学是重境界、图个体自由放达的理想主义的人生观。道家的人生哲学在思想表现形式上都是力图超越生命的有限而追求永恒，但在生命的过程中，要求人们把握客观与主观，坦然面对个体生命的喜怒哀乐，在顺应自然与世事变化的基础上寻求生命的意义，与儒家相比显得更加出尘而老练。[3]

道家认为文明增加了人们的欲望和痛苦，应当回到生命的本初源地，在无我无知无欲的思想引导下，跳出人生看人生，以超越的眼光看待生死，以大镇定与大冷静摆脱俗物的羁绊。如果用简单的几句话概括道家的人生境界或人生理想的话，这就是无为而治，莫与人争，少私寡欲，洁身自好，返璞归真。老子或道家人生哲学的最显著两个特点是：第一，处世谦下，善于保护自己。老子说：“是以圣人欲上民（欲为民上），必以言下之（言谈谦下）；欲先民（欲为民先），必以身后之（处事先人后己）。是以圣人处上而民不重，处前而民不害，是以天下皆乐推而不厌。以其不争，故天下莫能与之争。”（《老子·第六十六章》）由于待人处世谦下，所以当你居上位时，不被一般人看成负担，也不会被普通百姓伤害。他还说：“我有三宝，持而保之：一曰慈，二曰俭，三曰不敢为天下先。慈，故能勇，俭，故能广，不取为天下先，故能成器长。”（《老子·第六十七章》）这些文字所阐明的都是善于保护自己，不为人害的人生哲理。第二，洁身自好，追求自在。庄子最讲究人生哲理，他提倡人生要“逍遥游”，要自由自在，不受外界名物引诱，因而处世要做到“为善无近于名，为恶无近于刑”，只有这样，才“可以保身，可以全生，可以养亲，可以尽年”。（《庄子·养生主》）庄子讲述庖丁解牛的故事，旨在说明“以无厚入有间”“缘督以为经”的人生哲理。讲述“伐林”与“杀雁”的故事，旨在叙述一种“外乎材与不材之间”的处世哲理。还有《史记·老庄列传》

[1] 孔子．论语 [M]．郑州：河南人民出版社，2019:1-229。
[2] 艾新强．《论语》思想七题——国学研究系列之一 [J]．广西社会主义学院学报，2015(3):71-77。
[3] 温丽娟，齐勇．道家人生观与儒家人生观思想之比较 [J]．黑龙江社会科学，2019(4):43-47.

写楚威王聘请庄子为相，而遭庄子拒绝“终身不仕”的故事，目的也是宣扬道家洁身自好、不为物役、追求精神自由的人生哲学。

总之，道家人生观思想具有丰富的内涵，其身重于物的人生追求、返璞归真的人格理想、宠辱不惊的人生境界、谦下不争的处世之道等，无不显现着其人生观的绚丽光彩。尽管因鄙弃狭隘功利主义而崇尚虚无，因批判社会弊端而愤世嫉俗，走向悲观，因强调意志自由而忽视正确处理人际关系的必要，因蔑视文明的异化而否定科学文化的价值，但今天人们仍可以通过道家智慧找到历史的共鸣，它启迪人们不断反思生命的本质、生存的原则和生活的态度等重大的人生观问题。目前道家思维范式的“回归自然”被认为是战胜人类认知局限、知识再生和提升思维能力的关键。[1] 更重要的是，它启发人们重视自己的精神生活，引导人们逐步从身外之物的束缚中解脱出来，回归生命的本然状态，过一种真正属于人的生活，这丰富了中国传统的教育思想，为中国本土教育文化增添了独特韵味。

2.3 佛家

佛家文化慈悲圆融的内在澄明是华夏艺术文化的精神生态价值的组成部分。而佛家人生观作为中国人传统人文的三大模块之一，是沿着传统文化心理轨迹在守正创新中发现东方韵味的重要线索，体现了中国和谐文化的当代价值。[2]

佛家对人生的基本看法，源于释迦牟尼由于人生的痛苦和烦恼得不到解决而悟出来的道理，后来便成为佛家文化的基本人生观。佛家的正觉人生观，大致分为两大方面。一是正视人生缺陷，把握人生根本问题，以苦为师，发出离心，如实认识自己，明白人生的根本问题何在；二是珍视人生，发挥人的特征，识自性而发菩提心，创造应有的圆满功德和自在人生。[3]

佛家人生观表现在对人生的认识理念上，有代表性的是“四谛”:(1) 苦谛：说明世间是苦果；(2) 集谛：说明业与烦恼是苦的根源；(3) 灭谛：说明解脱与证果；(4) 道谛：说明离苦的道路。“十二因缘”:(1) 无明：一切烦恼的总称；(2) 行：一切行为；(3) 识：业识，为过去善恶业力所驱；(4) 名色：心识和形体；(5) 六根：眼耳鼻舌身意；(6) 触：即接触；(7) 受：即领受；(8) 爱：即贪染心；(9) 取：追求获取；(10) 有：前因后果；(11) 生：未来受报；(12) 老死：即老耄和死亡。“人生八苦”(1) 生；(2) 老；(3) 病；(4) 死；(5) 爱别离；(6) 怨憎会；(7) 求不得；(8) 五阴炽盛。“五蕴说”:(1) 色蕴：能感受到的各种有形物质；(2) 受蕴：因环境产生的心情；(3) 想蕴：积聚的思想；(4) 行蕴：身口意之善恶诸行；(5) 识蕴：对事物的辨别认知。[1] 佛家首先敢于正视人生诸苦，然后研求根本解决之道。就佛法而言，人生诸苦，只要换一个正觉态度，便变成了珍贵之物，成为征服的对象，乃至为济度众生而主动受苦，因见证苦性本空故，亦甘之如饴，

---

[1] 张杰，余红兵．反向认知：自然主体论的思维范式阐释［J］．外语与外语教学，2023(3):43-50。
[2] 王岳川．中国和谐文化及其当代价值［J］．新疆师范大学学报，2015(6):42-51。
[3] 黄东桂，宋金霞．佛教人生观探微［J］．广西社会主义学院学报，2006(1):56-58。

洒脱自在。其次，佛法所肯定的人道优胜之处在于聪明善思、富创造性；自主自制、勇于塑造；善能自觉，具有佛性。

佛家的人生观表现在人生的行为准则上有代表性的是“五戒”:(1)戒杀；(2)戒盗；(3)戒淫；(4)戒妄；(5)戒酒。“十善”:(1)不杀生；(2)不偷盗；)3)不邪淫；(4)不妄语；(5)不两舌；(6)不恶口；(7)不绮语；(8)不贪欲；(9)不嗔恚；(10)不邪见。“四摄”:(1)布施摄:乐于施舍施财施佛法；(2)爱语摄:以温和慈爱的善言慰喻；(3)利行摄:做奉献自我、利益众生的各种善事；(4)同事摄:亲近众生，同其苦乐，随机度化。行四摄须以“ 四无量心”为根本，才能表里合一。这四无量心是(1)慈无量心:予人以乐之心；(2)悲无量心:拔人之苦之心；(3)喜无量心:见人行善得乐则生欢喜心；(4)舍无量心:对一切众生一视同仁平等对待。六度:(1)布施；(2)持戒；(3)忍辱；(4)精进；(5)禅定；(6)般若。

在佛家眼中，佛就是已经觉悟的众生，众生则是尚未觉悟的佛。佛家倡导的人生观是面向芸芸众生的，其思想所蕴涵深邃的人生哲理，唯其博大精深，往往研究数十年也难窥其一斑。尽管如此，佛家人生观的宗旨是显而易见的，即旨在止恶防非，积极行善，净化自我。佛家文化是中国传统文化的重要组成部分，对构建社会主义和谐社会有积极的指导意义。佛家文化基本理念的当代教育价值体现在:(1)佛家文化的重“和”思想有助于社会的稳定与和谐。(2)佛家文化的财富观有助于人们的社会发展观由片面发展向科学。(3)认识传统佛家文化的当代价值有助于严格区分中华优秀文化与邪教的本质区别，提升人文素养。(4)佛家文化中克己淡欲，觉人利他的观念有利于提高人们的道德水准。[2]

三、价值观的沿革

价值观作为一种稳定的观念体系，是对各种关系及善恶、真假、美丑进行判断的标准与观点，内化于个体或民族的自觉意识，并通过人们的社会实践反映出来。不同的时代、不同的民族，人们的价值观往往不同，因此，价值观体系具有时代性。民族性和多样性。中国是一个历史悠久的文明古国，有着完整的文化体系和结构，儒佛道三家思想都是这个系统的重要组成部分。虽说以儒家思想作为主流价值观体系在我国表现出相对稳定的状态，但在不同的历史阶段表现形式又有所不同，中国的价值观有其自身的变迁脉络，特别是在历史发生变革的时期，价值观的沿革就更为显著。

3.1 传统价值观

中国传统价值观的现实基础是中国传统农耕文明、传统价值观的观念前提是“道”和“德”，传统价值观的核心内容是“仁者爱人”，传统价值观的根本精神是“自强

[1] 任宜敏．消极的抑或积极的？——佛教人生观辨[J]．佛学研究，2002(2):295-299。
[2] 刘衍永．论传统佛家文化的当代价值[J]．求索，2011(10):128-129。

不息”和“厚德载物”，传统价值观的规范体系是宗法制和礼制。中国价值观历史悠久，它萌芽于“三皇五帝”，孕育于夏商西周“三代”，形成于春秋战国时期，其官方形态确立于西汉武帝年间。其中的主导观念也处于不断流变的过程中，但传统社会也慢慢积淀了贯穿整个传统社会的主导观念。[1]

在浩如烟海的中国传统价值观念中，具有代表性的理念融合在不同的学派与文化哲思中。包括(1)追寻生命的内在意义。中国先哲没有把价值仅仅归结为主体的欲望、需求，而是看成每个事物固有的属性，认为事实世界之上有一个价值的世界，在此每个个体都是一个小宇宙，都秉承普遍的价值与道性，价值的实现离不开个体的修身自觉和内在超越，以不断体现和追寻生命的意义。(2)关注“群际”和“义利”。对社会群体的整体和谐发展的理想社会的追求也是持续的价值理想，要实现这种理想，在处理社会各层关系时理论上靠的是仁爱与忠孝、德政与纲纪、礼仪与教化的思想，实践上靠的是和而不同，明分使群，教导人们重义轻利，以存天理而灭人欲为君子境界，主张推己及人、以德服人。(3)胸怀家国天下。传统价值观中体现了很多对治国理政以及国家间关系的论述，体现在贵和少争、兼爱非攻、协和万邦、富国强兵、民为邦本及和而大同的社会理想之上，把和合与大同之世看成是人类社会的最佳状态，也是在传统上处理社会与和平问题的价值观的体现。(4)顺应自然天理。中国传统价值观早已认识到人类不是自然的主宰，要生存和发展必须遵循自然规律并与其共处共融。这样的思想体现在道法自然、理通万物、物各有宜、贵在有度、生生不息、开物成务的理念中，无不蕴含着对自然界的尊重和人类社会可持续发展的理念。

总之，中国传统的价值观首先存在着不同的实现路径。儒家关注的是人生境界和圣贤气象问题，将个体生命的价值实现与对“仁”“义”的追求结合在一起；道家注重的是天道的自然无为，认为人类社会的文明建构应该与天道相合，强调清静无为并养成一种善利万物、因势利导、随时而行的理想人格；其次中国传统价值观不仅限于社会的价值和人自身的价值等层面，而要上升至天地、宇宙价值的高度；此外，中国传统价值观强调个人的道德精神和价值，突出人在宇宙中的本体性和中心地位，体现了以人为本的价值观。 可以看出中国传统价值观关于理想人格、理想人际关系、理想国家与社会等问题的提出，是为了以一种文化价值理想来规范、引导个体之人与现实社会，以维护国家、社会与个人的和谐、健康发展。这对于当代社会的价值观建设，具有重要的启发和借鉴意义。[2]

3.2 近代价值观

中国近代价值观是对传统价值观的变革与继承的统一，因而是中国价值观体系的有机组成部分。中国近代价值观一方面批评了传统哲学中的迷信专制思想的部分，一方

[1] 江畅．中国传统价值观及其现代转化 [M]．北京：社会科学文献出版社，2020:1-21。

[2] 章伟文．试论中国传统价值观的当代意义 [J]．中原文化研究，2016(3):21-26。

面宣传西方资产阶级的新文化新思想，使得价值观体系从本体论、认识论、人性论到社会学说与传统价值观有了本质区别，具有与封建传统文化对立的鲜明启蒙性。[1] 启蒙性成为中国近代价值观的历史使命和基本特征。

中国近代价值观的启蒙性体现在近代思想的方方面面。(1) 在自然观上，用无神论取缔了天命鬼神论，利用推崇主体意识的近代心学把人说成是自己命运的主宰。(2) 在本体论上，用原子论、元素说和以太说等西方自然科学的新发现赶走了元气自然论，用丰富多彩的内心世界占据天理、同心的地盘。(3) 在认识论上，用“即物实测”的经验论原则取代了玄想、顿悟的直觉主义，认识论不再与道德修养术纠缠在一起，成为一个完全独立的领域。(4) 在辩证法上，用作用力与反作用力、吸引力与排斥力涤荡了阴阳的相互作用，使之升华为宇宙的普遍规律，而不再是个别现象和暂时状态。(5) 在伦理观上，抨击了传统的蒙昧主义和三纲五常的说教，断言人是有血有肉、有七情六欲的，其价值和意义在于追求幸福，它可以是人类行为的源泉和社会进步的动力。(6) 在政治观上，推崇社会契约论、天赋人权说，讴歌自由、平等和博爱思想。启蒙对中国近代价值观的影响是广泛的，集中地体现在近代价值观鲜明的主体特征，包括 :(1) 注重个体和个人的主观意志、情感好恶；(2) 重视感觉和感性经验，相信感觉在认识世界、改造世界和主宰世界中的决定作用；(3) 关注人的物质欲望和生理需求，人性本无善恶，在人们后天的所作所为中，苦乐是衡量善恶的标准；(4) 有个性有才能的人才是社会历史的主宰，是个人价值的体现。这种启蒙性和主体性从历史视角来看始终没有离开民族危机救亡中的价值求索。从“师夷长技以制夷”的理念到“以群为体，以变为用”的方略，再到“民权、人权、国权”的认知，再到“国民性”与爱国意识的觉醒，都是以放眼世界和民族生存为导向的。

从表面上看，近代对中国传统价值观造成冲击的是历史的变迁和资本主义工商业，而实际上更为根本的则是西方自由主义价值观。可以说中国近代的价值观以自然科学为根基，奋力呼唤主体价值，力图用自然和社会的双重属性来认知人性，试图对价值体系进行客观审视。近代中国价值观因其启蒙性和主体性，在历史的变迁中对民族意识的觉醒和爱国主义的升华都起到了铺垫作用。

3.3 当代价值观

自 20 世纪 20 年代之后，社会主义成为深刻影响中国近代历史进程的一种社会思潮，中国新文化派知识分子使得新文化运动时期的个体主义认同向五四运动以后的阶级认同和社会主义认同转变。20 世纪中叶新中国成立之后，社会主义精神作为中国现代价值观的鲜明旗帜，从独立自主自力更生，到全心全意为人民服务，再到民族复兴

[1] 魏义霞．中国近代哲学研究述评 [J]．哲学动态，1996(5) :8-10。

的道路探索，再到社会主义核心价值观的汇聚共识，正渐渐落实到社会的道德、制度、政策和活动，从而使之现实化为社会文化，转变成人们的内心信念和行为准则，形成了当代中国的价值观。

从意义和作用的角度来看，当代中国价值观是体现中国时代精神价值、充分展现中国国家形象和反映中国国家软实力灵魂的价值观体系。[1] 从实践基础和理论渊源来看，当代中国价值观是中国人民在参与中国特色社会主义伟大实践过程中形成的对价值关系的总体认识，是中国人民立足时代要求、实践要求和自身诉求，融社会主义核心价值观、中国传统文化价值、西方现代文化价值的诸多精华于一体所形成的价值体系，具有社会主义属性和当代中国属性。[2] 从本质和作用来看，当代中国价值观作为中国特色社会主义意识形态的重要组成部分，它既是社会理论的来源，是推动经济社会发展的动力，也有益于彰显中国特色社会主义话语权。[3] 当代中国价值观是以社会主义核心价值观为核心内容的社会主义价值观，作为核心内容的核心价值观也是成体系的。从党的讲话宣传精神来看，社会主义核心价值观是终极价值目标，核心价值理念和基本价值原则构成的有机统一的体系。终极价值目标就是党提出的“中华民族伟大复兴”，其基本含义就是“国家富强 、民族振兴和人民幸福”，其中人民幸福又具有更终极的意义。核心价值理念所倡导的 24 个字：富强、民主、文明、和谐，自由、平等、公正、法治，爱国、敬业、诚信、友善的价值理念传承着中华优秀传统文化的基因，寄托着近代以来中国人民上下求索 、历经千辛万苦确立的理想和信念，也承载着公民个人的美好愿景。[4] 中华优秀传统文化是社会主义核心价值观为引领的基因和源泉，但当代价值观不是对传统文化的复制，而是对传统文化的扬弃，是其适应社会主义和时代精神发展需要的整合、再造和创新。三个层面的每一个核心价值内容都是建立在社会主义制度基础上，体现社会主义性质，具有鲜明的和先进的社会主义新时代价值导向，这是传统文化焕发生机和时代价值的灵魂。

总之，要理解当代中国的价值观，需要到当代中国人民的社会实践和生活中去找根源。中国特色社会主义的探索与实践，让一个积贫积弱的文明古国焕发了青春，这给中国当代价值观产生了深刻的影响。社会主义旨在建立使每个人都能够得到自由而全面的发展，建立基于生产资料公有制的公平正义的社会价值理念。时至今日，中华民族的优秀文化始终深深熔铸在以爱国主义为核心的团结统一、爱好和平、勤劳勇敢、自强不息的伟大民族精神之中，并且孕育了具有中华民族独特意识、品格和气质的价值观念体系，这对中国传统教育理念的现代化发展也是一个重要的社会文化前提。

---

[1] 骆萍，孔庆茵．当代中国价值观内涵、意义与传播策略 [J]. 探索，2015(4):153-157。
[2] 刘民主，冯颜利．当代中国价值观的内涵探讨 [J]. 探索，2016(1):154-159。
[3] 陈国富．略论当代中国价值观 [J]. 探索，2015(4):148-152。
[4] 江畅，蔡梦雪．当代中国价值观概念的提出、内涵与意义 [J]. 湖北大学学报，2016(4):1-7。

第三节 人物故事中的美德取向

中国教育文化中，传统美德不仅是几千年的历史文化凝练而成的社会道德准则，也是华夏民族人文精神得以传承的核心灵魂，这些传统美德通过历史名人的人生故事在教育领域代代弘扬，对个人修身养性、家庭伦理乃至治国安邦都具有举足轻重的作用，对社会发展、文明进步产生了广泛且深远的影响。[1]

一、精忠报国

精忠报国源自儒家倡导的政治理念，最初记载“精忠报国”并弘扬的是宋代《宋史·岳飞传》，据载：岳飞之后背刻有尽忠报国，深入肤里，后被世人传为“精忠报国”，指的是以最纯粹的忠诚报效祖国。事实上，“精忠报国”作为一种爱国主义精神，在中华民族的历史上早已成为基本传统美德，呈现在各代爱国志士的人生故事中，深入教育、教化人心。

1.1 诸葛亮的鞠躬尽瘁

诸葛亮是三国时期最负盛名的政治家、军事家。他学识渊博，精于谋略，是蜀汉开国皇帝刘备的得力谋士。他由于在蜀汉政权的创立和巩固中功勋卓著，被后世称为智慧的化身。为了报答刘备的赏识与提携，诸葛亮为刘备筹划了立国的“隆中对策”。后来，刘备根据这一政治策略，联吴抗魏，在成都建立了蜀汉政权，并封诸葛亮为宰相。刘备去世之后，蜀国动荡不安，内忧外患。但诸葛亮励精图治，尽心尽责，不管事大事小，他都亲自过问。诸葛亮为了完成蜀国统一中国的愿望，曾先后六次亲自率领军队去攻打魏国，但都因为魏国军事力量强盛，最后只得以失败告终。公元 228 年冬天，诸葛亮又一次集结军队，出兵北伐。他带领将士积极组织进攻，但都没能够取得彻底胜利。最后诸葛亮累倒了，不幸病死在军营之中。诸葛亮留下的《出师表》《诫子书》《后出师表》等千古文章都在中国历史上有着深远的影响。其中《后出师表》的呈文分析了当时战争的形势，表达了诸葛亮自己的宏图大志，结尾时落笔写下了“臣鞠躬尽瘁，死而后已”这句感天动地的话语，这也是他一生励精图治、为国尽忠的总结。诸葛亮被安葬于定军山，谥号“忠武侯”。

“鞠躬尽瘁”的评价是对诸葛亮人物形象和精神符号的高度认可。他鞠躬尽瘁的前提是精忠报国，主要表现是凭借杰出的领导能力和指挥才华所建立的赫赫功勋，从治国理政到治军掌兵，他常常算无遗策、克敌制胜。他所提出的识人、养人、励人和用人原则，都与现代领导力理论有不谋而合之处，对现代组织领导者仍有启示意义。[2] 同时他作为智慧的化身，自比管仲、乐毅的文化主题被后世关注，成为记忆、传承、创新、

[1] 李火秀，邓琳．中国经典美德故事 [M]．杭州：浙江大学出版社，2018:1-4。
[2] 覃美静．诸葛亮领导力分析 [J]．领导科学论坛，2022(6):25-29。

传播中华优秀传统文化的重要内容，诸葛亮也成为后世学习的楷模，被敬为“千古名相第一人”。

1.2 王昭君的出塞和亲

王昭君与貂蝉、西施、杨玉环并称中国古代四大美女。王昭君原是汉元帝时期宫女，后远嫁匈奴呼韩邪单于。王昭君维护汉匈关系稳定达半个世纪之久，“昭君出塞”的故事千古流传。公元前 52 年王昭君出生于今湖北兴山县的一户平民之家，后以民间女子的身份被选入宫。由于不肯贿赂宫廷画师毛延寿，画像被画得并不美丽，因此没有被选入汉元帝的后宫。公元前 33 年正月，匈奴来朝请求娶汉人为妻。元帝遂将昭君赐给了呼韩邪单于，单于非常高兴，上书表示愿意永保边境安宁。王昭君抵达匈奴后，被称为宁胡阏氏。昭君和呼韩邪单于共同生活了三年，生下一子。单于去世后昭君向汉廷上书求归，汉成帝敕令“从胡俗”，依游牧民族收继婚制，复嫁呼韩邪单于长子复株累单于，两人共同生活十一年，育有二女。公元前 20 年，复株累单于去世，两年不到，王昭君病逝。她被厚葬于今呼和浩特市南郊，墓依大青山，傍黄河水，后人称之为“青冢”。由于昭君被称为民族关系史上的“民族友好使者”，乃至昭君葬地“青冢”也被赋予了独特的象征意义，因此王昭君形象也成为一种根植于历史记忆的文学建构，铸就了超越时空的文化典范。

昭君作为一个普通宫女，甘愿承担大汉帝国交托的重任，在匈奴生儿育女生活了多年，与匈奴部族融为一体。她不仅以其非凡的牺牲精神有力地维护了汉匈民族共同努力创下的和平大好局面，也在客观上大大促进了各民族经济的繁荣发展，同时她向世人证明了女子也能精忠报国。因此，在中国美德教育史上，王昭君早已不是一个简单的西汉和亲女性，而是世人心中一个永久的历史记忆，一个多民族共享的内涵丰富的文化符号，各族人民和知识界无不将昭君出塞视为民族友好团结的象征。[1]

1.3 林则徐的放眼世界

林则徐是晚清著名的政治家、思想家。1785 年，林则徐出生在福建一个清贫的教师世家，他的祖父和伯父都当过私塾先生，父亲也以教书为生。林则徐 4 岁入私塾旁听，在父亲的悉心教导下，他从小就立下了远大的志向。林则徐 19 岁考中举人，26 岁考中进士，历任官编修、江苏按察使、陕甘总督、湖广总督等职。公元 1838 年，林则徐被任命为钦差大臣，前往广州禁烟。千百年来，“中国” 与“夷狄” 的天下观主导了士大夫对国际事务的认知，西洋人及其文明被归入“夷狄” 之列。在这种背景下，林则徐能够顶住压力，以务实求知的态度去获取外来知识，主动认知西方。他一到广州就不论背景广揽人才，为了更加及时地获取国外信息，林则徐开官方译书之先河。除了主持翻译西方报刊和书籍外，他组织摘译的《四洲志》是近代中国人翻译的第一部世界地理著作，极大地扩宽了当时人们的国际视野。[1] 由于对西方文明和国际关系

[1] 周励恒．近代福建知识分子国际视野的形成与演变——以林则徐、严复为中心 [J]. 福建史志，2023(2):10-16。

的重视，这些知识在防备殖民主义侵略的斗争中起到了重要的参考作用。他随后在广州发布强硬的禁烟令，勒令英国的鸦片贩子在期限内交出全部鸦片。鸦片贩子想用钱财收买他，被林则徐狠狠痛斥："只要有一个百姓还受鸦片的毒害，我林则徐就寝食难安。"1839 年 6 月，林则徐将收缴的近 2 万箱鸦片在虎门公开销毁，沉重打击了英国鸦片贩子的嚣张气焰，向世界展示了中国人抵制鸦片的决心，维护了民族的尊严和利益。

作为虎门销烟的功臣，他领导军民与英军坚决斗争，他的著名诗句，"苟利国家生死以，岂因祸福避趋之"激励了一代又一代中国人为国家富强而奋斗。同时他主张学习西方科技和文化的思想，启示后人"知己知彼"的前提打开眼界，精忠报国的途径也可以是"师夷长技"，因而林则徐被称为中国"开眼看世界"第一人。林则徐的一生为子女们树立了良好的榜样。在良好家风的熏陶下，他的三个儿子都成长为国家的栋梁，林家后代更是能人辈出，大都为国家做出了贡献。

二、孝悌礼仪

孝悌礼仪是中华民族传统文化教育的核心与精髓。孝悌简言之是孝敬长辈、和睦兄弟。中国传统的孝悌道德包含"孝德"和"悌德"两个方面，"孝"与"悌"在内涵上是相互契合和相互补充的，"悌"与"孝"具有共同的精神内涵，即敬与顺。孝要求的是子对父的尊敬和顺从，悌要求的则是幼对长、弟对兄的尊敬和顺从。[2] 而礼仪则是儒家倡导以德立国的具体化。传统教育中的"三礼"即《周礼》《仪礼》和《礼记》形成了中华礼仪文化的完备体系，礼仪作为对民众行为的约束，是实现个人人格塑造，社会关系和国家和谐稳定的规范。近代以来在经历了现代自由、平等精神的洗礼之后，儒家伦理中的基本内容仍然可以作为现代社会的基本原则指导人们的生活。[3]

2.1 李密的辞官报恩

李密是西晋文人，他从小境遇不佳，自幼丧父，四岁时母亲改嫁，他幼时体弱多病，在祖母刘氏的抚养下长大成人。李密十分好学，博览五经，尤精《春秋左氏传》，以文学见长，年轻时曾任蜀汉尚书郎。魏灭蜀后，征西将军邓艾敬慕他的才能，请他担任主簿。李密以奉养年迈祖母为由，谢绝了邓艾的聘请。公元 267 年，晋武帝司马炎立太子，慕李密之名，下诏征密为太子洗马（官名）。诏书已下，郡县不断催促，这时，李密的祖母已九十六岁，年老多病。于是他向晋武帝上表，陈述家里情况，说明自己无法应诏的原因。这就是著名的《陈情表》。《陈情表》言辞诚恳，情真意切，晋武帝被李密对祖母的孝心感动，不仅同意暂不赴诏，还嘉奖了他孝敬长辈的诚心。李密在祖母去世服丧期满后出仕。在任河南温县县令时，他政令严明，政绩显著，以刚正见称。 李密本想到朝廷任职，施展自己的聪明才智，由于朝中权贵畏惧他的刚正，故

---

[1] 陈雪，杨春艳．王昭君影视形象传播研究［J］. 三峡大学学报，2021(3):99-103。
[2] 杨玉荣，梁东兴．中国孝悌传统及其现代转型［J］. 兰州学刊，2012(1):22-26。
[3] 韩星．孝悌之道与家庭伦理［J］. 学习与实践，2023(1):133-140。

朝中无人推荐。最后他只做了汉中太守，一年后罢官归田。后病卒，终年六十四岁。

李密为世人留下的《陈情表》历叙情事，俱从天真写出，无一字虚言假饰，既彰显了他的孝心又体现了他的智慧。魏晋时期，社会动荡，玄、佛盛行，在“忠”的观念淡化和混乱的形势下，“孝”被提到一个至高无上的地位，得到空前强化。在以“忠孝”治天下的礼仪传统里，要忠先须孝，李密的生长环境决定了他的孝心，而“孝心”是李密的立身之本。李密本想推辞做官，又要使晋武帝不怪罪是非常困难的，然而李密成功地作好了这篇文章。他陈述了自己孝祖母和报皇恩之间的重重矛盾，并逐一破解这些难题，因为以“孝”治天下是治国纲领，孝养祖母更是合情合理，这为“愿乞终养”给出了实在的理论根据。李密的辞官报恩让后人感受到中华礼仪中“情”的味道与“孝”的精神，其文章与行为成为传统孝悌教育的典范。[1]

2.2 杨时的程门立雪

杨时，是北宋著名的哲学家、文学家、官吏。杨时少年时就十分聪明，八岁能赋诗，九岁能作赋，当时知道他的人都称他为“神童”。他幼时先读的是佛学，少年时开始攻读儒学。公元1076年，高中进士却未赴任，而是专心研究理学，写出了著名的《列子解》。杨时出任徐州司法后投于程颢门下，专心研习理学，与程门立雪中的提到的游酢和伊焞、谢良佐共同成为程门四大弟子。公元1085年，杨时听说恩师程颢去世消息后悲痛万分，可在任上不能随意出行，于是便在寝门设灵大哭，并作哀辞。他四十岁时虽然在理学上已很有成就，依然选择投入恩师的弟弟程颐门下。一次，杨时与他的同学游酢一起去老师家请教问题。那天，正巧赶上下大雪，满天乌云，天寒地冻。当他们走到老师家门口时，才知道老师正在睡午觉。他俩为了不打扰老师休息，便恭恭敬敬地站立在门外等候。等了大半天，杨时的双脚都冻僵了，冷得浑身发抖，但他依然恭敬侍立，没有一丝疲倦和不耐烦的神情。程颐一觉醒来，从窗口发现侍立在风雪中的杨时和游酢，只见他俩通身披雪，脚下的积雪已一尺多厚了。程颐为他们诚心求学的精神所感动，耐心细致地回答了他们的问题。自那以后，程颐更加用心地向他俩传授学问，悉心教导。杨时历任浏阳知县、余杭知县，受到百姓的爱戴，也见证了王朝的腐败。公元1130年，他告老还乡后依然教育儿孙孝悌礼仪，直到83岁离世。

杨时的一生都以君子之风承上启下，尤其是在理学一道，他是“二程”与朱熹之间的过渡人物。杨时程门立雪的典故成为中国尊师重教礼仪的典范，朱熹也赞扬他“孔颜道脉，程子箴规，先生之德，百世所师。”后人常用“程门立雪”来比喻求学心切和对老师的尊敬。中国素以礼仪之邦闻名于世，2011年，“程门立雪”以民间文学的形式成功入选第三批洛阳非物质文化遗产名录。程门立雪的核心内容即“二程”文化的体现，也是中国教育文化中尊师重教的典型教材，是中华传统美德的精华所在。

[1] 王峰．李密《陈情表》文本解读四题［J］．文学教育，2022(34):134-136。

2.3 缇萦的救父之举

缇萦，姓淳于，是西汉时期临淄人。她的父亲淳于意喜欢读书，爱好医学。淳于意本来是一位地方官员，可是由于他的性格刚正不阿，又不喜欢官场的名利纷争，于是没多久就辞官回家，做起了专职医生。淳于意医术高超，远近闻名。但是由于他对封建王侯不肯趋承，拒绝为朱门高第出诊行医，被富豪权贵罗织罪名，送京都长安受肉刑。当时淳于意激愤地感叹："生子不生男，缓急无可使者。"缇萦有感于父亲的话，她要做一个男子能做的事情，毅然随父西去京师，上书汉文帝，痛切陈述父亲廉平无罪。奏章的内容大意是：我叫缇萦，是淳于意的小女儿。我父亲做官的时候，当地的人都说他是个清官。这回他犯了罪，被判处肉刑。我不但为父亲难过，也为所有受肉刑的人伤心。一个人被砍去脚就成了残废；被割去了鼻子，不能再接上去，以后就是想改过自新，也没有办法了。她在奏章中还表示自己愿意身充官婢，代父受刑。文帝受到感动，派人核查本案后宽免了淳于意，且废除了肉刑。缇萦以非凡的勇气和至诚的孝心，感动了高高在上的皇帝，不仅使父亲免于肢体伤残，而且改变了大汉朝的法律，造福天下苍生，这必然受到人们的颂扬和景仰。早在西汉末期，其事迹就被人们画于屏风，成为人们敬仰和学习的榜样，还被写入《列女传》。

缇萦的救父之举包含多方面的文化意蕴，后世的人们在传统文化美德传承和教育中可以从不同的角度去认识它、阐释它。缇萦能够感动汉文帝，成功救出父亲，除了她出众的智慧和杰出的辩说能力，还有她诚挚的孝心在"孝为至德"的中国传统社会中被高度认可。缇萦虽然没有像王昭君等人那样成为一个鲜明丰满的文学形象，但她的诚孝、机智、勇敢的品质，却受到人们的长久传颂，为美德教育增添了一段佳话。[1]

三、诚实守信

诚实守信是中国传统教育文化中的核心内容，长期被看作为人处世的基本道德规范。"信"泛指信用、信誉和信义。它要求人们要坚定诚实地对待个人、组织与社会。常言说，"人无忠信，不可立于世"，意思是说如果不讲忠诚信用，就不能够在社会上立足。因而，诚实守信是提倡人与人之间相互信赖，社会讲求信誉的重要前提，也是中华民族教育历程中历来尊崇的道德品质。

3.1 季札的挂剑之举

季札又称公子札、是春秋时吴王第四子，是可与孔子并提的圣贤，被尊称为"南季北孔"。历史上对他的评价有"明敏博洽的资禀，逊让君位的高风，诚信待友的德行，以民为本的思想"。据《史记》记载：一次，季札去访问各个诸侯国，他经过徐国时，拜见了徐君。刚一见面的时候，徐君就对季札随身佩戴的宝剑很感兴趣，但碍于面子，不好意思向季札索取。徐君的心思被季布知晓后，季布想把宝剑赠予徐君。可是，由

[1] 邢培顺．"缇萦救父"事件及后世的反响［J]．山东女子学院学报，2021(6):74-81。

于访问各国需要佩带剑等饰物，季布打算回徐国时再把剑赠送给徐君。想不到的是，当季布周游列国回来时，徐君突然生了一场严重的病，不幸过世了。季札非常伤心，他亲自到徐君的坟墓前，解下宝剑系在墓旁的树枝上。在场的侍卫对季布的行为很不理解，就问道："徐君已经死了，您还把剑挂在这里干什么呢？" 季札回答说："你不能这样说呀，刚和徐君见面的时候我就决定要把这把剑赠送给他了，我现在怎么能因为他死了就违背自己的心愿呢？" 侍卫听说后，对季札守信用的行为很是感动。后来，季札挂剑之举的事情便传开了。在季札死后，孔子还亲自为他题写了碑铭。

这一故事历经数千年仍被后人传颂，其背后所蕴含的信守承诺，不违初衷正是中华传统文化所强调的修身之要义。讲信誉，守承诺既是个人立足于世的美德也是职场竞争取胜的根本，这个故事对于现代社会教育的启示价值也是值得重视的。

3.2 晏殊的诚实公正

晏殊是北宋的政治家和文学家，也是婉约派著名词人之一。他自幼聪慧，十四岁以神童入试，曾任翰林学士，后官至宰相。他以词著于文坛，以兴办学校、培育人才而为天下所宗。晏殊少年时期的一则轶事彰显了他诚实公正的品格并被称颂至今。15岁时，晏殊不仅被大家称为"神童"，而且还得到了县令的推荐。他被推荐那天，前来参加考试的人超过三千，当晏殊看到试题竟发现题目是几天前自己做过的，兴奋之后他转念一想，认为这么做不仅有失公正，还有欺上瞒下的嫌疑。于是，就如实向主考官报告说："大人，这个题目我曾经练习过，请另外出题目让我作答吧。" 并且强调不换题目，即使考中了，也不算是真才实学，而换了题目做不好，说明学问还不够，也绝无怨言。监考官员觉得说得很有道理，就给晏殊换了题目。拿到新题的晏殊，看了几遍后略加思索，便拿起笔来一气呵成。这令监考人员惊叹不已，消息很快就传开了。皇帝听说这件事后，对晏殊的做法十分赞赏。他认为晏殊诚实守信，就赐予他"同进士出身"的荣誉。

宦海浮沉，晏殊并非是没有争议的名人，但他诚信竞争、诚实公正的品质是他名垂青史的前提。在文学上，他上承唐五代余绪，下启一代词风，这也奠定了他在教育上选贤任能，兴校教化，使教育事业由衰复兴的基础。晏殊的诚实公正助力了他为国兴学，培养人才的战略眼光和实干精神。[1]

3.3 商鞅的立木取信

商鞅是战国时期政治家、改革家、思想家，法家代表人物。他通过变法，在秦国实施严刑峻法，重农抑商，通过改革土地制度、行政税收制度使秦国一跃成为当时的强国。秦孝公死后，商鞅被公子虔诬为谋反，战败身死。商鞅在秦孝公的支持下主持变法成功，最主要的原因是树立"事皆决于法"的威信，这种法的威信来源于让民众意识到法的力量。在秦国处于战争频繁、人心惶惶之际，商鞅为了树立威信，推进改革，下令在

[1] 白玉成．晏殊换考题［J］．文史博览，2022(1):59。

都城南门外立一根三丈长的木头，并当众许下诺言：谁能把这根木头搬到北门，赏金十两。围观的人不相信如此轻而易举的事能得到如此高的赏赐，结果没人肯出手一试。于是，商鞅将赏金提高到五十金。重赏之下必有勇夫，终于有人站起将木头扛到了北门。商鞅立即赏了他五十金，以此来表明没有欺骗百姓。商鞅站在城楼上对大家说："你们都看到了，法令是算数的，今后，凡是按法令办事的人，都有重赏；违抗法令的人，都会受罚。"说完，就命人把新法令公布出来。这一举动，在百姓心中树立起了威信，之后大家都知道了商鞅的诚信和法令的威信，自此秦国慢慢强大起来，出现了路不拾遗、夜不闭户的太平景象。新法使秦国渐渐强盛，最终统一六国。[1]

商鞅的立木取信之所以成为他改革成功的良好开端，是因为他通过这一具体的范例展示了法规的力量，从而树立了执法者的威信。商鞅的命运也启示了后世的治理者与教育者："徒善不足以为政，徒法不足以自行。"[2] 法律只有以道德为支撑，才有广泛的社会基础而成为维系良治的良法。同时，商鞅的法治思想涵盖了法的制定、执行、普及各个环节，构成一个严密的逻辑体系，具有很强的理论性。这不仅影响了中国古代社会，其无诚信则无威信可言的理念对中国几千年尊师重道的教育文化及教育管理同样也有着深远的影响。

四、天道酬勤

天道酬勤是中国教育文化的精髓，取典于《周易》卦辞"天行健，君子以自强不息"和《尚书》"天道酬勤"。中国人的宇宙观相信天地就是宇宙，天高行健，地厚载物。中国教育常常从对乾坤物象的解释中引申出人生哲理，即人生要像苍天那样高大刚毅而自强不息，要像大地那样厚重广阔而厚德载物。"天道酬勤"作为教育理念，与"地道酬善、商道酬信、业道酬精"一起，成为中国传统哲学的最经典表达，引领着一代代中国人或独善其身，或兼济天下。

4.1 鲁班的精进学艺

鲁班是春秋时期鲁国人，著名工匠家，被后世尊为中国工匠师祖。鲁班出生木匠之家，从小就跟家里人做活。他学艺认真、做事细心，受到雇主们的赞赏。二十岁时已小有名气，他却不满足于现状，决心继续提高手艺。他听说终南山有位老师傅才高艺精，于是鲁班就离家寻访这位高人。他历经千辛万苦到了终南山，爬到山巅见一破屋，屋里斧子工具凌乱散落，一白发老翁正卧床休息。鲁班仔细收拾好工具后耐心等待老翁醒来。日落后，老翁醒来，经过一番问答，鲁班拜师入门。他先按照老翁的吩咐，把已经长满铁锈的工具一件件都磨得闪闪发亮。然后历经了砍大树、凿千眼、拆装模型的精进训练和勤学苦练，师傅对他非常满意。鲁班没日没夜地劳作苦练，学习了三

[1] 张倩茹．商鞅法家思想的政治实践——雷厉风行中的灵活与从容［J］．管子学刊，2022(3)：23-36。
[2] 徒善不足以为政，徒法不足以自行——法和道德关系的法哲学探析［J］．黑龙江社会科学，2007(4)：169-172。

年，把师傅的手艺都学会了。老师傅还要试试他，于是把模型全部毁掉，让鲁班重新造。鲁班凭记忆一件一件都恢复如初。老师傅又提出许多新模型让他造。他一边琢磨一边做，结果都按师傅要求制作完成。直到有一天，师傅把鲁班叫到眼前，告诉他手艺已成可以下山了，还把磨好的工具赠与他。鲁班虽舍不得离开师傅，可也只能含泪下山。他牢记师傅的话：永远不丢师傅的脸，不坏师傅的名声。从此鲁班用师傅给他的工具给人们制造了许多机械和器物，还收了不少徒弟。

中国流传着不少鲁班对建筑及木工等行业贡献的传说，许多被认为是他设计的工具及建造法则一直沿用至今。鲁班的名字之所以能成为中国古代劳动人民智慧的象征，是因为他品性中蕴含着精进学艺的精神。鲁班精神的内涵包括开拓创新、质量至上及勤奋好学、造福桑梓等要素，挖掘和传承鲁班精进学艺的精神在中国教育文化中始终具有超越时代的价值和深刻的现实意义。[1]

4.2 王冕的好学成痴

王冕，号煮石山农，是元代著名的画家、诗人、篆刻家。他出身于贫寒之家，没有殷实的家庭背景和广泛的社会关系，其才学技艺都是靠勤奋苦学积累而成的。王冕自幼好学成痴，他七八岁时，父亲让他去田埂放牛，他却偷偷地潜入学堂，听学生们诵读诗书，听后就默默记下来，天黑回家的时候却把牛忘在了田里。经常有人牵着牛来他家找其父亲理论，责备王冕放牛踩踏农田。父亲很生气，便鞭打王冕，但王冕依然如故，书还照听，牛还照忘。母亲见王冕对学习如此痴迷，便对丈夫说：“既然这样，就不如顺从孩子意愿，听其所为吧！”于是王冕离开家，在一间寺庙旁居住。他白天继续放牛，有空就在池塘边画荷花；入夜便悄悄地进入寺庙，坐在佛像的膝盖上，拿着书卷在长明灯下琅琅而读，直到天明。小王冕心性安适，仿佛不受杂念影响。浙东大儒、理学家韩性听说王冕的学痴举动感到惊奇，觉得此子有慧根，便收其为徒。后来王冕继承韩性衣钵，也成为一代名儒。韩性去世后，其门人对待王冕如同对待韩性一样恭敬。王冕虽然满腹经纶，才华出众，却因生性孤傲、鄙视权贵，屡试不第。于是他便把参加考试的文章全部烧掉，决意断绝功名利禄，隐逸清修，一心致力书画学问。后有人引荐他入仕为官，他却力辞不就，南回故乡，隐居会稽九里山，以卖画为生，终老田园。

王冕一生痴于诗画行文，除了在绘画、诗文方面造诣深厚，还学成了深厚的篆刻技艺。王冕一生与梅相伴，梅花是王冕的精神寄托，也是其艺术化身，以清远之气广布人间，流传后世。[2] 王冕好学成痴造就的文化底蕴使他能保持浓厚的平民色彩，独立不羁的人格追求，孤高自洁的人生态度，从而不仅成为中国文人理想的典范，也成就了传统教育文化中一抹靓丽的色彩。

---

[1] 宋守君，韩锋．鲁班精神对建筑类高校办学育人的启示［J］．山东高等教育，2014(12):82-88。

[2] 逸舟．王冕：一生只作墨梅香［J］．人民周刊，2021(18):86-87。

4.3 曾国藩的勤读思想

曾国藩，原名子诚，是清代名臣，他是一个治学严谨、博览群书的理论家和文学家。他出生于湖南湘乡市一个穷山僻谷的耕读人家，一生勤奋好学，以“勤”“恒”两字激励自己，教育子侄。谓“百种弊病皆从懒生，懒则事事松弛”。他抓住一切读书的机会，死前一日犹手不释卷。曾国藩从小酷爱读书、勤于读书，会根据环境和时世的变化选择合适的书籍，并将所学知识运用于实际生活中，这是常人无法企及的。曾国藩把读书分为“看”和“读”两大类，[1] 曾给自己订下了每天读书的十二条规矩，分别是：主敬、静坐、早起、读书不二、读史、谨言、养气、保身、日知其所无、月无忘其所能、作字夜不出门。曾国藩的这十二条读书规矩，前三条是为读书作准备的。第四、五、九、十、十一条是读书的方法；而第六、七、八、十二条看起来与读书关系不大，实质上是要求自己集中精力读好书，因而这看似关系不大的规矩，却是保证读书质量的重要手段。

曾国藩一生宦海戎马，无愧“立德立功立言三不朽，为师为将为相一完人”的称谓，这与他一生勤于读书坚持不懈的精神密切相关。他为勉励其弟曾国荃战后好好读书，以待厚积薄发的一副对联，“千秋邈矣独留我，百战归来再读书”充分反映了他的勤读思想，这不仅对于他一生的成就有着不可忽视的作用，也是每个时代学习者的至高境界，更是当代素质教育中不可或缺的传统文化养分。[2]

[1] 佚名．曾国藩论读书方法［J］．史学集刊，1996(2):79。
[2] 康凯丽．《曾国藩家书》的语言特点及传统文化传承与启示［J］．汉字文化，2022(24):190-192。

下篇

教育箴言赏析

第五章 学派思想选读

通过上篇的传统观念识悟，我们了解到中国传统教育思想不仅源远流长，积淀深厚，资源丰富，而且随时变迁、历久弥新、富有活力。更重要的是，这些传统的教育思想，由不同的学派传承，经过几千年历史的积淀，成果斐然，对于今天的教育，富有极大的理论价值和实践意义。本章将甄选历代代表性的学派思想加以呈现，力图凝练一幅较综合的图景，展现不同学派的思想精华与智慧火花。

第一节 治国与修行

儒家经典著作《礼记·大学》中明确提出："古之欲明明德于天下者，先治其国；欲治其国者，先齐其家；欲齐其家者，先修其身；欲修其身者，先正其心；欲正其心者，先诚其意；欲诚其意者，先致其知，致知在格物"。可见格物致知、诚意正心、修身齐家、治国平天下是中国教育的精髓与脉络，而治国平天下则是历代文人志士读书求学的最高理想。事实上，中国传统教育思想学派中的内容，无论是重入世还是出尘，最终都上升到了治国与修行的层面。

一、先秦百家的主张

先秦时期，随着我国古代社会生产的发展和社会的进步，学术亦出现了一个由"学在官府"到"学下私人"的转变，出现了诸子百家争鸣的局面。以儒家、道家、法家、墨家、杂家为代表的各学派，都在治国理念方面提出了自己的思想体系，对中国统治阶层数千年的培养方式和教育思维产生了深远影响。[1]

1.1 儒家

"教为刑先"。教化与刑罚的关系，是历代统治阶层都要面对的问题，就儒家学派来说，尤其主张先教化后刑罚，即教在刑先。认为德治优于法治。《论语·为政》说："子曰：道之以政，齐之以刑，民免而无耻，道之以德，齐之以礼，有耻且格。"用政令来引导，用刑罚来规范，老百姓仅仅做到不违政令，避免刑罚，而没有耻辱感。如果用德来引导，以礼来要求，老百姓就知道什么是耻辱，什么是荣光，就会身正行正。又说："为政以德，譬如北辰，居其所而众星共之。"用道德的手段来行政，就会得到人民的拥护，就像北极星那样，居其所而群星围绕。

"惠民之教"。儒家还主张统治者惠民、利民。《论语·雍也》载：子贡问孔子说："如

[1] 张祥浩．中国传统教育思想理论 [M]．南京：东南大学出版社，2011:14-100。

有博施于民而能济众，何如？可谓仁乎？”孔子回答说：“何事于仁，必也圣乎！尧、舜其犹病诸！”惠民、利民，广施博济，这是儒家的最高政治目标。《论语》里随处都可以看到惠民利民的思想。孔子曾评论子产说：“有君子之道四焉：其行己也恭，其事上也敬，其养民也惠，其使民也义。”行己恭是说待人谦逊，事上敬是说待上谨恪，养民惠是说爱利百姓，使民义是说节用民力。

“贵师重傅”。儒家认为，国家不能不尊师。“国将兴，必贵师而重傅；贵师而重傅，则法度存，国将衰，必贱师而轻傅，贱师而轻傅，则人有快，人有快则法度坏。”国家尊师重傅，法度就会得到推行，贱师轻傅，人们放纵情欲，法度就大坏。所以，“言而不称师谓之畔，教而不称师谓之倍。倍畔之人，明君不内，朝士大夫遇诸涂不与言”(《荀子·大略》)。在荀子看来，言而不称述老师就是背叛，教而不称述老师就是叛逆，背叛之人，明主是不接纳的，朝廷士大夫在路上遇见他也不会跟他交谈。

“保民而王”。在儒家看来，仅仅因为民众力量不可小觑而去“爱人”“爱民”是远远不够的，还必须用“仁政”和好的政策笼络民心，使民众心悦诚服地接受统治，实现“王道”的政治目标。孔子指出：“上者尊严而危，民者卑贱而神，爱之则存，恶之则亡，长民者必明此之要。”孟子进一步提出了“保民而王”的具体措施：首先是重视百姓的生存权利，改善其经济生活；其次针对大国君主“好战”的情况，提出善战者服上刑的主张，以达到消灭不义战争的目的；再次要关心民众疾苦，与民同乐。[1]

1.2 墨家

“圣人治天下必禁恶而劝爱”，这是墨家学派政治思想的核心，亦是其教育思想的核心。《兼爱上》说：“故圣人以治天下为事者，恶得不禁恶而劝爱。故天下兼相爱则治，交相恶则乱。”又说，圣人“不可以不劝爱人者此也”。他把劝爱看成是圣人的主要职责，亦即把教育天下人民兼相爱、交相利看成是圣人治天下的主要任务。

“古文节于身诲于民”。(圣王)自身节俭，(以身作则)教导百姓，因而天下的民众得以治理，财用得以充足。提倡节用、节葬、非乐，是墨家学派的特点，亦是其教育的特色。墨子认为，宫室房屋，只要能避风雨，挡霜雪，别男女即可，而不必费财力，穷极华丽。饮食只要做到果腹强身即可，而不必极五味，致远国珍异之品。衣服做到冬暖夏凉即可，而不必华丽靡费。

“率以尊天事鬼，其利人多”。墨子主张天志，即天有意志、感情、能赏善罚恶，能祸福于人。墨家认为，天对人民百姓的恩德是很优厚的，它创造了日月星辰，规定了春夏秋冬，又降下霜雪雨露，生长五谷桑麻，使人民有衣有食。而且，天还能管住天子，“天子为善，天能赏之；天子为暴，天能罚之。天子有疾病祸祟，必斋戒沐浴，洁为酒醴粢盛，以祭祀天鬼，则天能除去之。”(《墨子·天志中》)因此，天意不可违，顺天意，兼相爱，交相利，是天子需要遵循的道理。

[1] 汪志强．先秦儒家治国思想及其历史启示[J]．求实，2001(2):34-37。

“义者，善政也”。墨家主张，道义精神应当是从国家到个人普遍追求的一种价值理念。就个人而言，要以一种无私而利人利社会甚至“损己而益所为”的道义精神，去保护他人和社会的利益。就国家而言，要以道义精神作为选拔贤才的要求，要求贤才能够“举公义，辟私怨”。墨家以道义作为国家治理的信仰价值，确信它能够从精神信仰层面实现政府与民众价值追求的统一，并为这种追求提供内在的精神保障。[1]

1.3 道家

“万物莫不尊道而贵德”。老子教人尊道贵德。老子说：“道生之，德畜之，物形之，势成之。是以万物莫不尊道而贵德，道之尊，德之贵，夫莫之命而常自然。”（《老子·五十一章》）即道生万物，德养万物，而势成万物。所以万物莫不崇道而贵德。道德的尊贵不是谁赋予的，而是自然而然的。因此，老子指出，因为道德非常尊贵，所以圣人治国，士人治身，都要取法于道，取法于自然。“是以圣人处无为之事，行不言之教。”（《老子·二章》）圣人要以无为的态度去处事，以“不言”去教导老百姓。“为无为，事无事，味无味。”（《老子·六十三章》）即是说，以无为居身，以无为处事，以恬淡为味。“我天地不仁，以万物为刍狗；圣人不仁，以百姓为刍狗。”（《老子·五章》）天地自然生养万物，不刻意珍惜万物，圣人也要自然治理百姓，不去刻意作为。

“顺性而治，我无为而民自化”。这既是老子思想教育的目标，又是老子思想教育的方法。老子说：“我无为而民自化，我好静而民自正，我无事而民自富，我无欲而民自朴。”（《老子·五十七章》）即是说，我无为老百姓就会自我感化，我无为老百姓就会自我端正，我无为老百姓就会自我富有，我无为老百姓就会自我质朴。与倡导无为治国一样，老子也倡导无为治身，无为教化。顺性无为强调的是要遵循政治治理中那种由道支配的客观规律，顺应由道落实到个体身上所展现出来的自然而然之性，主张在因循和利用人性“自为为己”特征的基础上制定法度，其实质是给予民众一个自治自为的空间，这个过程的完成也是在道家推天道而明人事的原则下进行的。

“君子无辩”。道家有很典型的相对主义思想，教人齐物和齐物论。即把有差别的事物看成是齐一的，把不同的理论看成是同一的。《齐物论》说：“举莛与楹，厉与西施，恢诡谲怪，道通为一。其分也，成也；其成也，毁也。凡物无成与毁，复通为一。”在庄子看来，小茎和大柱，丑女和美女，宽大、狡诈、怪异、妖异等等是不同的，又是相同的，因为它们都是道的产物，所以一种事物的诞生的同时，也在走向毁灭。因此世上的所谓贵贱、大小、有无都无定质，没有标准，所谓物之不可分、言之不可辩。道家认为，万物都是道的产物，在道面前，万物尽管彼此不同，但说到底都是一样的，这种思想对一些国君的治国理念也有一定的影响。[2]

[1] 金小方．墨家治国理念与当代国家治理现代化［J］．河南社会科学，2016(6):78-83。
[2] 白延辉．黄老道家治国论的内在逻辑［J］．内蒙古社会科学，2019(2):42-47。

1.4 法家

“一教则下听上”。商鞅提出“圣人之为国也，一赏一刑一教，一赏则兵无敌，一刑则令行，一教则下听上。夫明赏不费，明刑不戮，明教不变，而民知于民务，国无异俗。明赏之犹至于无赏也，明刑之犹至于无刑也，明教之犹至于无教也。”(《商君书·赏刑》)就是说，圣人治理国家，要做到统一奖赏，统一刑法，统一教化。统一了奖赏，人民知道奖励的标准，作战就会无敌；统一了刑法，就可以使国人令行禁止；统一了教化，人民就会下听其上。明赏、明刑、明教以后，就会使民知民务，国无异俗，如此也就渐渐地达到无赏、无刑、无教的境地。

“以法为教，以吏为师”。韩非子提出“故明主之国，无书简之文，以法为教；无先王之语，以吏为师，无私剑之捍，以斩首为勇。是境内之民，其言谈者必轨于法，动作者归之于功，为勇者尽之于军，是故无事则国富，有事则兵强，此之谓王资。”(《韩非子·五蠹》)在韩非子看来，治国中明主对臣民实施的是法的教育，而不是文学诗书的教育。以法为教，须以吏为师，因为最熟悉法的是吏，而不是诗书之士。如果境内人民皆以法为规范，以功用为目标，就能做到国富兵强，天下无敌。

“毋以私好害公正”。《管子》认为废私立公是执法的保证。《管子·任法》曰：“不知亲疏、远近、贵贱、美恶，以度量断之。其杀戮人者不怨也，其赏赐人者不德也。以法制行之，如天地之无私也，是以官无私论，士无私议，民无私说，皆虚其匈以听于上。上以公正论，以法制断，故任天下而不重也。”意思是明主治国，必从公出发，而不能以私行。

“国强民弱，民愚则易治”。法家的富强之道也有其明显的局限性，战国时期，为了最大限度地强化君权，法家在致力于削弱贵族、大臣权力的同时，还力主采取“弱民”措施：“民弱国强，国强民弱。故有道之国，务在弱民。”(《商君书·弱民》)法家还主张愚民，“民愚则易治也。”尽管商鞅变法从法律上废除了井田制度，在一定程度上维护了民众的权利，但在法家的认识视野中，人民并不是国家的主人，而只是君主成就霸业的工具。历史角度地看，国民的愚昧落后正是君权神权、偶像崇拜得以产生的土壤。虽然这“可以行一时之计”(《史记·太史公自序》)，从长远看却钳制了人们的思想，妨碍了社会的真正进步。[1]

二、魏晋隋唐的思想

中国教育中的修行思想的演进与天人理念相关，呈现出敬天与崇拜人格化精神轮番交替的态势，同样也受到儒释道文化的交互影响：儒家提出“鬼神信仰，形质神用”；道家认为要“炼气养生，性命双修”；佛家主张“法无自性，业报承受”。[2] 儒家教

[1] 彭新武．先秦法家的治国理念及其现代性［J］．孔子研究，2023(1):14-25。
[2] 周克浩．《中国宗教思想通论》研究［J］．宗教学研究，2011(2):264-268。

人成圣，释家教人成佛，道家教人成仙。佛、仙、圣是三家宗教思想教育的基本目标。自魏晋到隋唐时期，统治者越来越看到了佛道的教化功能和社会功能，因而在儒学的独尊地位发生改变后，佛家的本土化及道家的传播共同形成与影响了这一时期的修行思想。

2.1 佛家

道安的思想。道安极重视佛教的教化。“如来兴世，以本无宏教”的意思是说如来创立佛教，是以本无论为基础的。人们都滞着在有形之物上，如果托心于空无，那么一切物累就没有了。这也是崇本息末的意思。类似的记载，还见于唐吉藏《中观观论疏》等。其实道安所谓的本无，就是大乘般若的性空。即谓诸法没有自性，皆为因缘和合而成，所以是空、是幻、是寂。“世尊立教，其法有三”的意思是说佛家的教化方法有三种。他在《比丘大戒序》中说：“世尊立教，法有三焉，一者戒律也，二者禅定也，三者智慧也。斯三者，至道之由户，泥洹之关要也，戒者断三恶之干将也，禅者绝分散之利器也，慧者齐药病之妙医也，具此三者，于取道乎何有也。”意思是说，佛家的教法有三种，一是戒律，二是禅定，三是佛理，三者是入道的门户。戒是断恶的利剑，禅是归一的利器，慧是医病的妙药，依此去做，就可以达到成佛了。[1]

慧远的思想。慧远作为净土宗之始祖，提出了形神问题是中国宗教思想的重要问题。“形灭神不灭”的意思是说灵魂不死，形灭而神不灭是佛家六道轮回三世报应的载体。慧远说：假令形神俱化，始自无本，愚智资生，同禀所受。问所受者，为受之于形邪？（《沙门不敬王者论》）如果形神同时生灭，那么人的智愚贤不肖就不好解释了。因为如果说这是由形决定的，则人人皆有其形，为什么会有智愚贤不肖的区别呢？此外，“善有善报，恶有恶报”的思想是佛教传入中国后，因果报应说的核心内容。慧远的《明报应问》说：“夫因缘之所感，变化之所生，岂不由其道哉！无明为惑网之渊，贪爱为众累之府。二理俱游，冥为神用，吉凶悔吝，唯此之动。”慧远在这里强调的是人世间善恶必有报应，这是因为人有无明和贪爱，无明就私身爱物，贪爱就恋生不已。如此则得失相推，祸福相依，心有善恶而报有罪福，因此善恶报应是自然而然的。

竺道生的思想。东晋佛教著名学者与高僧竺道生在金陵讲论《涅槃经》时提出了一不信因果没有慧根之人也能修佛的观点。所谓“阐提可以成佛”。在道生看来，“一切众生，莫不是佛，亦皆泥洹。”（《法妙法华经疏》）一切众生皆有佛性，皆可以进入涅槃或泥洹世界，亦即皆可以成佛。在佛教思想史上，关于一阐提是否可以成佛的问题，涉及是否人人都有佛性，众生是否都可以成佛的问题。竺道生认为众生都具有佛性，其思想拓展了佛教教化的阵地，直接影响了此后中国的佛教界，特别是推动了唐代禅宗的发展。

[1] 韩焕忠．道安思想的老子学底蕴［J］．湖北文理学院学报，2021(12):21-25。

天台宗的思想。天台宗作为中国最早的本土佛教，它的核心理念被概括在这八个字之中："一念三千，百界千如。"一念三千指众生的一念心就包含了三千种世间，心就是世界的本质，而百界即一百法界，为十法界自乘后之总数。意思是，每一法界皆是真如实相，换句话说人的一念可以到达任何地方，也可以参透任何机缘。这也是转念即菩提的道理。"止观法门"也是天台宗的重要思想，阐述的是教学法和修行法。所谓止，即禅定，意谓专注一心，扫除妄念。所谓观，亦即智慧，意谓增长佛智，弄懂佛理。在智顗看来，只有止观双修，实践和义理并行，才能到达佛门。

唯识宗的思想。唯识宗又称法相宗或法相唯识宗，创始者为玄奘，特别注重分析诸法的相状，故称法相宗，而分析的结果是诸法都离不开识。在宗教教育思想上表现出"转依成佛"，把转依看成是修道的途径。教人力破遍计所执性，回归圆成实，由此进入佛门，到达天国。《成唯识论》说："三种自性，皆不远离心、心所法。谓心、心所及所变现，众缘生故，一切皆名依他起性；一切皆名遍计所执。依他起上，彼所妄执我、法俱空，此空所显识等真性名圆成实，是故此三不离心等。"这即是说，一切"我、法诸种相状"都是心的变现，非有似有，所以此三性都不离心。唯识宗宗教思想的目标，即在使人实现转依，舍弃偏执地认为世界是实有的看法，而回归世界是幻是空的境界。

华严宗的思想。作为隋唐时期佛教中国化的重要成果，华严宗的基本思想即是"法界缘起"。所谓"法界"的法是指万事万物；界是指分界、类别，融摄一切万事万物称为"法界"。华严宗通常是在万物的本原、本体和众生具有的佛性的意义上使用法界这个名词。华严宗因奉《华严经》为主要经典而得名。十重玄门的思想是法藏华严宗教人修行成佛的基本理论。树立了十重玄门的观点，就有了佛智，可以到达天国。这一思想的核心指事物虽有差异却是相互依存，彼此重叠，相即相入，互不妨碍而和谐存在的。法藏的十重玄门理论，涉及诸多范畴。但基本的是诸法的互相包容贯通，但渗透的程度依事物摄取他物的能力而定。总之华严宗相信事物相即相入无碍自在，而差别之相历然分明，实具重重无尽缘起一体之关系。故观一微尘：可举法界而全收之。此诸事无碍玄妙不可思议的道理，就称作十玄门。[1]

禅宗的思想。禅宗认为"于自性中，万法皆见；一切法自在性，名为清净法身"。"一切般若智慧，皆从自性而生，不从外入，若识自性。一闻言下大悟，顿见真如本性"，提出了即身成佛的"顿悟"思想。作为禅宗代表经典的《六祖坛经》，主张"心性本净，佛性本有，觉悟不假外求，舍离文字义解，直彻心源"。慧能说：若起真正般若观照，一刹那间，妄念俱灭，若识自性。一悟即至佛地。(《坛经 · 般若品》)而与惠能相对立的禅宗北宗的神秀主张"诸恶莫作""诸善奉行""自净其意"，主张渐修。当然，惠能也不完全否认渐修。他说："法本一宗，人有南北，法即一种，见有迟疾。"[2]

---

[1] 赵纪斌．试论中古佛典序跋的佛家思想文化价值 [J]．学术探索，2019(8):145-149。
[2] 刘序琦．略论《太平经》思想的几个问题 [J]．江西师范大学学报，1983(3):37-44。

2.2 道家

《太平经》的思想。《太平经》内容博大，涉及天地、阴阳、五行、十支、灾异、神仙等。重新构筑了早期道教的“天人合一”思想。其宗教层面的主要思想是“兴善戒恶”。《太平经》说：“积善不止，道福起，令人日吉。为善亦神自知之，恶亦神自知之。”“真人前，今太平气临到，欲使谨善者日益兴，恶者日衰却也。”《太平经》认为，人活在世上，所以要兴善止恶，是因为为善为恶，皆有报应。《太平经》的善恶报应，也像佛家的三世报应那样，不一定是报于自身，“凡人之行，或有力行善，反常得恶，或有力行恶，反得善，因自言为贤者非也，力行善反得恶者，是承负先人之过，流灾前后积来害此人也。”《太平经》所谓善恶的涵义，抽象地说，是合不合天心、人意。《太平经》也区分了善师和恶师，认为师是天道的体现，而天道有盛衰、治乱，故人间也就有善师、恶师的区别，善师体现盛世，恶师体现衰世。[1]

陶弘景的思想。教人自善养生，得道成仙，是陶弘景道家思想的一个核心重要内容。陶弘景认为，生死寿夭，既是先天，亦是后天。他申明，他之所以收集前人的养生理论，就在于有补于群生，以期养性延命。陶弘景提倡的养生方法很多。但最重要的，则是服气、养神、保精。他说《服气经》曰：道者，气也。保气则得道，得道则长存。神者，精也，保精则神明，神明则长生。精者，血脉之川流，守骨之灵神也，精去则骨枯，骨枯则死矣。(《养性延命录下·服气疗病篇》)养生理论是陶弘景道教思想最重要的内容。生的无限延长即是仙。故养生之教推而极之，即是成仙之教。陶弘景认为神仙世界是存在的。他描述昆仑仙界说：“昆仑山上有九府，是为九宫，太极为太宫也。诸仙人俱是九宫之官僚耳。”从陶弘景所举的例子里，有服药而成仙的，有读道经万遍而成仙的，有经受神人考验而成仙的，成仙的途径可以不一，而成仙的结果则同。

寇谦之的思想。寇谦之作为北朝著名的道家代表人物，在推行道教教化的过程中，神道设教是他的基本思想。所谓神道设教语出《易·观》：“圣人以神道设教，而天下服矣”。神道即鬼神之道、神灵之道。“观卦”的意思是，圣人用鬼神之道对老百姓进行教化，以服天下之人。所谓“圣人法则天之神道，本身自行善，垂化于人，不假言语教戒，不须威刑恐逼，在下自然观化服从”，亦是此意。对道民进行思想教育，是道教传播的主要途径。寇谦之道民鉴于思想的中心是修善戒恶。这一点，他与儒家并无不同。寇谦之说：臣忠、子孝、夫信、妇贞、兄敬，弟顺，内无二心，便可为善，他把修德看成是修道的重要条件，把劝善看成是道教的基本内容。寇谦之提出道官进行道教教育的基本态度，一是态度要端正，二是要减轻道民的经济负担，如此才能最大限度地提高道教教育的实效，才能广泛地争取道徒，发展道教。寇谦之的道民教育思想是丰富的，他对道民教育在内容和方式方面均有所革新，以此奠定了他在南北朝天师道中的地位。[2]

---

[1] 释德安．华严宗发心思想与佛教的中国化［J］．法音，2021(9)：38-42。
[2] 张祥浩．中国传统教育思想理论［M］．南京：东南大学出版社，2011：221-268。

第二节 理学与功利

以孔孟伦理学说为核心的儒学，经长期的冲击，不断地被改造，至宋代开始，发展成了一个崭新的思想体系：理学（或称新儒学）。它融汇了佛教禅宗的唯心主义思辨和易经、老子、庄子的宇宙论，顺应了当时重整伦理纲常的历史需求，将产生万事万物的本源归结为一个“理”。从这核心思想出发，理学家们对礼仪秩序加以阐释，将“理”与“礼”的关系加以诠释，使“礼”归属于“理”的最高范畴。同时，我国教育的功利思潮不像理学那样有明显的传承体系，然而如果客观地还原古代教育思想和生活世界就会发现，通经致用的功利思潮在社会的影响不容忽略，其演进过程也为教育界带来丰富的启示 。[1]

一、宋元明清的理学思想

理学是宋元明清时期的孔学，理学的确立以周敦颐之学、“二程”之学、张载之学的兴起为标志，自北宋中期，经由南宋，直至元代，理学得以流传演变，并于内部产生了分立，之后不同的派别相互之间又出现了融合的趋势，其中的教育思想至今广被遵从。

1.1 司马光

司马光的理学思想是“以史为教，嘉善戒恶。重视历史教育”。司马光在《通鉴·魏记》中说：“正闰之论，自古及今，未有能通其义，确然使人不可移夺者也。臣今所述，止欲叙国家之兴衰，著生民之休戚，使观者自择其善恶得失，以为劝诫，非若《春秋》立褒贬之法，拨乱世反诸正也。”著史而辨别正闰，亦即一个王朝的正统与非正统，这不是史家的任务。他表明他著《通鉴》，旨在讲述国家的兴衰，生民的休戚，使读史者以善为榜样，以恶为教训，提高治理者的政治道德素养，以史为鉴，有益于治。司马光这一以史为教的用心，在《资治通鉴》一书里，是言之再三的。[2]

“风化清浊之源，在于选士制度”。所谓风化，又称风俗、风尚、教化，指社会的教育感化，历代相传而成的风尚和社会流行的风气、习俗。它为社会大多数人所遵尚。一个社会的风化如何，是清是浊，是与社会教化的好坏，社会政治的盛衰密切相关的。司马光极其重视社会的风化或教化，说：“教化，国家之急务也，而俗吏烦之，风俗，天下之大事也，而庸君忽之。夫惟明智君子，深识长虑，然后知其为益之大而收功长远也。”（《资治通鉴》卷六十八）他把社会教化并由此而形成良好的社会风气或习俗，看成是治国的首务。社会风化为什么有清有浊，有好有坏呢？司马光认为这与国家的

[1] 李雪辰．论宋代功利思潮的演进 [J]. 兰州学刊，2011(2)：18-22。
[2] 顾明远．《资治通鉴》中的教育故事 [J]. 中国教师，2018(5)：114-117。

选士制度密切相关。国家以德行取士，社会的风化就清明，国家以文辞选士，社会的风化就混乱。

"教子俭以养德"。注重家庭教育，也是司马光教育思想的核心内容，在《训俭示康》中，他告诫儿子司马康说："吾本寒家，世以清白相承，吾性不喜华靡。""众人皆以奢靡为荣，吾心独以俭素为美，人皆嗤吾固陋，吾不以为病。"在这里，司马光表白，俭素清白是他的家教传统。司马光指明，俭素清白是古来的美德，为孔子所提倡，作为有志之士，应以俭为美，而不应以侈为荣，司马光还列举出了历史上俭以发家，侈以败家的例子。作为宋朝一代名相，他以俭训示的教育思想，在后世产生广泛的影响。

1.2 二程

"生民之道，以教为本"。与传统的儒家一样，"二程"（程颢、程颐）作为宋明理学的鼻祖，主张治国以德教为本。认为"古者自家党遂至于国，皆有教之之地。民生八年则入于小学，是天下无不教之民也。既天下之人莫不从教，小人修身，君子明道，故贤能群聚于朝，良善成风于下，礼义大行，习俗粹美，刑罚虽设而不犯。此三代盛治由教而致也"（程颐《为家君请宇文中允典汉州学书》）。在二程看来，这是中国政治的传统，应该弘扬，而不应只重刑罚而不明教化，只重刑罚，那是达不到美风俗而成善政的。善治为什么必须兴教呢？二程认为，善治必须依赖人才，而人才是靠教育培养的。

"存天理，去人欲"。"存天理，去人欲"之说虽然由张载首先提倡，但还没有构成一个系统的理论。"二程"将之构成了一个系统的道德修养教育理论。"二程"所谓的天理，是指纲常伦理，因为这是得之于天的。"二程"说："天理云者，这一个道理，更有甚穷已？不为尧存，不为桀亡。"（《遗书》卷二）意思是天理是客观存在，不以人的主观愿望为转移的。他们认为所谓人欲是指人在物质和精神生活方面的过分追求及为人处世时的私心。"二程"把天理和人欲对立起来，说："视听言动说，非理不为，即为礼，礼即是理也。不是天理，便是私欲。人虽有意于为善，亦是非礼。无人欲即皆天理。"（《遗书》卷十五）至于存天理，去人欲的途径，"二程"提出了"闲邪存诚"。闲邪是防闲恶念，所谓存诚是说不自欺。存天理，去人欲是道德修养教育的内容，闲邪存诚则是方法论，二者都是"二程"道德理论的有机部分。[1]

1.3 朱熹

"圣人教人有定本"。被称为儒学集大成者的宋朝著名理学家朱熹多次强调所谓定本。意思是教育有固定不变的原则。朱熹又称这种原则为"大头脑"。他说："凡看道理，要见得大头脑处分明。下面节节，只是此理散为万殊。"（《朱子语类》·卷九·学三）在朱熹看来，圣人教人无不有他的定本和大头脑，即根本原则。而这根本原则又是什么呢？就是人伦道德。朱熹的《白鹿洞书院学规》，即其教人的定本。其中的父子

[1] 毛朝晖．二程理学的经学奠基及其结构性差异［J］．云南大学学报，2022(5):34-43。

有亲，君臣有义，夫妇有别，长幼有序，朋友有信，即为五教，是他教人的思想定本。而学、问、思、辨，是其穷理的定本。言忠信，行笃敬，惩忿窒欲，迁善改过，是其修身的定本；正其谊不谋其利，明其道不计其功，是其处事的定本；己所不欲，勿施于人，则是其接物的定本。穷理、修身处世，接物皆是其五教的定本在学行方面的推广。朱熹的教育思想和目标皆在于此。

“小学教以事，大学教以理”。朱熹把学校分为两个层次：小学和大学。小学与大学的区别，在于小学的教育是初步的，属于童蒙教育，而大学的教育则是高级教育。朱熹认为，小学的教育应以事为主，大学应以理为主。他说：“小学是直理会那事；大学是穷究那理，因甚恁地。小学者，学其事；大学者，学其小学所学之事之所以。”（《朱子语类》·卷七·学一）朱熹认为，小学必须教之以事，这是适应童蒙的年龄特征的。相对于小学而言，大学是指大学问之学，宋以后的书院，亦属大学。大学的教育是教之以穷理之学。他说：“大学者，大人之学也。明，明之也。明德者，人之所得乎天，而虚灵不昧，以具众理而应万事者也。”朱熹这里解释《大学》的明明德就是彰明天理。实际上是孔门的仁理，它流行于天地之间，充塞于宇宙之际，超越于万物之上而又内在千万物之中。[1]

1.4 许衡

“教在明人伦”。许衡作为元代著名的教育家，提出了教在明人伦的教育目标论。许衡说：明伦。明者，明之也。伦者，伦理也。人之赋命于天，莫不各有当务之责。如父子之有亲，君臣之有义，夫妇之有别，长幼之有序，朋友之有信，乃所谓天伦也。三代圣王，设为庠、序、学校以教天下者，无他，明此而已。盖人而不能明人之伦理，则尊卑上下、轻重厚薄淆乱，而不可统理。（《许衡集·小学大义》）人伦即人间的基本关系，这是得之于天而体之于人的，故又称天伦。许衡认为人如不能明白这一天伦，人类社会就会发生尊卑倒置，轻重厚薄淆乱，以至于祸乱相寻，人类沦为禽兽而已。所以自三代以来圣王皆设学校以教人伦，因此许衡把明伦视为教与学的主要内容和目标，认为天虽赋人以天伦，但人又禀气所生，禀得清气自然不妨碍天伦，如果禀受了浊气，或者禀受浊气多了，这就要妨碍天伦了，这就需要教化。

“教人之道，先务躬行”。许衡认为在知行中，行重于知。他提倡学要结合行。许衡说：“凡为学之道，必须一言一句，自求己事。先务躬行，非止诵书作文而已。”（《许衡集·语录上》）许衡认为读书的过程中，要结合自己的思想实际，凡有未能的，就应勉而行之，凡有不合的，就须警而改之。读书之有益，就在能够躬行。先王所以设学校教人，目的是有益天下之用。如不能以行引导人，仅以科目教人，就失去了先王设学校的初衷了。可以说，教人以行，结合自己的思想实际去读《六经》《语》《孟》等经典是许衡的一贯教学作风。[2]

---

[1] 林建峰．朱熹教育思想的哲学意蕴［J］．合肥学院学报，2016(2):17-22。
[2] 辛昕．论元初许衡的教育思想［J］．汉字文化，2022(4):188-190。

1.5 王夫之

“教以成性，教必有类”。作为明末清初的大思想家，王夫之有一个比较完整的思想教育理论的哲学体系。王夫之认为，人的形体是由天地阴阳五行秀气所凝成，而其性，则是气理所凝成，就气质而言叫作才，就气理而言叫作性。他提出了“习与性成”的观点。王夫之所谓习，一指风习，二指教习。风习是社会风气，教习是能使人成贤成圣的教育，风习与教习的区别在于风习影响人是不知不觉的，而教习影响人则是自觉的。而良好的风习和教习能成就人性，则又是一样的。王夫之说：“故恶人必不游君子之门，而君子必不取恶人而教。”(《读四书大全说》)。在王夫之看来，教必分清是善是恶，只有善人才予以教育，而对恶人，必不施教，这与天只给人类以聪明，而不给鸟兽以聪明是一样的道理。王夫子认为孔子的“有教无类”并不是不分善恶而教，而是教育者的调教应有一贯性，否则就会陷入不加拣别的教育观。

“天理即在人欲中”。天理人欲之辨是宋明时期道德修养论中的根本问题，也是思想教育中的根本问题。在宋明，正统的理学家无不以存天理去人欲为教。与正统的理学家相反，王夫之认为天理、人欲并不对立。《读四书大全说·先进篇》说：“凡诸声色臭味，皆理之所显。…… 倘须净尽人欲，而后天理流行，则但带兵农礼乐一切功利事，便于天理窒碍，叩其实际，岂非‘空诸所有’之邪说乎？”意思是天理人欲原不相对立，天理即寓于人欲之中，凡声色臭味即是天理的载体，如果灭尽人欲而后天理流行，岂不是将兵农礼乐等一切功利之事看成是天理的障碍，去掉这些障碍，岂不是空诸所有之邪说吗？当然，王夫之并不认为欲是可以放纵的，人的欲望只能在“天地之产”的可能内得到合理的实现，他既反对禁欲，又反对纵欲。这种理欲观，更易被大众所接受。[1]

二、宋代教育的功利思想

宋代的功利思想主要指反对虚谈性命、提倡实事实功的学派思想。针对理学的天理与人欲、义与利的对立观点，这学派注重功用财利，认为治国必以财用为基础，其思想上把“利”提高到了与“义”等同的地位，主张不能空谈道德仁义而忽略功利。[2]

2.1 李觏

“建国君民，教学为先”。宋朝著名思想家李觏极重视教育，认为建国君民，教育是第一等大事。其《安民策》说：“所谓安者，非徒饮之、食之、治之、令之而已也，必先于教化焉。教化之说何如？曰：夫俗士之论，未有不贵刑法而贱礼义也。”在传统的刑德之辨中，李觏是主张先德而后刑的。所谓安民，不只是解决人民的生计，而应该以教育为先，社会之所以有邪恶犯罪，都是失教的关系。李觏强调，重视教育是我国优良的传统。他还提出了改革教育的建议：“为朝家之计，莫若斥大七馆，使荐绅之

[1] 袁习渊，陈永富．王夫之教育思想初探 [J]. 文学教育，2008(9):132-132。
[2] 李雪辰．论宋代功利思潮的演进 [J]. 兰州学刊，2011(2):18-22。

族咸造焉；增修州学，使士庶人之秀咸在焉，择贤以为之师，分经以为之业，限以积久，毋得擅去。”意思是唯有扩大学校规模，广泛招收优秀学生，择贤为师，分经为业，延长时限，严格考试制度，从长考察，唯有这样，才能得到优秀人才。

“立人以善，成善在教”。李觏认为人性是可以造就的，关键在教。他强调“学校不立，教法不行，人莫知何人可师。道莫知何道可学。耳何以为正声？目何以为正色？口何以为正言？身何以为正行？明者幸而得之，昧者不幸而失之。”李觏认为，所谓教，其实是对人的自然欲望的调节。人的自然欲望不能说没有合理之处，这是他与传统儒者不同的地方，故一方面言，教不违背人性，另一方面，人的自然欲望也不能无限地让它发展，必须加以节度。李觏同样强调，圣人不应择民而教，对于地理决定论他颇不以为然，列举了很多历史中的故事以证明：英雄不以南北之分，而通过教育可以造就培养人才。

“礼者世教之主，教之本在师”。在教育的内容上，李靓突出了礼。李靓说：“礼者，生民之大也。”“天子之所以正天下，诸侯之所以治其国，卿大夫之所以守其俭，庶人之所以保其生，无一物而不以礼也。穷天地，亘万世，不可须臾而去也。”（《礼论・第六》）他把礼视为人道的最高准则，圣人治理天下的基本手段，士子修身的主要原则和社会教化的主要内容。他也充分重视教师在礼教中的作用。他说：“教之本在师。师者，所以制民命，其可以非其人哉？”在道德和思想教育中，教师是起主导作用的，故择师不可以随便。又说：“学校废，师不命于上，而学者自择焉。识不至，择不精，是能言之类莫不可师也。”（《广潜书・十五篇》）意思是学校废颓，思想混乱，在李靓看来，这都是由于择师不精，师非其人造成的。李靓提出了加强师德建设的要求：“以教育为职，以德行为先”。他指出教师不但要教书，而且还要育人，学生不仅要读书，而且要修德。

2.2 王安石[1]

“教之之道，为天下国家之用”。北宋改革家王安石强调培养天下有可用之才，并提出了教之之道，他说：“所谓教之之道何也？古者天子诸侯，自国至于乡党皆有学，博置教道之官而严其选。朝廷礼乐，刑政之事，皆在于学，士所观而习者，皆先王之法言德行治天下之意，其材亦可以为天下国家之用。苟不可以为天下国家之用，则不教也。苟可以为天下国家之用者，则无不在于学。”（《王文公集・上仁宗皇帝万言书》）王安石的教之之道，在制度的层面，就是设立学校。在内容的层面上，就是教以天下国家之用。除了学校以外，王安石还强调社会风俗对成才的影响。王安石说：“圣人上承天之意，下为民之主，其要在安利之。而能安利之要不在于它，在于正风俗而已。故风俗之变迁染民志，关之盛衰，不可不慎也。”与教之之道相联系的是取之之道、任之之道和养之之道，都体现了治国教育的功利主义思想。王安石以经世致用为学术

[1] 徐陶章，奕涵．大道为一：论王安石思想中的儒释交融［J］．上饶师范学院学报，2022(5):9-15。

研究之旨归，认为儒学和佛学的互补有利于促进社会发展与礼乐教化。

“变革之道，使学者专意经义”。对于当时学校的弊端，王安石有很深的认识。《王文公集·上仁宗皇帝万言书》说：“方今州县虽有学，取墙壁具而已。非有教导之官，长育人才之事也。唯太学有教导之官，而亦未尝严其选。朝廷礼乐刑政之事，未尝在于学。”王安石指出，当世的学校，所教完全脱离实际，凡朝廷礼乐刑政等有用的学问，均被排除在学校教学之外，学校只去教授课试文章。即令学好了，亦不足为天下国家之用。如此空耗岁月，实际上是摧毁人才。因此提出了改进学校教育的意见，其《乞改科条制》说：“宜先除去声病对偶之文，使学者得以专意经义，以俟朝廷兴建学校，然后讲求三代所以教育选举之法，施于天下。”王安石的这一奏疏，提出了教育改革的根本目标和任务是兴建学校，复三代教育选举之法，改革现有的诗赋记诵为主的应试教育取士制度，选拔学以致用的人才。

“为师之道，传之以心”。王安石重视教师的作用。他说：“君不得师，则不知所以为君；臣不得师，则不知所以为臣。为之师，所以并持之也。”他相信治天下固然要用圣人之道，但圣人之道还要人来弘扬，由此而言，教师不是可有可无的。对于社会教化，王安石则提出了善教的问题，所谓善教，指在位者对民众的感化，应该说服而不是压服。不善教是指在位者对民众采取压服而不是说服的方法。王安石认为，凡有资格教化民众，为人师的人都应采取前一方法而不应采取后一方法。王安石这一说服而不压服、感化而不强制的教育方法，是传之以心，也是有利于社会秩序与教育实效的方法。

2.3 陈亮

“教不违性，养成其才而充其气”。南宋思想家陈亮认为学校的作用，是在培养人才，鼓舞士气。他说：“天子设学校于行都，使之群居切磨，朝暮讲究，斥百家之异说，而不以为诞，言当今之利害而不以为狂，所以养成其才而充其气也。”他主张国家必设学校教卿大夫子弟，如此朝廷才不乏可用之才。为了造就有用之才，陈亮主张教育不应违背人性。他在《陈亮集》卷四中说：人所共有的本性，能完全得到满足，就是富贵尊荣，反之就是危亡困辱。但人的欲望能否得到满足这不是由自己决定的，而要制定礼乐刑政以进行调节，故所谓礼乐刑政的礼教，也是根据人性而定的，所以礼乐刑政之教，应该既是对人性的节制，又是顺应人的自然之性和生活欲望。在陈亮看来，理学家的性命之学，存理去欲之教是完全违背人性和人才培养的，不去道德性命之学，存理去欲之教，则人心无从正，风俗无法淳，人才必然凋敝。他建议教育要明师道，播仁义，不拘一格地使用人才。如此，则国家可兴，天下可平。

“教以成人之道，不教以醇儒自律”。陈亮主张教育要以成为济世人才为目标，而不能约束在使人成为纯粹的儒者之中。他坦言：“亮以为学者，学为成人，而儒者亦一门户中之大者耳。秘书不教以成人之道，而教以醇儒自律，岂揣其分量则止于此乎？不然亮犹有遗恨也。”（《陈亮集》卷二十）。在陈亮看来，朱熹的成人之道，并不值得追求，他觉得真正的成人应该是于内追求仁义道德的修养，对外则注重实际功效，做到仁智勇德具备，由此才能与天地并立。与传统儒家相比，陈亮的“成人之道”具有鲜明的务实与功利特色。在他看来，成人之道的人格特征不同于传统的醇儒，而是首先把义利、理欲统一于一体的主体，其次兼具仁、智、勇的德性，再次还要具有强烈的社会责任感和道德使命感。所谓当得世界轻重有无，将个人价值与社会价值、道德价值与功利价值统一起来。[1] 陈亮思想中的成人之道是一种理想人格的构建，对现代教育的精神文明具有举足轻重的实践意义。

2.4 叶适[2]

“所用在于所养”。叶适在治理和教化方面相较于程朱理学是具有鲜明的功利色彩的。叶适重视社会治理的功效，强调惠通工商，以国家之力扶持商贾，流通货币。统观叶适思想，“功利”是作为实现国家社会治理的手段，究其本源仍是为“王道”服务。他说：“天下之物养之者必取之，养其山者必材，养其泽者必渔，其养之者备，则其取之者多，其养之者久，则其得之者精。夫其所以养之者，固其所以为取也。”意思是所用必赖所养，自然界如此，人类社会更是如此。欲用才必先养才，欲取士必先养士。至于如何养育，叶适强调学官自身的素质，学官自己有良好的素养，才能谈得上教民成才，他说：“明恕而多通，吏之所以自教，节廉而少欲，吏之所以自养。故自养自教更急于养人教人。”

“所教必有所用”。叶适主张教师要教人以道义，但是义与利并非不能相容。他认为如果道义排斥功利，道义就是无用的虚语，进而提出了教与政，学与用相合一的思想，说：“文章高下，未有不与事称者。”所谓“事”即现实政事，为文必有益于教化、关乎时事。叶适强调文章的内容须备义理，尤其是科举之文必须坚持务实的导向。他批评说：“彼学也，此政也，学与政判然为二。”（《叶适集·经总制钱》）意思是当今所教所学是先王之道，而一旦为官为吏，所事则与所学毫无关系。在校是学，所事是政，视学、政为二途，这又怎能不造成人才颓废，政治衰败？因此叶适认为科举、制策与治学必须“务实”，要以实践为前提，反对空谈，这与其治国思想一脉相承。基于此，他认为学者治学修身，首先应务实。

第三节 心学与实学

心学和实学都是中国教育和哲学发展的重要学术支脉。《哲学大辞典》中将“心学”与“陆王心学”统归为一，由南宋陆九渊创立，明王守仁进一步发展。此派在哲学世界观上认为心是世界之根本。[3] 而实学的概念在中国其实由来已久，它一方面是儒家入世实用思想的体现，贯穿于儒家教育思想；另一方面，它又是在特定历史时期产生

[1] 曲爱香．陈亮“成人之道”思想及其现代价值［J］．甘肃社会科学，2013(3):40-43。
[2] 田萌萌．论叶适思想的“致用”指向［J］．北京社会科学，2022(3):45-54。
[3] 方克立．中国哲学大辞典［M］．北京：中国社会科学出版社，1994:387。

的对儒家文化的反思和批判的形式，是作为社会新思潮消解儒学的经院性而成为庶民文化的“革新”因素。了解心学和实学的代表人物及其核心思想对于了解中国教育文化有很大的帮助。[1]

一、宋元明清的心学思想

宋元明清时期的心学思想是强调心为价值之源的孔学流派，明王守仁在《象山全集·叙》中说：“圣人之学，心学也。”由此，后世学者，称由陆九渊和王守仁开创的这一学派为心学学派，以区别为以程朱为代表的理学学派。心学与理学的基本区别，一是心学倡言心本体，有别于理学的理本体；二是心学思想教育理论的特点，是强调受教育者的主体性，心学认为思想教育，旨在扩充和引发人的先天良知本性，而不是教以人性所本无的东西。

1.1 陆九渊[2]

“存心、养心、以求放心”。陆九渊是南宋著名哲学家、教育家。他的心学思想开启了明代中后期平民儒学的先河。他认为，所谓教育，在本质上是教人，在于使人保存和涵养自己的良心，在良心被蒙蔽或丢失的时候，要教人把它找回来。陆九渊说：“孩提之童，无不知爱其亲，及其长也，无不知敬其兄，先王之时，庠序之教，抑申斯义以致其知，使不失其本心而已。尧舜之道不过如此。此非有甚高难行之事，何至辽视古俗，自绝于圣贤哉！”（《陆九渊集·贵溪重修县学记》）即是说，所谓教育，就在于教人自存其心，不失本心。为什么教人只在教人存心、养心和求放心呢？陆九渊认为，这是因为心即理。他说：“心，一心也，理，一理也。至当归一，精义无二，此心此理实不容有二。”意思是理不在心外，不是充塞于天地之中，而只在心里。仁、义、礼、智、信都是心的不同展现。求仁求义，即求心所包含的理，知是知非，也是知心所包含的理。还强调，一个人如果良心本性迷失，存心养心最重要的，就是要把迷失的良心本性找回来，故人可怕的不在其有所陷溺，而在其自弃而不求，故教人存心、养心，还必须教人求放心。

“学当有师，师承须正”。与儒学传统一脉相承的是，陆九渊认为，人不当师心自用，学当有师。他说：“学者大病，在于师心自用。师心自用，则不能克己，不能听言，虽使羲皇唐虞以来群圣之言毕闻于耳，毕熟于口，毕记于心，只益其私，增其病耳。为过益大，去道愈远，非徒无益，而又害之！”（《与张辅之》）意思是学者如果师心自用，纵然熟读圣贤之书，闻圣人之言，亦只能增其私而大其过。他强调求师的好处，在于老师能在学业上给予有秩序的指导，不使学者读书漫无边际，无所至止。凡是无所师授得来的知识，不过是一些杂驳没有统贯的知识，谈不上学问的。陆九渊还强调，

[1] 潘畅和．对中国实学的哲学诠释［J］．延边大学学报，2009(2):53-56。
[2] 陈寒鸣．从君子文化的视角论陆九渊心学的意义［J］．齐鲁学刊，2019(6):50-58。

学当有师，但师承要正，不能师事异端。他认为“天下正理，不容有二。若明此理，天地不能异此，鬼神不能异此，千古圣贤不能异此。”陆九渊还认为，虽说学必求师，但明师难求，不可必得。在未得到明师的指点之前，学者也不能虚耗光阴，而要随时努力。

“辨志为尚，德育为先”。陆九渊认为，圣贤之所以为圣贤，就因为他们在艰难困苦的条件下不堕其志，孔子虽无事业上的成功，但其志向高远，宏毅不拔，不愧为圣人。他说：“人惟患无志，有志无有不成者。”（《陆九渊集·语录》）人如有志向，那是没有什么事情做不成的。故教人，要教人首先立志。陆九渊的这种思想，与孟子的辨志是一脉相承的。同时，陆九渊教人，以“尊德性”为先，他认为，德才或德艺相较，德无疑重于才艺。究其原因，是德是一个人安身立命的基础。“士庶人有德，能保其身，卿大夫有德，能保其家，诸侯有德，能保其国，天子有德，能保其天下。无德而富，徒增其过恶，重后日之祸患，今日虽富，岂能长保？”（《杂说》）陆九渊强调读书要以心地洁净为前提，否则书读得越多，危害也就越大。

“自立为主，减担为方”。自立谓自己做主，不依附旁人。陆九渊对子弟说：“请尊兄即今自立，正坐拱手，收拾精神，自作主宰。万物皆备于我，有何欠阙。”（《陆九渊集·语录下》）意思是人都是自己的主人，要有自立的气概，自我主宰的度屋，不必扶墙靠壁，只要心地洁净，即令不识字，亦不妨碍他堂堂正正地做一个人。故教人，首先是教他做一个人，然后才是读书学艺。同时，陆九渊教学，崇尚简易，减负的方法。他曾作诗说：“易简工夫终久大，支离事业竟浮沉。”他不主张给学生看许多传注，只看古注也就够了。这一教学法，他称之曰减担，认为唯有减担，才可提高效能，造就一代人才。

1.2 王守仁[1]

“以明伦为宗旨”。王守仁作为集心学之大成者的思想家、军事家、教育家，传承了我国古代儒家的教育传统，他的“心学”体系反映了明代的时代面貌。他说：“古圣贤之学，明伦而已。尧舜之相授曰：人心惟危，道心惟微，惟精惟一，允执厥中，斯明伦之学矣。”（《万松书院记》）在王守仁看来，教育的宗旨就在于阐明伦常，亦即父子有亲，君臣有义，夫妇有别，长幼有序，朋友有信，人伦之外的教育，都是异教，人伦之外的学问，都是邪说。依人伦而行，就是治世，背人伦而行，就是乱世。这种以明伦为宗旨的教育思想，在王阳明全集里，是随处可见的。王守仁强调，教以明伦，看似容易，其实很难。说其容易，这是因为人伦之知是人的本性良知，即使是孩提之童，亦无不知爱其亲而敬其兄，所以教以明伦，并不是从外面把伦常之理灌注人心。而是通过教育，引发人类本性内原已具有的东西。说它至难，是因为要做到人伦的极致，虽圣人亦有不能尽的时候，更不要说一般的平民百姓了。王守仁强调，明人伦，重要的不在讲明人伦，而要在行动上实践人伦。这就要求教师自为师范，率先垂范，作出

[1] 刘建国．王守仁“心学”体系的内部结构［J］．长白学刊，1985(2)：11-14。

表率。否则，教师即使讲得头头是道，也是苍白无力，难以令人相信的。

“发其志意，开其知觉”。王守仁强调启蒙教育，即把道德教育摆在教育的首位，使儿童从小就养成良好的道德品质，主张以诗礼读书去栽培儿童，“诱之以歌诗发其志意，导之习礼以肃其威仪，讽之读书以开其知觉。”(《训蒙大意》)当然，诗礼的教育要根据童蒙的年龄与心理特征进行，而不应以教士人诗礼的方法进行。庄子曾把仁义道德与人性对立起来，而王守仁则因循人的自然性情进行道德教育，这种观点更加高明。王守仁批评当世的启蒙教育完全违反了儿童的生理和心理特点，这样做的结果，造成儿童“视学舍如囹狱而不肯入，视师长如寇仇而不欲见”，又怎么能引导好儿童呢?王守仁的思想富有施教者的智慧，符合儿童心理发展的规律，值得后人珍视。

“知行合一”。王守仁认为认识事物的道理与实行其事，是密不可分的。知是指内心的觉知，对事物的认识，行是指人的实际行为。它既是阳明文化的核心，也是中国古代哲学中认识论和实践论的命题。受这一思想启示，中国的传统教育哲学认为，人的外在行为受内在意识支配，由衷向善(知)的人，才有外在自发的善行，所以说知行合一。王守仁的知行合一包括“知中有行，行中有知。以知为行，知决定行”。王守仁极力反对道德教育上的知行脱节及“知而不行”，突出把一切道德归之于个体的自觉行动，这是有积极意义的。同时，他相信道德是人行为的指导思想，按照道德的要求去行动是达到“良知”的功夫，在道德指导下产生的意念活动是行为的开始，符合道德规范要求的行为是“良知”的完成。这种知行合一思想主要是讲内心“省察克治”的唯心主义道德修养学说。他所谓不曾被私意隔断的知行本体，就是指“见父自然知孝，见兄自然知弟，见孺子入井自然知恻隐”的良知，认为“致吾心之良知于事事物物”就是行。他的“致良知”即知行合一，就是“去恶为善”“去人欲，存天理”的功夫。

1.3 黄宗羲

“道德与事功一体”。作为明末清初著名思想家和政治家，黄宗羲的心学与其政治思想之间的关联，首先体现在其“道德与事功一体”的儒学观，就思想史脉络而言，则体现出作为近世新儒学两大支柱的心性、事功之学的交汇转化。他心学的教育与政治意义亦集中体现在“天人之道”的维度。他说：“自仁义与事功分途，于是言仁义者陆沉泥腐，天下无可通之志”“岂知古今无事功之仁义，亦无不本仁义之事功”。[1]以人事积极承接天理，是黄宗羲论“天人之际”的精义所在。君子之于天命，在持中守正、居易以俟之外，更应主动承接、积极实现，不仅要有“俟命”之品节，更应具备“造命”之担当。一方面，超越的心灵之维为政制革新、法度损益提供了重要精神支持；另一方面，黄宗羲认定天意必由民意而见，反对宿命论与灾异说，主张士君子通过自身的实践与修为来积极承当天运，从而展现出一种持循天理、勇于担当的经世精神和更加积极的教育与政治意识。[2]

---

[1] 黄宗羲．明儒学案(卷47)[M]．杭州：浙江古籍出版社，2005:408-409。
[2] 顾家宁．王霸之辨与天人之际：黄宗羲心学的政治之维[J]．天府新论，2017(5):52-60。

“理为气之理”。黄宗羲理气观的基本主张是“理气合一”，反对“理气二分”。理气关系是宋明理学的基本命题，黄宗羲反对“理气二分”的观点是基于其批判“知、行”分离的功夫论，他从本体论上论证“理为气之理”和“气为理之气”的基本观点，提出了对理气问题的新认知。黄宗羲思想形成的深层原因是明代中期阳明学兴起之后产生了很大的社会影响，其一个基本的主张是“知行合一”，即反对空谈“知”，而不去做实在的修德行为。针对此流弊，黄宗羲针对一些儒家学者在修圣贤学时只重“知”、重“悟”而不重“行”、重“功夫”的做法进行质疑，主张应该继承王阳明“知行合一”的思想，那么从本体论上来讲，“知”与“行”的合一必须要求“理”与“气”的合一。黄宗羲认为：明朝灭亡的根源在于伦理秩序的崩溃；而伦理秩序崩溃的根源在于人心失去理之主宰，是理气相分所致。理与气的关系是一体之两面，本来就是一物，只是因为人们观察角度的不同给予不同的名字而已。他说“心无本体，功夫所至，即其本体”。这一思想强调了存在的真实内涵，反对将理性抽离现实生活。同时，“理为气之理”的思想为明代理学中的悟道与行道之辨提供了全面论证，将儒学发展方向从悟“向内返本复初”之道引向践行“向外结合历史与人事”之道。[1]

二、清代教育的实学思想

所谓实学，即经世致用之学，这一学派认为学问须有益于国家人民之用。实学作为一种学术思潮，与清谈心性相对立。清代实学派倡导亲身习行践履，注重实际知识。实学思想认为，客观实际存在的事物，是认识的基础，所以读书不能离事离物，因为只有这些实用知识是有益于国计民生，临事可以济世应用的。

2.1 包世臣

“兴废之故系于人”。包世臣是清代著名的实学思想家，对当时的社会情况、民间疾苦、诸般时弊有比较深入的了解。他相信“人事修，天运变”。只要上下齐心合力，及时采取变革措施，是可以“拨乱反正”的。如何“拨乱反正”？包世臣认为，首先应弄清社会出现乱象和危机的根源。他说：“天下事，必灼见弊之所极，与致弊之源，而后能为救弊之策。”包世臣还曾提出过一项带有原则性的“以渐而进、积小成大”方针：主张从基层的制度改革和行善政以完善社会现状。包世臣还提出过“创意改制”的主张，其中，建立“审官院”的建议颇有价值。他呼吁士人自觉以“民事”为事，使儒学满足社会人群的需要，解决社会现实问题，所表述的乃是改造传统儒学，使儒学实学化的诉求。[2] 虽然由于当时中国封建制度的种种弊端尚未充分暴露，新的思想尚未传入中国，包世臣的改良思想存在一定局限性，但他的“兴废之故系于人”的务实思想对于各时期的中国教育具有重要的现实意义。

[1] 陈杨．明清之际哲学转向的气学视野 [J]. 现代哲学，2019(5):153-160。
[2] 张锡勤．包世臣经世思想述评 [J]. 学术交流，2010(7):8-12。

“凡民事皆士事也”。包世臣认为，教育者和知识分子，不论是“谈性命”的“高者”，还是“矜词章”的“卑者”，都算不上是真正的“士”。真正的士应是实学实用，以自己的所学为国为民办事的人。他认为士所以列于四民之首，是因为士能通农、工、商诸学，并能运用自己所学的知识指导、推动农、工、商业的发展。他希望广大知识分子自觉认识并承担起自己的社会责任，在生产、流通和社会管理方面起到自己应起的作用。为促使知识分子经世致用，他曾建议科举考试“罢八股，以明经术、策时务二事应之。”(《包世臣全集》)包世臣以满足“人需”释儒，以为民办事释士。他针对儒学不能满足“人需”，士人漠视且不通“民事”的弊端进行改革的思想对于后世的教育理念有积极的启示作用。

2.2 颜元

“教以习行为重”。清初思想家颜元是清代实学的代表人物，他是个极重视实践教育的教育家，他一生反对静坐读书，崇尚实践，主张教学以习行为重。[1]其《存学编》说：“即诗、书、六艺，亦非徒列坐讲听，要惟一讲即教习，习至难处来问，方再与讲。”颜元指出，传统教育一个最突出的弊病就是脱离实际，所以他主张以实学代理学。颜元所谓的习行，意为“做”，具有现代教学所讲的实习、实行的意义。为什么教必以习行为重呢，颜元认为客观实际存在之物是构成人们知识的实际内容，只有亲自实践一番，才能掌握知识，即使学习理论知识，也只有经过习行，才能化理论知识为自己的知识。否则，“心中醒，口中说，纸上作，不从身上习过，皆无用也！”(《存学编》卷二)。况且，教学是为了应用，而人的精力有限，在讲读中耗去一分，在习作中就少却一分，纸墨上多耗费一分，实行中便少一分。

“教以动不教以静”。在中国古代，儒道两派的思想家，大多数以静教天下，而不是以动教天下，因为他们的道德本体是静而不动的。在颜元看来，晋宋的苟安，佛老的空无，理学的静坐，是造成人才殆尽圣道消亡，国家衰弱的根本原因。唯有动，才能强身强家强天下，他对这一点是深信不疑的。他再三强调：“养身莫善于习动，夙兴夜寐，振起精神，寻事去作，行之有常，并不困疲，日益精壮。”又说：“人不做事则暇，暇则逆，逆则惰，惰则疲，暇、逆、惰、疲，私欲乘之矣！”(《颜习斋言行录》)意思是人如果静而不动，多有暇日，就会养成懒惰的习惯，私欲就会随之而生。只有动而不惰，才能朝气勃勃，精神振奋，如此，私欲也就无从而生了。颜元的结论是：“宋元以来儒者皆习静，今日正可言习动！”(《颜习斋言行录》)从而把王夫之的主动的教育思想，又向前推进了一步。

“教以实不教以虚”。所谓实，是指实用和应用知识和道德实践，所谓虚，是指天道性命之学。“教以实不教以虚”是颜元教育的又一基本原则。颜元认为，实是天道、地道和人道。他说天地之道是实不是虚，世界是实不是虚，佛说空，老说无，但佛老

[1] 陈凤．颜元实学思想对当今高校道德教育的启示［J］．新丝路，2023(9)：115-117。

不能使天无明，地无山川，人无耳目，故人生天地之间，虽有官运不济，亦必以实文、实行、实体、实用为天地造实绩，而不能像宋儒那样，宽衣博带，袖手交谈性命之理，负天地之气数，坏民物之安阜。颜元的教学，是以实习为特征的。在他主持漳南书院时，把书院设为六斋，前四斋的文事、武备、经史、艺能都是类似于今日的应用实用之学。书院虽然也设理学斋和帖括斋，这是当时的时尚，不能完全取消，但颜元把这二斋的门开向北面，以示此二斋并不重要。

“教以儒不教以文”。所谓儒，是指孔子创立的学派。教以儒，是指教以儒学、儒术。所谓文，是指文章、文艺。不教以文，是说不教以文章做法。颜元把儒与文加以区分，甚至加以对立。他说："夫儒者，学为君相百职，为生民造命，为气运主机者也。"(《颜习斋言行录》卷二)意思是儒是以实学为事，以经济事业为功的，而文人则以文章为学，二者有天壤之别。对当世社会的尚文而不重儒，颜元提出了激烈的批评，他说："且学所以明伦耳，故古之小学教以洒扫、应对、进退之节，大学教以格致、诚正之功，修养治平之务。民舍是无以学，师舍是无以教，君相舍是无以治也"。意思是后世不讲明伦之学，不讲应用、进退之节，不讲格致诚正之功，国家取士专以文为据，学校劝课亦以文为功，父兄相劝，朋友相磋，亦即文字而已。如此，又怎能治天下国家呢？颜元的这些实学思想，都饱含着他对世道的关切和对教育改革的深思，在当时是极其难能可贵的。

2.3 李塨[1]

“教必不言性天”。作为颜元学派的传人，李塨继承了教人以实不以虚的传统，认为圣人是以实用教人，而不以玄虚的性与天道教人的。其《周易传注序》说："天之事在化育，人之事在经纶。天而不为天之事，而欲代人经纶，则天工废，人而不为人之事，而专测天化育，则人绩荒。"圣人为什么不教人性天之道而只教以人事呢？李塨认为，其原因就是性天即在人事之中，或者说，理并非孤悬一物，它只在人事之中。与颜元一样，李塨也尖锐地批判宋儒以理为教而不以物事为教："有物有则，离事物何所为理乎？且圣道只在其然，故曰：不见那物事，不能时习，与异端窈窈冥冥，其中有物等语，不宛同一旨乎！"他认为离下学即无所谓上达，离物事即无所谓道理。把道或理看作是独立一物，这只是佛老的思想，而不是儒者的传统。因此他同他的老师颜元一样相信“理在气中”，他说“夫事有条理曰理，即在事中。"(《论语传注问》)这一思想是“教必不言性天”的体现，也是李塨对唯物论思想的重大贡献。

“致知在格物”。李塨继承老师的“解格物具有习行道德、人伦、技艺的意义”这一传统，强调大学之教虽是教理，但不能离物。他理解大学的格物以《周礼》三物(六德、六行、六艺)为物，以亲习其事为格。所谓格物，也就是学习道德人伦技艺之事。为什么学必兼习其事，教必不离物呢？李塨认为，所谓学，就是学其事，习其事。这些都

[1] 陈山榜．李塨及其著作[J]．河北师范大学学报，2013(9):31-35。

离不开现实生活中实际的事物。李塨说："谓之物者，则以诚、正、修、齐、治、平皆有其事，而学其事皆有其物，《周礼》礼乐等皆谓之物是也。"致知在格物者从来圣贤之道，行先以知，而知在于学。[1]他以行路打比方，认为"不知不能行，不行不可谓真知"，同时还说"知之一，行之一，明分为二事是也，必先问清路，然后可行"。正因为对"格物致知"和"知"与"行"的关系作了如此理解，他把"知"与"行"看作是并行的两个方面，凸显出其学术思想辩证客观的特征。

[1] 张祥浩．中国传统教育思想理论 [M]．南京：东南大学出版社，2011:326。

第六章　经典名言拾味

从前几章的阅读中读者不难发现，中国传统教育在长期发展过程中，教育典籍浩如烟海，教育思想也丰富深邃。在教育典籍辈出的历史长河中，其遗言余旨，蔚然可观。其中有些长期以来广为流传，成为教育格言，宏博精深，充满哲思，历代执教者莫不视为教育的宝筏，每加引录，以教诲后学。本章所选经典名言多来自《中国历代名人名言》[1]及《中国古代名言词典》[2]。虽然“群言百家，不可胜览”，在本章中的拾味难免挂一漏万，但相信从为学与修身、世情与哲理这几方面品味经典名言，将是传承中华优秀传统文化的有效途径。

第一节　为学与修身

中国教育文化中的儒者之“学”的第一要义，就是“修身”。所谓“修身”，不仅仅是道德修养或道德教育，而是以“天—人”“物—我”“身—心”一体而相通为前提，在物我感通、身心相守中成就“诚于中，形于外”的饱满人格。中国古代有着丰富的为学与修身之道，旨在通过各种学习的理念与法门提高个体的心性修养，不断完善自身的学问，塑造出完美的人格，兼具美德与智慧，获得不为物所役的自由和圆满。

一、秦汉前后时期

1.1　为学

博学而笃志，切问而近思。（《论语·子张》）

玉不琢，不成器；人不学，不知道。（《礼记·学记》）

博学之、审问之、慎思之、明辨之、笃行之。（《礼记·中庸》）

大博学而详说之，将以反说约也。（《孟子·离娄下》）

温故而知新，可以为师矣。（《论语·为政》）

博学而日参省乎己，则知明而行无过。（《荀子·劝学》）

吾尝终日而思矣，不如须臾之所学也。（《荀子·劝学》）

吾生也有涯，而知也无涯。（《庄子·养生主》）

故师之教也，不争轻重尊卑贫富，而争于道。（《吕氏春秋·劝学》）

强勉学问，则闻见博而知益明；强勉行道，则德日起而大有功。（《举贤良对策》）

[1] 尹邦彦，尹海波．中国历代名人名言 [M]．南京：译林出版社，2009。

[2] 钱厚生．中国古代名言词典 [M]．南京：南京大学出版社，2010。

乌号之弓虽良，不得排檠，不能自任；人才虽高，不务学问，不能致圣。(《说苑·建本》)

故学者如登山焉，动而益高；如寤寐焉，久而益足。(《中论·治学》)

宝玉之山，土木必润；盛德之士，文艺必众。(《中论·艺纪》)

盖文章，经国之大业，不朽之盛事。年寿有时而尽，荣乐止乎其身，二者必至之常期，未若文章之无穷。(《典论·论文》)

文章者，所以宣上下之象，明人伦之叙，穷理尽性，以究万物之宜者也。(《文章流别论》)

读书百遍而义自见。(《三国志·魏志》)

思风发于胸臆，言泉流于唇齿。(《文赋》)

恒患意不称物，文不逮意。(《文赋·序言》)

人好学，虽死若存；不学者，虽存，谓之行尸走肉耳。(《拾遗记》)

盛年不再来，一日难再晨。及时当勉励，岁月不待人。(《杂诗》)

文章当从三易：易见事，一也；易识字，二也；易读诵，三也。(《沈隐侯集》)

人乃有贵贱，同宜资教，不可以其种类庶鄙而不教之也。(《论语义疏》)

1.2 修身

饭疏食，饮水，曲肱而枕之，乐亦在其中矣。(《论语·述而》)

天作孽，犹可违；自作孽，不可活。(《尚书·太甲》)

必有忍，其乃有济。(《尚书·君陈》)

仁者以财发身，不仁者以身发财。(《礼记·大学》)

诚者，非自成己而已也；所以成物也。(《礼记·中庸》)

人之有德于我也，不可忘也；吾有德于人也，不可不忘也。(《战国策·魏策四》)

厚者不毁人以自益也，仁者不危人以要名。(《战国策·燕策三》)

良药苦于口而利于病，忠言逆于耳而利于行。(《孔子家语·六本》)

欲速则不达，见小利则大事不成。(《论语·子路》)

志忍私，然后能公；行忍情性，然后能修。(《荀子·儒效》)

不厚其栋，不能任重。(《国语·鲁语上》)

善不由外来兮，名不可以虚作。(《九章·抽思》)

大行不顾细谨，大礼不辞小让。(《史记·项羽本纪》)

人必其自爱也，然后人爱诸；人必其自敬也，然后人敬诸。(《法言·君子》)

欲人勿闻，莫若勿言；欲人勿知，莫若勿为。(《上书谏吴王》)

面一旦不修饰，则尘垢秽之；心一朝不思善，则邪恶入之。(《女诫》)

君子之行：静以修身，俭以养德。非淡泊无以明志，非宁静无以致远。(《诸葛亮集·诫子书》)

勿以恶小而为之，勿以善小而不为。(《三国志》)

立身之道，与文章异：立身先须谨重，文章且须放荡。（《梁简文帝集》）

洗心而革面者，必若清波之涤轻尘。（《抱朴子·用刑》）

二、唐宋前后时期

2.1 为学

黑发不知勤学早，白首方悔读书迟。（《劝学诗》）

读书破万卷，下笔如有神。（《杜少陵集》）

书山有路勤为径，学海无涯苦作舟。（《治学名联》）

古之学者必有师。师者，所以传道、授业、解惑也。（《师说》）

二句三年得，一吟双泪流。（《题诗后》）

自古文士，不独知己难得，而知人亦难也。（《诗话》）

共君一夜话，胜读十年书。（《伊川先生语》）

古之能为文章者，真能陶冶万物，虽取古人之陈言入于翰墨，如灵丹一粒，点铁成金也。（《答洪驹父书》）

为学之道，必本于思。思则得知，不思则不得也。（《晁氏客语》）

纸上得来终觉浅，绝知此事要躬行。（《冬夜读书示子聿》）

无一事而不学，无一时而不学，无一处而不学，成功之路也。（《朱子语类》）

问渠哪得清如许？为有源头活水来。（《观书有感》）

学诗者以识为主：入门须正，立志须高。（《沧浪诗话·诗辨》）

人之不可以不学，犹鱼之不可以无水！而世至视若赘疣，岂不甚可叹哉？（《陆九渊集·与黄循中》）

一语天然万古新，豪华落尽见真淳。（《论诗·绝句》）

桃花岁岁皆相似，人面年年自不同。（《琵琶记》）

2.2 修身

土相扶为墙，人相扶为王。（《北齐书·尉景传》）

人患不知其过，既知之，不能改，是无勇也。（《五箴序》）

不自满者受益，不自是者博闻。（《省心录》）

凡百事之成也在敬之，其败也必在慢之。（《资治通鉴》）

专心致意，毕力于其事而后可。（《梦溪笔谈》）

富贵不淫贫贱乐，男儿到此是豪雄。（《秋日》）

瓜田不纳履，李下不整冠。（《乐府诗集·君子行》）

常人所欲在富，君子所贵在德。（《杂说》）

成人不自在，自在不成人。（《鹤林玉露》）

有则改之，无则加勉。（《集注》）

慈悲胜念千声佛，造恶徒烧万炷香。（《琵琶记》）

信者，人之根本，人而无信，大不可也！（《西厢记》）

三、明清前后时期

3.1 为学

天下之至文，未有不出于童心焉者也。（《焚书·童心说》）

诚以学不立志，如植木无根，生意将无从发端矣。（《寄张世文》）

读万卷书，行万里路。（《画旨》）

学者有段兢业的心思，又要有段潇洒的趣味，若一味敛束清苦，是有秋杀无春生，何以发育万物？（《菜根谭》）

攻人之过毋太严，要思其堪受；教人之善毋过高，当使其可从。（《菜根谭》）

若要功夫深，铁杵磨成针。（《蜀中广记》）

一寸光阴一寸金，寸金难买寸光阴。（《三宝太监西洋记》）

非学无以广才，非静无以成学。（《增广贤文》）

耕读各勤本业，何难平地为山。（《醒世要言》）

凡作文，必须一篇之中，并无一句一字是杂凑入来。（《西厢记汇评》）

盖天下之书，诚欲藏之名山、传之后人，即无有不精严者。（《水浒评》）

文贵工，不贵速。（《聊斋志异·织成》）

性痴则其志凝，故书痴者文必工，艺痴者技必良。（《聊斋志异·阿宝》）

少年读书，如隙中窥月；中年读书，如庭中望月；老年读书，如台上玩月，皆以阅历之浅深，为所得之浅深耳。（《幽梦影》）

发前人未发之论，方是奇书。（《幽梦影》）

夫文未有繁而能工者，如煎金锡，粗矿去，然后黑浊之气竭而光润生。（《与程若韩书》）

学者功夫不勤苦，而欲有所得，犹农夫不耕耘，而望有获也。（《困学录集粹》）

作文之心如人目。（《儒林外史》）

敢为常语谈何易，百炼工纯始自然。（《论诗十二绝句》）

书到用时方恨少，事非经过不知难。（《济公传》）

世事洞明皆学问，人情练达即文章。（《红楼梦》）

熟读唐诗三百首，不会吟诗也会吟。（《唐诗三百首序》）

知识是引导人生到光明与真实境界的灯烛。（《危险思想与言论自由》）

依傍和模仿，决不能产生真艺术。（《且介亭杂文末编》）

3.2 修身

人无礼而何为，财非义而不取。（《水浒传》）

为人不可忘本。（《水浒传》）

马逢伯乐而嘶，人遇知己而死。（《三国演义》）

义不负心，忠不顾死。（《三国演义》）

女无明镜，不知面上精粗；士无良友，不知行步亏逾。（《明心宝鉴》）

处世须存心上刃，修身切记寸边而。（《西游记》）

遇方便时行方便，得饶人处且饶人。（《西游记》）

千日行善，善犹不足；一日行恶，恶自有余。（《西游记》）

富贵功名，前缘分定，为人切莫欺心。（《西游记》）

扫除心上垢，洗净耳边尘。不受苦中苦，难为人上人。（《西游记》）

有麝自然香，何必当风立。（《客座赘语》）

君子闲时要有吃紧的心思，忙处要有悠闲的趣味。（《菜根谭》）

径路窄处，留一步与人行；滋味浓的，减三分让人尝。（《菜根谭》）

遇忙处会偷闲，处闲中能取静，便是安身立命的功夫。（《菜根谭》）

学好，千日不足；学歹，一日有余。（《三宝太监西洋记》）

饶人半著岂为低，省受许多闲气。（《醒世要言》）

律己宜带秋气，处世宜带春气。（《幽梦影》）

成德每在困穷，败身多因得志。（《寒松堂集》）

平生不作皱眉事，世上应无切齿人。（《增广贤文》）

一失足成千古恨，再回头已百年身。（《隋唐演义》）

惟大英雄能本色，是真名士自风流。（《儿女英雄传》）

强不知以为知，此乃大愚；本无事而生事，是谓薄福。（《格言别录——〈格言联璧〉录写》）

自觉心是进步之母，自贱心是堕落之源。故自觉心不可无，自贱心不可有。（《自觉与自贱》）

做人和写文章一样，包含不断地修正。（《非梦集·黑魇》）

第二节　励志与世情

在中国教育文化史中，“励志”与“世情”是代代相传的核心理念。所谓“励志”，《辞海》中的解释就是“奋发志气，把精力集中在某方面”，《现代汉语词典》将之解释为“勉励志向”。[1] 而“世情”的概念在中国文化中是指“世态人情”及“时代风气”。从历代经典名言中，可以看到中华关于励志与世情的传统教育既充满着中华民族的入世奋斗的精神，又蕴含着待人处世的隽永智慧，使无数学人能够在求学、修身、养德、处事中树立理想、适应社会，从而达到更高的生命价值。

[1] 涂道勇，肖翠．关于励志教育的研究综述 [J]．学理论，2015(35):186-188。

一、秦汉前后时期

1.1 励志

天行健，君子以自强不息。 （《周易·乾》）

大道之行也，天下为公。（《礼记·礼运》）

敖不可长，欲不可从，志不可满，乐不可极。 （《礼记·曲礼》）

择任而往，知也；知死不辟，勇也。 （《左传·昭公二十年》）

朝闻道，夕死可矣！ （《论语·里仁》）

三军可夺帅也，匹夫不可夺志也。（《论语·子罕》）

士不可以不弘毅，任重而道远。 （《论语·泰伯》）

穷则独善其身，达则兼济天下。（《孟子·尽心》）

志不强者智不达，言不信者行不果。 （《墨子·修身》）

仁人之所以为事者，必兴天下之利，除去天下之害，以此为事者也。 （《墨子·兼爱中》）

志之难也，不在胜人，在自胜。 （《韩非子·喻老》）

路漫漫其修远兮，吾将上下而求索。（《离骚》）

少壮不努力，老大徒伤悲。（《乐府·长歌行》）

大风起兮云飞扬。威加海内兮归故乡，安得猛士兮守四方。（《大风歌》）

人固有一死，或重于泰山，或轻于鸿毛。（《报任安书》）

不飞则已，一飞冲天；不鸣则已，一鸣惊人。（《史记·滑稽列传》）

有志者事竟成。（《光武帝临淄劳耿弇》）

老骥伏枥，志在千里；烈士暮年，壮心不已。 （《龟虽寿》）

壮士何慷慨，志欲威八荒。（《咏怀》）

百炼而南金不亏其真，危困而烈士不失其正。（《抱朴子·博喻》）

刑天舞干戚，猛志固常在。（《读山海经》）

1.2 世情

上善若水，水善利万物而不争。处众人之所恶，故几于道。（《老子·第八章》）

祸兮福之所倚，福兮祸之所伏。（《老子·第五十八章》）

轻诺必寡信，多易必多难。 （《老子·第六十三章》）

信言不美，美言不信。 （《老子·第八十一章》）

小人闲居为不善。 （《礼记·大学》）

人心之不同，如其面焉。 （《左传·襄公三十一年》）

三人行，必有我师焉：择其善者而从之，其不善者而改之。 （《论语·述而》）

人欲见其所不见，视人所不窥；欲得其所不得，修人所不为。 （《列子·仲尼》）

积于柔，必刚；积于弱，必强。 （《列子·黄帝》）

时有满虚，事有利害，物有生死。 （《韩非子·观行》）

祸在于好利，害在于亲小人。　（《尉缭子·十二陵》）
一死一生，乃知交情；一贫一富，乃知交态。　（《史记·汲郑列传》）
生年不满百，常怀千岁忧。　（《生年不满百》）
天下良辰，美景，赏心，乐事，四者难并。　（《拟魏太子邺中集诗序》）
一人得道，鸡犬升天。　（《神仙传·刘安》）

二、唐宋前后时期

2.1 励志

大丈夫宁可玉碎，不能瓦全。　（《北齐书·元景安传》）
欲穷千里目，更上一层楼。　（《登鹳雀楼》）
老当益壮，宁移白首之心。穷且益坚，不坠青云之志。　（《滕王阁序》）
千淘万漉虽辛苦，吹尽狂沙始到金。　（《浪淘沙》）
出淤泥而不染，濯清涟而不妖。　（《爱莲说》）
不患人之不能，而患己之不勉。　（《上仁宗皇帝言事书》）
君子之所取者远，则必有所待；所就者大，则必有所忍。　（《贾谊论》）
人生到处知何似？应似飞鸿踏雪泥。　（《和子由渑池怀旧》）
谁道人生无再少？门前流水尚能西！　（《浣溪沙·游蕲水清泉寺》）
海阔凭鱼跃，天高任鸟飞。　（《诗话总龟》）
将相本无种，男儿当自强。　（《神童诗·劝学》）
生当作人杰，死亦为鬼雄。　（《夏日绝句》）
不是一番寒彻骨，争得梅花扑鼻香？　（《琵琶记》）
事业要当穷万卷，人生须是惜分阴。　（《琵琶记》）
与义不与利，记恩不记仇。　（《君子行》）

2.2 世情

宁走十步远，不走一步险。　（《三侠五义》）
疑人莫用，用人莫疑。　（《旧唐书·陆贽传》）
凭君莫话封侯事，一将功成万骨枯。　（《己亥岁》）
无官一身轻，有子万事足。　（《借前韵贺子由生第四孙斗老》）
近水楼台先得月，向阳花木易为春。　（《残句》）
世情薄，人情恶，雨送黄昏花易落。　（《钗头凤·世情薄》）
相识满天下，知心能几人？　（《事林广记·警世格言》）
万两黄金未为贵，一家安乐值钱多。　（《琵琶记》）
莫道是非终日有，果然不听自然无。　（《琵琶记》）
沉舟侧畔千帆过，病树前头万木春。　（《酬乐天扬州初逢席上见赠》）
不塞不流，不止不行。　（《原道》）

物极则反，数穷则变。（《本论》）

人有悲欢离合，月有阴晴圆缺，此事古难全。（《水调歌头·丙辰中秋》）

人间私语，天闻若雷；暗室亏心，神目如电。（《事林广记·警世格言》）

善有善报，恶有恶报；不是不报，时辰未到。（《来生债》）

三、明清前后时期

3.1 励志

恩仇不辨非豪杰，黑白分明是丈夫。（《水浒传》）

同心报国，青史留名。（《水浒传》）

粉身碎骨全不怕，要留清白在人间。（《石灰吟》）

能闲世人之所忙者，方能忙世人之所闲。（《幽梦影》）

创业固难，守成不易。（《增广贤文》）

莫道人行早，还有早行人。（《三侠五义》）

好风凭借力，送我上青云！（《红楼梦》）

清者自清，浊者自浊。（《衣珠记·赠剑》）

施恩不图报，无求而自得。（《警世通言》）

天地生才有限，不宜妄自菲薄。（《老残游记》）

有缺点的战士终竟是战士，完美的苍蝇也终竟不过是苍蝇。（《华盖集·战士和苍蝇》）

心事浩茫连广宇，于无声处听惊雷。（《无题》）

3.2 世情

忍得一时之气，免得百日之忧。（《增广贤文》）

近水知鱼性，近山识鸟音。（《增广贤文》）

天下大势，合久必分，分久必合。（《三国演义》）

天下动之至易，安之至难。（《三国演义》）

夫过者，自大贤所不免；然不害其卒为大贤者，为其能改也。（《改过》）

世上伤心无限事，最难死别与生离。（《儿女英雄传》）

树高千丈，叶落归根。（《官场现形记》）

友者，俭岁之粱肉，寒年之纤纩也。（《今世说》）

人人好公，则天下太平；人人营私，则天下大乱。（《老残游记》）

假作真时真亦假，无为有处有还无。（《红楼梦》）

人生莫受老来贫。（《红楼梦》）

室雅何须大，花香不在多。（郑板桥对联）

第七章　名人家训举隅

在中国传统教育理念中，因为“人必有家，家必有训”，所以中国的家训传统，自古及今，源远流长；也因为尊长敬祖的文化风尚，所以中国历来重视家庭教育，许多古圣先贤，将他们一生的智慧都浓缩成教导子孙的家风家训，将他们用一生所经历的世间炎凉和识悟的思想精髓毫不保留地教诲奉献给自己的子子孙孙。随着时代的发展，中国家训典籍中所包含的教育内容逐渐丰富，囊括家庭生活和人生智慧的方方面面。[1] 可见，历代家风家训，是祖先们为后代点亮的一盏心灯，也是在“家天下”的文明模式中，反映出不同历史时期社会教育主流的明镜，其中不仅承载着丰富的教育理念，也承载着华夏文明独特的历史智慧与人生箴言。作为华夏民族的子孙，饱含虔敬之心，通过研读和传承历代经典家风家训，让更多的人得到先贤们的教诲之益，让更多的中华儿女沐浴先贤的光芒，是开启智慧、提升教育、创造幸福美好人生的有益之举与厚福功德。[2] 本章将从修身处世、齐家立业两个教育层面展现这些用殷殷之情与岁月智慧凝练的中华理想家风与精神财富。

第一节　修身处世

中国传统的家书家训几乎无一例外，都是以教导修身为本。其最主要的内容是向子孙进行修身教育，教育子女通过修身养性，塑造品学兼优的完美人格，做一个德才兼备的好人。修身之道的内容主要包括慎独自律、忠信仁厚、立德正心、谦虚谨慎、持节重义、养心节欲、延年益寿等诸多方面。在日常生活中，如何待人接物，如何处理好各种复杂的社会人际关系，也是中国传统家庭教育通过家书家训反映出的一项重要内容。中国历代家训总体而言都强调与人相处时要谨言慎行、诚实守信、宽厚忍让、与人为善等基本处世原则。[3]

一、修身名家与名篇

修身而后处世。在历代家书家训中，教导后代如何修身往往是被置于家庭教育的首位，从《钱氏家训》《孔氏祖训箴规》《王阳明家书》《安得长者言》的教诲中，我们都能够读到修身在家庭教育中的重要性。

[1] 郦波．中华家训智慧［M］．天津：新蕾出版社，2014:4。
[2] 王馨．中国家风家训［M］．北京：台海出版社，2017:1-2。
[3] 于奎战．中国历代名人家风家训家规［M］．杭州：浙江人民出版社，2017:1-6。

1.1 钱镠：《钱氏家训》

钱镠，字具美，杭州临安人，吴越国的开国国君。钱镠在唐末为镇海军节度使，后被中原王朝封为吴越国王。钱镠在位期间，采取保境安民的政策，经济繁荣，文士荟萃，文艺也著称于世。民国十三年(1924)，吴王第三十二孙钱文选根据先人的《八戒》和《末戒》，总结出《钱氏家训》。

持躬不可不谨严，临财不可不廉介。

(意思是：要求自己不能够不谨慎严格，面对财物不能不谨慎廉洁。)

尽前行者地步窄，向后看者眼界宽。

(意思是：只知往前走的处境会越来越窄，懂得回头看的见识会越来越宽。)

能改过则天地不怒，能安分则鬼神无权。

(意思是：能改过自新那么天地也不再生气，能安守本分则鬼神也无可奈何。)

读经传则根柢深，看史鉴则议论伟。

(意思是：熟读典籍才会功底深厚，了解历史才能谈吐不凡。)

1.2 孔尚贤：《孔氏祖训箴规》[1]

孔尚贤，字象之，号希庵，孔子第63世孙。他立志要“远不负祖训，上不负国恩，下不负所学”。万历十一年(1583)，孔尚贤为了规范族人言行，在先祖遗训和反思自身的基础上，颁布了具有纲领性质的族规《孔氏祖训箴规》，成为此后孔氏家族世代传承的家规家训。孔尚贤在《孔氏祖训箴规》中开宗明义地指出：“我祖宣圣，万世师表，德配天地，道冠古今。子孙蕃庶，难以悉举。故或执经而游学，或登科而筵仕，散处四方，所在不乏。各以祖训是式，今将先祖箴规昭告族人……”这部《孔氏祖训箴规》条例共计10条，其中不乏修身处世的行为准则，将“崇儒重道，好礼尚德”等孔门传统作为家规的重要内容。同时要求孔氏后人无论身处何地、从事何种职业，都要遵守“克己秉公”“读书明理”等家规。在漫长的历史长河中，孔子的八德之训、孔尚贤的《孔氏祖训箴规》培育了孔氏族人温文尔雅、正直无私的品格，也塑造了他们崇德尚贤、廉洁礼让的风尚。《孔氏祖训箴规》的精要内容包括：

祖训宗规，朝夕教训子孙，务要读书明理，显亲扬名，勿得入于流俗，甘为人下。

(意思是：早晚以祖宗传下的规矩教导训诫子孙，一定要让他们多读书明白事理，显名称誉千世，光耀祖宗。不得入于流俗，甘居他人之下。)

凡有职官员不可擅辱。如遇大事，申奏朝廷，小事仍请本家族长责究。

[1] 中央纪委监察部网络中心．中国家规[M]．北京：中国方正出版社，2017:3-10。

（意思是：凡是有职务的官员不可独断专行。如果遇到大事，应向朝廷陈述申报，小事仍然请本家族长责问追究。）

崇儒重道，好礼尚德，孔门素为佩服。为子孙者，勿嗜利忘义，出入衙门，有亏先德。（意思是：崇儒重道，好礼尚德，向来是孔门传统。作为孔氏子孙，不能见利忘义，不能做出有损祖先德行的事情。）

子孙出仕者，凡遇民间词讼，所犯自有虚实，务从理断而哀矜勿喜，庶不愧为良吏。（意思是：孔门子孙中有为官者的话，凡是遇到民间诉讼，因案件自有虚实，务必理性判断，怀哀怜之心，切莫自鸣得意，但愿不愧为贤能的官吏。）

1.3　王阳明：《王阳明家书》[1]

王阳明，名守仁，字伯安。浙江绍兴府余姚县人，明代著名思想家、教育家和军事家。官至南京兵部尚书，一生虽历经坎坷，但崇德尚义，文韬武略，成就卓著。在王阳明看来，修身与齐家、治国、平天下是一体的，不分轻重，忽视任何一方都不能达到至善。如果儒学忽视治人，只重视修己，那它就会变得和老庄一样，重视出世、超脱和独善其身。如果儒学忽视修己，只重视治人，那它又会变得和法家、纵横家一样，重视功利和权力。前者虽然纯真，但却容易忽视现实；后者虽然重视现实，却缺乏纯真。王阳明留下的家书融入了他从小接受"蒙以养正"教育的点点滴滴，也寄托着他对后代子孙的谆谆教诲。其中的精要内容包括：

"幼儿曹，听教诲：勤读书，要孝悌；学谦恭，循礼仪；节饮食，戒游戏；毋说谎，毋贪利；毋任情，毋斗气；毋责人，但自治。能下人，是有志；能容人，是大器。凡做人，在心地；心地好，是良士；心地恶，是凶类。譬树果，心是蒂；蒂若坏，果必坠。吾教汝，全在是。汝谛听，勿轻弃！"

（意思是：孩子们啊，你们要听从教诲：勤奋读书，孝顺父母、敬爱兄长；要学习谦恭待人，一切按照礼仪行事；饮食要节制，少游玩；不要说谎，不要贪利；不要任情耍性，不要与人斗气；不要责备别人，但需管住自己。能够放低自己的身份，这是有志气的表现；能够容纳别人，这才是有大的度量。做人，主要在于心地的好坏；心地好，才是善良之人；心地恶劣，是凶狠之人。譬如树上结的果子，它的心是蒂；如果蒂先败坏了，果子必然会坠落。我现在教诲你们的，全都在这里了。你应该好好听从，不要轻易放弃。）

"夫学，莫先于立志。志之不立，犹不种其根而徒事培拥灌溉，劳苦无成矣。""夫志，气之帅也，人之命也，木之根也，水之源也。源不浚则流息，根不植则木枯，命不续则人死，志不立则气昏。是以君子之学，无时无处而不以立志为事。"

---

[1] 于奎战．中国历代名人家风家训家规[M]．杭州：浙江人民出版社，2017:11-20。

（意思是：学习，没有比先立下志向更重要的。不确立志向，好比栽树不栽培它的根而徒劳地对树木进行培土浇灌，辛苦却不会成功。志向，就如气的统帅，人的性命，树的根本，水的源头。水源不疏通，水流就会停止，树木无根就会枯萎，性命不延续人就会死，人不立定志向就会气质昏浊。所以君子做学问，无时无处不以立志作为要务。）

“汝在家中，凡宜从戒论而行。读书执礼，日进高明，乃吾之望。吾平生讲学，只是“致良知”三字。仁，人心也；良知之诚爱恻怛处，便是仁，无诚爱恻隐之心，亦无良知可致矣。汝于此处，宜加猛省。”

（意思是：你在家里，一切行事应该遵从训诫。勤读诗书、执守礼制，一天比一天进步，这才是我对你的期望。我平生讲学，就“致良知”三个字。仁，指的是人心；因良知而引发的诚意、真爱、悲痛、忧伤，这就是仁，没有诚爱恻隐之心的，也就达不到良知。对此，你应该深深地自省。）

“昔人云：‘脱去凡近，以游高明。’此言良足以警，小子识之。”

（意思是：古人说：“要远离那些庸俗的人，应该与那些高明的人交朋友。”这句话说得好，足以作为警示，你们这些小孩子一定要懂得这个道理。）

1.4 陈继儒：《安得长者言》[1]

陈继儒，字仲醇，号眉公，明代著名文学家、书画家。29岁弃秀才功名，携家人隐居于松江小昆山，后移居东佘山，潜心文学与书画艺术。他与当时的沈周、文徵明、董其昌一起被合称为“四大家”。重视家教、家风的陈继儒写有一部具有劝喻训导性质的家训著作《安得长者言》，将他长期立身行道的感悟，传给后世子孙。全文以格言形式出现，共录有122条，主要包括行善积福、慎独寡欲、修德向贤、宽恕待人等内容，这种清言体的家训并不多见，堪称格调清新、哲思隽永，对当时和后世都产生了重要影响。

吾不知所谓善，但使人感者即善也；吾不知所谓恶，但使人恨者即恶也。

（意思是：我不懂什么叫善，只知道令人感动的事就是善；我不懂什么叫恶，只知道令人痛恨的事就是恶。）

静坐然后知平日之气浮，守默然后知平日之言躁，省事然后知平日之费闲，闭户然后知平日之交滥，寡欲然后知平日之病多，近情然后知平日之念刻。

（意思是：潜心静坐以后才知道平日里心浮气躁，缄口不言以后才知道平日里言多语躁，省视俗事以后才知道平日里枉费闲心，闭门谢客之后才知道平日里交游太滥，清心寡欲之后才知道平日里多欲伤身，通达人情之后才知道平日里观念执拗。）

[1] 曾礼军．陈继儒《安得长者言》的训喻导向与晚明士风[J]．安康学院学报，2012(1):67-70。

士大夫不贪官，不受钱，一无所利济以及人，毕竟非天生圣贤之意。盖洁己好修，德也；济人利物，功也。有德而无功，可乎?

（意思是：士大夫不贪恋做官，不贪取金钱，这是好品德，但如果一点儿都不帮助别人，也不是圣贤所希望的。洁身自好，修身养性，这是德；帮助别人，有益社会，这是功。只积德而不建功，能行吗？）

读书不独变人气质，且能养人精神，盖理义收摄故也。

（意思是：读书不仅能改变人的气质，而且能涵养人的情操，大概是因为真理道义能凝聚人的精神吧。）

闭门即是深山，读书随处净土。

（意思是：闭门谢客就像隐居深山，专心读书随处可入清净刹土。）

夫不言堂奥而言界墙，不言腹心而言体面，皆是向外事也。

（意思是：不谈论学问而只讲究门派，不谈论思想而只讲求面子，这都是只重外表不重实质的事。）

二、处世名家与名篇

中国文化十分重视人与社会的关系。人生天地间，懂得如何为人处世既是中国教育文化的重要内容也是各个家庭家训及家庭教育的核心目标，中国家庭教育的经典名篇大都围绕着这一永恒的主题。

2.1 袁黄：《了凡四训》[1]

袁黄，字庆远，后改了凡，浙江嘉兴府嘉善县人，明代思想家。他卓有异才，对天文、术数、水利、军政、医药等皆有研究。他的《了凡四训》是结合了自己亲身的经历和毕生学问与修养，为了教育自己的子孙而作的家训。此书劝人积善改过，强调从治心入手的自我修养，阐明了“命自我立，福自己求”的思想，并现身说法，结合儒释道三家思想以自身经历体会阐明此理，鼓励向善立身，慎独立品，自求多福，远避祸殃。该书自明末以来流行甚广，影响较大。

易为君子谋，趋吉避凶；若言天命有常，吉何可趋，凶何可避？开章第一义，便说：“积善之家，必有余庆。”汝信得及否?

（意思是：《易经》替宅心仁厚的有德之士筹谋如何趋向吉祥、避开凶险的道理。如果说上天所定的命运是固定的，那如何可以趋吉避凶呢？《易经·坤卦》上说：能够经常行善的家庭，必定会有多余的福报传给子孙。你是否能信这个道理呢？）

至诚合天，福之将至，观其善而必先知之矣。祸之将至，观其不善而必先知之矣。

[1] 于奎战．中国历代名人家风家训家规［M］．杭州：浙江人民出版社，2017:165-175。

今欲获福而远祸，未论行善，先须改过。

（意思是：一个人如能以至诚心来待人处世，那么就与天道相吻合。福报将要到来时，只需看他的善行，就必能预先得知；而灾祸要降临时，只需看他的恶行，也必定能预测得到。现在如果想要得到福报而避开灾祸，在还没有讲到行善之前，必须先从改正过失做起。）

尘世无常，肉身易殒，一息不属，欲改无由矣。明则千百年担负恶名，虽孝子慈孙，不能洗涤；幽则千百劫沉沦狱报，虽圣贤佛菩萨，不能援引。乌得不畏?

（意思是：这个世间，一切都不是恒常；肉体是很容易消亡的，只要呼吸停止，肉身就不再归我所有，这时想要改过也没有办法了。到这种地步，在明显的世间果报上，将须担受千百年的坏名声而遭人唾骂，虽然有孝子慈孙善良的后代，也洗刷不掉恶名；至于在阴间还要历经千百劫里在地狱里受折磨，纵然是圣贤佛菩萨也无法救助、接引。这种恶报怎能不惧怕呢？）

何谓劝人为善?生为人类，孰无良心?世路役役，最易没溺。凡与人相处，当方便提撕，开其迷惑。譬犹长夜大梦，而令之一觉；譬犹久陷烦恼，而拔之清凉，为惠最溥。韩愈云："一时劝人以口，百世劝人以书。"

（意思是：什么是劝人为善呢？我们作为一个人，谁会没有良心呢？然而，在这茫茫的世间路上，为了追求名利而劳苦不息，这是最容易堕落的。因此，凡是与大众相处，每当发觉有这种现象，就必须巧妙地予以提醒，来解开人们的迷惑。就像是让人在漫漫长夜的大梦之中尽快清醒过来一样。又譬如像是帮助人们从长久烦恼当中解脱出来使之身心清凉自在。这种恩惠最为广大普遍。唐朝韩愈曾说："口说道理来劝人，只能短时间惠及极少数人。要长久普遍地劝导世人，则须写成书籍来流传。"）

2.2 张英：《聪训斋语》[1]

张英，字敦复，号乐圃，安徽桐城人，清代名臣。曾任翰林院掌院学士、文华殿大学士兼礼部尚书等职。先后充任纂修多部著述，一生清廉为官，谦恭礼让，终生让路，不失尺寸，其德行操守堪为世人楷模。所著《聪训斋语》主要讲述治家、读书、修身、择友、养生、怡情，是一部语句平实、思想深刻的传世家训。

读书者不贱，守田者不饥，积德者不倾，择交者不败。

（意思是：认真读书的人会受到别人的尊敬，谨守田产的人不会受到饥饿的威胁，积德行善的人不会倾覆倒下，慎重选择交友对象的人不会一败涂地。）

读书可以增长道心，为颐养第一事也。

（意思是：读书可以养成客观看待事物之心，是颐养心性的第一等事。）

[1] 韩婷婷，王芳明.《聪训斋语》与家风 [J]. 月读，2022(8):35-39。

读书须明窗净几，案头不可多置书，读书作文，皆须凝神静气，目光炯然。出文于题之上，最忌坠入云雾之中，迷失出路。多读文而不熟，如将不练之兵，临时全不得用，徒疲精劳神，与操空拳者无异。

（意思是：读书需要有窗户明亮、案几洁净的环境，桌案上不能放太多的书。读书写文章，都要凝神静气，眼光要明亮。文章的重点要标注于书页上面，最忌掉进云里雾里，找不到出路。读的文章很多但如果不能深入理解，就像将领不操练士兵，打仗时全用不上，白白浪费精神，跟打空拳的人没什么两样）。

古人有言："终身让路，不失尺寸。"老氏以让为宝，左氏曰："让，德之本也。"

（意思是：古人说："一生谦让的人，不会有任何损失。"老子把忍让当成宝贝，左丘明也说："谦让是道德的根本。"）

言思可道，行思可法，不娇盈、不诈伪、不刻薄、不轻佻。

（意思是：说的话要值得人们称道，做的事要值得人们效法，不骄傲自满，不狡诈虚伪，待人不挑剔无情，举止要稳重。）

2.3 张廷玉：《澄怀园语》[1]

张廷玉，字衡臣，号砚斋，安徽桐城人，大学士张英次子。历任礼部尚书、户部尚书、吏部尚书、保和殿大学士、首席军机大臣等职。张廷玉受教于乃父张英的家训，在为人处世中受益匪浅。他温文尔雅，学识渊博，立身唯谨，理政以慎，刑尚宽平，受时人称赞，后成为整个清朝唯一配享太庙的汉臣。其所著《澄怀园语》是张廷玉修身处世、齐家为政的经验总结。

凡人看得天下事太容易，由于未曾经历也。待人好为责备之论，由于身在局外也。"恕"之一字，圣贤从天性中来；中人以上者，则阅历而后得之。

（意思是：凡是把一切事情看得太简单的人，是因为他阅历太浅。喜欢责备别人的人，是因为自己没有处在局内。"恕"这个字是有德行的人自然表现出来的；中等资质以上的人，只有在经历后才能认识到。）

一言一动，常思有益于人，唯恐有损于人。

（意思是：每说一句话、每做一件事都要想着能对人有益，最怕损害他人利益。）

与其于放言高论中求乐境，何如于谨言慎行中求乐境耶？

（意思是：与其在高谈阔论中寻求快乐，还不如在谨言慎行中寻求快乐。）

居官清廉乃分内之事。为官第一要廉，养廉之道，莫如能忍。人能拼命强忍不受非分之财，则于为官之道，思过半矣！

---

[1] 王伟，张琳．《澄怀园语》官德思想及其启示 [J]. 江苏师范大学学报，2017(5):121-125。

（意思是：为官清正廉洁是应该的。做官首要就是廉洁。保持廉洁的品行，最要紧的是能忍。人如能忍住而不接受非分财物，那么他对于为官之道就已经了解一大半了。）

天下之道，宽则能容，能容则物安，而己亦适。

（意思是：在世界上为人处世，以宽厚待人则能够包容许多事物，而包容本身则容易使人安稳顺利，这样自己也容易适应自在。）

2.4 颜之推：《颜氏家训》

颜之推，字介，生于江陵，是中国是南北朝时期文学家、教育家。学术上，颜之推博学多识，一生著述甚丰，今存《颜氏家训》和《还冤志》两书。《颜氏家训》成书于隋文帝灭陈国以后，隋炀帝即位之前（约公元 6 世纪末），是颜之推记述个人经历、思想、学识以告诫子孙的著作，共有七卷，二十篇。[1]

士君子之处世，贵能有益于物耳，不徒高谈虚论，左琴右书，以费人君禄位也。

（意思是：大丈夫立身处世，贵在能做一些有益于人的事，不能光注重高谈阔论，附庸琴书风雅，而浪费了君主给予的俸禄和职位。）

君子之立己，抑亦如之。至诚之言，人未能信，至洁之行，物或致疑，皆由言行声名，无余地也。

（意思是：君子立身行事，大概和这种情况一样。最诚实的话，别人是不会容易相信；最高洁的行为，别人往往会产生怀疑，都是因为这类言论、行动的名声太好，没有留余地造成的。）

《礼》云："欲不可纵，志不可满。"宇宙可臻其极，情性不知其穷，唯在少欲知足，为立涯限尔。

（意思是：《礼记》上说："欲望不可放纵，志向不可自满"，天地之大，也可到达它的极限，而人的天性却不知道穷止，只有寡欲而知足，才可划定一个界限。）

世人多蔽，贵耳贱目，重遥轻近。少长周旋，如有贤哲，每相狎侮，不加礼敬；他乡异县，微藉风声，延颈企踵，甚于饥渴。

（意思是：世人多有一种弊病，看重耳闻的传言却轻视所见的事实，重视遥远的而非身边的事情；同周围年长年少的人周旋，如身边有贤哲之人，总是给予亲昵或侮辱，不予以礼敬；但对于他乡的人事，稍闻一点风声，就伸长脖子踮起脚尖如饥似渴地向往。）

止凡人之斗阋，则尧舜之道，不如寡妻之诲谕。

（意思是：在阻止俗人的吵架争斗方面，尧舜圣贤的教导还不如妻子的劝解有用。）

[1] 孙疏文．传统文化视域下的《颜氏家训》内涵及其当代传承［J］. 汉字文化，2022(23):187-189。

巧伪不如拙诚。

（意思是：奸巧伪诈不如笨拙而诚实。）

第二节 齐家立业

齐家立业是中华民族重视家庭教育和家风传承的主要方面。家风的形成往往是一个家族齐家立业思想在生活教育中的体现，再经过家族子孙代代接力式的恪守祖训，流风余韵，代代不绝，就形成了一个家族齐家立业中鲜明的道德风貌和审美风范。齐家立业的家训往往浓缩了作为一个家族智者、长者的杰出代表的丰富人生体验，凝练成一个家族代代传袭下来的家族文化风格，饱含深厚的爱子爱家之情感与寄托，具有广泛而深远的教育意义。

一、齐家名家与名篇

在从“正心修身”到“齐家治国”的中国教育思维中，“齐家”是志在四方与兼济天下的重要前提与保障，一句家和万事兴的格言突显了齐家在中国教育及文化生活中的核心地位。

1.1 王羲之：《金庭王氏族谱 · 旧序》[1]

王羲之，字逸少，是东晋时期著名书法家，有“书圣”之称。他历任秘书郎、宁远将军、江州刺史，后为会稽内史，领右将军，世称“王右军”。清乾隆年间重修《金庭王氏族谱》时，时任嵊县教谕的周咨询把口耳相传的王氏家训写入《金庭王氏族谱》序文之中，此外《金庭王氏族谱》“凡例”一节还载有 26 条族规，从治国的高度、国与家的关系开篇，最后落实到如何做人。王氏后人认为，祖上的家规家训也是一笔很大的精神财富，作为后人，在弘扬书艺的同时，更要不断完善家规，用家规家训的精神内涵去教育激励下一代。

上治下治，敬宗睦族。

（意思是：国治家治，家国同治；孝敬长辈，和睦家族。）

执事有恪，厥功为懋。

（意思是：管事办事，讲究法度；谨慎严密，遵守规矩。立功尽职，人之本分；不应自傲，更需努力。）

敦厚退让，积善余庆。

（意思是：品行忠厚，礼让三分；多做善事，造福子孙。）

[1] 于奎战．中国历代名人家风家训家规 [M]. 杭州：浙江人民出版社，2017:50-58。

我族素称仁厚之乡、礼仪之族，倘有不肖子孙犯奸作盗，败坏彝伦，玷辱宗风者，家长会众开祠重惩；若其怙终不悛，会同十递送官，尽法重处，削去谱传，不许复入。

（意思是：我们家族一向以仁厚知礼节著称，倘若有不肖子孙作奸犯科、败坏伦理道德，辱没宗族风尚的，由族长集合族人在祠堂里对其施以重罚。如果还不知悔改，就会同邻里将其押送官府，按照律法从重处理，并删去他的谱牒传记，不许他再入族谱。）

1.2 司马光：《温国文正司马公文集》

司马光，字君实，号迂叟，陕州夏县人，是北宋政治家、文史学家。司马光位极人臣历经四朝，受人景仰，一生著作等身，注重家庭教育。他认为，“欲治国者，必先齐其家”。他把家庭教育提升到影响国家和社会的政治高度，所著《温公家范》全面系统地阐述了治家方法、修身之道和为人处世的道理，形成了独立完整的家庭教育理论体系，堪称中国家训史上的典范之作，影响和教育了无数后人。[1]

彖曰：“家人有严君焉，父母之谓也。父父，子子，兄兄，弟弟，夫夫，妇妇，而家道正。正家而天下定矣。”

（意思是：彖辞说：“一个家庭里有威严的家长，即父亲和母亲。父亲要像个父亲，儿子要像个儿子，兄长要像个兄长，弟弟要像个弟弟，丈夫要像个丈夫，妻子要像个妻子，这样家道就端正了。家道端正，天下也就安定了。”）

《大学》曰：“古之欲明明德于天下者，先治其国；欲治其国者，先齐其家；欲齐其家者，先修其身……自天子以至于庶人，壹是皆以修身为本。其本乱而末治者否矣，其所厚者薄，而其所薄者厚，未之有也！”此谓知本，此谓知之至也。所谓治国必先齐其家者，其家不可教而能教人者，无之。

（意思是：《大学》说：“古代那些要想弘扬光明品德的人，先要治理好自己的国家；要想治理好国家，先要管理好自己的家庭；要想管理好家庭，先要修养自身的品性……从天子到普通百姓，都要将提高自身修养作为根本。本乱而末治，那是不可能的。该重视的不重视，不该重视的重视，如果本末倒置，想立家治国是不可能的！”这才是抓住了事物的根本，这才是最高的智慧。要想治理好国家必须先管理好自己的家，也就是说，如果连家都管理不好而想去治理国家，这是不可能的。）

夫生生之资，固人所不能无，然勿求多余，多余希不为累矣。使其子孙果贤耶，岂蔬粝布褐不能自营，至死于道路乎？若其不贤耶，虽积金满堂，奚益哉？多藏以遗子孙，吾见其愚之甚也。

（意思是：人赖以生存的生活必需品固然不可缺少，但不要过分贪求，过分就会成为累赘。假如子孙后世真的贤能，他们怎么会连粗粮粗布都不能自己求得，以至于冻

---

[1] 陈君慧．中华家训大全 [M]．哈尔滨：北方文艺出版社，2013:168-215。

死饿死在路边呢？假如子孙无能，即使满屋堆满了黄金，又有什么用呢？所以，祖辈们储藏过多财物留给子孙，我觉得是非常愚蠢的。）

平生衣取蔽寒，食取充腹，亦不敢服垢弊以矫俗干名，但顺吾性而已。众人皆以奢靡为荣，吾心独以俭素为美。

（意思是：我一向穿衣只求抵御寒冷，吃饭只求填饱肚子，也不敢故意穿肮脏破烂的衣服以表示与众不同，以此取得人们的赞扬，只是顺着我的本性行事罢了。许多人都以奢侈浪费为荣，在我心中却以节俭朴素为美。）

然则贤圣皆不顾子孙之匮乏耶？曰：何为其然也？昔者圣人遗子孙以德以礼，贤人遗子孙以廉以俭。

（意思是：难道古代那些先贤都不管子孙的贫困了吗？有人说：他们为什么不给后代留下很多财产呢？（那是因为）古代圣人留给子孙后代的是高尚的品德与严格的礼法，贤人传给子孙的是廉洁的品质和朴素的作风。）

1.3 苏氏家族：《苏氏族谱亭记》等[1]

苏氏家族是北宋年间在成都平原西南的四川的名门家族，诞生了三位著名的文学家，他们就是名闻天下的“三苏”（苏洵、苏轼、苏辙）。父子三人在文学上造诣极深，受优良家风的影响，父子三人的立身操守也都光明磊落、清正廉洁，关心国家命运，同情民间疾苦。苏氏家族门风笃厚，苏洵、苏轼、苏辙父子三人皆留下了大量有关齐家治家的家训文字、诗词。

少而孤，则老者字之。贫而无归，则富者收之。而不然者，族人之所共诮让也。

（意思是：如果有年纪幼小的孤儿，那就由族中成年人来抚育。如果有贫穷而无家可归的人，那就由族中富有的人来收养。要是有不这样做的人，那么全体族人都要来谴责他。）

事父母极于孝，与兄弟笃于爱，与朋友笃于信…… 薄于为己而厚于为人。

（意思是：侍奉父母要极尽孝心，兄弟之间要互助关爱，与朋友相处要坦诚守信……对自己要严格要求，对别人要宽宏大量。）

苟非吾之所有，虽一毫而莫取。

（意思是：倘若不是我应当拥有的东西，即使是一丝一毫我也不会去求取。）

以此进道常若渴，以此求进常若惊，以此治财常思予，以此书狱常思生。

（意思是：用这方砚台学习圣贤之道，应当经常是如饥似渴的；用它追求上进，应

---

[1] 于奎战．中国历代名人家风家训家规 [M]. 杭州：浙江人民出版社，2017:78-89。

当经常有所警醒；用它书写治理财政的规章，应当经常考虑多给民众利益；用它书写狱文，应当经常想到多给犯人悔过自新的机会。）

1.4 杨慎：《杨氏族谱》等[1]

杨慎，字用修，号升庵，四川新都人，祖籍庐陵。明朝著名文学家，明代三才子之首。他一生为官清廉、刚正不阿。杨慎一生勤奋好学，博览群书，著述多种，均有较高的学术水平。杨慎家族，历来清白传家，至今仍保存着许多世代相传的家规家训，如《杨氏族谱》中，除记录着杨氏先祖清廉为官的事迹外，也记载了杨氏的家规家训。在优良家风的影响之下，杨氏家族人才辈出。

家人重执业，家产重量出。

（意思是：子孙后代要守业尚勤，努力做事业，方可生财兴家；要崇尚节俭，量入为出，方可传承家产。）

家礼重敦伦，家法重教育。

（意思是：治家的礼仪在于敦睦人伦，对父母要孝顺，夫妻关系要和睦，兄弟之间要友爱；治家的礼法在于重视教育，增长后人智识，提升族人才干。）

茅屋是吾居，休想华丽的。画栋的不久栖，雕梁的有坏期。只求他能遮能避风和雨。再休想高楼大厦，但得个不漏足矣。淡饭充吾饥，休想美味的。膏粱的不久吃，珍馐的有断时。只求他粗茶淡饭随时济。再休想鹅掌豚蹄，但得个不饥足矣。

（意思是：茅草房是我的住处，不要想华丽的。再富丽堂皇的屋子也会有坏的时候，能遮风避雨便够了。不要老想着住高楼大厦，不漏就足够了。粗茶淡饭能够充饥，不要想着吃美味的食物。精美珍奇的食物不常有。只求粗茶淡饭能随时有。不再想鹅掌猪蹄，只求不饿就足够了。）

丑妇是吾妻，休想美貌的。只求她温良恭俭敬姑婷。再休想花容月色，但得个贤惠足矣。蠢子是吾儿，休想伶俐的。聪明的惹是非，刚强的将人欺。只求他安分守己寻生计。再休想英雄豪杰，但得个孝顺足矣。

（意思是：我的妻子不必过于美貌，漂亮俊俏未必是好事。只希望她能够温和善良、谦恭节俭并且孝顺父母长辈就好。我的孩子也不必过于精明，有时候过于聪明和刚强也未必是好事。只希望他能够安分守己找到自己谋生的办法，孝顺长辈就足够了。）

临利不敢先人，见义不敢后身。

（意思是：面对有利可图的事，不敢抢在别人的前面去谋取；看见应伸张正义的事，不敢躲在别人的后面去回避。）

---

[1] 赵聃洪智．杨慎家族家风文化及其时代价值［J］．楚雄师范学院学报，2022(6)：17-23。

1.5 朱用纯：《朱子家训》[1]

朱用纯，字致一，自号柏庐，明末清初江苏人，著名理学家、教育家。朱柏庐自幼致力读书，曾考取秀才，后居乡教授学生，并潜心研究程朱理学，主张知行并进，躬行实践，一时颇负盛名。所著《朱子家训》又名《治家格言》，是以家庭道德为主的启蒙教材，精辟地阐明了修身治家之道，是一篇家教名著。其中，许多内容继承了中华优秀传统文化的精华，居身务期质朴，教子要有义方，勤俭持家，邻里和睦等，为历代儒客尊崇，在今天仍然有现实意义。

父之所贵者，慈也。子之所贵者，孝也。

（意思是：作为父母，最可贵的品格，是慈爱。作为子女，最可贵的品格，是孝顺。）

见老者，敬之；见幼者，爱之。

（意思是：见到老年人，要尊敬他们。见到年幼的孩子，要爱护他们。）

勿以善小而不为，勿以恶小而为之。

（意思是：千万不能因为善行很小就不做。千万不能因为恶行很小而去做。）

处世无私仇，治家无私法。

（意思是：处理公共事务，不应掺和私仇。处理家事，不能掺杂私心。）

诗书不可不读，礼义不可不知。子孙不可不教，童仆不可不恤。斯文不可不敬，患难不可不扶。

（意思是：不可以不阅读古代圣贤的经典，不可以不了解各种礼仪规范和道德规则。不可以不教育子孙后代，不可以不关爱仆人属下。一定要敬畏传统文化，尊重有文化的人，也一定要帮助遇到灾祸和有困难的人。）

二、立业名家与名篇

在中国历史长河中，不乏以建功立业为理想的优秀人物和励志思想，这种充满追求富有力量的教育理念从知名历史文化人物的家训中都能够找到语重心长的箴言，有的已成为脍炙人口的名篇佳句。

2.1 范仲淹：《诫诸子书》等[2]

范仲淹，字希文。祖籍邠州，后移居苏州吴县。北宋时期杰出的政治家、文学家。范仲淹在地方治政、守边皆有成绩，文学成就突出。他倡导的“先天下之忧而忧，后天下之乐而乐”的思想和仁人志士节操，对后世产生了深远影响。范仲淹治家严谨，专门撰写《诫诸子书》等教育子孙后代，教导族人要正心修身，积极行善，后有《范

[1] 朱杰人．朱子家训 [M]．上海：华东师范大学出版社，2014:3-13。
[2] 于奎战．中国历代名人家风家训家规 [M]．杭州：浙江人民出版社，2017:154-165。

文正公文集》传世。

且温习文字，清心洁行，以自树立平生之称。当见大节，不必窃论曲直，取小名招大悔矣。

（意思是：平时要多读有益的书，清心寡欲，洁身自好，以此树立良好的品德，不要玷污自己的名声。同时要注意培养自己高尚的节操，不要随便讨论别人的是非曲直，虽博得一时小名，却招致日后更多的烦恼和懊悔。）

勤读圣贤书，尊师如重亲。

（意思是：要多读圣贤书，尊敬老师要像尊敬自己的父母一样。）

礼义勿疏狂，逊让敦睦邻。敬长舆怀幼，怜恤孤寡贫。

（意思是：做事要以礼义为先，不能恃才傲物，要处处谦逊，与邻居搞好关系。要尊老爱幼，怜孤恤寡，帮助穷人。）

谦恭尚廉洁，绝戒骄傲情。字纸莫乱废，须报五谷恩。

（意思是：要谦虚恭敬，廉洁自律，戒骄戒躁。写过字的纸不要随便乱扔，要对养育我们的五谷粮食怀有感恩之心。）

先天下之忧而忧，后天下之乐而乐。

（意思是：在天下人忧愁之前先忧愁，在天下人快乐之后才快乐。）

莫道官清无岁计，满山芝术长灵苗。

（意思是：不要说为官清廉勤勉，无法用岁月来衡量，且看满山的草药长出新苗，一方土地郁郁葱葱。）

2.2 顾炎武：《日知录》《亭林文集》等[1]

顾炎武，字忠清，江苏昆山人，因故居旁有亭林湖，学者尊其为亭林先生。顾炎武是明末清初杰出的思想家、经学家、史地学家和音韵学家，与黄宗羲、王夫之并称为明末清初“三大儒”。顾炎武虽然漂泊一生，甘守清贫，却博学多识，治学严谨，他为后人留下的经世致用的立业思想和胸怀天下的爱国情怀，深刻影响了后世学人。

必存济世安民之志，而后可以考古论今。

（意思是：先要有服务社会安抚百姓的志向，才能安心研读圣贤书和谈古论今。）

保天下者，匹夫之贱，与有责焉耳矣。

（意思是：保护国家这件事，每一个老百姓都有义不容辞的责任。）

[1] 于奎战．中国历代名人家风家训家规 [M]．杭州：浙江人民出版社，2017:175-185。

今日者，拯斯人于涂炭，为万世开太平，此吾辈之任也。

（意思是：今天，拯救人民于水深火热之中，为子孙万代开创太平基业，是我们的责任。）

不忘百姓，敢自托于鲁儒；维此哲人，庶兴衰于周雅。

（意思是：心中不忘天下百姓，才称得上是儒家学者；唯有这样的贤人，才能将传统文化从颓废中振兴起来。）

不登权门，不涉利路。

（意思是：不攀附权贵之门，不涉足贪利之路。）

某虽学问浅陋，而胸中磊落，绝无阉然媚世之习。

（意思是：我虽然学问浅陋，但襟怀坦白，绝无曲意逢迎别人的习惯。）

文之不可绝于天地者，曰明道也，纪政事也，察民隐也，乐道人之善也。若此者，有益于天下，有益于将来，多一篇，多一篇之益也。若夫怪力乱神之事，无稽之言，剿袭之说，谀佞之文，若此者，有损于己，无益于人，多一篇，多一篇之损矣。

（意思是：文章不能消失在天地之间，是因为它可以阐明道理，记述政事，体察百姓困苦，乐于称道别人的善行。像这样的文章，有益于天下，有益于将来，多一篇，就有多一篇的好处。至于那些满篇都是怪异、勇力、叛乱、鬼神之事，荒诞无稽的言谈，抄袭剽窃的言论，对人阿谀奉承的文章，像这样的文章，对自己有害，对别人无益，多一篇，就有多一篇的危害。）

2.3 爱新觉罗・玄烨：《庭训格言》[1]

清圣祖爱新觉罗・玄烨是清朝定都北京后第二位皇帝，年号“康熙”。玄烨八岁即位，在位六十一年，建树甚多，其守成、创业之功绩举世公认。《庭训格言》是雍正八年胤禛追述其父在日常生活中对诸皇子的训诫而成，共二百四十六条，包括修身、为政、立业、待人以及日常生活中的细微琐事。康熙十分珍视天下与家业，渴望能传之千秋万代，自信生命中的智慧与体会对子嗣后人都有益处，这使《庭训格言》具体生动而真实。

凡人于无事之时，常如有事而防范其未然，则自然事不生。若有事之时，却如无事，以定其虑，则其事亦自然消失矣。古人云：“心欲小而胆欲大。”遇事当如此处也。

（意思是：人无事的时候，要像有事的时候那样谨小慎微，这样自然安然无事；有事的时候，要像无事的时候那样淡定不焦虑。古人说：“越是细心谨慎，越是胆大有气魄。”遇到事情应当以这样的心态处理。）

[1] 钱国旗，王娟娟．从《庭训格言》看康熙帝的文化思想［J］．新疆大学学报，2021(6):73-79。

凡人于事务之来，无论大小，必审之又审，方无遗虑。故孔子云："不曰如之何、如之何者，吾末如之何也已矣。"诚至言也！

（意思是：对于发生的任何事情，无论是事大还是事小，一定要十分谨慎，仔细地观察和研究，这样才不会留下后患。因而孔子说："遇事不先问几个'怎么办''如何办'的人，我最后也要对他所办的事说'该拿这件事怎么办啊！'"这的确是至理名言！）

《大学》《中庸》俱以慎独为训，是为圣第一要节。后人广其说，曰："不欺暗室。"所谓暗室有二义焉：一在私居独处之时，一在心曲隐微之地。夫私居独处，则人不及见；心曲隐微，则人不及知。

（意思是：《大学》《中庸》都把慎独作为重要要义，是成为圣贤的第一要节。后来人们也常说"不因在暗室而轻率疏忽"。慎独有两个方面，一是在自己独处的时候，二是在我们内心的隐蔽之处。这两个地方都是只有我们自己能察觉而别人看不到的地方。）

道理之载于典籍者，一定而有限，而天下事千变万化，其端无穷。故世之苦读书者，往往遇事有执泥处，而经历事故多者，又每逐事圆融而无定见，此皆一偏之见。朕则谓当读书时，须要体认世务；而应事时，又当据书理而审其事。宜如此，方免二者之弊。

（意思是：在典籍上记载的道理，只有那么多，但天下的事情变化多端，无穷无尽。因此世上刻苦读书的人，往往遇到事情执拗拘泥，不懂变通，那些经历事情多的人，往往遇事圆滑而没有确定的见解，这两种人都带有片面性。我认为在读书时，一定要大量经历治世的事务，在应对事情时，就根据书本知识反复研究那个事情。只有这样，才能免于这二者的弊端。）

2.4　郑板桥：《郑板桥家书》等

郑板桥，字克柔，人称板桥先生，江苏兴化人。清代著名的文人画家。曾任范县、潍县知县。为官清正廉洁，勤政爱民，颇有政绩。辞官后客居扬州，以卖画为生，为"扬州八怪"之一。《郑板桥家书》作为中国古代"齐家"文化的经典之作，蕴含着丰厚的人文思想：博爱众生，中庸宽和。传世以来，深受好评。在清代，有人评价《郑板桥家书》"曲尽人情，多见道语""语语真，肝肺搓牙，跃然纸上"。[1]

凡人读书，原拿不定发达，然即不发达，要不可以不读书。立意便拿定也，科名不来，学问在我，原不是折本的买卖。

（意思是：一个人读书求学时，并不知道将来能否飞黄腾达。但是，即使将来不能飞黄腾达，也不可以不读书、不求学。一旦拿定这个主意，即使考不中科举，但也获得了学问，这也是得大于失，是个不亏本的买卖。）

[1] 李鸿渊．论郑板桥家书的人文思想及其意义 [J]．北京理工大学学报，2009(5)：106-110。

昔有人问沈近思侍郎如何是救贫的良法，沈曰读书。其人以为迂阔，其实不迂阔也。东投西窜，费时失业，徒丧其品，而卒归于无济，何如优游书史中，不求获而得力在眉睫间乎！信此言，则富贵；不信，则贫贱。亦在人之有识与有决，并有忍耳。

（意思是：曾有人问沈近思侍郎，改变贫穷面貌的好办法是什么？沈侍郎回答说："读书。"这个人认为沈侍郎迂腐，不合时宜，其实沈侍郎并不迂腐。与其东奔西走求人求官，耗费时间耽误学业，又丧失人品，归来时又一无所得，不如在书史之中悠游岁月，不求有所得，但得到的好处就在眼前。相信沈侍郎这句话，就能富贵；不相信，就贫贱终身。其中关键就在于一个人有没有这样的见识和决心，并能持之以恒而已。）

设我至今不第，又何处叫屈耒？岂得以此骄倨朋友！敦宗族，睦亲姻，念故交，大数既得。

（意思是：假如我至今为止没有考取进士，又能到哪里去叫屈？怎敢因为自己当了官就在朋友面前自高自大！我们要厚待族中亲人，与亲友处好关系，关心旧时朋友，大概就是这样。）

岂非富贵足以愚人，而贫贱足以立志而浚慧乎？

（意思是：难道不是富贵的家境使后人愚钝，而贫困底层的家世足以使人树立志向培养智慧吗？）

2.5 曾国藩：《曾国藩家书》

曾国藩，字伯涵，号涤生，是晚清时期的政治家、文学家。他曾推进洋务运动，引进西方的军事和技术，被称为晚清中兴名臣之一。《曾国藩家书》是曾国藩的书信集，成书于 19 世纪中叶，记录了曾国藩前后三十年的翰苑和从武生涯，近一千五百封。所涉及的内容极为广泛，是曾国藩一生的主要活动及其治政、治家、治学之道的生动反映。曾氏家书行文从容镇定，形式自由，随想而到，挥笔自如，在平淡家常中孕育真知良言，具有极强的说服力和感召力。[1]

吾人只有进德、修业两事靠得住。进德，则孝悌仁义是也；修业，则诗文作字是也。此二者由我作主，得尺则我之尺也，得寸则我之寸也。今日进一分德，便算积了一升谷；明日修一分业，又算余了一文钱。德业并增，则家私日起。至于功名富贵，悉由命定，丝毫不能自主。

（意思是：对于我们而言，只有进德行和修业两件事靠得住。进德就是传统的仁义孝悌，而修业就是诗文写作。这两件事是由我作主，一分耕耘一分收获。今天提升了功德就像是积累了一升粮食；每天修了一分学业就如同赚了一文钱财。德业都有精进则家族兴旺。至于功名富贵都是命定的，我们不能作主。）

[1] 于奎战．中国历代名人家风家训家规 [M]．杭州：浙江人民出版社，2017：296-305。

人苟能自立志，则圣贤豪杰何事不可为？何必借助于人？我欲仁，斯仁至矣。我欲为孔孟，则日夜孜孜，惟孔孟之是学，人谁得而御我哉？若自己不立志，则虽日与尧、舜、禹、汤同住，亦彼自彼，我自我矣，何与于我哉？

（意思是：人如果自己能树立远大志向，就能像圣人豪杰一般成就大事，何必借助他人的力量？孔子说，只要自己愿意实行仁，仁就可以达到。只要自己想要成为孔孟般的圣人，那么就日夜孜孜不倦学习，谁又能阻止得了我呢？但如果自己没有志向，即使日夜与诸多圣人住在一起，也是各不相干，影响不到自己的。）

若事事勤思善问，何患不一日千里？

（意思是：如果事事能够勤思善问，又何必担心不每天都突飞猛进，取得巨大的进步呢？）

凡人一身，只有“迁善改过”四字可靠；凡人一家，只有“修德读书”四字可靠。此八字者，能尽一分，必有一分之庆；不尽一分，必有一分之殃。

（意思是：人这一生，也只有按照“迁善改过”这四个字来做才能长久，即弘扬传播正道而不断改正自己的过失；一户人家，只有按照“修德读书”这四个字来做才可安稳，即修行品德读书进取。这个原则能达到一分就有一分的福报，若缺失一分则有一分的灾祸。）

凡行公事，须深谋远虑

（意思是：大凡是办公事，应当想得周到看得远。）

功名之地，自古难居。

（意思是：从古至今，功名高位均是一个难待的地方。）

盖无故而怨天，则天必不许；无故而尤人，则人必不服。感应之理，自然随之。

（意思是：无故而怨天，天必然不答应；无故而尤人，人定然不服气。天人感应的规律，应该遵从跟随。）

凡将才有四大端：一曰知人善任，二曰善觇敌情，三曰临阵胆识，四曰营务整齐。

（意思是：将领均应具备四大才能，一是知人善任；二是善于猜测敌情；三是临阵时有胆有识；四是营中事物要治理整齐。）

默观近日之吏治、人心及各省之督抚将帅，天下似无戡定之理。吾惟以一勤字报吾君，以爱民二字报吾亲。才识平常，断难立功，但守一勤字，终日劳苦，以少分宵旰之忧。

（意思是：我默默观察最近的吏治、人心及各省的总督巡抚将帅，天下好像没有安稳的迹象。我只能用一个勤字来效忠，用爱民两个字来报答父母。因我的才识很普通，所以很难建功立业，只能遵守一个勤字，终日劳累，以稍微减轻些担忧。）

读书以训诂为本，作诗文以声调为本，事亲以得欢心为本，养生以戒恼怒为本，立身以不妄语为本，居家以不晏起为本，作官以不要钱为本，行军以不扰民为本。

（意思是：读书以训诂为本，作诗文以声调为本，服侍长辈以得欢心为本，养生以心境平和为本，立身以慎言为本，居家以早起为本，做官以不贪腐为本，行军以不扰民为本。）

从古帝王将相，无人不由自立自强做出，即为圣贤者，亦各自有自立自强之道，故能独立不惧，确乎不拔。

（意思是：所有的帝王将相，无不是自立自强。就是圣人、贤者，也都有自立自强的方法，因此能够独立而没有恐惧，坚忍不拔。）

第八章　大学校训简览

校训是学校教育理念、治学风格的高度概括，是学校办学传统与育人目标的集中体现，是最能反映学校特色和教育价值取向的根本标志之一。对校训的一般定义是：学校为训育上之便利，选若干德目制成匾额，悬之校中公见之地，是为校训，其目的在使个人随时注意而实践之。校训从小处而言是校园文化建设的重要内容，从大处来看也是一个地区教育文化与精神的体现。校训传达承载的大学文化既是社会文化的重要组成部分，又折射着一个国家教育的价值取向及发展水平。[1]

第一节　校训文化概述

校训作为办学理念和学府精神的体现，离不开长期积淀的传统教育理念，越来越受到教育文化研究者的重视。20 世纪 90 年代以来，不同研究从教育学、语言学、文化学视角研究校训与大学理念、校园文化、校道德建设的关系，以及校训的教育功能。由于认识到校训的重要性，各学府在精心打造自身形象、 提升文化品位的同时，不断努力在校训上凝练思想，使之既能代表本校文化，又能独具特色。因此，综合诠释校训文化对于我们理解一个地区的高等教育文化概况十分必要。[2]

一、校训的渊源

任何类型的大学都是教育文化和环境的产物。作为学校教育手段之一及彰显教育理念的校训也不例外，它并不单纯是奇思妙想的结果，它的形成和它一贯继承的传统思想和教育历史是分不开的。

1.1 思想渊源

我国古代没有出现“校训”二字单独成词的先例，它不像“家训” 那样在古籍中早已单独构成词组。在教育文化不断发展的过程中，校训的形成和它一贯继承的教育思想是分不开的。中国校训的思想之源是“家庭为本位、人伦为基础”的伦理文化和“天下为公、太平大同”的教育理想，表现为“主德求善”和“和谐稳定”的思想。 我国现代意义上的校训是可以追根溯源的，我国古代就有了校训的雏形。

中国文化不讲或很少讲脱离伦理型学说的智慧、知识和真理，以重视道德伦理灌输为主旨，偏重于塑造“道德型”“伦理型”的理想人格设计，疏于“智力型”“实验型”

---

[1] 沈永社．中国大学校训校风师风学风大全 [M]．北京：金城出版社，2015:1-3。
[2] 王彩霞．中国学校校训研究 [M]．太原：山西教育出版社，2015:1-3。

人才的培养。中国古代所谓的“学问”，不是有关客观世界的纯认识，而是如何安身立命与治国平天下的道德信条和经世之学。有关宇宙论、认识论等对于客观世界的探讨都是从属于或落脚于道德问题的基点上，以修身为本，以齐家治国平天下为目的，自觉地以道德规范维护上下尊卑的社会秩序。基于“和谐稳定”，中国教育强调集体主义和爱国主义。儒家伦理强调个人对于社会义务重于权利的观念，在这种观念的熏陶下，中国人形成了对民族和国家的高度责任感和义务感，使整个中华民族具有强大的生命力和凝聚力。国家和谐稳定的集体利益伦理造就了一批甘心为国分忧、为国捐躯、为正义献身的英勇人物，也培育出以集体为重、克己奉公的情怀。这样的思想在校训中的一个具体体现就是强调精忠爱国。

1.2 历史渊源

中国古代校训的出现大约可以追溯到书院时期。早期书院主要担负收藏、校勘、整理图书的任务，而书院作为一种新的教育制度的确立则是在宋代。[1] 尤其到了南宋，书院办学条件有了很大的改善，本身的功能也更加齐备，形成系统的规章制度，所以使最终确立体现自己风格、地位和办学特色的院训成为可能。南宋朱熹的《白鹿洞书院揭示》对书院教育的目标宗旨、为学之序、 修身、处事、接物的基本要求等都作出了明确的规定，是书院建设的纲领性文件。后世许多学校的校训都取材于此，可以说此揭示是一种办学理念、教育宗旨或办学目标，是校训的主导思想。后来揭示传至朝鲜、日本，被奉为院规、校训，其影响深远。《白鹿洞书院揭示》和“忠孝廉节”院训以碑刻的形式公诸于讲堂，镶嵌于壁，悬挂于门楣，它们言简意赅，便于学生记忆。在它们的影响下，后世也涌现出了一批精品院训，它们对仗工整、富有内涵，成为我国现代校训的原型。我国古代虽然并未出现明确的“校训”的概念，但是出现了校训的实体，而“校训”是从日本引进的新名词。“校训”这一实体在中国面临的问题是没有一个固定统一的中国式名称。甲午战争以后，从日本引进了“校訓”一词，这是一个“日语的回归汉字借词”，该词的引入使得教会大学乃至后来的新式大学中的校训实体有了明确的中国式称谓——“校训”。在日本“校训”名称和教会大学校训实体的启发下，我国古代校训转型为现代校训。另外，和“校训”一样，“校风”也是从日本引进的新词语，且早于“校训”出现。校训成为学校的教育制度并为我国近代新式学校普遍采用和接纳后，中国涌现出了一大批富有传统文化意蕴和时代特点的著名校训。由于中国的教会大学早于我国新式大学而出现，上海圣约翰大学校训“光明与真理”和东吴大学校训“养天地正气，法古今完人”是我国教会大学中最早的校训。

总之，在本土教育历史上，富于文化意蕴且深远久长的校训所传递的文化道德信息，随着时间的推移一定会融入民族血液之中。 中国现代意义上的校训是伴随中国近代教育的开始而出现的，而近代教育则是在西方文化的硬性渗透下被动开始走上缓慢的发

[1] 王彩霞．中国学校校训研究 [M]．太原：山西教育出版社，2015:9-18。

展道路的，并且是一条从高等教育到中等教育的下延式发展道路。

二、校训的形式

校训作为教育文化的产物其形式具有一定的特征与规律。它的表现形式与语言特征反映了一个地区或学校的基本风尚、审美导向和教育模式。[1]

2.1 表现形式

中国古代典籍中的格言句式对中国学校校训的形式有很大影响，如《学记》中的“化民成俗，其必由学”等精神理念，尽管不是现代意义上的校训，但“四言八字” 的语言表达方式影响了近代大学校训的形式结构。近现代教育的一大批校训都采用这种“四言八字”形式。同时还有以下三种形式影响着中国学校校训的形式：家训、对联和碑刻。

如前一章节所述，中国社会是“家庭本位”的社会，家训在教育中有着很高的地位。我国古代家训的形式对校训有一定的影响。周武王最先用“铭”教子。“铭”是古代家训的一种文体，将训诫内容刻在器物上，以供子孙经常观看，这为后世家庭、学校、社会的伦理规范奠定了基础。“铭”的形式比较直观，通俗易懂，有助于缺少生活经验的青少年由感性认识上升到理性认识，较快地明白寓于其中的深刻道理。唐代的家训以诗歌形式出现，讲求工整、对仗、押韵，故称诗训。诗训形象生动，委婉动听，重在以情动人，以物喻理。在明清家训发展过程中，还出现了格言、箴铭、警句、歌诀体裁的家训。明代中后期，伴随着通俗文化的兴盛，新的家训形式通俗简短，近似白话，便于记诵。而清代的家训大多是饱含深意的哲言睿语，它们言简意赅，言近旨远。家训从铭到诗到格言、警句的发展，对校训的形式具有很大的启发意义，为它提供了可借鉴的样板。[2] 同样，我国自古书写对联的传统讲求对仗工整、押韵，尤其一些格言对联对立志、治学、修身、明理等有高度的概括，对校训形式的启示很大。尤其书院楹联作为一种特殊的形式，言简意赅，是一种精练的文体和文学艺术，起着长篇大论和课堂活动无法起到的作用。此外，将经典金句刻在石头上的碑刻也是中国式教育传播的特有形式。中国不仅名山大川景地有石刻碑文，地方的学府门口也有石刻碑文，这大概对后世校训以碑刻形式出现有一定的关系。帝王赐匾后或悬挂或张贴或碑刻等形式，对后人要把校训张贴、悬挂于学校显眼的地方等做法都有显著启示。我国本身固有的这些形式，对校训的发展成型有很大的影响，它们可以被看作是古代校训的原型。

由此可见，中国校训的主要表现形式是基于中国传统经典著作和传统文化中的教育内容，引经据典，以源于家训、对联和碑刻的形式和讲求对仗工整的优美简洁的语言表现出来，成为一种表达学府精神和教育理念的最直接标识。

---

[1] 曹梦．大学校训文化探析［J］．文教资料，2016(28):59-60。
[2] 徐少锦，陈延斌．中国家训史［M］．西安：陕西人民出版社，2003:781。

2.2 语言特征

总体而言，中国校训中的语言特征是：语音上节奏分明，声韵和谐，虽绝大多数不合平仄，但整体读来依然抑扬顿挫，朗朗上口；词汇上用词考究，多选褒义词，精练简洁，内涵丰富；从句型和修辞而言，多数的校训没有标点符号，没有主语，没有连词，却是表意完整的句子，这是校训所独有的语言现象，反映了汉民族重简约、重意合、重领悟的“三重”思维特点；校训中的句型大多是均衡对称的，且美辞迭出，体现了汉民族追求和谐、追求美的传统心理特点。[1]

从句式而言，新中国成立前的校训句式除一言四字、四言八字占大的比重外，其他句式基本是平分秋色，基本保持比例平衡协调。新中国成立前的校训句式和种类也是五花八门。一言句式校训随着时间的推移慢慢减少，而被二言、四言句式校训所取代。这在新中国成立后、改革开放前的校训上表现得最为明显。改革开放后，“二言八字”校训句式明显下降，随之突显的是“四言八字”校训句式，而其他种类繁多的句式也大量涌现，还出现了之前没有的新句式，如三言、七言、八言、十言，甚至还有一句话的形式，种类更加丰富。从用词而言，中国校训用语非常丰富，可以说校训的用词体现了中国人的思维特征。中国哲学中存在“动词思维”[2]的倾向在校训中同样显著：如二言句式校训用语中的“团结”“创新”“爱国”“求是”“笃行”“奋进”“拼搏”“开拓”等都采用动词用法；四言句式校训如“敬业乐群”“致知力行”；五言句式校训如“养天地正气、法古今完人”“立一等品格、求一等学识、创一等事业”等句式都是采用动词用法。当然，一言校训不管是什么时期基本是以形容词和名词为主，如“诚”“朴”“忠”“勤”“慎”“敬”等形容词和“智”“礼”“义”“公”等名词。改革开放后，一些现代语汇也渐渐成为校训的来源，形成了混合式的语言特征，既有古典语词，又有现代语词。此外，中国大学校训的隐喻涉及最多的是水隐喻、土地隐喻、工具隐喻、石隐喻、道路（旅行）隐喻、植物（种植）隐喻等，反映出了一定的教育文化认知传统。

总之，中国校训的语言特征不仅仅集中反映了中国人的传统思维方式和教育认知，也是体现汉语的音韵、结构、修辞之美的重要窗口，这些语言特征使校训成为中国学府对外传播教育文化的特别名片与载体。

三、校训的内涵

大学校训的内涵反映的不仅是教育的典范和理想，还是一个学校办学历史以及时代精神的缩影，结合时代内涵的校训可以成为大学不断发展与进步的不竭动力。校训的内涵可以从它的本质和价值去解读。

---

[1] 刘庆华．校训语言研究 [D]．南京：南京师范大学，2008:20-33。
[2] 牟正甫．试析《论语》的动词思维——以“问政”为核心 [J]．佳木斯大学社会科学学报，2009(1):7-8。

3.1 校训的本质

自从“校训”这一概念从日本引进后，有关校训本质的探讨也层出不穷。一些学者首先把校训归结为训育，并使校训成为训育的标的。随着研究的深入，一些学者认为校训本质不能脱离国家的教育方针，应选取名言、警句或国家的教育方针中的语句作为学校的座右铭。对校训本质的进一步明晰表现为一些学校从自身办学特点出发，让校训体现学校的精神和奋斗目标，使校训成为教育学生的重要内容，总体上强调学校是制定校训的主体。

在近代，我国教育史上曾出现“训育”“训导”等概念，后来随着社会的发展，这些概念又被“德育”所取代，尤其是“训育”“训导”不常见了。随着时代的变迁，校训定义发生了变化。它不再局限于训育内容，而是根据学校的具体特点，选取名言、警句或国家的教育方针中的语句作为学校的座右铭。这样，校训不仅注重精神内核的引领作用，而且注重外在形式的影响作用。把校训上升为教育方针的校训定义是以《世界教育大辞典》所列校训的本质为代表的：“校训是根据国家和地方教育委员会法定的教育目标，同时考虑各学校的历史、传统、地区性、学生的实情等条件，发挥学校的自主性而制定的具体教育方针，要旨与涉及道德人格形成的教育观念。”[1] 至此，校训的本质进一步发展变化为，从学校自身办学特点出发，对学生进行道德上的教育，体现学校的精神和奋斗目标，强调学校是制定校训的主体。时至今日，学界普遍把校训看成是一种准则、行为规范、奋斗目标，认为校训是学校文化建设努力要达到的一种理想状态，是学校文化的灵魂，是学校办学理念、治校精神的反映。总之，校训的本质是在办学实践基础上根据一定社会目标要求拟定的，以表征传统精神和办学特色，并对师生行为具有导向性、规范性和勉励性作用的经高度凝练而成的一种办学格言。[2] 校训是学校精神文化的高度概括，具有整齐性、美感性、激励性、长期性和时代性等特点。

3.2 校训的价值

校训在教育文化中的价值体现在它和学校文化诸要素的关系以及对学校文化的引领。“学校文化”既在于一种精神性的引导，也在于一种独具的制度方式的保证。[3] 它不是孤立存在的，它和其他亚文化一起构成社会文化，它引领其他亚文化，并对社会文化起着一种导向作用。学校文化作为一种文化含量最高的高层次文化，是在文化继承和创新过程中形成的融合了学校精神和个性表达的特殊文化结构，也分为物质、观念、制度和行为文化四种。而观念文化如校训、办学理念、校风、教风、学风，是学校物化形态的精神统领。学校观念文化的培育和弘扬是学校文化建设的核心所在，是学校文化存在的前提，而校训正是学校育人的一种方式和手段，学校观念文化的培育和弘扬可以通过校训来入手。

[1] 平塚益德．世界教育大辞典 [M]．长沙：湖南教育出版社，1989:505。
[2] 王刚．关于大学校训本质的探讨 [J]．高校教育管理，2011(2):23-27。
[3] 丁钢．学校文化与领导 [J]．全球教育展望，2004(3):6-12。

校训和校风、教风、学风的关系是航向与航程的关系。校训是学校办学思想的集中体现，是学校办学的灵魂，在学校工作中应处于统领地位，并通过校风、教风、学风等形式来体现。许多学校在长期的办学过程中，基于时代要求、学校传统、学科特色，形成了既具有各自特色，又富有时代特征的校训。校训在长期的学校文化实践中一经被师生共同接受，就会自然而然地被他们自觉发扬，从而演化、升华为代表学校整体价值追求的学校精神，形成学校整体文化的最高层次，成为奏响包括校风、教风、学风的学校文化之歌的主旋律。校训，读之似望见大海上的灯塔、苍穹间的灿星，它最能彰显一所学校的办学特色。步入校园，跃入眼帘的往往是赫然醒目的校训，校训以其独特的表达方式、深刻的文化内涵成为学校文化之魂，它以无形的控制力、感染力、凝聚力，在学校文化建设中发挥着其独特而巨大的作用。

总而言之，校训的价值在于以其独特的表达方式、深刻的文化内涵构筑着学校文化之魂，传承着学校文化，把握着办学方向，锻铸着师生灵魂，弘扬着学校精神，同时体现着办学者高度的社会责任感和强烈的历史使命感，升华着教育者独特的价值传承和永恒的人格魅力，是一种教育文化和人格追求的浓缩。

第二节　特色校训枚举

在崇尚科学、教育的今天，人们每当读到一所学校的特色校训，精神都为之一振，无不为之用词之精当、熨帖、厚重而折服。校训使人印象深刻，受益良多。因为许多学校经过若干年的积淀，已经形成了反映自身文化和地区特色的学校精神，这种精神历经锤炼已成为学校的品牌而深入学校的骨髓。本节将以中国不同特色的代表性高校为枚举范例[1-2]来展示中国教育文化的取向。

一、华东地区高校

1.1 上海

复旦大学（博学而笃志　切问而近思）

同济大学（严谨　求实　团结　创新）

上海交通大学（饮水思源　爱国荣校）

华东师范大学（求实创造　为人师表）

上海大学（自强不息　道济天下）

东华大学（崇德博学　砺志尚实）

上海应用技术大学（明德　明学　明事）

[1] 教育部思想政治工作司．百所高校校训校徽校歌汇编 [M]. 北京：中国人民大学出版社，2012:1-333。

[2] 沈永社．中国大学校训、校风、师风、学风大全 [M]. 北京：金城出版社，2015:1-306。

1.2 江苏

南京大学（诚朴雄伟　励学敦行）

东南大学（止于至善）

苏州大学（养天地正气　法古今完人）

中国矿业大学（崇德尚学）

江苏大学（博学　求是　明德）

扬州大学（坚苦自立）

河海大学（艰苦朴素　实事求是　严格要求　勇于探索）

1.3 浙江

浙江大学（求是创新）

浙江工业大学（厚德健行）

中国美术学院（行健　居敬　会通　履远）

宁波大学（实事求是　经世致用）

浙江师范大学（砺学砺行　维实维新）

中国计量大学（精思国计　细量民生）

浙江中医药大学（求本远志）

1.4 安徽

中国科学技术大学（红专并进　理实交融）

合肥工业大学（厚德　笃学　崇实　尚新）

安徽大学（至诚至坚　博学笃行）

安徽农业大学（团结　勤奋　求实　创新）

安徽财经大学（诚信博学　知行统一）

安徽建筑大学（进德　弘毅　博学　善建）

安徽医科大学（好学力行　造就良医）

二、华北地区高校

2.1 北京

清华大学（自强不息　厚德载物）

中央财经大学（忠诚　团结　求实　创新）

北京外国语大学（兼容并蓄　博学笃行）

北京航空航天大学（德才兼备　知行合一）

北京理工大学（德以明理　学以精工）

中国农业大学（解民生之多艰　育天下之英才）

北京师范大学（学为人师　行为世范）

中央民族大学（美美与共　知行合一）

2.2 天津

南开大学（允公允能　日新月异）

天津大学（实事求是）

河北工业大学（勤慎公忠）

天津中医药大学（进德修业　继承创新）

中国民航大学（明德至善　弘毅兴邦）

天津外国语大学（中外求索　德业竞进）

天津商业大学（笃学　弘毅　明德　济世）

2.3 辽宁

大连理工大学（团结　进取　求实　创新）

东北大学（自强不息　知行合一）

中国医科大学（政治坚定　技术优良）

东北财经大学（博学济世）

辽宁大学（明德精学　笃行致强）

沈阳农业大学（团结　勤奋　求实　创新）

2.4 吉林

吉林大学（求实创新　励志图强）

东北师范大学（勤奋创新　为人师表）

长春理工大学（明德　博学　求是　创新）

延边大学（求真　至善　融合）

东北电力大学（勤奋　严谨　求实　创新）

长春大学（知行合一　诚信至善）

北华大学（崇德尚学　自强力行）

2.5 黑龙江

哈尔滨工业大学（规格严格　功夫到家）

东北林业大学（学参天地　德合自然）

黑龙江大学（博学慎思　参天尽物）

哈尔滨师范大学（敦品励学　弘毅致远）

东北石油大学（艰苦创业　严谨治学）

哈尔滨商业大学（求真至善　修德允能）

2.6 山东

山东大学（学无止境　气有浩然）

中国海洋大学（海纳百川　取则行远）

山东师范大学（弘德明志　博学笃行）

青岛大学（明德　博学　守正　出奇）

山东科技大学（惟真求新）
济南大学（弘毅 博学 求真 至善）
烟台大学（守信 求实 好学 力行）

三、华西地区高校

3.1 四川

四川大学（海纳百川 有容乃大）
西南交通大学（精勤求学 敦笃励志 果毅力行 忠恕任事）
成都理工大学（穷究于理 成就于工）
四川师范大学（重德 博学 务实 尚美）
四川美术学院（志于道 游于艺）
西南民族大学（和合偕习 自信自强）

3.2 陕西

西北工业大学（公诚勇毅）
西北大学（公诚勤朴）
陕西师范大学（厚德 积学 励志 敦行）
长安大学（弘毅明德 笃学创新）
延安大学（立身为公 学以致用）
西安外国语大学（爱国 勤奋 博学 创新）

3.3 重庆

重庆大学（耐劳苦 尚俭朴 勤学业 爱国家）
西南大学（含弘光大 继往开来）
重庆医科大学（严谨 求实 勤奋 进取）
重庆邮电大学（修德 博学 求实 创新）
西南政法大学（博学笃行 厚德重法）
重庆师范大学（厚德 笃学 砺志 创新）
重庆工商大学（厚德博学 求是创新）

3.4 甘肃

兰州大学（自强不息 独树一帜）
西北师范大学（知术欲圆 行旨须直）
兰州理工大学（奋进求是）
甘肃农业大学（敦品励学 笃志允能）
西北民族大学（勤学 敬业 团结 创新）
兰州财经大学（博修商道）

四、华南地区高校

4.1 广东

中山大学（博学　审问　慎思　明辨　笃行）

南方科技大学（明德求是　日新自强）

暨南大学（忠信笃敬）

南方医科大学（博学笃行　尚德济世）

深圳大学（自立　自律　自强）

华南师范大学（艰苦奋斗　严谨治学　求实创新　为人师表）

广州大学（博学笃行　与时俱进）

4.2 福建

厦门大学（自强不息　止于至善）

福州大学（明德至诚　博学远志）

福建师范大学（知明行笃　立诚致广）

华侨大学（会通中外　并育德才）

集美大学（诚毅）

福建农林大学（明德　诚智　博学　创新）

福建医科大学（勤奋　严谨　求实　创新）

4.3 云南

云南大学（自尊　致知　正义　力行）

昆明理工大学（明德任责　致知力行）

云南师范大学（刚毅坚卓）

大理大学（博学达真　大德至理）

云南民族大学（格致明德　弘道至善）

云南财经大学（好学笃行　厚德致远）

云南中医药大学（崇德和合　博学敦行）

4.4 中国港澳台地区

香港大学（明德格物）

香港中文大学（博文约礼）

香港城市大学（敬业乐群）

香港浸会大学（笃信力行）

澳门大学（仁　义　礼　知　信）

澳门科技大学（意诚格物）

台湾大学（敦品　励学　爱国　爱人）

五、华中地区高校

5.1 湖北

武汉大学（自强　弘毅　求是　拓新）

华中科技大学（明德厚学　求是创新）

华中师范大学（求实创新　立德树人）

武汉理工大学（厚德博学　追求卓越）

华中农业大学（勤读力耕　立己达人）

湖北大学（日思日睿　笃志笃行）

5.2 湖南

湖南大学（实事求是　敢为人先）

中南大学（知行合一　经世致用）

湖南师范大学（仁爱精勤）

湘潭大学（博学笃行　盛德日新）

南华大学（明德　博学　求是　致远）

吉首大学（以人名校　以业报国）

5.3 河南

郑州大学（求是　担当）

河南大学（明德新民　止于至善）

河南师范大学（厚德博学　止于至善）

河南理工大学（明德任责）

河南农业大学（明德自强　求是力行）

河南中医药大学（厚德博学　承古拓新）

5.4 江西

南昌大学（格物致新　厚德泽人）

江西师范大学（静思笃行　持中秉正）

江西财经大学（信敏廉毅）

江西农业大学（团结　勤奋　求实　创新）

南昌航空大学（日新自强　知行合一）

景德镇陶瓷大学（诚朴恕毅）

第三节　中西校训比较

校训不仅是一所学校文化的灵魂，也是一方文化教育理念的浓缩体现。校训文化与本国传统文化之间存在着一种无法割裂的原初性关联，与其社会基础、宗教信仰和文化思潮密切相关，与其创校背景、历史流变、价值取向及民族意识等在本质上是一脉相承的。由于历史、文化、社会环境等的差异，中西方学校的校训各有特色，而中西方教育价值的取向也体现在校训中。因此，比较中西方校训文化，对于了解中西方教育价值观的差异，发现传统教育文化特征及建设新时代校园文化有着重要的意义。

一、文化之源的比较

任何文化现象差异的背后都存在着思维方式和文化产品形式的差异。中西方校训差异的根源在于教育思想的差异和语言文化表达形式的不同。[1]

1. 思想之源

(1) 中国校训的思想之源

中国校训的思想之源首先是“主德”“求善”的道德性思想。中国文化是以儒家文化为主体的求善的道德性文化，即“德性文化”。它很少讲求脱离伦理型学说的智慧，所谓的“学问”，不是关于客观世界的纯认识，而是如何安身立命与治国平天下的道德信条和经世之学。有关宇宙论、认识论的探讨，都是从属于或落脚于道德问题的基点上。 这样的“德性文化”决定了我国学校的校训总是以德为先，智为德服务。校训的内容都是围绕“德”来确立，如“勤”“诚”“敬”“公”等反映德育的字眼，另外还有很多它们的同义词。这样的校训随处可见，俯拾即是。其次是“重稳定”“重和谐”的整体性思想。儒家把天、地、人看成统一的整体，以“天人合一”为最高境界，认为和谐才是世界的永恒规律。重稳定、重和谐和重整体思想的表现之一就是强调爱国家、忠于祖国，做到“以国事为己事，以国权为己权，以国耻为己耻，以国荣为己荣”，表现出为国分忧，立志报国的满腔深情。爱国主义至上突出表现在新中国成立前的“教育救国”和新中国成立后的“教育兴国”运动。再次是“自强不息”“刚健有为”的革新思想，这推动了一种积极乐观的生活态度，讲求不断追求完善的体魄、学识、技能和道德。

(2) 西方校训的思想之源

西方校训的思想之源首先是“主知”“求真”的科学性思想。西方文化将认识与道德论相区分，道德让位于真理，真理面前人人平等。智慧作为希腊传统道德中的最高

[1] 王彩霞．试探中西校训之差异 [J]. 大学教育科学，2006(1):82-84。

境界，也一直为哲学家们所关注。他们的“主知”思想对西方文化和教育发展的影响是经久不衰的，也可以看作是“主知”“求真”校训的精神本源。“主知”思想为后来大学理念的形成奠定了基础，英国的纽曼在《大学的理念》一书中指出：“大学是探索各种知识的场所。”传授知识和探索学问是大学和其他场所的本质区别。其次是“重神”的宗教性思想。西方文化可谓是“宗教文化”。特别是中世纪时期，宗教势力十分强大，兴办任何事情都须以上帝为旗帜，大学的一切活动都要体现宗教的意志，即便是制定校训也不例外。最有代表性的是英国牛津大学的校训“主启吾智”，它彰显出中世纪宗教对大学的影响，强调“启示”是知识和真理的源泉。[1] 再次，是“自治”“自由”思想。对于西方现代大学而言，大学自治既是其理想所在，也是它确保学术独立的命脉所在。从中世纪大学的自治可以看到现代大学自治传统的萌芽，这种自治权和学术自由权对西方的大学理念产生了深远的影响。

(3) 形式之源

中国校训的形式之源：如前概述中所说，我国古代家训的形式对校训有一定的影响。最早的家训通过“铭”将训诫内容刻在器物上，以供子孙经常观看。唐代出现讲求工整、对仗、押韵的“诗训”，明清家训以格言、箴铭、警句、歌诀等形式为主。这些家训风格清新，大多是饱含深意的哲言睿语，言简意赅，言近旨远，耐人寻味。我国古代的对联对校训的形式也有一定的影响。对联讲求对仗工整、押韵，以潜移默化的方式传达着严肃的哲理和文化意蕴。尤其一些格言对联，对立志、治学、修身、友善、处事、齐家、明理等有高度的概括，这些对校训形式和内容的影响也是深远的。

西方校训的形式之源：《圣经》已成为西方传统文化的一部分，所以西方校训受到《圣经》的影响。因为掌握的材料有限，人们大都推测西方大学的校训形式可能是得到《圣经》中“十诫”的启示。《圣经》中认为：无所不能的上帝向希伯来人传谕了十诫，并将十诫内容写在两块石板上。西方校训的实体受此启发，大学校训也通过实物的形式被固定下来。

二、校训特征的比较

中西方校训虽然有着很多共性，但由于思维方式和表达形式的不同，其特征存在着差异，主要表现在语言特征和内容特征的不同。

2.1 语言特征

中西思维方式的差异影响着校训语言的特征，分别体现在词汇、句法和修辞的特点上。[2]

[1] 严明，陆云云．出国留学一本通 [M]．北京：化学工业出版社，2010:235-239。
[2] 张竞碧．中西大学校训之比较研究 [J]．湖北工业大学学报，2009(3):97-99。

【词汇特点】

总体而言，中西方校训语言的共同点是简洁、通俗、凝练，具有一定的稳定性。最显著的差异是：中国校训对仗工整，言简意赅，而西方校训用词自由，表述客观。中国的校训多以动词词组为主，多采用一言两字，二言四字，四言四字，二言八字，其中二言八字最多。而西方校训则多采用句子和名词结构的形式，自由洒脱，不太注重押韵和对仗，折射出西方人追求自由的理念。中国的动词占主导地位的校训反映了较强的实用主义精神；而西方的名词占主导地位的校训有着更多的思辨色彩；中国校训强调主观性，涵盖的内容较多；西方校训则注重客观性，校训内容相对集中，往往只涉及一到两层含义。例如哈佛大学的校训：真理；耶鲁大学的校训：光明与真理。

【句法特点】

中国大学校训的句法特点比较单一，主要是动词性平行结构与名词性平行结构。而西方大学校训结构多样化，以下列四种结构为主：一是名词性平行结构。这种结构内容直白，简洁，给人印象深刻，这点与中国大学校训相同。例如西点军校的校训：职责　荣誉　国家。二是以介词开头的句子。这种句子阐明在某一特定条件下要达到的目的，从而彰显校训与众不同。 如英国剑桥大学的校训：此地乃光明与神圣。三是陈述句。这种结构采用了 A 是 B 的格式，结构简单，易于记忆。例如：英国牛津大学的校训：上帝指引我们迈向光明。四是祈使句。这种结构采用祈使句形式，号召、劝慰人们，让人感到亲切，催人上进。例如：美国加利福尼亚伯克利分校的校训是“寻求知识之光”。

【修辞特点】

中国大学校训在长期的演变过程中，深深打上了传统文化的烙印，渗透了诗歌、对联、碑刻的语言和形式，具有言简意赅、形式工整、语言押韵等特点。首先中西方大学校训都喜欢通过隐喻来表达，这是最明显的一个相同点。如斯坦福大学的校训是“自由之风吹拂”。 北京林业大学的校训是“养青松正气，法竹梅风骨”。其次对偶是中国大学校训中使用最多的修辞手法，这与中国人喜欢四平八稳的性格息息相关。当然，这种对偶既可是严式对偶，即字数、词性、平仄等严格相对。也可以是宽式对偶，即字数、结构等相同或相似。校训基本上是宽式。再次，中西方大学校训用明喻表达得不多，但也有体现，例如：加拿大多伦多大学校训是“像大树一样茁壮成长”。阜阳职业技术学院校训是“上善若水”。总的来说，西方大学校训修辞手法的运用要比我国的丰富，除了上述明喻、隐喻外，还有拟人，例如华盛顿大学西雅图分校：是知识让我们走到一起。借代，例如麻省理工学院：既会动脑，也会动手。这些修辞手段的运用，体现了校训语言的美学法则，给人以美的享受。[1]

[1] 成晓艳，韩文祥，成长江．中西方教育价值观的差异——对校训的分析与思考［J］. 继续教育研究，2007(6)：119-120。

2.2 内容特征

中西方大学校训在内容上有许多相似点。比如两者都强调厚德、求知、求真、创新、爱国等；两者都喜欢用“大词”。“大词”是一种通俗的说法，泛指语言的长词、难词、生僻词等，其正式程度以及语域皆高于一般词汇。但是中西方校训的内容上的不同特征也反映出了不同的教育文化传统。

【中国校训的内容】

中国的大学校训大都引经据典，如《论语》《大学》《中庸》《周易》《汉书》《孟子》《礼记》等传统经典巨著，并对这些传统文化进行现代诠释，使校训在新时期闪耀着古代经典文化的光芒。因此，有理由相信：中国大学校训很好地继承并发展了我国古代的优秀文化传统。由于受到传统文化，特别是儒家文化的影响，中国的校训内容具有强烈“主德求善”的道德主义倾向；“重集体、重和谐”的整体主义取向；“主张直觉静思”的体悟学习传统，以及注重意志修炼的教育态度取向。当这些取向表现在中国学校的许多校训中，“德”“品”“团结”“静思”“弘毅”就成为高频度的关键词。如南开大学的校训“允公允德，日新月异”；大连理工大学的“团结、进取、求实、创新”；江西师范大学的“静思笃行，持中秉正”；武汉大学的“自强、弘毅、求是、拓新”都反映了这样的讲求修行德性的教育文化传统。

【西方校训的内容】

西方的校训从内容来源来看，大都受《圣经》的影响。基督教是西方文化的母体，《圣经》已经成为西方传统文化不可或缺的一部分，毫不夸张地说，西方的大学校训在一定程度上都打上了《圣经》的烙印。所以许多西方大学的校训带有浓厚的宗教色彩，受《圣经》的影响颇深。这些校训具有“追求知识，信仰宗教”的历史痕迹；“个人主义，崇尚自由”的文化风尚以及“平等意识，自我意识”的人文特征。

三、校训文化的启示

中西校训研究可以让我们看到文化对比的普遍规律：文化产品的背后是文化理念，文化现象的背后是一方水土长期积淀而成的教育结果，而比较与借鉴始终是教育文化共生发展的有效途径。

3.1 校训背后的教育文化

通过比较中西方校训的文化之源及内容特征，可以看出它们都继承和发扬了各自的传统文化，受各自民族文化的感染和熏陶，反映出了风格各异的教育文化背景。[1]

通过中西校训形式之源的比较，可以看出中西方大学校训在形式上的相通之处：都是通过实物的形式，通过引经据典来体现，通过箴言、格言、德目、训诲等语言形式悬挂于学校的显眼之地来宣扬其校训文化，体现着当地的社会需求、文化根脉、育人

[1] 王彩霞．试探中西校训之差异[J]. 大学教育科学，2006(1):82-84。

理念、价值取向和学校愿景。然而，由于中西方思维特点和语言习惯的差异，校训也反映出了中西教育文化的主要差异：西方“主知”、中国“主德”；西方“求真”、中国“求善”；西方“重神”、中国“重伦”；西方“崇自由”、中国“崇稳定”；西方“尚自我”、中国“尚整体直觉”；西方“善对立思辨”、中国“善实用”；同时中国的校训动词性强，反映了较强的规范教育和经世精神；而西方的名词性为主的校训有较多的思辨色彩，它注重对事物的探索与内在引导。究其原因，是因为中西教育精神的价值取向有所不同。中国教育文化的价值取向注重境界而西方重视宗教精神；中国推崇圣贤人格而西方重视真理探寻；中国主张乐群培养而西方尊重个性发展；中国更加重视“求公”的集体主义德性文化是源自超越生命的美学境界，而西方偏向“求是”的个性主义知性文化是源自二元对立的文化特质。[1] 在中国教育文化中，服务社会和追求境界的教育求公价值取向明显。中华境界滥觞于易经哲学，看重孟子同乐思想中审美价值的普遍性和公共性。比较而言，由于受柏拉图理念理论、亚里士多德演绎法，以及之后的培根归纳法、笛卡尔直觉理性的影响，西方教育文化明显地具有极为鲜明的二元对立的特质。二元，即主体和客体，或精神与物质。尽管二元因其相互依存和转化的关系被忽略而往往被分裂和对立起来，但却是西方大学求是价值取向的主导和对科技的推动力。

3.2 校训文化的教育启示

中西方校训反映出的教育文化各具特色，体现的是各自的办学理念和精神风貌，具有长期性和继承性，代表了一个国家的教育理想。分析比较中西方校训背后不同的教育文化有助于我们以跨文化的视角理解中西教育文化的差异，借鉴世界一流高校的理念精华，反思我国教育理念的不足，这对丰富我国未来校训建设和教育文化的内涵具有现实意义。

通过对中国代表性大学校训的分析，可以清晰地看到，中国教育文化在儒家传统理念的引领下非常注重个人知行的和谐以及个人与社会的和谐。甚至为了追求个人身心的和谐而强调自强不息式的不懈进取，为了社会的和谐而强调牺牲自我的奋斗，实现个体身心和人与社会的和谐。这一目标体现了中国君子追随圣贤止于至善的传统教育的精髓与儒家特有的公德性文化价值。[2] 通过对西方一流大学校训文化的属性与渊源分析，可以发现主要有四种类型：“神谕”（宗教取向）、“求真”（知识与学术取向）、“服务”（社会取向）、“个性化”（创新取向）等，体现出了发展性、学术性、公益性以及新奇性的价值目标。[3] 教育研究者通过对中西方校训文化的对比看到了各自的文化底蕴与价值，也提出了中国校训理念有待完善的方面：校训雷同现象比较明显，“求

[1] 李剑．大学校训的中西差异：超越生命与二元对立［J］．国家教育行政学院学报，2013(9)：16-19。
[2] 周谷平，陶炳增．近代中国大学校训——大学理念的追求［J］．清华大学教育研究，2005(2)：95-101。
[3] 韩萌．世界一流大学校训文化的属性、类型及价值目标［J］．教育科学，2019(1)：68-74。

实、创新、团结、严谨”出现的概率比较高；德性教育目标的普遍呈现使得教育具体目标的个性被淡化。因此有学者提出了校训文化的提升方向[1]：首先是加强重视人的个性与全面发展。由于中国传统文化及近代特殊的历史条件，强调了人的社会属性与责任，而相对忽略了人的自然属性与个性，个体身心的全面发展需继续加强。其次是重视美育的教育文化地位。近代以来，大学校训直接指向现实世界、功利世界和意义世界，充满了“真”与“善”的要求，却缺乏“美”的内容。这不仅因为“美学”是个外来词语，更主要是因为中国传统的“美德”思想更多强调的是心灵美，“美”被“德”概括了。再次是回归传统自然和谐理念。中国哲学自古十分强调人与自然的和谐关系，认为人与天地万物同为一气所生，互相依存。但由于近代以来中国的问题，主要是社会和人的问题，受其影响，现代中国校训中彰显着精英济世、科技救世的实用情结，与自然和谐共生的传统理念相对淡化，存在着“自然缺位”的现象。在新时代背景下，中国人文的精神、青山绿水的价值以及可持续发展的意识已然成为当代中国教育文化的重要内容，因此人的全面发展、美的人文精神以及环境的可持续发展理念在当代校训文化中的弘扬显得至关重要。

综观中国大学的校训文化，可以看到中国教育文化的传统精髓以及近代社会文明发展的进程。更可以看出中国大学教育受现实世界的影响，除了语言上传承了儒家的经典名言，也将教育目标更多地指向意义的世界。基于经济的快速发展与物质水平的提高，伴随“灵魂跟上脚步”的呼吁，教育的人文本质重新被置于显著的地位。自近代以来，大学取代传统宗教或传统文化的精神机构而成为一个国家开展科学人文学问事业，推进真理探求的主打领域。但是面对现代文明所固有的现代性病症，许多大学都面临着沦为高等职业培训所的困境。[2] 哈佛学院前院长的著作《失去灵魂的卓越》反思的正是学校如何在功利性机制中忘记教育宗旨的。如果教育文化只仅仅关注职业知识技能的传承，办学目标只是为社会输送专业人才，那么教育将失去本来的精神而只会输送善于将自己融入社会体系的作为精致的利己主义者的专业人员。相反，教育的本来精神是保存传扬并丰富一个民族的文化精神，这需要青年人的活力及追求真理的自由与勇气。因此，在吸收当代社会先进技术的同时，不忘守护教育文化的人文精神本质，建设具有中国特色的现代校训文化已成为当代教育的需要和呼唤，而在此过程中作为大学精神和大学文化精髓的大学校训必将发挥重要作用。

[1] 宋永忠，姜晓云．中国大学校训百年[J]．江海学刊，2008(3):204-210。
[2] 王德峰．认识自我与世界代序[Z]．开启问学求真之路，2023。

On Chinese Traditional Educational Culture: Perceptions and Proverbs

YAN Ming YU Yue
Translator: YAN Ming

Preface

For years, I've been a proponent of the Platonic midwife approach to education, while practicing this very philosophy, I always disapprove of the educational approach of drilling and spoon–feeding. In my classes, in my conversations, I frequently define this type of education as "anti–education." In recent years, I have devoted myself to the English translation of Chinese classics and histories, and I have often come into contact with the educational thought of the ancients. When I got the research and translation manuscript of *On Chinese Traditional Educational Culture* sent to me by Professor YAN Ming, I felt as if the wind of wisdom in education blowing from the grand history of China. It is therefore a great honor for me to write the preface to this book.

This book is the result from the joint efforts of Professor YAN Ming and Headmistress YU Yue. With profound knowledge and keen insight, they have conducted in–depth research and wonderful interpretation of traditional Chinese educational culture, and finally completed this masterpiece that is helpful to the current foreign language education and cultural spreading. I know Professor Yan Ming is an expert in language education, but what I value more is her personality as a poet, whose poems are full of meaning of Zen. With such a state of mind, she can naturally comprehend the essence of education.

This book consists of two parts, which complements and confirms each other. In the first part,"Comprehension of the Traditional Perceptions", from "The Main Outlines of Chinese Culture" to "The Cultural Foundation of Education in China", to "The Cultural Characters of Chinese Institutes", and "An Overview of Chinese Educational Culture", it reveals the essence of Chinese traditional educational culture. The second part of "Contemplation of the Educational Proverbs" from "The Selected Readings of Schools and Thoughts" to "The Comprehension of Classic Proverbs", from "The Essentials of Famous Family Instructions" to "The Scanning of University Mottoes", it vividly shows the multi–dimensional space and rich connotation of Chinese traditional educational culture. In today's globalization, the value and significance of Chinese traditional educational culture are becoming increasingly prominent. It is not only an important way for Chinese and foreign readers to appreciate Chinese history and society, but also a crucial resource to build a harmonious society and promote social progress. It is in this context that this work comes into being. It intends to present and interpret to more people the Chinese traditional educational culture through in–depth research and translation, so as to better inherit, develop and spread this valuable cultural heritage.

With their profound learning and keen insight, Professor YAN Ming and Headmistress YU Yue have carefully identified and outlined the essence and connotation of Chinese traditional educational culture for us. Their research is not only in-depth, but also comprehensive, integrating theoretical knowledge with practical inspiration, not only bearing the history, but also facing the reality for better predicting the future, therefore it provides a new perspective for us to understand and appreciate Chinese traditional educational culture. This book is not only important on the study of the Chinese traditional educational culture, but also significant for spreading Chinese traditional educational culture as a tool. I believe that both readers interested in traditional Chinese educational culture and scholars engaged in relevant research will benefit a lot from this book.

Here, we should be grateful to Professor YAN Ming and Headmistress YU Yue for their hard work, their research and translation has opened a door to the profound world of traditional Chinese educational culture for the readers. We are also thankful to all those people involved in the publication of this book, whose work has made it possible to present the very book to the world. I hope that this book can arouse the attention and hot discussion from readers, can be placed on the desks of scholars, and be studied in the classrooms, so as to further promote the research and dissemination of traditional Chinese educational culture.

Finally, once again, I sincerely recommend this book to all readers who love Chinese humanist spirits and educational culture, whether you are a reader with a deep interest in it or a scholar engaged in related research, you will get deep inspiration and rich rewarding from this book. Let us deeply understand and appreciate the charm of traditional Chinese educational culture through reading this book, and jointly inherit and carry forward this valuable cultural heritage.

ZHAO Yanchun

June 22, 2023 at Meilan Lake

Introduction

In the post–pandemic era of internationalization of education competition, The "cross–cultural transmission competence" of humanities has gradually become a key word in the context of "Chinese culture going global". From the consensus that "cultural identity is the deepest identity" in the cultural circle, to the awakening of "cultural turning" in the field of translation research, to the development of educational linguistics with the concept of "language integrating with education", the whole situation makes"Chinese humanistic spirit" and "cultural transmission" the popular terms in contemporary times. However, the natural science research style in humanities caused by the mainstream of "micro–quantitative experiments" and "linguistically based research" has deeply revealed the tendency of "feelings of Tao" giving way to the tools of Qi" in the educational world; as the goal of local cross–cultural education has just changed from "international vision of understanding the world culture" to "international value of promoting the Chinese culture", the works from "top–down project research" are still far more than those of "bottom–up analytical popularization", western fashion followers and imitators are more popular than the traditional local explorers and inheritors in educational culture field. Therefore, the qualitative research of Chinese traditional educational culture and its cross–cultural and interdisciplinary transmission need to be strengthened and deepened.

The best way to understand a civilization is to interpret the essence of its traditional culture of education. As an exploration on the integration of educational linguistic concepts and cultural translation, as well as the result of cooperation between ideological courses in college and educational practice in society, this work focuses on the inheritance, research and translation of traditional Chinese educational culture, so as to present the traditional Chinese education that rooted in the land of China for thousands of years to Chinese and foreign readers with cultural ideas and educational proverbs in bilingual form. The first part,"Comprehension of the Traditional Perceptions", consists of four chapters:"The Main Outlines of Chinese Culture" "The Cultural Foundation of Education in China" "The Cultural Characters of Chinese Institutes", and "An Overview of Chinese Educational Culture". The second part of "Contemplation of the Educational Proverbs" is composed of four chapters:"The Selected Readings of Schools and Thoughts" "The Comprehension of

Classic Proverbs" "The Essentials of Famous Family Instructions" and "The Scanning of University Mottoes". The design of the writing is based on the high–frequency topics, famous figures, classic works and authoritative documents of traditional Chinese educational culture. Although it cannot cover all aspects, it tries to learn from and highlight the essence, with concepts and examples, reflection and promotion. It adopts the interdisciplinary perspectives of pedagogy, culturology and linguistics as a whole, through literature review, inductive speculation and translation practice, it manages to conform to the call of cultural convergence and market demand of traditional humanistic acquisition in a view of "seeing the world through the classics". While analyzing the quintessence of traditional education and culture to Chinese and foreign readers, it emphasizes the four major characteristics: The two–way integration of concepts and proverbs, the dual perspectives of language and culture, the dual orientations of academics and general knowledge, and the double–effect practice of foreign language and education. So the basic principles of the writing are:

1. restoring the traditional footprints of Chinese culture by taking history as a clue;
2. taking classics as the core to condense the essence of vast educational culture;
3. presenting colorful elements of education in China with bilingualism as the carrier;
4. sorting out important themes of authoritative literature based on scientific methods.

Thousands of years of history in China is full of its colorful species of culture, endless insightful wisdom emerges on this land; and the education course is endless for a world of harmony and prosperity. Cultural prosperity is in the rise, we are lucky to live at this flourishing age to view vast territory of our motherland and review the details in its long history. Viewing through the long river of Chinese education and cultural history is like overlooking the vast Chinese land with wise thoughts and brilliant chapters, thus we realize the impermanence of the human society and the eternity of knowledge and wisdom. Although our writing may only be like the footprints on snow and mud in this changing world, we would like to draw a scenery of the splendid educational landscape on a certain piece, and seek to reflect the local culture with a bright color. Writing so far, our hearts are filled with emotion, beyond the window the clouds are light and breeze is blowing. Before submitting the book for publication, the sentimental thoughts and views at this moment can be expressed in a few lines, and here are our blessings to the colleagues who keep tireless spirit in the educational field.

A Scene at the Desk

Light fragrance of green tea is flowing,
Thoughts from mind and pen keep flourishing.
What breeds my white hair outside window?
Which still decorates the spring branches smiling.

Many thanks to the famous scholar and translator Professor Zhao Yanchun of Shanghai University for his insightful preface and careful guidance, every time we communicate, the enlightenment of his poetic style in education and the power of his translation in literature is deeply felt; and our gratitude also goes to the editors and teachers of Donghua University Press for their hard work. We are even more grateful to all the friends for such good fortune that gave us inspiration in the process of shaping the work. In this era with the information explosion, technology surge, fierce competition, and abundant materials, it is you who still care for the unquantifiable humanistic feelings in traditional culture, and jointly inherit the connotation of virtue and poetry in Chinese education together with countless forefront educators. Although the work is not expected to become a towering tree in the humanistic spiritual home of China, hopefully it can be used as a leaf of reed grass, swaying and accompanying Chinese and Western readers through time and space to dialogue with sages, to meditate and explore the true nature of education, and then jointly look up to the infinite starry sky of culture and education above the land of China.

There is no ending for modification in the writing, and the work is far from perfect, we sincerely hope that readers can criticize and correct it without reservation.

The authors

2023.06

Fengxian Bay College Town, Shanghai

Contents

Part II Contemplation of the Educational Proverbs

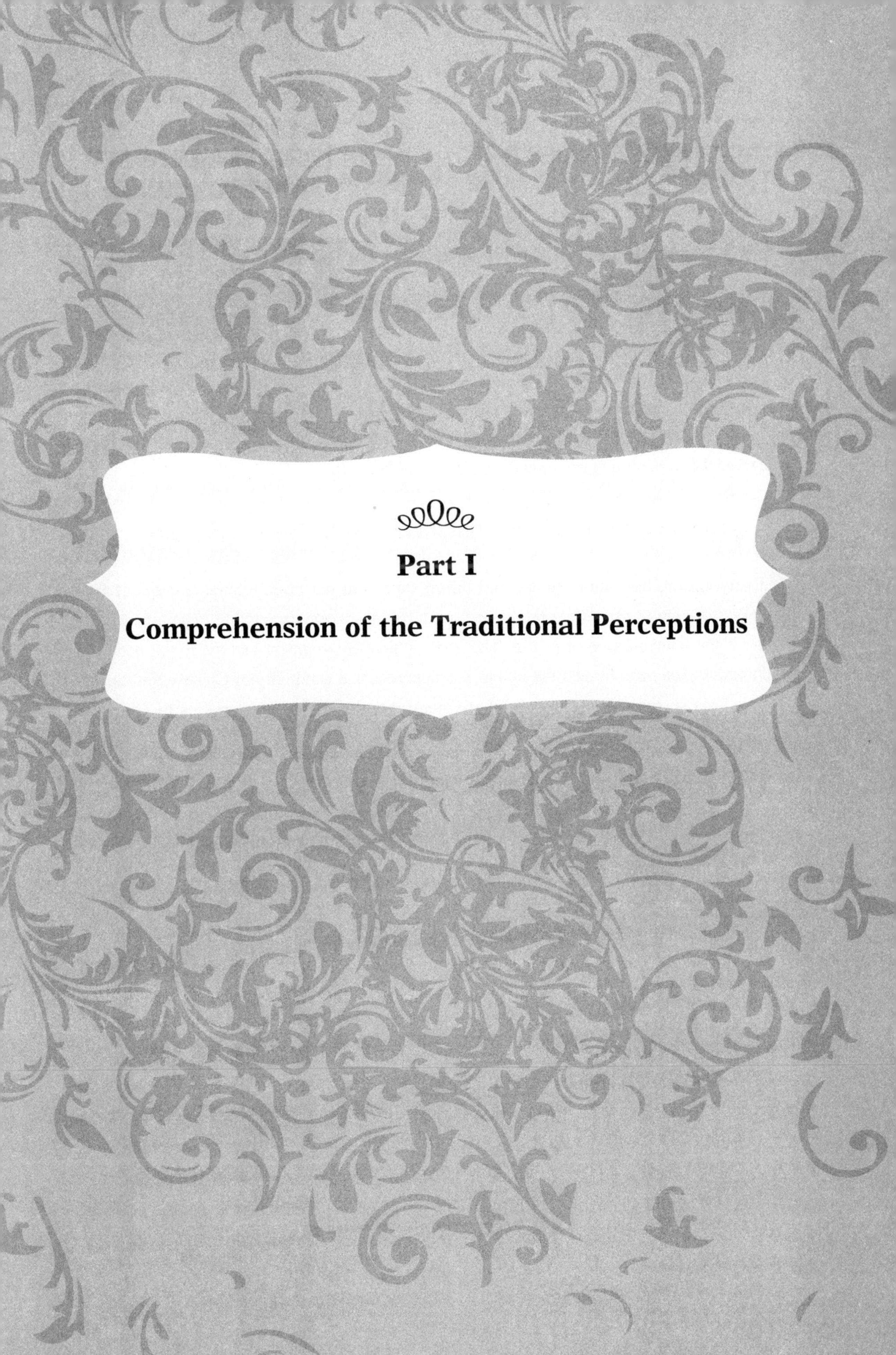

Part I

Comprehension of the Traditional Perceptions

Chapter One The Main Outlines of Chinese Culture

Chinese culture is one of the world's oldest cultures, tracing back to at least five thousand years ago. The area in which the chinese culture is dominant covers a large geographical region in eastern Asia with customs and traditions varying greatly between provinces, cities, and even towns as well. Important components of Chinese culture include ceramics, architecture, music, literature, martial arts, cuisine, traditional opera, philosophy and religion. The development and trace of Chinese culture is certainly influenced by geographical environment,national history and social convention, meanwhile, it also in return deeply influences the formation of traditional educational culture.

Section One The Environment and Initial State of Culture

Every culture has its birthplace and initial state, and the initial characteristics of the birthplace of culture often determine the formation of a particular culture. The essence of culture is the humanization of nature. The geographical environment and the living patterns of Chinese region have formed the richness, uniqueness and continuity of Chinese traditional culture. This section mainly expounds the natural and social characteristics of Chinese traditional culture from two aspects: the river civilization and the clan system.

I. The Great River Civilization

Archaeology has proved that the homeland of Chinese culture is around middle and lower reaches of the Yellow River, especially the region of Shanxi and Henan Province today, the Yellow River is therefore called the mother river of Chinese ethnic people. However, Chinese culture came into being in a diversified way, it is combined and integrated by ethnic people and in different dimensions, which is based on the geographic conditions of large territory, color ful landform and rivers that differentiate the changing landscapes in north and south regions. The various rivers have played a decisive role in the development of agricultural civilizations in China: the Yangshao culture, Dawenkou culture, Longshan culture and Erlitou culture in the Yellow River basin; the Hemudu culture, San Xingdui culture in the Yangtze River basin; and the Hongshan culture in the Liao River basin have been the typical examples of the initial state of Chinese agricultural civilizations bred by the great rivers.

Many of the ancient civilizations that emerged during the Axial Agehave since declined and disappeared from the annals of history. Only Chinese civilization has kept continuing to inherit its vitality and tradition through ups and downs, vast territory with complexity of geographic forms and the two great rivers with their cultures parallel and complementary is part of the important reasons. The old saying of "the precipitous north and the beautiful south; the solemn north and the cozy south; the tough north and the elegant south; the austere north and the gorgeous south" is the summary of the vigorous culture of the Yellow River and the splendid culture of Yangtze River. When the Yellow River Basin was facing the civilization declining because of over assart, terrible climate and the wars against nomadic tribes, the culture of Yangtze River basin became the resort of treasure, foods and humanity with its natural advantages. On the other hand, once the Yellow River Basin near the northern land was invaded through by the nomadic tribes, the Yangtze River as a natural moat with potential cultural and economic resource would provide the Chinese people with the foundation for defensing and rejuvenation. Blessed with the inheritance and creation of the Yellow River culture around Yangtze River Basin, the gist of the Chinese traditional culture has been kept and brightened, the nourishing and protecting from the two great rivers is definitely the precondition for the ever lasting and spreading of the Chinese civilization.

The unique river civilization in China is a natural terrace for agricultural economy, which is a basic form for Chinese cultural development as well as the earliest industry on this land. The agricultural economy from the river civilization has been evolved with the social division of labour, which further divided its agriculture into crop farming and stock farming , thus agricultural civilizations in China has been further differentiated into a muti–dimensional structure, and this general environment has deeply influenced the development of national culture. In such a vast territory, traditional Chinese culture is usually divided into different subcultures in each region, and there are different traditional cultural artifacts and symbols. Such distinctions give rise to the old Chinese proverb:"the folkway varies within ten li, the custom varies within a hundred li".

II. The Clan System

Patriarchal Clan is one of the most important dimensions to understand the Chinese society. Clan refers to people who live together and are related by blood. It is also a social community organized to participate in the festival. The patriarch usually presided over the sacrificial activities. As the ancestral place of worship, ancestral halls play a central role. With the shift in the development of ancient Chinese feudal society, family rights and the central monarchy forces, especially the class interests represented by the patriarch, changing and the spectrum of interests, the clan system in different historical periods showed different characteristics.

The basic elements of a clan include: keeping the patrilineal kinship of the members; taking the family as the basic unit; living together in a stable residential area, and obeying the organizational principles under the clan leader. People with the patrilineal kinship are called clansman, but the organizational principles determine whether a group is a clan system. A clan usually owns a common place for offering sacrifices for ancestors: the ancestral temple. The development of Chinese clan history from Zhou Dynasty to Qing Dynasty can be divided into four periods according to the changing roles of the clan leaders: the Pre–Qin Period, The Han and Tang Dynasties, the Song and Yuan Dynasties and Ming and Qing Dynasties.

The long historical clan system culture created by ancient China is closely related to its social ideal of harmony, stability, cohesion and unity. The patriarchal clan system and the clan ethics have long been the most striking cultural features of ancient China. In ancient China, the clan system was abolished in the Qin Dynasty, but it reemerged among high–standing families in the Han Dynasty and spread to common people after the Tang Dynasty. It is generally agreed that the hierarchical preference structure embedded in the clan system helped to increase trust and cooperation among people. It helped people to take collective action by themselves and also opened a back door to influence government decisions. In this sense, the clan system probably also helped to prolong the political institutions for two thousand years.

Section Two The History and National Character

China has a long history, it is just like a surging river, which breeds colorful scenery along its banks. The development of the Chinese nation in the history has its distinct characteristics. The Chinese civilization,which has demonstrated a unique cohesion and endured for thousands of years, is closely related to the spiritual structure, as wells as the ways of thinking and acting of this nation. This section will briefly review the historical track and national character of Chinese civilization.

I. The Historical Track

Generally speaking, Chinese civilization, as one of the independent civilization sources, has a clear evolution trajectory, indicating a diversified development with the central plain as the core and resulting in the feature of mutual penetration and integration. As has been mentioned above, China's ancestors nurtured by the river civilization and an agriculture–dominant economy gradually entered the new threshold of civilization from a stable agriculture society in ancient times, and the clan chiefs transformed into a new ruling class centralizing diverse powers. Thus, the kindred ties and state administrative system fused into an underlying structure of the society; resulting in a trend of inward concentration, stronger human relations, communal living, and centralized power.

Relying on advanced productivity; production mode and the great unity, ancient China created a brilliant civilization marked with four great inventions, playing a leading role in the world over a long period. The Xia, Shang and Western Zhou Dynasties represent the early states and bronze civilization in China. The Spring & Autumn and Warring States Periods witnessed the vassals contending for hegemony and various social reforms. In the Qin and

Han Dynasties, a unified country emerged in China. In Wei, Jin and Southern and Northern Dynasties, China experienced political division and national integration. With the time of Sui and Tang Dynasties came a prosperous and open age in the Chinese history. Song and Yuan Dynasties are the special period for diverse cultural collisions and great socio–economic development. Then China confronted the prosperity of farming civilization and crisis before modern times when entered the period of Ming and Qing Dynasties before the Opium War. The Opium War interrupted the independent development of China. China was invaded and insulted by western powers and forced to ink a series of unequal treaties to cede territory and pay indemnities, falling into a colonial and semi–colonial abysm. During the one century old modernization from the Opium War, Chinese people continuously promoted the development of national industry and culture through the struggles against the imperialism, feudalism and bureaucrat capitalism. The Revolution of 1911 led by Dr. Sun Yat–sen overthrew the Qing Dynasty, and profoundly publicized the concepts of democracy and republic. Then the New Democracy Revolution under the leadership of the Communist Party of China pointed a socialist future for the bourgeois revolution and won the victory of national independence and liberation.

October 1, 1949 witnessed the founding of the People's Republic of China, inaugurating a new historic era toward socialist modernization. After a zig–zagging exploration, the reform and opening–up path with Chinese characteristics was finally established. This path strengthened the construction of democracy and laws, established a socialist market economy and actively participated in international competition and cooperation, striving for a sustainable development and an affluent, democratic, cultural and harmonious society.

II. The National Character

The national character is a spirit of the nation's common spiritual structure and behavior. The Chinese nation has formed its unique character during its development of thousands of years. The building of the national character is deeply influenced by ancient myths, confucianism and the different geo–cultures. In other words, these elements are the intrinsic genes of the Chinese national character, which continue to develop and interact even after thousands of years.

2.1 Ancient Myths

First of all, there is always an attitude of God worshiping in the traditional character of Chinese people. The mythology created by the ancient ancestors played an obvious role in cultivating their characters of nature revering, being grateful and working with perseverance. Many lofty characters can be found among the supernatural beings, who selflessly experienced many hardships to save the suffering people. Nuwa, who healed the sky with colorful stones; Shennong, who taught people to farm and tasted countless herbs; Pangu, who sacrificed himself to create the world for people; and Xingtian, who held a great rebellious spirit, to name just a few, all have reflected the ancient ancestors'personality of tough, selfless and hardworking.

2.2 Confucianism

Second, Confucianism has a profound influence on Chinese national characters. The main thoughts of Confucian include observing and understanding the universal moral principles of human beings, which is based on the hierarchic system in Chinese society, and are reflected from the virtues of benevolence, justice, politeness, intelligence and trust. In such a cultural climate, Chinese people have learned to refrain themselves and keep etiquette, endure humiliation for greater mission, and practice introspection in a moderate way. As valuing justice above material gains, Chinese people get used to be prudent and contented in poverty and moderation while devoting to morality, they are completely convinced with the standard social convention. On the other hand, Confucianism cares about social reality and the fate of the nation, the individual destiny is to be connected with the rise and fall of the nation, that adds the sense of historical mission and social responsibility among Chinese intellectuals.

2.3 Geo–culture

In addition, affected by geo–cultures, Chinese ethnic people boast two aspects of cultures: farming cultures in southern China and nomadic cultures in northern China that symbolized by cattle and horse respectively. The life of Chinese ethnic people are closely connected with cattle and horses, the metaphor of "southern cattle and northern horses" implicates the real qualities and characters of the Chinese people. The technique of the plough pulling with cattle began in Spring and Autemn Period, in the southern part of China where farming is the main mode of production and life, cattle were regarded as the important helpers people rely on for a living, the character of the cattle has even become that of the farmers. Chinese people often assimilate and encourage themselves with the qualities of cattle, actually, the confucianism also takes the virtues of cattle for self–cultivation. The style name of one disciple of Confucius "Ran Geng" is "Zi Niu" meaning "little cattle". In modern times, the Chinese still take the cattle as spiritual model. The well–known saying from the great writer Lu Xun (Zhou Zuoren) is: Head bowed, like a willing ox, I serve the people. In northern China, horses are the crucial part of people's lives. The Mongolian, the Tibetan, and Man Minority people in their earlier days all lived in the typical nomadic culture with horse–worship customs. Horse–worship also exists in the ideas and folk activities of many ethnic groups, including the Han. The cultural images of horses in various mythologies and proverbs symbolize divinity, counter–evil force, authority, monarch, soul bringer, immolation and auspiciousness. The phrase "the spirit of dragons and horses" well declares the high status of the horse in the same breath of the national totem. In a word, the cultural character of the people in north and south parts of China carries the quality and spirit of hard working and daring perseverance like cattle and horses, which has long become the token of Chinese national soul.

As can be seen, after the long process of communication and integration influenced by traditional concepts, the mainstream thoughts of Confucianism and the geo-cultures, the ethnics in China have developed the comprehensive, multivariant, complementary and even contradictory characters: featured with gratefulness, reverence and unyielding will; kindness, politeness and high ambition; diligence, simplicity and perseverance.

Section Three The Tradition and the Social System

The cultural development of a region cannot be separated from its deep-rooted traditional concepts and social systems, which is reflected in the life attitudes and ways of members from various social groups. The ancient Chinese social tradition of "the common fate and structure of family and state" has become the political foundation of the mainstream cultural concept, and also constitutes the social value system of traditional Chinese society with ethics as the core. This cultural concept emphasizes centralism and harmony, while this social system is composed of consanguineous relationship and the conscience system.

I. Centralism and Harmony

The concept of centralism and harmony constitutes the traditional structure and development mode of Chinese society. The replacement, development and struggle ideal of successive dynasties are built and reincarnated around such traditional system, and this traditional idea has also influenced the educational culture of the past dynasties.

1.1 Centralism

By retrospecting the Chinese cultural tradition, one may find the "Centralism" in China has a long history. Ever since the beginning of Chinese civilization, the Chinese ethnics have formed the tradition of "one common ancestor, one authority, and one center". The "Centralism" culture considers polycentric culture as the root of social turmoil. Xun Zi once said: One authority makes sense, two authorities cause roils; since the ancient time, no stable society has been lasting with two monarchs. The traditional Chinese society never tempted to build an administration that is multiple and lateral, instead it kept trying to manage the power relations vertically, and centralize it into the hands of the monarch, so that the uni-direction power manipulation is firmly formed. Vertically, the power structure from the concept of "centralism" is also radially one directional, the subordinate has to absolutely obey the superiors, namely "justice is used to correct the behaviors of people, it must be carried forward from the above, not from the bottom". The "Centralism" concept from traditional Chinese society has helped to form The "Center" mode of thinking and value orientation, in which everything has a center or heart, so that the name of the nation is literally meant to be "the central nation". In the book *On China* by Shi Jie in Song Dynasty: "The nation located in the middle of the world is called the central nation". "China" or "Chunghwa" means the center of the world. The cultural trace of "Centralism" is also seen in the natural and social life of

Chinese people. For example: the sky in the nature, the sun in the universe, the center of the space and the gold in materials, the father of a family, the dragon of the animals, the heart of internal organs, the number of nine, all symbolizing and reflecting The "centralism" value orientation and mode of thinking of Chinese people.

1.2 Harmony is Paramount

In retrospection of the Chinese social tradition, one will find the most welcomed philosophy is to rule the world towards harmony by virtues and propriety. *The Book of Changes* clearly annotated this belief by calling the natural and perfect harmony as "Tai He" (the extreme harmony). Later the Confucianists inherited and spread the tradition and stated that "Tai He" covers all the meaning of harmony. The famous scholar in Ming Dynasty Wang Fuzhi said:"Tai He" means the extreme harmony. There was no inharmony before the universe came into being, after the world came into being, the harmony is not to be lost, this is called the extreme harmony. After more than two thousand years, such tradition has internalized into and guided our minds and behaviors, and made the focus and essence of our culture as cultivating orders, expanding and appreciating the relationship of harmony. Almost a century ago, when the well known German sinologist Richard Wiehelm who translated *The Book of Changes* talked about the differences between Europe culture and Chinese culture, he stressed the inclusiveness of Chinese culture and the expansivity of Europe culture, arguing that Chinese culture is flexible with more tenacity. The Chinese culture has repeatedly turned calamities into blessings and further carried itself forward, the great vitality reflected from history is the result from the rule and belief that "the opposing forces will finally integrate and achieve the harmony". Thus it can be seen that the nature of Chinese traditional culture is founded on the belief of harmony and reasons that permeating in the natural and social mechanisms.

II. Consanguineous Society and Conscience System

Clan society and conscience system have played a far–reaching role in maintaining and stabilizing the Chinese social order, and have become an important premise in the long history of China and the traditional educational culture, and also reflect the significant characteristics of Chinese thinking.

2.1 Clan Relationship

Influenced by the geo culture and economic factors, the traditional Chinese social structure is formed according to the family relationship. As an agricultural society, Chinese people built stable community with the blood relationship at very early historical period. On the other hand, there was little invasion for the comparatively closed geographic environment, China ended the primitive society in a gradual way, during this process, it was hard for the communities to break away from the family dominated society. China continued its clan system based on the blood relationship till the Western Zhou Dynasty, that is why the

Chinese society was originally in the form of acquaintances and connections. In a micro-view, Chinese society can be seen as the family connected acquaintance society with the main body of myriads families. In the society, the parents and children are the closest unit of such relations. That is to say this mode is the basic one for people to build and develop the social connection and communication. So to speak, blood relation is the key element to the relationship of people in China. The whole society is developed on the base of "family center" till it totally becomes a "world of acquaintances". Obviously, it is the social constructional model in which the nation and the families are highly united. In view of such a model, various social relations and events can be annotated completely. Likewise, the Chinese social system had long been basically settled since the feudalistic Western Zhou Dynasty was found, in this system the emperor was the only super authority and the officials of different levels are increasing downward with plebs as the bottom layer, so that the lasting system are called The "pyramid" model. Structurally this system is characterized with closeness and domestic affection, the whole society as well as the administration systems are graded strictly by the closeness of the family ties within the clan system.

2.2 Conscience System

Based on this clan relationship, the whole social system in China is ruled and governed by human operation instead of law system, relying on humanity education and conscience system with a long history. The concepts of "parent-like local chief" "elders and betters" "respected teachers" "respected magistrate" are all the culture-loaded words from the clan relationship and the conscience system that reflecting the traditional philosophy in China: conscience centered and virtue oriented. For the traditional spirit of Chinese society is not religious doctrines but the experience of lives, which is part of the humanity education that bestowed people with a peaceful life and a lofty mindset. The conscience system of the Chinese society has been inherited and enriched by Confucianism. It defined and maintained the distinction between a man of virtue and a man of meanness while arguing that the distinction is not based on family background or social position, but on the personal capacity and virtues. In this social system, people's "body and behaviors" are believed to be guided by their "mind and manners". Therefore, in the cultural behaviors of the Chinese people, the best way to convince and tame people is the conscientious psychological influence, for The "conscience system" and "human relations" are inseparable. Mencius once said:"the benevolent has no enemy", the statement reveals the fundamental belief of The "conscience system". A review of the conscience system and education tradition helps find the focus of humanistic knowledge and the features of great virtues. Confucius asks his followers to be erudite in classic works and stresses the education of humanity, behaviors, faith, and integrity, among which the virtue education with The "manner" and The "benevolence" as the focal content and "filial piety" as the key word becomes the principal line of all the Chinese ideological system, mutually enforcing the cultural tradition of "harmony between man and culture" and Chinese ethnic intellection of "keeping harmonious relationship".

Chapter Two The Cultural Foundation of Education in China

In view of education, the concept of China refers not only to its geographical meaning, but more about its culture. The Chinese people reproduce and create on this land from generation to generation the cultivated colorful and unique traditional culture and philosophy permeating in all walks of life in their material culture, behavioral culture, systemic culture and spiritual culture. Such traditional culture and philosophy are the foundation of the development of its education.

Section One The Traditional Cultural Influence on Education

Many of the requirements and norms advocated by Chinese educational culture can always find its trace in traditional culture. During thousands of years of historical development, these traditional cultures have provided numerous spiritual and material examples of local education in terms of the unique life philosophy, linguistic charm and cultural symbols, maintaining extremely strong vitality and becoming the extremely precious wealth.

I. The Philosophy of Life

Traditional Chinese philosophy is a philosophy of "life". In view of such value, heaven is the source of all living things. According to The *Book of Changes* (*Yijing*), the continuous creation of life is change; and the great virtue of heaven and earth is creating life. Mencius said,"(One should) love one's family, and love the people of every family in the world." Generations of learned people in China have carried on the idea of "heaven and earth giving birth to all lives", and thus keep emphasizing love for and kindness toward all living things. It is not uncommon to find the thoughts in Chinese educational field that love starts from loving one's family and other people, to loving all living things in the world. Humans and other living things are of the same kind and are equal with each other. In a letter to his family, Zheng Banqiao (1693—1765), a great painter of the Qing Dynasty, wrote that he loved all living things in the world, be it an ant or an insect. This, he said, was The "will of heaven", and that human beings should understand heaven's will. Related to such a philosophy is the eco–aesthetics of traditional Chinese culture. Ancient Chinese thinkers regarded nature, with human beings included in it, as the world of life. All living things in the world have their own life and state of being. From such appreciations, people could feel great spiritual delight, according to such philosophers. Confucian scholars in the Song and Ming dynasties all enjoyed observing the state of being of living things. Love for all living things in the world and appreciation for their state of being can often be found in ancient works of art and literature. Dong Qichang (1555—1636), a famous painter of the late Ming Dynasty, explained that, most artists enjoyed a long life because everything they observed was full of life. Chinese artists never paint dead animals. The birds, fish, insects, and flowers are all full of vitality under their brushes. Ancient Chinese literature illustrated a similar focus. In the poems of the Tang and Song dynasties, when Chinese poetry reached the apex of development, birds and flowers were often depicted as if they had human feelings. In *Strange Tales from Make–do Studio* (*Liaozhai zhiyi*), by Pu Songling (1640—1715), human beings and other living things are described as being of the same kind. Many of the stories tell of love between men and beautiful women incarnated from plants or animals.

II. The Charm of the Language

The numbers of Chinese language learners across the world have been on the rise in recent years. While those used to phonetic languages often find Chinese characters difficult to learn, some learners may experience the gratification of discovering historical and cultural elements in the process. Extensive research has revealed that Chinese language possesses many advantages over other languages. Written Chinese is based on a set of ideogram characters, from a single word one may obtain a wealth of information about its hidden meaning, the evolution history and the related phrases. Historians can decipher damaged ancient characters carved on bones and shells, this is not possible for other Latin languages. To express the given idea, the Chinese version is always the shortest, the most accurate, and the most effective one.

In a narrow sense, Chinese language is impressive with its characters known as the symbols of sentiment. Some pictographic symbols of Chinese characters express people's keen observation and experience of the world. This is why some European poets have found Chinese characters inspiring to their imagination. The poetic allusions are not without basis. Take the character 旦 for example, the upper part is a sun symbol, while the lower part represents the horizon. In other words, the character indeed stands for "the sun rising on the horizon" . The name of a famous university in Shanghai, Fudan, is composed of the characters 复 and 旦 , meaning "Day after day, the sun is rising on the horizon". A number of characters containing 旦 as an element all relate to the rising or setting of the sun. For example, the original complex form of the character for "east" 東 , looks like the sun rising from a forest. The character 暮 was originally written as 莫， resembling a scene of the sun setting into a forest. The left part of the character 明 was originally the symbol for "window", while the right part stands for "moon." Thus, 明 depicts a scene of the moon shining through the window. Is this not a poetic conception? The original complex character for "beauty" is written as 麗 . It resembles two deer running side by side on a mountain, a beautiful scene.

In a broad sense, Chinese language has a long history and special influence.The ancient written history of China had been caved onto the bone or shell in Oracle Bone Script, 甲

骨 文 in Chinese, with the history over 5,000 years. An important ancient written record is The Bamboo Annals, 竹书纪年 in Chinese, which can be dated back to 296 BC. This is a diachronic record written on bamboo, about the growth history of ancient China, it records the historical facts and events ranged in chronological order, as in a time line. When the movable type printing technology had been improved by clay movable types, the weakness of unevenness of wooden type was overcome. This printing technology greatly reduced the cost and time of book publishing and helped improving the ancient Chinese language reading and education. In 1924, the modernizers persuaded the government to choose the standardized Peking dialect as the standard national language, with a standardized grammar and vocabulary written in Chinese characters. Mandarin then became the official language of China and it was called "National Language". On the other hand, in 1950's the Central Government of The People's Public of China had standardized Chinese characters by two means, first by the reduction in the total number of standardized Chinese characters to around 7,000 commonly used Chinese characters; secondly, by structural simplification of character forms, this gave birth to Simplified Chinese. The educational language of Beijing Dialect and the simplified spoken and written characters form modern standard Chinese, which is, as the name implies, a "universal language". The language now has become the main media and carrier for education and cultural communication for at least one fifth of the people in the world and also an important language in the human history.

III. The Implication of Cultural Symbols

No discussion about Chinese culture is complete and vivid without mentioning of its typical symbols. In this part just a few cultural symbols are to be illustrated to form a general impression of some Chinese legacies and artworks, these symbols have some profound and typical implication on traditional education in the long history.

3.1 The Great Wall

The Great Wall is the most typical cultural symbol of China. Through more than 2,000 years from the seventh century BC to the 16th century AD, 19 dynasties built parts of the Great Wall, adding up to over 20,000 kilometers. With many gaps along the Wall, the section of MuTianYu in Beijing is the best preserved. Although the Great Wall is unmatched in size, quality and difficulty in building, it is considered a symbol of Chinese culture that yearns for peace. Suffering from the devastating damage of wars, people realized that building a wall to protect lives was better than burying the dead in trenches. The construction of the Great Wall was extremely hard labor, sometimes even at the cost of life itself. Compared with bloody wars, however, people would rather choose the former. Thus the Great Wall was built with the basic goal of safeguarding peace. It represented Chinese people's longing for a peaceful life, and it did play a significant role in history. The cultural value of the Great Wall includes the labor and wisdom of the Chinese people to defend peace, the vitality and essence of human beings as an objective object. It also includes the identity as a cultural symbol existing in the collective memory of the Chinese people, the indomitable spirit of the Chinese nation and the characteristics of the Chinese civilization, even today, the existence of the Great Wall is also a lasting symbol and reminder for its peace–loving citizens and educators home and abroad.

3.2 The Temple of Heaven

The Temple of Heaven located in Yongdingmen inner Street, is the world's largest temple complex, composed of three altar walls, five groups of buildings, nine altar doors, forming a grand pattern of the south and north circle, with the solemn manner of "Cangbi temple to heaven", it is another symbol of Chinese tradition. Careful visitors will notice the centripetal structures of the two main buildings, the Circular Mound Altar and the Hall of Prayer for Good Harvests. This type of architecture gives one a sense of reaching up to heaven while ascending the steps. When you ascend the steps to the altar, no matter from which of the four directions, you find yourself entering a centripetal world. On the top tier, you find a round stone at the center that represents the heart of Heaven and is aptly called "Heavenly Heart Stone". The tablet representing heaven was placed on this stone when the emperor offered oblations on the Winter Solstice. Ancient Chinese believed that people could communicate with heaven, and the Temple of Heaven was built to enable this. When you stand inside the outer wall of the Imperial Vault of Heaven, and speak into the wall, a friend farther away along the wall can hear your voice; it's like talking to people on the phone. This phenomenon, due to the much shorter length of the sound waves compared to the radius of the round wall, gave rise to the nickname "echo wall" for the outer rim of the Vault. The echo of sound at the Circular Mound Altar and the Imperial Vault of Heaven is evidence of what our forebears considered to be at the center of the world and communicating with heaven.

3.3 Porcelain

"Porcelain" has the same name as China in English. This proves that people have long known of China's relationship to porcelain. In other words, porcelain is seen as the calling card of Chinese culture, and is of great significance in the history of Chinese civilization. Porcelain was invented by Chinese ancestors on the basis of long–term pottery production. China is one of the earliest countries in the world to make and use pottery, and porcelain is a major and unique invention from China. The data obtained from archaeological excavations prove that as early as about 20,000 years ago, our ancestors began to consciously and purposefully make and use pottery. With the help of modern scientific and technological means, experts in the field of cultural relics museums and science and technology set the time of the invention of porcelain in the Eastern Han Dynasty. Chinese porcelain has been favored by artisans for generations because of its clear color, pure raw materials, elegant design and exquisite production. This calling card represents the crystallization of Chinese culture and the embodiment of the aesthetic pursuits of the Chinese people. Chinese people love crackle ware because they love nature's unique craft. Porcelain is an artificial art, but what it most defies is nothing other than artificiality. Chinese porcelain also pursues painting effects. Porcelain ware usually contains images from landscapes as well as bird–and–flower paintings. Chinese people believe that ultimate beauty is simple and natural; anything that is affected and over–polished runs contradictory to this philosophy. As representative of Chinese porcelain, blue–and–white porcelain displays a world of conciseness and elegance, serenity and purity. Most Chinese porcelain ware embodies the characteristics of Confucian aesthetics. In its pursuit of gentleness and refinement one senses the aesthetic propensities of Confucianism; through its implicit and reserved artistic style one discovers the reserved nature of Confucian aesthetics.

Section Two The Cultural Sources of Educational Philosophy

Philosophy of education is a subject that studies the basic problems of education from philosophical viewpoints and methods. It is a study of the law of education, reality and practice of education for the purpose of cultivating the ideal and desirable human beings. It is also the establishing and shaping of the educational spirit of the time. Therefore, educational philosophy plays an important role in the orientation and development of education. This section will present the cultural sources of Chinese educational philosophy from the perspectives of traditional Chinese philosophy, ethics and basic values. This section will present the cultural sources of Chinese educational philosophy from the perspectives of traditional Chinese philosophy, ethics and basic values.

I. The Philosophy and the Ethic

The position which philosophy has occupied in Chinese cultural education has been regarded as comparable to that of religion in other civilizations. In China, philosophy has been every educated person's concern. In the old days, if a man were educated at all, the first education he received was in philosophy. When children went to school, the Four Books which consist of *the Confucian Analects, the Book of Mencius, the Great Learning, and the Doctrine of the Mean,* were the first ones they were taught to read. The Four Books were the most important texts of Neo–Confucianist philosophy. Sometimes when the children were just beginning to learn the characters, they were given a sort of a textbook to read. This was known as the *Three Characters Classic,* and was so called because each sentence in the book consisted of three characters arranged so that when recited they produced a rhythmic effect, and thus helped the children to memorize them more easily. This book was in reality a primer, and the very first statement in it is that "the nature of man is originally good". This is one of the fundamental ideas of Confucianism philosophy.

People have been accustomed to think that there were three religions in China: Confucianism, Taoism, and Buddhism. But Confucianism, as we have seen, is not a religion. As to Taoism, there is a distinction between Taoism as a philosophy, which is called Tao chia (the Taoist school), and the Taoist religion (Tao chiao). Their teachings are not only different; they are even contradictory. Taoism as a philosophy that teaches the doctrine of following nature, while Taoism as a religion teaches the doctrine of working against nature. For instance, according to Lao Tzu and Chuang Tzu, life followed by death is the course of nature, and man should follow this natural course calmly. But the main teaching of the Taoist religion is the principle and technique of how to avoid death, which is expressly working against nature. The Taoist religion has the spirit of science, which is the conquering of nature. If one is interested in the history of Chinese science, the writings of the religious Taoists will supply much information. As to Buddhism, there is also the distinction between Buddhism as a philosophy, which is called Fo hsiieh (the Buddhist learning), and Buddhism as a religion, which is called Fo chiao (the Buddhist religion). To the educated Chinese, Buddhist philosophy is much more interesting than the Buddhist religion. It is quite common to see both Buddhist monks and Taoist monks simultaneously participating in Chinese funeral services. The Chinese people take even their culture philosophically. At present it is known to many westerners that the Chinese people have been more concerned with the ethic than other people are, this is a core concept in Chinese educational culture. For instance, in one of his articles, "Dominant Ideas in the Formation of Chinese Culture, Professor Derk Bodde says: "They [the Chinese] are not a people for whom religious ideas and activities constitute an all–important and absorbing part of life. It is ethics (especially Confucian ethics), and not religion (at least not religion of a formal, organized type), that provided the spiritual basis in Chinese civilization. All of which, of course, marks a difference of fundamental importance between China and most other major civilizations, in which a church and a priesthood play a dominant role". Chinese people do not had much concern with religion because they have had so much concern with philosophy. They are not religious because they are philosophical. In philosophy they satisfy their craving for what is beyond the present world. In philosophy also they have the super–moral values expressed and appreciated, and in living according to philosophy these super–moral values are experienced.

According to the tradition of Chinese philosophy, its function is not only the increase of positive knowledge (information regarding matters of fact), but the elevation of the mind—a reaching out for what is beyond the present actual world, and for the values that are higher than the moral ones. It was said by the Lao Tzu: "To work on learning is to increase day by day; to work on Tao is to decrease day by day". It shows that in the tradition of Chinese philosophy there is a distinction between working on learning and working on Tao (the Way). The purpose of the former is the increase of positive knowledge, that of the latter is the elevation of the mind. Philosophy belongs in the latter category.

The main spirit of Chinese philosophy is both idealistic and realistic, and very practical, the task of Chinese philosophy is to accomplish a synthesis out of these antitheses. The man who accomplishes this synthesis, not only in theory but also in deed, is the sage. The spiritual achievement of the Chinese sage corresponds to the saints achievement in Buddhism, and in western religion. His character is described as one of "an internal saint and an external king". That is to say, with his inner sageliness as his nature, he accomplishes spiritual cultivation; with his kingliness as his style, he functions in society. It is not necessary that the sage should be the actual head of the government, he is just to be the active role in his society. It is the mission of Chinese education philosophy to develop such a character, with which ethics plays a big part.

II . The Basic Values of Teachings

In the history of Chinese civilization, from the Xia, Shang and Zhou Dynasties to the Qing Dynasty, the traditional Confucianism, Buddhism and Taoism undoubtedly occupied the dominant position of Chinese culture. From the contention of a hundred schools of thoughts in pre–Qin Dynasty to the unification of the First Emperor of Qin who unified and deposed a hundred schools of thoughts and respected Confucianism, until the invasion of the West in modern times, the overall situation with Confucianism, Buddhism and Taoism dominating the ideological situation of Chinese culture and ideology, was basically fixed. The Chinese elite people have been wandering through entering the world, being away from, and abandoning the world. Confucianism governs the world, Buddhism governs the mind, and Taoism governs the body, while obtaining a super stable and balanced state, thus making the lifeblood of Chinese civilization continue along with its basic values.

2.1 Confucianism

Confucianism is defined as the system of ethics, education, and statesmanship taught by Confucius and his disciples, stressing love for humanity, ancestor worship, reverence for parents, and harmony in thought and conduct. It is one of the various schools of pre–Qin philosophy created by Confucius, and gradually developed to a complete Confucianism system. Since then, it dominated the Chinese ancient thoughts and had great influence upon China, Southeast of Asia, or even the world. Confucianism has left Chinese people a rich literary heritage known as the Four Books and Five Classics. For six centuries these texts became the elementary requirements of Chinese education in the feudal society and served as the basis of the civil service examination by which scholars were selected for official posts at various levels of the government. The ethical principle of Confucianism is its discovery of the ultimate in the moral character of human relationships in which Confucius offered the solution for the ills and evils of his day. Confucius' central doctrine is that of the virtue of Ren. Ren is translated variously as goodness, benevolence, humanity, and human–heartedness. In short, Ren means affection and love. Confucius is regarded as The "Great and Revered Teacher", a teacher for all generations. From the dawn of civilization to the Revolution of 1911, he has so deeply influenced the daily life and thought of the Chinese people that he is respected as the moulder of the Chinese mind and character. His thoughts and teaching are taken as the symbol of traditional Chinese culture and national spirit. It can be summed up in these eight words: loyalty and piety, affection and love, faithfulness and righteousness, peace and harmony, as pointed out by Dr. Sun Yat–sen.

2.2 Buddhism

Buddhism is another important source of the Chinese educational philosophy. The Buddhist way of life of peace, loving, kindness and wisdom is just as relevant in Chinese education today as it was in ancient India. Buddha has explained that all our problems and suffering arise from confused and negative states of mind, and that all our happiness and good fortune arise from peaceful and positive states of mind in view of Buddhism, after we die our very subtle mind leaves our body and enters the intermediate state, or 'bardo' in Tibetan. In this subtle dream–like state we experience many different visions that arise from the karmic potentials that activated at the time of our death. These visions may be pleasant or terrifying depending on the karma that ripens. Once these karmic seeds have fully ripened they impel us to take rebirth without choice. Buddhism believes that every action we perform leaves an imprint, or potential, on our very subtle mind, and each karmic potential eventually gives rise to its own effect. Our mind is like a field, and performing actions is like sowing seeds in that field. Positive or virtuous actions sow the seeds of future happiness, and negative or non–virtuous actions sow the seeds of future suffering. This definite relationship between actions and their effects–virtue causing happiness and non–virtue causing suffering – is known as the 'law of karma'. An understanding of the law of karma is the basis of Buddhist morality.The coming of Buddhism to China from India was a great event in the development of Chinese culture and of Buddhism itself. After a long period of assimilation, it established itself as a major system of thought as well as a religious practice, contributing greatly to the enrichment of Chinese philosophy and exercising and enduring influence on the Chinese popular religion and on the mind and character of the Chinese people as well as Chinese education.

2.3 Taoism

Taoism is a native Chinese culture. Like Confucian culture, it has exerted great influence on Chinese people's ideological, political, economic and cultural life. In many ways the doctrines of Confucianism and Taoism complement each other, running side by side like two powerful rivers through later Chinese thought and literature in education. The Taoists made Lao Tzu their supreme god, taking *Dao De Jing* as their cannon, with Zhang Daoling, the founder, as the Sect's Heavenly Teacher. During its popularization since its birth, Taoism had long been a kind of high–level culture, and widely pursued by the upper–class society. Consequently, many leaders of Taoism had gained great respects from the imperial governments. Lao Tzu held that everything was linked with and dependent on one another. Each pair of yes and no, easy and difficult, long and short, etc. was a contrastive unification. If one side didn't exist, there wouldn't be the other. He also asserted that the two opposite sides could be converted. Meanwhile, dissatisfied with the social reality of in–fighting and hard life, he advocated a society of a small country with a small population and no communications with neighboring countries. Many of his viewpoints and principles of life such as the weak overcoming the strong, holding oneself aloof from worldly success, emptying the heart of desire, adopting an easy–going manner, retiring at the height of one's career, being selfless and modest, etc. have exerted great influence on the Chinese mind and education and have been applied to politics, economy, military affairs, culture, business, and social intercourse.

Confucianism, Buddhism and Taoism are the foundation and lifeblood of Chinese civilization and it is a basic narrative for exchanges and mutual learning among human civilizations. The international dissemination of Confucianism, Buddhism and Taoism is a new cultural approach for introducing Chinese culture to the world. The essence of the thinking of the three teachings can be summarized with the key words in following table: It can be seen that although the traditional thoughts of Confucianism, Buddhism and Taoism have different focuses, the viewpoints of benevolence and harmony, positive pursuit of goodness, harmony in the world and in diversity, and the unity of heaven and man all reflect the value pursuit and spiritual realm of the Chinese nation in a similar way, while highlighting the distinctive Chinese character and wisdom.

Tab.1 The Essence of the Thinking of the Three Teachings

The Teachings / The Parameters	Confucianism	Buddhism	Taoism
The Nature	The Spirit of Gumption	The Determination of Devotion	The Respect of Natural Regularity
The Tenet	Benevolence, Righteousness, Courtesy, Wisdom and Trust	Abstain from All Evil and Pursue All Good Conducts	Self-cultivation and Being Free from Vulgarity
Outlook on Life	Keep Active, Strive for Achievement.	Love All Creatures and Devote Selflessly	Take the Course of Nature and Improve Oneself
Outlook on World	The World is a Stage for Talents	The World is a Reflection of One's Inner-world,Good or Evil	The World is a Harmonious Realm for Human and Nature
Core Values	Self-fulfillment in Creation	Purify the Mind and Verify the Causality in Self-devotion	Integration of Nature with a Perfect Self
Philosophical Tendency	The Worldly Philosophy	The Philosophy with Worldly Means and Etherealv Minds	The Ethereal Philosophy

Section Three The Evolution and Features of Education in China

According to the statistics of Chinese educational cyclicity, the education industry in ancient time already had its climax one after another. The lasting tradition transferred to the modern mode at the end of Qing Dynasty. Tang and song dynasties saw the two peaks in China's ancient education history. However, since the beginning of modern times , education development in China has been influenced more by western systems and thoughts.

I. The Historical Traces

The historical trace of Chinese education is actually a condensed picture of the development of Chinese culture in the long history. The formation of educational culture is always the product of a certain era and history, and can only be truly understood if it is placed in the historical time and space at that time.

1.1 The General Context

In the early period of Qin Dynasty, Confucius and Mencius laid the foundation of Confucianism education in China. Contention of a hundred schools of thought led by Confucianism and supplemented by other cultivation formed a basic system of education in China. In the late period of Warring States, Xuncius comprehensively summarized the educational thought of Confucianism while adopting the rationalism from Legalism, his efforts in teaching paved the way for the renaissance of Confucianism in period of the Western Han Dynasty. Initiated by Dong Zhongshu and other scholars, the imperial court set up the educational policy of "Worshiping Confucianism Only". Since then the leading position of Confucianism education had been kept till the end of Qing Dynasty. Due to the efforts of scholars of Neo–Confucianism , Confucianism education reached a climax in Song Dynasty. In the period of Wei and Jin Dynasties, Metaphysics learned from Confucianism and Taoism , its features of naturalism and individual–respecting affected the minds of learners and educators in the Northern and Southern Dynasties as well as Sui and Tang Dynasties, thus changed the position of Confucianism to some extent. The education at that time appeared to be diversified and colorful. Since its introduction to China in the Eastern Han dynasty, Buddhism was gradually accepted by intellectual circles, and its popularity reached its peak in Sui and Tang Dynasties. Due to the spreading and efforts of scholars in Sui and Tang Dynasties, the metaphysical thought of Confucianism and Taoism were well adopted by Neo–Confucianists in Song and Ming Dynasties, and perfectly integrated into the Confucius educational thoughts. With the eastward transmission of western sciences, some Confucius scholars with wide perspective automatically adjusted their minds and advocated the tradition of studying for application,and presented the educational doctrine of pragmatism, thus preparing for the period of transformation to modern education in China. However, the Neo–Confucianists who stressed the traditional ethics–centered education still had great influence, so that the modernization of education in China was confronted with many obstacles. The complete modernization of education in China was actually one century late than the western countries. The outbreak of the first Opium War in 1840 and the establishment of the Peking Institute (the Imperial College of Translators) in 1862 are regarded as the mark of the beginning of the modern history of Chinese education. The first modern school in China appeared in 1862, the new educational system was established in early 20th century. The popularization of natural and social science education happened just after the new educational system was established in 1922, for the various features of modern education was increasingly seen in China. The educational modernization in China was passively completed in a haste, the historical situation was quite different from that in western countries.

1.2 The Important Stages

The development of Chinese education has experienced some important stages. The first period is the primitive education, which is connected with people's labors. The ancient texts have recorded the religious activities and totem worshiping, which were inherited by education. The end of the clan society witnessed the appearance of school education of "family learning" , but such schools were monopolized by the clans. The second period saw the development of Chinese characters and schools. The earliest characters found in China were inscriptions on bones and shells and later on bronze wares. There are also inscriptions on bamboo slips, wooden slips and on cloth and silk. The invention and application of paper in Eastern Han Dynasty and art of printing in the 11th century exerted great influence on the development of school education. According to the classic books, the earliest schools were called "Yang" "Xu" "Xiao", the school system appeared at the end of clan society and the early time of slave society. The third period began when the private schools were originated by confucius, who set up private school and enrolled students to teach poetry, calligraphy, rites and music. He also brought his students to tour the various countries as a huge teaching group in late spring and autumn period. After the dynasties of Warring States, Qing, Han,Wei and Qin, the private schools boasted new development. Apart from the secular schools, there were private religious schools of Buddhism and Taoism. After Tang and Song Dynasties, the private schools were diversified with more styles and names, and held an important position in the educational history of China. What is worth noticing is that though the Chinese education also changed with the changing dynasties, the policy of "respecting Confucianism only" had not changed since the Western Han Dynasty till facing the impact of the modern time. The fourth period began with the establishment of imperial examination system, it is a combined system of human resource selection and education. The imperial examination system was set up in Sui and Tang Dynasties, it gave ordinary people the opportunities of becoming a government official through examinations and motivated the people for active learning and formed a tradition of attaching importance to education. On the other hand, it enforced the style of scholasticism and rigidified the school education. The fifth period started with the influence of the westernization movement and the modernization movement. Since China was forced to open its gate by the Opium Wars, the ruling class has gradually recognized China's situation of lagging behind western countries in military, science, economics and education, they began to advocate the westernization movement with "taking western technique for practice on the basis of Chinese traditional culture and knowledge" as its guiding doctrine. For the first time, China set up foreign schools, mainly foreign language schools, industrial schools and military schools, and sent the first batch of overseas students. The modernization movement in late 19th century was initiated by intellectuals with bourgeoisie innovation thoughts. They called for the abolition of imperial examination system, the innovation of educational mode, the introduction of western science and technology and the cultivation of practical talents. The abolition of imperial examination system and the popularization of modern schools were the results of such movements. In 1905, the imperial examination system which had a history of 1300 years was finally abolished, the western educational system and the content of science and technology were introduced in China. The sixth period came with the impact of the May 4th movement. The slogan of science and democracy shook the traditional education of feudalism. The modern vernacular Chinese became the teaching language in schools, the education process was approachable in view of daily lives of people, thus paved the way for the popularization of mass education. The plebeian education movement was carried out, the equal right for male and female in education was advocated, the scientific education methods were praised, these social movements all dramatically changed the educational tradition in China. Ever since the foundation of the People's Republic of China, many reformations have taken place in education field, specially since the opening up policy was implemented in 1978, the educational reform and development in China has been in a new period, the educational tradition with the new Chinese style is coming into being. In the course of the development of Chinese education, the traditional philosophy with its unique views of political education, unity of moral and intellectual education and inner cultivation orientation has been continuously created and innovated and exists in the modern education in a changed form. It has a huge and profound impact on the development and characteristics of Chinese education.

II. The Traditional Characteristics

What the Chinese educators has stressed since ancient time are affinities and harmony, instead of the cultivation of creativity. Therefore, the educational thoughts and systems in different times are inclusive ,connected and inherited. The educational tradition and climax are continuous and lasting. On the other hand, there existed weakness in the educational mechanism, making it copying itself instead of improving itself, and finally resulted in the confrontation with many obstacles in transmission and reformation. Like other Chinese culture tradition, education in China has diachronic changes in its development. However, while being compared with other countries, there are synchronic characteristics that are inherited and connected in Chinese education tradition, they can be summarized as below:

The first is the unification of the politics and the education. The most obvious feature of this is the combination of education and talent selection, which is reflected in the imperial examination system. Such a system enrolled and distributed official positions according to the result of unified examination. Such a tradition was even typical in revolutionary base area, the education focused on cadre training, the students in schools are both learners and leaders, and enjoyed the treatment of state civil servants. The second is the ethic–centered tradition. Chinese culture is guided by moral philosophy, it also applies to education in which the morality and self–cultivation is highly stressed. For a long time,"self–cultivating, family regulating, state ordering and governing the great land perfectly" was the supreme ideal in Chinese education career, which held great humanistic spirit and stressed the social functions of teaching. The third is the classic texts–oriented tradition, technology was long ignored. This is closely related with the ethic–centered tradition. Historically, school education in China attached importance to political tactics, the knowledge of production skills was hardly concentrated, such tradition directly impeded the development of scientific technology in China, and still hinders the improvement of vocational and technical education today. The fourth is the concentration of scholastic teaching of classic knowledge. Rote learning has been the mainstream method in traditional teaching, as described in an old saying:"If one read the three hundred Tang poems over and over again, you will be able to chant some of them at least" . Such a method might be helpful in consolidating the basic knowledge, but it is to the disadvantage of cultivating critical thinking and creativity. The fifth is the tradition of respect for teachers. For the long history of attaching great importance to education, Chinese people hold the tradition of respecting the teachers. In China, there has been the tradition of "regarding the teacher as a parent even if one has been taught for just one day", meaning the teacher should be respected as a parent. The well–known"Essay On Teachers" from the famous scholar Han Yu in Tang Dynasty summarized the missions of a teacher as "propagating doctrines, imparting professional knowledge and resolving doubts", while emphasizing the teacher's dignity. This everlasting tradition of respecting teachers is undeniably influenced by the educational value of Chinese people. In short, the Chinese educational tradition has the characteristics of the combination of politics and education, non–religious orientation, moral cultivation, inheritance of the classics, respecting for teachers and teaching, etc., and there are also deficiencies worthy of reflection, such as separation from production, neglecting technological creation and old–fashioned indoctrination.

Culture is the carrier of national spirit, and education is the driving force of national progress. Understanding the characteristics of Chinese educational and cultural traditions is conducive to cultivating the consciousness of blending educational and cultural reference under the background of education globalization competition. And it is of importance to constantly reflect and forge ahead for generating new impetus for the educational and cultural development.

Chapter Three The Cultural Characters of Institutes in China

Since the end of the 20th century, the academic world in China began the research on cultural characters of institutes. Here the institutes mostly refer to academic and education institutions and universities. Meanwhile, the topic of "cultural characters of Chinese institutes" involves Chinese culture, educational history, and spirits of university, theories on school management and other concepts. The achievement from researchers in this field has presented colorful perspectives for a profound understanding of educational culture in China.

Section One The Basic Structure of Chinese Institutes

The basic structure of Chinese institutes here mainly refers to the school education in the social system. From the Jixia Academy in the Warring States Period to various schools of basic education and institutions of higher learning in modern society, the basic structure of Chinese institutions of higher learning reflects not only the educational system of Chinese society, but also the ideological changes in educational culture.

I. The Educational System and the Chinese Institutes

The basic concept of Chinese institutes here refers to the school education in society. The educational system in Chinese history has experienced several transitions. At the early period of feudal society, the ruling class began to build and run schools for cultivating their supporters and assistants, with the process and purpose of talent selection and official admission.

In Han Dynasty, the selection system was separated from and paralleled with school education. Since the Sui and Tang Dynasties, the imperial examination system gradually took the place of selection and recommendation system, so that schools became the dependency of the examination system. After Song Dynasty, for the nominal nature of the official institutes, private schools were increasingly popular, academies of classical learning coexisted with the imperial institutes. The private academies are the specific organization of cultural education, it is a certain result from the cultural accumulation, research and creation around book collection and correction, writing and inscription, reading and teaching by Chinese ancient scholars. The private academies are also the traditional place for education activities and research communication. The form of traditional academies is both the combination of high and basic education, and also the outcome of the integration of exam–oriented and quality–oriented education, the result of the cooperation of official institutes and the private schools.

The classic academies have existed for more than a thousand years, and were the gathering place for scholars to pursue their studies. The original purpose of academies in China was to cultivate scholars and literati, to transform social traditions, to civilize village people and to harmonize the society, therefore academies in China held great social functions.

In the history of China, the educational institutes and system belong to the superstructure, and is the outcome of certain historical era. When the function of social mechanism (the state/the folk elite/the society) was lost in modern times, the educational modernization in China as an agricultural country was slow in a separated and fragmented way, so was the way of institutes. The institutes established for enriching the country and increasing its military force have experienced a long process of development from "taking western technique for practice on the basis of Chinese traditional culture and knowledge" to "acting completely on international convention". Just as what Professor Ji Xianlin said: The Chinese educational tradition which originated from the imperial colleges (Tai Xue) in feudal China to imperial academy (Guo Zijian) to imperial university and finally to the modern university, is continuous and coherent. From the perspective of development process of Chinese universities, they are formed and built in the inclusive assimilation of Chinese culture from the very beginning, and are still influenced deeply by Chinese culture. It is reasonable to say that the Chinese culture generated and gestated the universities in China, and they are essentially the very existence of the Chinese culture.

II. The Educational Culture in Chinese Institutes

The forming of the educational culture in Chinese institutes is correlated with "the view of high education" in Chinese culture. The view of high education here refers to the basic thoughts and concepts in Chinese culture, these are the soul of the classic education in ancient China. The ancient concepts of high education mostly originated from Confucianism. The cultural origin of Chinese institutes is "learning to be oneself" that taking human as the center of logic. Human refers to the learner himself, or "ego". The concept of "ego" is different from the individuality in western culture. On the contrary it aims at achieving the extreme selflessness: the absolute perfection, quite in line with "self–cultivating, family regulating, state ordering and great land governing"."Learning to be oneself" lies in taking learning as the fundamental principle, taking learning as the fundamental principle depends on educating people with virtues, and educating people with virtues is for serving the society. In other words, the basic purpose of education is the the ethic and academic achievement, however the ethic education has to be based on the social functions, which is the center concept of Chinese traditional education philosophy, it originated from Confucius and guided the school culture for a long history. During the Southern Song Dynasty, the avocation from Zhu Xi and other scholars made the philosophy a universal concept. The outlet of the educational culture in Chinese institutes is "officialdom for good scholars", a culture of talent education for the government and society. If "learning to be oneself" in *The Analects* focuses on the happiness of learning and loftiness of one's character that reflecting the artistic beauty of education, then "officialdom for good scholars" is a practical technology facing the reality, an outlet for scholars that learning for oneself. It is true that officialdom for good scholars became popular since Confucius teaching, but the fixation and institutionalization of officialdom for good scholars was attributed to the imperial examination system and its educational institutes. The supreme ideal of educational culture in Chinese institutes is to illustrate virtue; to renovate the people; and to pursue the highest excellence. In *On the History of Chinese High Education*, Professor Tu Youguang concluded that the philosophy of *Great Learning* is the law of ancient Chinese high education. Being called as law means it is followed and kept by educators through the history of Chinese ancient high education. Since the universities were set in modern times, countless scholars have tried to annotate the philosophy of Chinese high institutes based on the Great Learning Philosophy, focusing on illustrating virtue and renovate the people so as to stress the ethical education and social functions.

To sum up, the educational culture in traditional Chinese institutes is based on "learning to be oneself" to demonstrate the ethicality, taking the outlet of "officialdom for good scholars" to meet its practicability, and keeping the ideal of "illustrating virtue, renovating the people and pursuing the highest excellence" to greatly show its transcendentality. Therefore, the traditional Chinese institutes regard virtues, practicability and goodness as the priority for education. Without doubt, the neglect of materials and technology, the side–effect of lacking of system construction is also obvious.

Section Two The Cultural Evolution of Chinese Modern Universities

It is observed from the traditional culture of Chinese institutes that among the three teachings, Confucianism is the one that has the biggest impact on the forming of cultural characters and spirits in traditional education. The changes of modern society and cultune also have a great impact on the culture spirit of universities.

I. The Spiritual Guidance of Confucianism

In the process of pursuing world–class universities, Chinese institutions do not want to lose their "individuality" in order to pursue "commonality" and lose their cultural foundation. Therefore, Confucian culture has become the spiritual symbol of safeguarding cultural identity in the cultural change of contemporary Chinese universities.

1.1 Core Position

Internationalization and localization are the two ends of the balance in the process of continuous advancement of universities in modern society. Internationalization is the accelerator of university progress, while localization is the steering wheel of university progress. The concept of a world–class university reflects the norms and values of the leading research universities in the world, especially those in the United States and Western Europe. In the pursuit of world–class education, Chinese universities do not want to lose their individuality in pursuit of commonness and thus lose the cultural traditions.Today, the talent view of Chinese universities is in line with the Confucianism advocated by Confucius, and university culture is often inspired by the wisdom of Confucianism in traditional culture. Contemporary liberal education is not only an idea of university education, but also a mode of talent cultivation. Its goal is to cultivate a complete person with broad vision, comprehensive understanding, humanistic spirits and graceful feeling. Its spiritual guidance is coherent with the key concept of Confucianism, in inheriting the doctrines of "self–cultivation; family regulating; state–governing; world–harmonizing" it has been regarded as the classic thought for its dual meaning of self–actualization and social responsibility. From the fact that classics of Lao Tzu and the *Analects of Confucius* are still required to read among contemporary college students, we can see that Confucianism is still of great significance today. The concept of "universal harmony" in Confucianism mentioned in the previous section not only contributes to the talent cultivation in universities, but also will make special contributions to the peace and development of human society. As a concept of integrated meaning, it contains at least four levels: the harmony in nature, the harmony between human and nature the harmony among human beings, the harmony between man and himself physically and mentally. The four levels of "universal harmony" are still the gist of modern general education and social life in China.

1.2 The Cultural Essentials

The traditional culture represented by the Confucian civilization has never been absent in the humanistic education of Chinese universities. Confucianism not only pays attention to self–cultivation, but also emphasizes "the great impact of education in civilizing people into good tradition and customs". Obviously, the primary task of Confucian education is to teach humanistic culture. Under the background of educational globalization, whether it is in the disputes between instrumental rationality and humanism in university culture, or in the choices between educating people or improving techniques, Confucian culture has undoubtedly provided spiritual coordinates for all–round development of human beings. In addition, traditional Confucianism is the source of Chinese university culture; In such tradition , the personality of a scholar, the values and the practice of the values are embodied by a stable Taoist style, and demonstrated with the doctrines of "benevolence, righteousness, propriety, wisdom and trustworthiness", this has become the internal gene of Chinese intellectuals and university spirit passed down from generation to generation. Such a culture requires intellectuals not only to improve themselves, but also to have a broad mind and actively spread the university culture and educate the people around them. As the saying goes,"a scholar should aim at the path of enlightenment and benefit the world", which shows that the spirit of a university should not be closed and selfish, but open and beneficial. This is not only the traditional ideology of scholars for thousands of years in China, it also plays an important role in shaping the spirit of Chinese universities in successive dynasties as the earliest spiritual source of contemporary Chinese universities. Many universities have extracted the spiritual values from the Confucian culture in forming the university spirit with its own characteristics. The spiritual coordinates of this Confucian tradition with Tao as its center while taking "benevolence, righteousness, propriety, wisdom and trustworthiness" as its creed can be shown in the figure below:

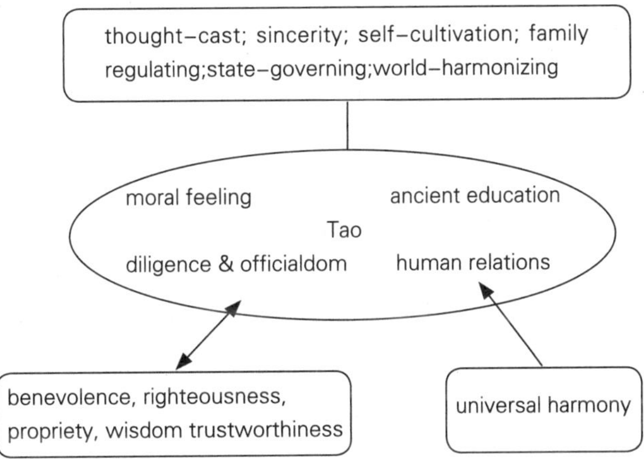

Fig. 1 The Spiritual Guidance of Confucianism

II. The Connotation Evolution of University Spirit

The evolution of Chinese university spirit is inseparable from the development of local education and culture. In the process of the rise and fall of state power, the traditional Confucian elite's sense of social responsibility was stimulated. In the modern Chinese context, it is not difficult to find that the university spirit integrated with western culture can also find its source in traditional Chinese culture.

2.1 Main Contents

The university in the modern sense originated from Europe in the Middle Ages, but a longitudinal study of China's ancient education will find that although the ancient Chinese society did not have the form of a university in the modern sense, it did have the reality of a university in the modern sense. The Jixia Academy in the State of Qi in the Warring States Period, the Imperial College in the Han Dynasty and the academies established by the Imperial College in the Tang Dynasty are all ancient Chinese universities, which were responsible for the inheritance and development of traditional Chinese culture. For more than two thousand years, they have acquired the spirit of a university in the modern sense. China's traditional cultural education has always paid more attention to social and ethical relations, and The "moral integrity" of the ancient Imperial School of China has also influenced the modern sense of university. After the Opium War, Chinese and western cultures began to exchange and conflict on a large scale. The traditional spirit of "taking the world as their own responsibility" became undoubtedly the rich source of the spirit of Chinese universities under the modern and humiliating situation, which is exactly in line with Mencius's "thrive in calamity". Under the guidance of "traditional Chinese values aided with modern western technology" China's higher education began to learn and imitate the western countries in a comprehensive way. In the process of the exchange and integration of Chinese and western cultures, Chinese universities gradually formed the university spirit with Chinese characteristics. It can be seen from the above elaboration that Confucian culture is the spirit of Chinese traditional universities. The main spiritual connotation and evolution of Chinese university education is embodied with the ideas of "moral supremacy" "autonomous spirit" "free administration""compatibility" "national spirit" "democracy and science".

2.2 Evolution Process

Influenced by Confucian culture, the essence of ancient university education and academy education in China lies in The "understanding of human ethics", that is, to make students understand and abide by various ethical norms among people in the feudal society. Modern Chinese universities actively absorb western education thoughts and draw lessons from western educational experience while still placing moral education in an important position. The spirit of autonomy is one of the main spirits of modern universities, which originated from western medieval universities. In fact, the spirit of autonomy has long existed in ancient Chinese universities. The academies that sprouted in the late Tang Dynasty, formed in the Five Dynasties, and became powerful in the Song Dynasty were mostly founded by the folk organizations, and the economy and management were relatively independent. The heads, deans and lecturers of those colleges came from the public, their genuine ability and knowledge were attached to great importance. There was a rule that if one is not qualified for the position, he will be replaced on a quarterly basis, which reflected the obvious spirit of autonomy. In the early days of the establishment of modern university system in China, Tsinghua University only took ten years to become a world–renowned university after the establishment of the undergraduate department in 1925. The most important reason is the independence of the university and the faculty governance, which are the lifeblood of modern universities. The spirit of freedom and compatibility in universities is a necessary condition for the development of modern higher education. In China, this spirit was first embodied in the Jixia Academy of the State of Qi in the Warring States Period, which was the earliest institution of higher education in the history of Chinese education that carried out free lecturing and independent running of schools. Later private schools and academies inherited the fine tradition of freedom and compatibility, carried out the open–up policy and advocated free lecturing. This spirit was the most prominent in the reform of Peking University in modern times. The national spirit with patriotism as the core is the core cultural tradition of the Chinese nation. The principles said by Mencius that "Neither riches nor honors can corrupt him; neither poverty nor humbleness can make him swerve from principle; and neither threats nor forces can subdue him" are followed by ancient universities. While inheriting Chinese culture, ancient Chinese academies also had a strong national spirit. The main feature of Bailuzhou Academy, which nurtured the national hero Wen Tianxiang, is to honor the past sages and cultivate integrity. In the Ming Dynasty, the motto of "I hear the sounds of the wind, the rain and the reading, I care for the things of my home, my country and the world" has still been widely read and appreciated. The national spirit of modern Chinese universities was formed along with the patriotic movement of saving the nation from extinction, which was mainly manifested by the consciousness of social distress and social participation arising from the strong sense of social responsibility and mission. The fate of Peking University, Tsinghua University and Sun Yat–sen University in modern times has been closely linked with the rise and fall of the nation, which is an example of the national spirit of Chinese universities. Both the concepts of science and democracy were introduced from the west in modern China. Therefore, the spirit of science and democracy in Chinese universities has been gradually formed and developed along with the development of modern history of China. After the eastward transmission of western sciences in the late Qing Dynasty, western ideas of democracy and science began to enter the country. Kang Youwei, Liang Qichao, and Tan Sitong as leaders of the Reform Movement, introduced and publicized the western idea of civil rights and sciences. As the first person who systematically introduced western thoughts, Yan Fu, a thinker and translator, made the most remarkable achievements in the process of publicizing democracy and science. He partly paved the way for the May 4th New Culture Movement. With democracy and science as two banners, the May 4th New Culture Movement inherited and surpassed its predecessors to a great extent. In 1906, Zhao Tianlin, the president of Beiyang University, proposed the school motto of "seeking truth from facts", which is also the most direct embodiment of the pursuit of scientific spirit.

On the basis of inheriting the core cultural tradition of the Chinese nation and the experience of running a school in ancient times, modern universities in China have gradually developed by absorbing and integrating western culture and school management ideas. At the same time, modern Chinese universities were under the background of great powers' aggression, social turbulence, regime changes and social reforms. The party–oriented education of the Kuomintang government before new China; socialist transformation of university model in line with Soviet Union at the beginning period of new China; the ten–year Cultural Revolution as an unprecedented catastrophe are all the the main restraining factors for the spiritual development of Chinese universities. Therefore, in a hundred years of time, Chinese universities have experienced three transitions: referring to the American higher education model, comprehensive copying of the former Soviet Union model , and building the spirit of institutions of higher learning with Chinese characteristics by referring to the experience of universities of various countries. It is particularly important to deal with the relationship between inheriting and innovating; university autonomy and the national will as well as the balance between localization and internationalization.

Section Three The Cultural Concepts of Famous Universities

The famous universities in a region not only bear the responsibility of cultivating talents, but also represent the cultural concepts of a locality and lead the direction of future education. Prestigious universities often show their cultural values through masters and pass on their educational styles and ideals through special cultural symbols. This section will briefly review the historical footprints of some famous Chinese university presidents and the typical cultural symbols of some well known universities.

I. The Footprints of Prestigious Presidents

Famous universities are often associated with the glittering names of presidents. It is the same in China as in other countries. It is like Cai Yuanpei to Peking University, Mei Yiqi to Tsinghua University, Zhu Kezhen to Zhejiang University, and Guo Bingwen to Southeast University. They are all like stars in the night sky. Under their advocacy, great changes have taken place in China's higher education from thought to practice. They were active in innovation, pioneering and enterprising, leaving a strong cultural feature and rich practical experience for the development of China's higher education.

1.1 Cai Yuanpei

Cai Yuanpei once said: the universities shall boast classic works and great scholars. In many universities, idealism and the materialism co–existed in philosophy , romanticism and realism keep pace with each other in art and literature, the inculcation and free styles are both seen in teaching, the theories of motivation and utility are paralleled in ethics, and optimism and pessimism are both accepted in cosmology, this is the general principle of freedom of thought, and the reason why universities are so called. When he was president of Peking University, Cai Yuanpei employed teachers based on their academic attainments and merits. As long as the teacher has a high academic level, other worldly conditions are not important. He took six "Regardless of..." as his principles: regardless of faction; regardless of age; regardless of educational background; regardless of seniority; regardless of nationality and regardless of political views. Thanks to his efforts, Peking University at that time gathered a number of national first–class scholars. In liberal arts, Chen Duxiu was appointed director of literature science, working with other faculty members including Li Dazhao, Lu Xun, Hu Shi, Qian Xuantong, Liu Bannong, Shen Yinmo and the like. In disciplines of science, Xia Yuan, Li Siguang, Yan Renguang, Ren Hongjun and Li Shuhua, who were famous physicists at that time, were selected.

1.2 Mei Yiqi

When Mei Yiqi was the president of Tsinghua University, he announced that a university should be set up for two purposes: one is to gain knowledge, the other is to cultivate talents. He believed that the so-called great universities are not about having big buildings, but about owning great scholars. He showed respect to his teachers by practice and was highly respected by his professors. During Mei Yiqi's term of office in Tsinghua University and when he led Southwest Associated University, he tried every means to recruit more talents and improve the treatment of professors, so that a galaxy of talents gathered in Tsinghua campus, among them are Chen Yinque, Zhao Yuanren, Zhu Ziqing, Wen Yiduo and Qian Zhongshu, as well as Feng Youlan, Jin Yuelin, Wu Han, Li Da, Zhang Dainian and other masters of the social sciences.There are also Xiong Qinglai, Ma Daqiu, Hua Luogeng, Qian Weichang, Qian Xuesen, Zhou Peiyuan, Liang Sicheng, the founders of mathematics, natural science and engineering science.

1.3 Kwok Bingwen

When he was the president of Southeast University, Kwok Bingwen advocated the balancing of four aspects in running a school, among which the balance between humanities and science included equal treatment of all kinds of academic ideas and the advocation of academic freedom. At that time, Nanjing was still under the rule of warlords, but in Nanjing higher normal school, professors could openly introduce all kinds of new thoughts and theories, not only socialist Marxism, but also the Three People's Principles, National Reformism, thus forming a situation of coexistence and free contention of a hundred schools of thought. At the same time he developed and perfected the training policy of "three aspects of education" and advocated improving simultaneously the students' talent, body, spirit, moral and knowledge by virtue, intellectual, and physical education. In particular, he advocated to develop students' thinking and application ability as the standard, help students gain both general knowledge and specialized skills, so as to achieve a balance between generalists and specialists.

1.4 Jiang Menglin

After Jiang Menglin succeeded as the president of Peking University, he still insisted on the principle of academic freedom. He claimed that the university was set up for the study of higher learning, so freedom of thought should be the standard. The famous "controversy of science and mystery" further proves his idea of maintaining academic freedom. He requested that various committees, such as the administrative council, academic affairs office and general affairs office, be set up under the president. Its core is to continue to adhere to the principle of professor governance, supplemented by a sound organization. He presided over the formulation of the *University Organization Law*, which still reaffirmed the democratic management of professors.

1.5 Zhu Kezhen

When Zhu Kezhen was president of Zhejiang University, he made a good research on the educational system and educational ideals of ancient and modern times, China and other countries. He advocated all–round development of students, emphasizing not only moral education, but also intellectual education and physical education. He proposed to train students to be generalists with high faith, law–abiding spirit and healthy body. He has always advocated a generalist education, believing that college education not only gives students comprehensive knowledge, but more importantly cultivates students' various abilities.

II. The Culture Symbols of Famous Universities

Since its birth, Chinese institutions of higher learning have developed under the influence of moral education, which was stipulated by the educational purpose of the Ministry of Education at that time, which called for "The emphasis on moral education, the supporting of utilitarian and military education, and the aesthetic education as the supplementary part for morality". The tenet of the university as imparting profound academic knowledge, cultivating talents with great knowledge, and meeting the demands of the nation in *The Principle of Higher Learning* basically settled the main direction of Chinese universities. The cultural symbols of traditional elite schools that have developed since modern times are considered to be embodied in the school–running philosophy, campus scenery and students' feelings. Let's take the following universities as the examples.

2.1 Peking University

Peking University, is formerly known as the National Peking University in 1912 with Yan Fu as its first president and later Cai Yuanpei as his successor. During the May 4th Movement, Peking University became famous as a new cultural center, it witnessed historical changes over the past hundred years after several brilliant periods. Peking University's traditional educational philosophy is to engage in politics and encourage patriotism, and to enlist all schools of academy. Through the practice of generations of Peking University students, the spirit of Peking University has been further developed and interpreted by the cultural character of "the world is for the public and great virtue is for the growth". From the perspective of campus scenery, Peking University has always been known as the university next to the imperial palace. From the Red mansion to the Beach and to the library, the buildings of old Peking University are antique and exude a unique temperament of classical culture. Even after moving to Yan Garden, what remains unchanged is still the charm of its unique royal architectural style. The scene of "The watchtower with double wings in the cloudy imperial city, and the crowded city and spring trees in a rainy day" might be the unique cultural symbol of Peking University. Peking University is a blend of the free–flowing traditional Chinese academies and the highly academic German universities of the late 19th century. People may feel the open and inclusive spirit and feelings rooted in Chinese culture from the first building with modern sanitary and hot water equipment, to the student uniform of the campus life, and finally to the fashion of traditional robes.

2.2 Tsinghua University

Tsinghua University was formerly known as Tsinghua Xuetang, a preparatory school for students studying in the United States. It was funded by the Boxer Indemnity returned by the United States. From imitating the colonization cultural character of the United States at the beginning to adding Chinese cultural elements, Cao Yunxiang and Luo Jialun established the direction of basing the university on the Chinese cultural foundation in the process of the integration of Chinese and western cultures. Finally, the two ideas of the school management were highlighted: Attaching great importance to sports and showing great respect to excellent scholars while combining eastern and western cultures. To trace the cultural symbols of Tsinghua University is just like what the song of the university has expressed: On the one hand, to integrate the east and the west; the past and the present; on the other hand, to stand by virtue without questioning the social background. Its campus culture contains the traditional Chinese spirit of great harmony, the spirit of unremitting self–improvement and the spirit of pursuing knowledge. The monuments in its campus scenery are seen as distinctive. The typical ones are the 3.18 Broken Stele and the Wang Guowei Monument. The 3.18 Broken Stele at the foot of the north hill of Tsinghua University is made from a remnant of white marble columns. It was built to commemorate the death of Wei Jiesan during a patriotic demonstration. His last words were:"My heart is quite relieved, but when is the time for China to get stronger?" Tsinghua is always proud of its students with patriotic spirit. The Wang Guowei Monument is located at the foot of the hill behind Qinghua Garden. The inscription was written by Professor Chen Yinke. The monument erected by Tsinghua University for the late Qing Dynasty legacy scholar of Chinese culture, it shows that its campus culture respects the master and maintains the personality of independent spirit and free thought even in the period of party education.The campus life of Tsinghua students is characterized by distinctive spirit of sports and self–discipline. Student rules are an essential part of campus life, all aspects related to the students' daily life, classes, learning, rewards and punishments need to be within the scope of the management regulations, and the elimination rate of the students is high. Although the Tsinghua campus lacks the free atmosphere of Chinese ancient academies, it reflects the strict spirit of the traditional imperial examination system.

2.3 Southwest Associated University

Southwest Associated University was a university that started and ended with the Anti–Japanese War. After the July 7th Incident, the national Peking University, Tsinghua University and the private Nankai University were moved to Changsha and Kunming respectively, renamed the National Southwest Associated University, and became a university with an independent spirit and cultural character until its disintegration in 1946. The school philosophy of Southwest Associated University is based on Chinese culture while seeking to integrate Chinese and western culture. In addition, attaching importance to the gaol of higher education, practicing of general education is a concrete interpretation of the cultural character of "Great virtue and practical knowledge" in Southwest Associated University. The campus scenery of Southwest Associated University is often associated with the monument of National Southwest Associated University on which Feng Youlan composed inscription when the three universities were separated. The inscription describes the history of the university, praises the spirit of Associated University, and traces the traditional significance of Chinese culture. The inscription clearly approves the Chinese culture, attributing the victory of the Anti–Japanese War to the long history of China, and attributing the inclusive spirit of the Southwest Associated University to the democratic essence of Chinese culture. In view of the campus scenery, the phenomenon of teachers and students traveling together is another campus cultural symbol of the University. Zhao Ruihong has talked about the phenomenon with the following lines: Teachers and students can talk freely and argue over tea time, they often wander and chatting together on holidays. During the weekends, the University dormitory often witnessed students pay visits to professors for consultation, the endless stream of students formed a unique scenery of the campus. And the time and the chatting in tea house also became the peculiar language for students in Southwest Associated University. Reading, arguing and discussing the world's affairs in the tea house not only showed the tradition of classical learning of academy students who care about everything in the world, but also demonstrated the monastic realm who are spiritually far away from the hustle and bustle, which reflects the unique feeling of the students of Associated University. Later, many scientists and litterateurs as school fellows said that they deeply missed the experience of tea house chatting in the University, from which the unique charm of this campus cultural symbol is clearly seen.

Chapter Four An Overview of Chinese Educational Culture

Thousands of years of Chinese history have witnessed countless customs and cultures, as well as political harmony and endless enlightenment. The Long history of Chinese education and culture is like the bird view of the boundless Chinese territory, there are many wise thoughts and glorious chapters leaving the eternal morality with various expressions, although it might be a glimpse of the Chinese educational style, an overview of it can certainly reflect the eternal light of the very local culture.

Section One The Cultural Landscape in a Comparative View

When comparing the cultural characteristics of the East and the West, some scholars believe that Chinese traditional culture is a kind of "internal learning" that adjusts the relationship between the human society and the self, while western culture is a kind of "external learning" that adjusts the relationship between the self and the outside world. Therefore, Chinese traditional education culture is regarded as a culture of virtue that advocating morality, while educational culture in western countries is a kind of intellectual culture advocating rationality. The eastern and western educational cultures do have different focuses on value orientations which also reflected in the educational purposes. From the perspective of comparison, the fundamental characteristics of the five thousand years of Chinese traditional education appear more prominently: the cultivation of people is based on morality and culture, thus having formed the unique Chinese Confucian orthodoxy as a sort of educational culture.

I. Contrasts of Traditional Ideas

Any fruit of culture cannot be separated from the soil bearing the cultural ideas. The differences between Chinese and western educational ideas directly affect the characteristics of educational culture and the education and development of people in the cultural environment. Understanding the basic concepts of Chinese and western education helps to reveal the root causes of the differences between Chinese and Western educational cultures.

1.1 Chinese Education Philosophy

In the history of Chinese educational thoughts, there are many academic and cultural schools represented by Confucianism, Buddhism and Taoism.The educational value orientation of Confucianism, Buddhism and Taoism constitute the unique form of the educational values in China, and also has a significant and lasting influence. As the symbolic representation of the feudal political framework, Confucian culture's educational value orientation has obvious characters of utility. Confucianism attaches great importance to the role of education, almost all of their principles examine the value of education from the perspective of the state and society. Of course, educators in ancient times did not ignore the relationship between education and human beings, but they mostly expounded the effect of education on human beings from the the perspective of abstract human nature. From the similar theory of human nature of Confucius to Mencius and Xun Zi's argument of good or evil human nature, and then to the later mixed theory and the three levels of human nature, although their understanding of human nature has been quite different, they have the same understanding of the role of education, believing that human nature can be perfected through education to achieve the goal of stabilizing social order. In this way, the political and moral values of education become the motivation of educational practice, and meeting social needs is the purpose of education. The Confucian educational concept boasts a profound influence on China's feudal society. To receive education is to display talents and realize one's ambitions in the future. This has long become the consensus of dignitaries and ordinary people in the Chinese society . Ever since the establishment of the imperial examination system, the value orientation of "Officialdom is the natural outlet for good scholars" has been firmly imprinted in Chinese people's thoughts.

Unlike Confucianism, the educational value and influence of Buddhism and Taoism were not in line with the official education in feudal China, and the influence of their educational values was mainly in personal practice. Although there are different emphases in different historical stages and regions, the basic view of Buddhism is that all life is bitter, and the fundamental purpose of its education is to cultivate oneself and become a Buddha. The distinctive characteristic of Chinese Buddhist theory is that it pays attention to the nature of mind away from delusion. If the Tiantai and Huayan schools embodied the mind mainly as a tendency, then the Zen school initiated the idea that "mind is Buddha" and attributed everything to the mind and nature, and the cultivation of the mind was developed to a new stage, which echoed the educational thought of "keeping the law of nature and eliminating human desires" in neo–Confucianism theory in the Song and Ming dynasties. Another prominent feature of the Buddhist theory in China is the equality theory of "all living beings have the Buddha nature" as the mainstream of the Buddhist nature theory, which happens to coincide with the traditional Chinese thought that "all men can be Yao and Shun", and also assists the Confucian educational idea that ordinary people can also emulate sages. The core of Taoist educational thought is "Tao". Although "not expressible, not observable" it can only be felt and understood in a natural way, the Taoist idea of pursuing a natural state in accordance with human nature and nature is the consensus of people on Taoism conforming to the law of the world. The value orientation of the way to nature and the concept of the unity of all things also has a great influence in the course of Chinese traditional education. In intellectual education, Taoism holds that "the wisdom of the great is seemingly foolish, and the approach of the wise is seemingly ignorant", which helps the educated to dilute the pursuit of utilitarianism and respect self–consciousness. In moral education, Lao Tzu opinion that "the universe of saints is not emotional" is the typical one that distinguishes between superior and inferior virtues and opposes hypocrisy of benevolence, and it holds the righteousness against formalism. In aesthetic education, the Taoist saying "the loud sound is hard to hear, the great view is invisible" embodies the pure spirit of simplicity.

Although Confucianism, Buddhism and Taoism each has their own emphasis, they also share something in common. First, all these schools tend to attach importance to moral education without exception: The Confucian benevolent government is based on "virtue of the governors" and "kindness of the people"; The Taoist sage is good at "saving people" and saving the world; The Buddhism tenet of "pursuing all benevolence" and "refraining from all malevolence" are all classic moral–centered education. Second, they shared awareness of caring for life: The Confucian concept of "self–cultivation" and "self–improvement"; the Taoist idea of "the unity of heaven and man" and "the precious rebirth of self"; and the Buddhist compassion of "kindness grief" and "universal salvation", these are all the interpretation of the rebirth spirit in Chinese traditional education. Mr. Nan Huaijin once explained the three schools of Chinese culture in this way:

Confucius created a grain store, without a grain store, bread and steak is not enough to eat and will cause weakness. Taoism is a drugstore, not feeling sick, you do not need to go to the drugstore, but it is a must for the sick. The Buddhism is like department stores, people will go shopping in department stores if they have a full meal and no illness, which is necessary for living a life. The metaphor of these three stores is a high generalization of the miniature of traditional Chinese education styles and social thoughts, and reflects the traditional concepts of education on this very land.

1.2. Western Education Philosophy

Like the Chinese cultural tradition, the western cultural tradition is also the soil for the formation and growth of its educational tradition. The development of western educational tradition, especially those in Europe and America, shows the following characteristics: theologization, humanism and psychology–oriented. These characteristics can be seen from the great influence of the five western educational masterpieces. They are Plato's *Utopia*, Comenius' *Grand Pedagogy*, Rousseau's *Emile,* Herbart's *General Pedagogy*, and *Dewey's Democracy and Education*.

In the Utopia, Plato proposed standard of cultivating the supreme ruler through education, trying to make him a superman who surpasses all egoistic desires, that is, a man with divinity. It is the core of Plato's educational thought to lead people rationally close to divinity. Plato regarded the human mind as a complex whole composed of three parts: desire, spirit and reason, from a low level to a high level in state of cultivation. Reason includes the determinants of justice, wisdom and virtue. In Plato's view, the basic function of education is to train human nature to be intelligent and self–control in order to get close to God. Later in the Roman period, neo–Platonism combined eastern mysticism with the Christian view of science, believing that true cognition comes from faith. Later Aquinas established the theological system of scholasticism, which further combined Christianity and Platonism, and made reason and faith more consistent. By the time of Comenius, after the rise of the Renaissance, humanitarian ideology began to emerge. Comenius declared in *Grand Pedagogy* that man was the most sublime, perfect and beautiful of all creation.

Comenius combined divinity and humanity, and established an educational theory that both praised the divinity and advocated human nature, he insisted on relying on Godship and emphasized following the laws of nature. In the practice of education, Comenius stressed the parallel between natural way and artificial training, and paid attention to the harmonious development of human nature. Then in the 18th century, Rousseau accepted the idea of naturalistic education, and wrote the immortal chapter *Emile,* as a result, he opened up the humanistic way in the development of education science. Rousseau pointed out in *Emile* that the cause of education is the first of all human undertakings, and then he called for the method of education to "be suitable for people and the human minds". Rousseau greatly developed the thoughts of natural education from Comenius since the Renaissance. By nature, Comenius meant the objective nature, while Rousseau meant the nature of human beings. The work of Herbart led the development of western education towards the psychology–oriented period. Herbart lived in the era of the Great Philosophical Revolution in Germany, and he used philosophy in educational practice all his life. Herbart regarded all human activities as the activities of various ideas, and the ideas and their mutual functions as the basis of psychological activities. At the beginning of the 20th century, Herbart's *Theory of General Pedagogy* became the authority in education. At the same time of the prevalence of Herbart's theory, Dewey's theory also came into being. At the beginning of the 20th century, Dewey's *Democracy and Education* was published, while criticizing and inheriting the theories of almost all educators since ancient Greece, and it put forward many valuable opinions. Dewey combined functionalism and instrumentalism with social organism and systematically discussed the nature, process and value of education, among them, the most important aspect has been the psychological development of the interest, meditation, experience and cognition of human beings.

II. Differences in Educational Philosophy

As can be seen from the above traditional Chinese and western educational philosophy, although there are similarities, the characteristics of either part are obvious with focuses respectively. In terms of form, Chinese education attaches great importance to identity, while western education to diversity, Chinese education stresses lasting stability, and western education cherishes the spirit of reform and innovation; Chinese education values authority while western education values equality; In terms of content, Chinese education attaches great importance to humanity while western education emphasizes science.

2.1 Differences between Chinese and Western Education Forms

First of all, China is a country with group culture of collectivism as its main cultural concept. The consciousness of collectivism among Chinese people comes from the agricultural living style of small–scale peasant economy. This mode of production makes Chinese people accustomed to collective work, and this typical situation, which has been established by convention, has created the cultural psychology of collectivism among Chinese people. In culture of collectivism, the overall interests of the group are the only reference and the motivation of all individual interests. What Chinese people care about is what others think of them. They consciously restrain their words and deeds with universally recognized codes of moral behavior to gain the approval of their communities and society.

The Confucian concept of "harmony with differences" is a concrete expression of the above concept. Unification is the main theme of Chinese education, that is, educational activities are carried out with unified content and single method of evaluation mechanism. The ancient Chinese imperial examination system and the contemporary college entrance examination system reflect this kind of educational thought to a certain extent. The basic characteristic of western culture is individualism. In educational field, individual value and dignity, individual characteristics and differences are especially emphasized, western culture advocates novelty and encourages unique style. This ideology encourages the pursuit of diversity and creates the western education that characterized by diversity and coexistence of diverse ideas."Diversity" is well represented in western education systems. The campus teaching atmosphere is natural and flexible, with neither teachers nor students having to follow many mandatory rules. In particular, humanistic education after the Renaissance has made it a consensus to choose useful and beneficial knowledge for children's education. Dewey's educational thought after the 20th century emphasizes the idea that understanding knowledge in activities makes individuals become active subjects to control their own experience and construction. Secondly, thousands of years of agricultural economy in China has developed a deep–rooted concept of "coherence" in traditional culture. It is reflected in education as the educational outlook and academic values of economic applications. Chinese education emphasizes the importance of basic knowledge because it requires long–term stability. As the saying goes,"great oaks grow from little acorns". It is the basic idea of Chinese education to stress the importance of basic knowledge and classical academic tradition. On the contrary, western culture in education encourages unique and multivariant ideas, so that they do not emphasize basic knowledge and predecessors' classics, but seek to develop new styles, appreciate novelty and inspire innovation and adventure spirit. Thirdly, the traditional Chinese culture with Confucianism as the core has always advocated the hierarchical concept of the distinction between the superior and the inferior, the older and the younger, which is reflected in the educational thought of the traditional "dignity of teachers", in other words, teachers undertake the tasks of knowledge spreading , professional teaching and problem solving, and are regarded as the academic authorities that students should worship and learn from. This is conducive to a civilized and orderly study environment, but is also a hindrance to the cultivation of independence and critical thinking. Under the influence of egalitarian educational thought, teachers in the west play the role of guiders and equal partners for students in the educational process, therefore, learners' pursuit of knowledge and intelligence goes beyond the compliance with the social hierarchy and becomes more challenging and independent.

2.2 Differences between Chinese and Western Educational Content

The Chinese educational content with humanity as the main line originates from the traditional concern about the relationship between nature and man. The different thoughts and orientations of the relationship between nature and man have formed the different understanding of the relationship between education, human education and nature, as well as the different concepts of the value of natural knowledge and humanistic knowledge, thus the situation that humanistic education has been attached more importance than science education for a long time in the history of traditional Chinese education, which is reflected in the morality–oriented characteristics of Chinese traditional education, general knowledge is subordinate to the needs of moral education. For instance, Confucius education includes four aspects of the key points: literature knowledge, norms of conduct, being loyal to the duties and being trustworthy."Children should be filial to their parents, love their teachers, be careful and faithful in what they say, be friendly with all, be close to those who have a kind heart, and if they have any energy left, they can devote it to the study of culture". In the Confucian education system, moral education always comes first. Under its influence, Chinese traditional education embodies strong ethical and value concepts in teleology curriculum view and methodology. Respecting the sages and the classics and valuing morality over technology reflect the thought of Confucian education as the foundation of humanistic knowledge system in which science, engineering, medicine and agriculture are regarded as inferior in a subordinate position. It was only after modern times,"with the introduction of the western scientism trend of thought", that Chinese people's favor and respect for scientific and technological knowledge came into being in the process of the analysis and reflection about military failure. The emphasis on science in western education stems from their special focus on the difference between man and nature. Western education also emphasizes the relationship between human and nature and the role of scientific knowledge in human's healthy growth and social development while advocating human–centered science education. This is reflected in The "intelligence–oriented" characteristics of western education. The importance of wisdom has been emphasized since ancient times. Socrates believed that "virtue is knowledge", that "virtue is an attribute of the soul" and Plato and Aristotle attached great importance to "rational" education, in their views, students' physical, emotional and intellectual development is necessary, and the most important thing is to facilitate the rational (intellectual) development. Therefore, education content in western culture is relatively extensive, involving a lot of natural science knowledge.

2.3 The Cultural Origins of the Difference between China and the West

In addition to the influence of social factors such as politics, economy, military and ethnic customs, the differences between Chinese and western traditional educational ideas are also determined by the political, philosophical and talent views of educators themselves.

Chinese Confucian educationists emphasize the relationship between human and society, combining talent training with political needs, and advocating the cultivation of political talents who are proficient in human relations. This kind of talent must live up to social moral standards through self–cultivation. In view of this "benevolence", moral education is formed as the axis of the system in education. Education is to teach people how to behave like a man, to emphasize self–affirmation, to achieve the realm of saints through "self–cultivation". This kind of self–cultivation is dominated by its own ethics and morality, which can exclude the thought of gods and spirits in the educational content, making religion and theology subordinate to the imperial power and sages in the Chinese educational tradition. However, this view of ethical education as a decisive factor in human life limits the development of empirical science. Confucian educators advocate introspection rather than outward exploration of the law of the universe, which is reflected in the educational content that education is disjointed from natural science and the educational content excludes scientific and technological knowledge. In a sense, the development of natural science has been limited by an overemphasis on the role of morality. The ancient Greek educators also emphasized the relationship between man and nature, while advocated the cultivation of a harmonious and perfect man with wisdom. Based on the view of "truth", the content includes moral, intellectual, physical and aesthetic aspects, among which intellectual education must be the mainstream, only with extensive knowledge, can one develop rational soul, thus making the education content relatively comprehensive. This view had a positive impact on later generations, especially on the development of European culture and science, and laid a foundation for the emergence of some ideologies in the Renaissance period. On the other hand, due to the emphasis on the adaptation to the natural development of human beings, the characteristics of students at different ages have been taken into account as the determination of education content; which also provides the basis for the establishment of the modern school system. However, western educators in ancient time regarded the purpose of education as to enable people to reach The "world of ideas " and develop the so–called "rational soul". In their opinions, whether a person is perfect or not should be judged by whether he has reached the realm of "god". This is reflected in the educational content from the Middle Ages to the Enlightenment period, there kept being many mysterious idealism concepts, until humanism and scientism entered the mainstream trend of western education.

Thus it can be seen that the origin of the differences between Chinese and western educational value is: Chinese education attaches great importance to the harmony between self and society , to the applied value of knowledge and the secularism of education; While western education pays more attention to individual freedom and subjective consciousness, and stresses the inherent value of knowledge and the religious nature of education .

III. Dialogues between Chinese and Western Cultural Figures

Although Chinese and western cultural celebrities have been far apart from each other, they have respectively left classic wealth in their countries and produced immortal influence. This section chooses the representative cultural celebrities of China and the west in the same historical period for comparing, through the contrastive study of their styles and ideas, this section intends to show the different styles of Chinese and Western educational culture.

3.1 The Spiritual Qualities of Confucius and Socrates

As the leading roles of the cultural axis era, Socrates and Confucius had a great influence on the construction of their respective axis culture and education. Both of them actively devoted in the field of history with a messianic mentality.Socrates compared himself to a gadbee in Greece, his own existence is the spur on the nation to forge it ahead. Confucius was also ambitious with the proclamation:"if the phoenix does not fly, and there is no nice picture in the Yellow River (a sign of saint's mission), my life will be over". Later generations witnessed that both of them played the role of the father of ethics for their own nation with their efforts in a lifetime. Although both left no written works, they devoted themselves to the cause of education by vigorously cultivating young learners with heuristic teaching approach.

Although they have a lot in common, their educational and cultural styles are quite different. First, they have different political orientations. Although both of them had great motivations for salvation, Socrates only fixed his ideal in the spiritual field and never had the intention of becoming an official. After a deep reflection and summary of ancient Greek culture, he put forward the slogan of "know yourself" and reached the conclusion that virtue is knowledge, and realized the great "Ethical Turn" for ancient Greece. Although he focused on and thought about human affairs and practical philosophy, he did not show much affection to political practice. Unlike Socrates, Confucius was passionate about political practice and traveled around the world actively seeking out opportunities to take office. Confucius once said that if any monarch put him in an important position, the situation of the rite system destruction in Eastern Zhou Dynasty would be completely changed. In one year time people can see the obvious governance effect, three years' time may witness the social stability and prosperity. Eventually he got neither attention nor position, hence he devoted himself to the studying and teaching of *The Five Classics*: the book of songs; collection of ancient texts; the rites; the book of changes; the book of music; and the spring and autumn annals, on which he placed his deep affection and ambition. The differences of political orientation between

Confucius and Socrates led to the divergence of cultural purport between the east and the west. Firstly, Confucianism has a strong motivation for worldly affairs and fame, while western culture is relatively detached, truth for the sake of truth, seeking more for free and independent personality. Secondly, the ways of thinking were different , Socrates is synchronic thinking oriented, while Confucius is diachronic thinking oriented. Diachronic thinking is closer to historicism and conservatism than synchronic thinking, hoping to find the answer to the problem from studying history, Confucius held a typical narrative style of ancient history. Therefore, Zhang Xuecheng a historian and thinker in Qing Dynasty commented:"Events and facts have solid grounds, but the principles are amorphous. Therefore, The *Five Classics* taught by the Confucius are based on the laws and regulations of the previous kings, and he never deviates from the events and facts to merely follow the principles. This shows that Confucius's style of "Following the way of Yao and Shun (Chinese ancient chieftains), imitating the system of King Wen and King Wu of Zhou", which was so helpful in digging preaching examples in history. Synchronic thinking is a kind of essentialism thinking because of its free and lively, three–dimensional sense and creativity. According to Russell (a British philosopher), the Socratic way of inquiry is limited by knowledge and works well in logic learning. In essence, the Socratic way does not exclude knowledge because it involves the means of inductive and synthetic thought. Thirdly, both of them were good at using heuristic teaching in the way of education, but there have been great differences in essence. Socrates emphasized the presupposition of the definition (essence) in the discussion, or the ultimate end of the discussion is essence. This determines that Socrates' discourse is a truth–seeking process of thought. This process is also a form of intellectual game in which the conversationalist feels intellectual pleasure, although often the discussion does not have a definite outcome. Although Socrates compared himself with a criticizer, he was still rather modesty in his pursuit of truth. He first admitted that he had no idea what he was discussing, and then posed questions for the others to find the answers. The purposes and core of his talk are truth. They were playing the game of chasing the truth, and Socrates' way of speaking really reflected the dialectical spirit. On the contrary, Confucius' way of thinking was diachronic and had a strong contextual tendency, so he used examples to achieve the purpose of ethical education in teaching. And the historical example had been accomplished facts, waiting for more people to convince and imitate. It proves that history plays a very important role in education and it also reflects the immersion teaching process. *The Analects of Confucius* fully embodies the authority of discourse and the dignity of doctrine, undoubtedly, it didn't need further exploration for answers, and applied to the gentleman style of Confucianism.

As the spiritual leaders of the cultural axis era, the two completely different ways of thinking, political orientations and teaching modes have nurtured and forged two kinds of cultural spirits with great differences. The differences and influences are manifested in many aspects in the long history.

3.2 Mencius and Aristotle's Views on Teachers

As two other masters of the Axis age: The teacher images represented by Mencius and Aristotle have reflected the differences in the development of Chinese and western education. Mencius, as the representative of Oriental Chinese traditional culture, paid great attention to cultivating talents who could be used for practical purposes. He required teachers to have both moral integrity and practical ability, to be good guiders for students, and to build a good atmosphere for respecting teachers while honouring disciplines. Comparatively speaking; Aristotle, the representative of ancient Greek and western culture educator, paid great attention to cultivating all–round talents, teachers were required to possess specialized knowledge and to form a free and equal teacher–student relationship.

As for the status of teachers, Mencius equated teachers with kings. To elevate the status of teachers to a higher level, he said "God blesses the people by providing them with kings and teachers", it reflects the important status of the scholars and their desire to participate in politics. Mencius said,"A master instructs others in order; Scholars also take rules as a good craftsman". It means teachers and learners should follow the principles in what they are doing. This shows that teachers should set up certain principles and standards for students in teaching. Of course, Mencius also pointed out that "A good workman can teach others rules, but can not teach skills directly"; and that "The gentleman leads but does not express opinions, as if he can leap in the middle of the road, talented people will naturally follow". He did it just right, and capable people will learn from him. This also shows that Mencius thought that teachers were only the guiders in teaching, and the key lied in the improvement and training of students' self–cultivation. Differently, Aristotle regarded education as an important means to build a city–state governed by talents. He said that "a city–state should be a collection of many individuals, and only education can make it unified as a group". At the same time, influenced by Aristotle, it has been believed in the west that the human mind is just like a wax block or white paper, everything is with the possibility of development, to make people's potential into reality, we need to rely on education and teachers, and pay attention to the guidance of teachers. In other words, students should learn from wise people in order to acquire knowledge and skills, so teachers should play a leading role in the process of education. As for the quality of teachers, Mencius proposed three conditions for teachers: 1. Good moral quality. Mencius proposed that the content of education should be the feudal patriarchal system of five morality, with the human ethics as the center, so he advocated to constrain desire, to examine oneself, to know the shame and correct mistakes, to cultivate noble spirit, and to strengthen one's will. In this way, teachers should be morally noble. 2. Extensive and specialized knowledge. Mencius said, to study extensively and expound at length is thus to return to the point where one can annotate the main essence. Mencius said,"The value of erudite and detailed explanation equals to the reverse: a concise clear conclusion" that is, a teacher should have profound knowledge, and be able to explain in detail, and then in a comprehensive understanding, he should summarize the brief meaning. Therefore, profound knowledge is the basic quality necessary for a teacher. 3. The self cultivation. Mencius required teachers to love education, to be devoted to their duties and to be exemplary professionals. Mencius not only expressed his love for education by saying "It is the one of the three types of happiness (the other two are the safety of family, and a clear conscience) to educate the world's talents", but also quoted the saying of his disciple Gong Zichou that "a teacher must teach the students in the right way" to stress the significance of setting good examples for their students. As to Aristotle, his requirements for teachers fall into two categories: 1.The professional knowledge. Aristotle divided the content of knowledge or education into two categories: those suitable for free people to learn and those not suitable for free people to learn. And the knowledge imparting of free subjects suitable for free people requires the teachers of deep and specialized knowledge. 2. The education–loving quality. In the prosperous period of Alexander's reign, Aristotle did not indulge in the official status, but engaged in teaching and scientific research activities in the lyceum he founded for more than ten years. During this period, he seldom involved in politics, which proves Aristotle's love for education. As for the teacher–student relationship, Mencius put more emphasis on respecting teachers and valuing the Tao, that is, students' respect for teachers. Mencius once said: walking slowly and behind the elders shows respect for the elder people, and it's disrespectful to get ahead of an elder. What Mencius expected was that the whole society would form a good atmosphere in which students respect their teachers. Aristotle put more emphasis on the principle of "teaching benefits teachers as well as students" in the teacher–student relationship. He loved his teacher Plato, but he also put forward the maxim that "I loved truth more". He was not blindly obedient, and did not hesitate to put forward different views. Aristotle's teaching was mostly in the form of walking and playing in the woods with students while discussing knowledge together, which made him and his followers known as The "School of Freedom and Equality", reflecting the concept of paying attention to freedom and equality between teachers and students.

Mencius and Aristotle, as masters of the cultural axis era, reflected the similarities and differences between Chinese and Western educational cultures. The core value of Chinese teacher culture is morality, noble teacher's ethics, high accomplishment is our primary requirement for teachers, the cultural tradition of respecting teachers has been inherited in its unique form. On the other hand, the core value of western culture is wisdom. The pursuit of knowledge and truth, the knowledge and specialization of teachers are the important requirements in western education.

3.3 Zhuangzi and Rousseau's Educational Thoughts

Zhuangzi and Rousseau are both excellent masters of education, and they both found the phenomena of antinomies (A contradiction between two propositions) in the process of human civilization. Their educational views respectively represent the peak of natural education in China and the west. Although they lived in different times and regions, the comparison of their views on naturalism education has long been a hot topic in the academic world.

What they had in common is that they both criticized and questioned the type of education that suppressed humanity, advocated that education should conform to the laws of nature and human nature, and held a negative attitude to science and technology. In Zhuangzi's view, the development of human society was the continuous destruction of nature by human behaviors which is no different from "bridling a horse and a cow". As for knowledge, Zhuangzi believed that knowledge could lead to confusion and contention, and could easily be used by wrong doers. Therefore, Zhuangzi believed that the only solution was to abandon cleverness and return to simplicity. Zhuangzi was critical of the educational thought advocated by Confucianism and thought it was against human nature.

Therefore, Zhuangzi proposed in his book *The Main Keys to Keeping Healthy* that one should follow the natural vein as usual, meaning that everything should follow the path of nature, and education is no exception. And in his book *The Ultimate Bliss*, it was pointed out that only by adapting to the personality of the educational object can interest be aroused and the potential be brought into full play so as to achieve the goal of self–transformation. Zhuangzi believed that the use of technology destroyed the nature of world, he said: Conspiracy and strategy may not be upright and could cause people to become restless, which is not the right way to be achieved. Similarly, Rousseau believed that "under the feudal system, all our wisdom is the prejudice of slaves, and all our habits are enslaved to torture and contain us. Civilized people are bound by education and system from the cradle to the grave in the slave state". He argued that traditional classical education focused only on theology and the humanities, which were boring and narrow minded, developing only one aspect of the child. On how to implement natural education, Rousseau advocated that education should follow children's nature and operate according to the law of nature.He advocated the implementation of negative education to children, using the principle of natural consequences of education, to prevent children's fallacy thoughts. Rousseau also made it clear in his *On Whether the Revival of Science and Art would Contribute to Social Morality* that science and art is poison to morality when they corrupt the good of mankind. There are also differences between Zhuangzi's and Rousseau's views on education. First of all, their theories point to different objects. The purpose of Zhuangzi's education is to help becoming a sage, a sage is the one who achieves the realm of absolute freedom."The sage, reflects the original beauty of heaven and earth and realizes the laws of all things". Rousseau's natural education is to cultivate citizens. Rousseau described the ideal citizen in *Emile* as the combination of the advantages of the nobility and the bourgeoisie at that time. He should be a "citizen" in the modern sense who is rich in knowledge, healthy in body and mind and independent in thoughts. The second is the different understandings of age stages in education. Zhuangzi's discussion of natural education is from the perspective of a whole person, without dividing the learners into children and adults, let alone dividing the growth process of people into several periods for education. However, Rousseau divided children's education into four stages and advocated that education should be carried out according to different stages of children's development. Thirdly, their philosophical basis of educational theories are quite different. Zhuangzi relied on "Tao" and he made it clear in his *Zhi's Trip to the North* that: Is there anything that was born before heaven and earth? The creator of the world itself cannot be part of the world. This immaterial concept is considered by Zhuangzi to be the most fundamental "Tao". Different from Zhuangzi;Rousseau relied on sensory experience. He believed that since the knowledge that perceived by the human mind was the gateway to sensation, the original rationality of human beings was derived from sensory experience. Finally, their understandings of the role of education were different. While Zhuangzi advocated the doctrine of silence, simplicity and inaction, and denying the positive role of education, Rousseau, denied education that went against children's nature, but on the other hand, he fully affirmed the role of education, believing that it is education that leads to the differences between people. He stated in *Emil* that "all we need for growth is to be given by education".

In view of the relationship between man and nature, though both Zhuangzi and Rousseau emphasized the harmony and unity between man and nature, they are different on the basis of philosophy concerning monism and dualism. As far as the social ideal is concerned, they all expressed their yearning and pursuit for freedom and equality, yet different in the ways of realization as the different beliefs of the most virtuous world and the contract society respectively. In terms of aesthetic attitude, although they both advocated the existence of simplicity and authenticity and reject alienation, yet they reflected the differences of content learning in ways of observing things: by Tao or by virtue. Zhuangzi's nihilism that goes with nature and Rousseau's idealism that goes back to nature has not been the leading edge or mainstream in history, but they both called for the return to nature of humanity and society, which has great significance for modern education.

Section Two The Spiritual Core of the Educational World

As is known to all, the core of traditional Chinese education in the past dynasties is the ideological education among people. In the spirit of Chinese education, whether among royal family or ordinary people, regardless of different dynasties and schools, it is the main task for the ideological education to train people to form an ideal world view, outlook on life and values in line with the requirements. It also permeates into various contents of the real society and education culture at all times, thus forming the unique philosophy in spirit of the Chinese nation.

I. The Microcosm of Worldview

The world view of "unity of nature and man" is a basic concept held by most philosophers in traditional Chinese philosophy from pre–Qin to Ming and Qing Dynasties.This makes Chinese culture emerge and grow in a broad and harmonious environment from the very beginning. The definition of heaven can be understood from three aspects, the first is the physical heaven, opposite to the earth, it can also be considered as the contemporary view of nature. The other is the spiritual heaven. It has a dominant role in the fate of people and everything in the world. The third is the moral aspect, which is the supreme truth that all things in the world must obey and recognize. In the history of education, many sages and scholars had differences on the definition of heaven, but they invariably believed that the idea of "unity of heaven and man" expressed an internal relationship of unity between man and nature. Such a world view is not only reflected in the writings of scholars and educational ideas, but also vividly manifested in the concept of time and space, folklore stories and human society of the Chinese people.

1.1 Aesthetics in Time and Space

In the context of agricultural civilization, the relationship between human and nature is often a beautiful landscape in China. It has long been taught and learned among the courts, the schools of learning, and the plebeians. Both solar terms and festivals, as part of the humanistic education , they reflect people's delicate feelings towards a period of time and a place of soil. The "24 solar terms" form a knowledge system and social practice formed by the Chinese people through observing the annual movement of the sun to understand the changing laws of the seasons, climate, phenology and other aspects of the year. The ancient Chinese divided the annual motion track of the sun into 24 equal parts, each part is a"solar term", collectively they are referred to as "24 solar terms". Specifically they include: Start of Spring, Rain, Awakening of Insects, Vernal equinox, Qingming, Grain Rain, Start of Summer, Small Manchu, Grain in Ear, Summer Solstice, Minor Heat, Major Heat, Start of Autumn, End of Heat, White Dew, Autumn Equinox, Cold Dew, Frost's Descent, Start of Winter, Minor Snow, Major Snow, Winter Solstice, Minor Cold, Major Cold. The 24 solar terms guide traditional agricultural production and daily life, and are an important part of the traditional Chinese calendar system and its relevant practical activities. In the international meteorological organization circle, this time recognition system is praised as "China's fifth invention". From the popular traditional poems, people can unconsciously experience the influence of solar terms on the thinking and life of Chinese people. For example:

Late Spring
Yuan Zhen
A quiet day, blinds sparse, swallows cheep,
dust whirled on the steps, two sparrows fight.
To shut the door at dusk a wind does sweep;
all flowers fall in silence, no one at sight.

A Poem with Rhyme of My Guest in Mountains at Start of Summer
Wen Tianxiang

Back to the world of streams and stones,
with sun and moon I'm staying.
The scene of summer permeates deep valleys,
spring is shining in everything.
Enjoying the poetry and drinking,
the light mood is beyond the earthliness being,
A series of sound music could be,
the solution to the factitious wind of annoying.

Song of Autumn
Liu Yuxi
Since olden days we feel in autumn sad and drear,
but I say spring cannot compete with autumn clear.
On a fine day a crane cleaves the clouds and soars high,
it leads the poet's lofty mind to azure sky.

Thinking of Home on Winter Solstice Night at Handan
Bai Juyi
At roadside inn I pass the winter solstice day,
clasping my knees, my shadow is my company.
I think, till dead of night my family would stay,
and talk about the wayfaring me, poor and lonely .

Poets did not deliberately emphasize ecological harmony and solar term culture, but ancient poetry is full of the inter–flow between people and nature, heart and time, as well as emotion and outside world. When tasting these classic poems, readers can not only experience the beauty of nature and time but also the ideal living state that is following nature and beyond vulgarities with a sense of national cultural identity that the Chinese literati yearn for with mutual affinity. This kind of aesthetic appreciation from literature spreads in the living environment and the education field of Chinese people while transcending time and space, it enriches the spiritual connotation and enhances the national cohesion. In the folk proverbs, one also feels the cultural elements of a solar term which reflects the unique lifestyle and civilization concept of the Chinese nation. For example:

A fine day in Start of Spring, the effortless work in ploughing;

From the Awakening of Insects to Vernal Equinox, one should be busy transplanting rice seedlings;

From Frost's Descent to Minor Cold, one should turn the ground to freeze insects;

For a bumper year, autumn harvest is the key;

If the food is not cold during the Qingming Festival, god will hail to retaliate;

After the summer solstice, the daytime is getting shorter and shorter.

Solar term proverbs come from the summary of the practical life experience of Chinese agricultural laborers in the past dynasties. They are passed down from generation to generation and tested repeatedly, shining with the light of wisdom and the vision of observing the world. The 24 solar terms seem to reflect the ancient culture of farming life, but in modern society, they still present great vitality in mirroring the time and space aesthetics of the Chinese people and the feelings of their home and country. Various solar terms not only continue to guide people's agricultural production and influence related dietary customs, but also keep enriching and inheriting in educational thoughts and actions generation after generation. Since modern times, farmers around the country have constantly modified and improved the agricultural proverbs related to solar terms according to the changes of temperature, precipitation and phenology, and localized the 24 solar terms in line with their own environments. For example, the old peasant proverb says "Qingming ends snow, grain rain prevents frost", indicating that after grain rain, the cold weather is basically over. Now in some regions, it is changed to "grain rain, there is frost but no snow, the sowing of multigrain should not be delayed", it has become a new foundation for arranging farming. In addition to the practical values, the 24 solar terms continue to be inherited today because they contain the fresh cultural genes of the Chinese nation. It imperceptibly interferes with our cognition of the colorful world, and subtly affects our experience of the vast universe. For example: Qingming Festival was originally a solar term to remind farmers to hurry up their spring ploughing, later it gradually integrated into the customs of the Cold Food Festival, forming the two representative festival customs of worship and outing. As time changes, there formed other contents like a profound pursuit of the distant, of the memory of the ancients, and a cherished recollecting of the martyrs."Qingming Festival" carries the unique consciousness of life in the Chinese nation, which is still guiding people's behavior today and has great educational significance.

The ideas like "what do you do in different solar terms and what can be predicted by different weather conditions" have penetrated into the cultural root of the Chinese nation. They help to make the spirit and material life of the Chinese people rhythmically beautiful while reflecting the wisdom of respecting nature and adapting to the weather. In short, the 24 solar terms are "the punctuation from nature that the Chinese people use to enrich their life", they function as a set of "human–nature induction device" in their collective view of the world, it stands through the ancient and modern time, and is always full of brilliance and vitality.

1.2 The Spirit from Mythologies

The concept of divinity in Chinese world view is reflected in mythologies and folklore, which is not only diversified in themes, but also unique and beautiful in language styles. It is a very important branch of traditional Chinese culture. From the perspective of ancient Chinese culture, Chinese people have held the concept of ghosts and gods for a very long time. Myth is also the beginning of Chinese people's cognition of the world, the embodiment of national spirit, and the soil of the earliest literature, art and national belief.

Chinese ancestors believed that heaven and God could not be separated. The Chinese myth of Genesis provides the basis for understanding the unity of heaven and God. First, they believe their ancestors were animalistic gods, second, The "God of heaven" has the power above all creatures to control the forces of nature. During the Yin and Shang Dynasties, the religious concept changed from "respecting God" to "respecting etiquette", Confucius' cultural thoughts reflect the nature of historical transition. Traditionally, heaven, as the embodiment of God, was an elusive force above nature, as human society developed, people began to recognize the greatness of their inherent nature, therefore,"humanism" began to be publicized, and thus religion was transformed into a "humanistic religion" or "moral religion". Since Confucius separated the concept of heaven and God, Chinese culture has moved from "between God and man" to "unity of heaven and man". When it reflected in the theory of God's will, the destiny is connected to morality,"Heaven" has become the metaphysical source of human nature and humanity from the bottom up through the way of life. People on earth seek good fortune and avoid evil through the communion of spirits and ancestors, or gain the legitimacy of ruling the dynasty; the king on earth represents not only the whole dynasty, but all the people under his rule. Therefore, The "mandate of Heaven" must also hold the nature of the collectivism."Unity of man and nature" means that man and nature unite, which is the human nature that man finally reaches transcendence through continuous cultivation in reality. This transcendence is the spirit of the Chinese nation and is reflected in the many fairy tales and characters collected in *The Classic of Mountains and Seas and Nanhuai Zi.* For example: Gun faced the enormity of the flood and dared to bear the heavy mission of flood control and save the people.He tried every means to control the flood, after his death , his son Yu took over his mission so that the task of flood controlling will be followed and continued.In the end, Yu succeeded in controlling the flood by living in harmony with nature; Pangu's "life after death" story also embodies individual transcendence in the way of the unity of heaven and man.The greatness of Pangu lies not only in his hard work day after day and year after year to open up the world, but also in the fact that he did not forget to give birth to everything under heaven when he was about to fall,with his own behavior, he explained to the ancestors the image of the god of creation and embodied the philosophy of "unity of heaven and man" in ancient China. These are examples of individual transcendence. Facing the collapse of the sky and the earth, Nüwa went to the Kunlun Mountains to gather colored stones, she cut the feet of huge turtles to erect four poles of the heavens, killed the black dragon to help Jizhou, and gathered reed ash to stop the polluted water, every feat of her has been earth–shattering, like the myths of "Houyi shooting down the sun" and "Jingwei reclaiming the sea," this story reflects the efforts and courage of the ancestors to transform nature in the face of terrible disasters, and is an example of the transcendence of nature. Gonggong was a hero who dared to fight against the Emperor of Heaven. He went beyond the dilemma and continued to fight after being frustrated, breaking the pattern of the old society, despite the defeat, he still won spiritually as a hero. The myth of the Cowherd and the Weaver Girl transcends the marriage custom of ordinary people, and the business mode of ordinary marriage. Although separated by the Milky Way, they have been loyal to each other for a long time. These are examples of social transcendence. After the Xingtian rebelled against the Emperor of Heaven and was beheaded, he continued to fight in defiance with the nipples as his eyes and the navel as his mouth; After Nezha cut his own flesh to return his mother and bone to his father, his regeneration of "green lotus root as bone and lotus leaf as clothing" reflects the persistence of transformation, these are examples of spiritual transcendence. The unity of heaven and man in Chinese mythology embodies not only the transcendent spirit but also the deity of virtue, which is concentrated in sacrifice and dedication, which is inherited from the creation myth. Heroes in the legends are almost all incarnations of sages. They are solemn and kind and have the will to save people. They are never selfish, and the spirit of dedication is their virtue. For example: Shen Nong could not bear to see people suffering from sickness, so he tasted all the herbs in the world, and finally died of poisoning; Kuafu, in order to chase the sun, and prevent people from suffering, began his difficult journey till finally sacrificed his life, his cane turned into a peach forest. In order to prevent the people from suffering from floods, Yu devoted all his life to the flood control, three times he passed his own house without entering, he abandoned his small family for the big homeland. The gods in Chinese legends seem far away from the human world and do not bother the daily routines. Most of them have no desires, no human weakness and feelings. They are the embodiment of supreme power, virtue, omniscience and omnipotence. This kind of divinity represents the model of people's yearning for perfect personality. This kind of divinity, combined with the concept of natural law, gradually forms the initial pursuit of extremely noble personality and the motivation to human nature in Chinese education culture.

In a word, Chinese mythology contains the beginning of national thoughts and explains the resistance consciousness and transcendent spirit of the early people in adapting to nature and the world. This spirit has influenced generation after generation of Chinese descendants, showing the ideological culture of the Chinese nation from the attachment of "respecting heaven and serving God" to the transcendence of "unity of heaven and man", and then it has developed beyond the individual, beyond nature, beyond society, and finally beyond the spirit itself, it is transcended from outward to inward, and finally reached the supreme state of "unity of nature and man". The spirit in Chinese mythic stories not only expresses the aspirations of our ancestors to conquer nature and transform society, but also reflects the indomitable and unyielding spirit of the Chinese nation. It is also the essence of the initial belief of the Chinese nation and a vivid portrayal of the world view of "the unity of nature and man".

1.3 The World in Yin and Yang

The four seasons, the notion of Yin–Yang and five elements are cultural concepts with typical Chinese characteristics. If the 24 solar terms are a complete calendar formed on the basis of the traditional"four seasons and eight festivals", then the theory of Yin–yang and five elements has compatibility with the concept of the four seasons. When Chinese ancestors explained the movement of heaven and earth and the alternation of four seasons, they introduced the concepts of Yin and Yang and five elements. Lao Tzu can be said to be the first person to explain the concept of Yin and Yang from the height of philosophy. *Lao Tzu(Chapter Forty–two)* says:"All things tend to the direction of the sun, and Yin and Yang mutually agitated into a new harmonious body". The concept of Yin–yang, the five elements and the four seasons have their own origins, and independent development, the theories gradually influenced and penetrated each other, and there was a tendency of confluence in the Spring and Autumn period. In the middle and late Warring States period, the scholars of Yin and Yang school integrated and unified these concepts while forming the theory of Yin and Yang and the five elements, which became the theoretical tool and mode of thinking for Chinese people to understand and explore the universe and life. So far, the germination, generation, development and finalization of Chinese culture in many fields all contains the concept of Yin–yang and five elements theory, emphasizing the interchanges of Yin–yang and Qi in breeding all things in the universe.

The theory of Yin–yang and the five elements originated from the keen insight and deep understanding of the ancient laboring people about themselves, nature and society. In essence, Yin and Yang refer to the contradictory unity and dynamic balance of things, and the unity of opposites and dynamic balance are the basic choice of the operating quality of all things. The thought of five elements is actually a profound understanding and grasp of the internal elements and the relationship between objects. The five elements first appeared in the *Book of Documents*, The "five" of the five elements is written as " X " in oracle bone inscriptions, meaning the intersection and fusion of all things in heaven and earth; The "elements" of the five elements is written as " 行 ", which is like a cross–road connecting all directions. The five elements actually represent the basic sequence and law of the elements and functions of the five objects. It's like a simplified model of the world, while constantly absorbing the spiritual elements of such doctrines as Confucianism, Taoism, legalism and agriculturalism, it has been developed and perfected by Jizi, Guan, Zou Yan, Dong Zhongshu, Liu Xiang and others and finally gained the characteristics of ancient basic materialism and dialectics. The theory of Yin–yang and the five elements regards yin–yang as the most basic manifestation of things, the unity of contradiction as the original driving force for the change and development of all things, and believes that everything in the universe is composed of five elements such as gold, wood, water, fire and earth, all of which follow the two objective laws of coexistence and elimination, the theory regards the fluctuation and rotation of Yin–yang and the five elements as the theoretical basis of the cosmological view. The basic meaning of the theory of five elements lies in the continuous operation of the order and relation among the internal elements of things and among things, and the characteristics of five elements is the basic law for analyzing the attributes of things and the relation between things. For example, anything that is vigorous, outward, rising, high, warm and bright belongs to Yang; all relatively static, internal, falling, low, cold, dark are Yin. In addition, wood is characterized of growth and development, fire is characterized of warmth and luxuriance, is characterized of breeding and inheritance, gold is characterized of transformation and convergence, and water is characterized of irrigation and extending downward. According to the characteristics of the five elements, the theory of Yin–yang and five elements deduced the interaction between the five elements, namely: Sheng, Ke, Cheng, and Wu."Sheng" means the interpromoting relation in five elements, like wood promotes fire, fire promotes earth, earth promotes gold, gold promotes water, water promotes wood as the order and the cycle, it is endless."Ke" means the inter–restriction relation in five elements, like wood restricts earth, earth restricts water, water restricts fire, fire restricts gold, gold restricts wood as the order and the cycle, it is endless."Cheng" refers to a series of abnormal reactions caused by one of the five elements restraining too much."Wu" means one of the five elements is too weak to restrain the corresponding element and cause the anti–effect. The core ideas of Yin–yang and five elements theory are overall correlation, harmonious balance, mutual connection, dynamic development, following the law and learning from nature. Its concentration is embodied in unity, integrity and self–adjustment. Once an element is too strong or too weak, it will cause abnormal reaction of the five elements, and things will lose their dynamic balance, thus affecting the harmonious development of the world.

The theory of Yin–yang and five elements is rooted in the Taiji chart and life experience. It is a kind of scientific and harmonious dialectics. Yin and Yang is an abstract summary of the two opposite and unified aspects or two basic attributes of objective things, and the five elements are five different stages of the relative changes of Yin and Yang. The theory of Yin–yang and five elements has been widely used in the field of traditional Chinese medicine and educational thinking and has shown a far–reaching influence, it can be concluded that this mode of thinking reflects the world view in Chinese traditional culture and folk life, it mirrors people's appreciation to the symbiotic cooperative relationship of all things, and it still manifests significant enlightenment for modern education.

II. The Essence in View of Life

In Chinese culture, the so–called view of life is regarded as "the way to be a person" or"the strategy to handle life", which refers to how to view life, spend life and arrange life, in other words, view of life refers to the concerns from the survival and living, to the meaning and belonging of life. In short, the core of view of life is the ultimate concern of life ideal, to understand the traditional outlook on life of a culture, one should not only understand the social and historical essence of the culture, but also experience the humanistic spirit and goal behind the particular culture. The philosophy of Confucianism, Buddhism and Taoism, which is the most influential philosophy in Chinese traditional culture, boasts a great influence on the educational purpose and cultural characteristics of Chinese history.

2.1 Confucianism

Confucianism has always been dominant in Chinese traditional culture, and its philosophy of life is a realistic outlook on life that emphasizes morality and progress. The life consciousness of Confucianism is mainly manifested in the understanding of human nature and the search for ideal life, especially the real pursuit of the value of life and the moral perfection for the meaning of life. Life view of Confucianism is a moral type one, one is required to be filial, respectful, sincere, to love people and keep benevolent (*The Analects of Confucius–XueEr*). The core Confucian concepts of benevolence, justice, propriety, wisdom, trustworthiness, gentleness, kindness, courtesy, frugality, accommodation, courtesy, generosity, trustworthiness, sensitivity, and virtues are the basic norms and creeds of human life, which are the Confucian moral standards for human behavior.Those who can adhere to the above exercises in their own daily life and take them as their principles are The "sages" and "men of high ambition and benevolence" praised by Confucianism,they were able to die to achieve virtue, sacrifice for righteousness" and devote their lives for practicing the moral norms stipulated by Confucianism. Another prominent characteristic of Confucian life philosophy is to seek progress and utility. Learners of Confucianism are all realists, the pursuit of the eternal value of the moral reality is their ideal personality in real life. Throughout his life, Confucius rarely talked about human nature destiny, and never talked about ghosts and spirits. He always taught his disciples to learn, forge ahead and strive in real life. Confucius once said:"I am such a man, diligent to forget eating, happy to forget worry, did not feel the aging was coming." He often instructed his disciples to be"tireless in learning and teaching"."There is always a teacher in the company of three, choose the merits and learn from them, and change the demerits"(*The Analects of Confucius–Shu Er*). Confucius always taught people to live a meaningful live and to take a positive attitude towards life. He once counseled earnestly:"It is lamentable to eat all day and do nothing! (*The Analects of Confucius, YangHuo*)" , he also took running water as a metaphor to inspire people to cherish their time and do something meaningful. Confucius said by the river:"The passage of time is just like the flow of water ,which goes on day and night"(*The Analects of Confucius–Zi Han*). Based on the teachings of Confucius, Zeng Zi discussed the positive idea of " There is much to do and a long way to go in life", he said,"An upright man should have a broad and strong mind. There is much to do and a long way to go. Isn't benevolence a duty and heavy mission? Isn't it a long task to the end of one's days?" (*The Analects of Confucius–Tai Bo*) . Confucianism believes that righteousness is more important than profit. It emphasizes that "thinking about righteousness when one sees the profit", that "righteousness is the essence", that "profit should be taken after righteousness", and that "righteousness comes first before profit". Confucianism also highly appreciateds the value of spiritual ideal personality, Mencius said,"Live with a wide perspective in the world, establish the right position in the world, and behave in a right way in the world. If one is successful, and let the people share it, if one is not successful, then walk one's right way alone. Wealth can not confuse his thoughts, poverty can not make his moral wavering, power can not make his will yield, thus one can be called a man of ambition and action" (*Mencius–Teng Wen Gong*). The emergence of patriots and national heroes in the past dynasties, as well as the reputation of "ancient civilization" and "Land of rites", are closely related to the influence of Confucianism.

In short, the tenet of the Confucian View of life is "benefiting all the people in the world", and "altruism". Confucianism always emphasizes the importance of the interests of the state and the nation, requires individuals to obey the whole, and concerns the harmony of interpersonal relations, national unity and social peace. The core of the Confucian philosophy of life is to attach importance to the spiritual realm and to believe that the spiritual needs of human beings are higher than the material needs. This thought is fully reflected in the ideal of life, attitude and cultivation of life. It plays a great role in shaping the ideal personality of "aspirational man" and "great man", and also facilitates the pace of edifying national character and promoting spiritual civilization.

2.2 Taoism

Different from Confucianism, life philosophy of Taoism is an idealistic view on life that emphasizes the realm and aims at individual freedom. Taoist view of life tries to transcend the limitation of life and pursue eternity in the form of ideological expression, however, on the journey of life, people are required to grasp the objective and subjective sense of life, calmly face the joys and sorrows of individual life, and to seek the meaning of life on the basis of conforming to the changes of nature and the world, which is more detached and aloof than life view of Confucianism.

Taoism believes that civilization increases people's desire and pain, so they should return to the original state of life. Under the guidance of anatman and undesire, they should keep their perspective out of life and observe life, understand life and death with transcendent vision, and get rid of vulgar fetters with great composure and calmness. If one has to summarize the realm of life or life ideal of Taoism with a few simple words, that is: govern by non–interference, argue and fight with nobody, preserve one's moral integrity, recover one's original simplicity. The two most remarkable characteristics of Lao Tzu or Taoist philosophy of life are: first, behave oneself with modesty, be good at self–protection. Lao Tzu said: If a sage wants to be above the people, he must show his modesty to the people in his words; If he wants to get ahead of the people, he must stand behind the people. Therefore the people do not feel burdened and hindered when sage is above or ahead of them; consequently people are never tired of respecting and supporting him. To this kind of contention, the world can not contend with it. (Chapter 66 of *Lao–Tzu*) As a result of treating people and doing things modestly, so when in the upper position, one is not considered a burden by ordinary people, and will not be hurt by people. He also said:"I have three treasures, which I particularly cherish: the first is kindness, the second is thrift, and the third is not daring to be the first in the world. Because of love, I can be brave and fearless, because of thrift, I can appreciate the wide world, for not daring to be the first , and I can grow freely to be useful (Chapter 67 of Lao–Tzu). These words are all about the philosophy of self–protection, and not to be harmed by people. Second. Preserve one's moral integrity and pursue freedom. Zhuangzi was particular about the philosophy of life. He advocated" *A Happy Excursion*" in life;one should be free and away from the temptation of external names, so people should conduct themselves in the society as follows:"Don't be famous for being good, and do not get punishment for doing evil." Only in this way,"can one be safe and complete, be supporting the family and living a long life (Zhuangzi–*Master of Health Preservation*)" . When Zhuangzi told the story of Paoding dismembering cattle, he was to illustrate the life philosophy of "work with skill and ease and follow the natural vein as the usual method" . When he talked about the story of "deforestation" and "killing wild geese", the purpose is to annotate the life philosophy of "being between talented and mediocre". There is also a story in *Records* of the *Grand Historian–Biography* of *Lao Zhuang* that King Wei of Chu tried to hire Zhuangzi to be his prime minister, but Zhuangzi refused to be an official for life. The purpose of such writing is also to promote the Taoist life philosophy of preserving one's moral integrity, not live for worldliness, and the pursuit of spiritual freedom.

In brief, the Taoist view of life boasts rich connotation, the view that pursuit of life is more important than that of materials, the ideal of returning to the simple and true personality, the realm of life beyond favours or humiliation, and the modesty approach to life all present the special inspiration with their brilliant view of life. Despite there exist some negative aspects of Taoist view of life, like the worship of nothingness for dismissing narrow utilitarianism, the pessimistic and cynical attitude for criticizing the ills of society, the ignoring of proper needs of handling human relations because of the emphasis on freedom of will, dismissing the value of scientific culture because of the dissimilation of civilization; people can still find historical resonance from the wisdom of Daoism today, for it keeps enlightening people to reflect on the essence of life, the principle of survival and life attitude and other important issues of life views. At present, the Taoist paradigm of "returning to nature" is considered to be the key to overcome human cognitive limitations in the process of knowledge regeneration and intellectual improvement. More importantly, it inspires people to attach importance to their own spiritual life, and guides people to gradually free themselves from the bondage of external things, return to the natural state of life, and live a real life belonging to human beings.This enriches the traditional Chinese educational thoughts and adds a unique charm to the Chinese local educational culture. More importantly, it inspires people to attach importance to their own spiritual life, and guides people to gradually free themselves from the bondage of external things, return to the natural state of life, and live a real life belonging to human beings. This enriches the traditional Chinese educational thoughts and adds a unique charm to the Chinese local educational culture.

2.3 Buddhism

The inner clarity of Buddhist culture's compassion and harmony is an integral part of the spiritual ecological value of Chinese art and culture. The Buddhist outlook on life, as one of the three modules of Chinese traditional humanities, is an important clue to discover the oriental charm from the innovation with integrity along the track of traditional cultural psychology, and it reflects the contemporary value of Chinese harmonious culture. The basic Buddhist view of life originated from the truth that Sakyamuni explored and realized from the unsolved pains and troubles of life, and later became the basic outlook on life of Buddhist culture. The Buddhist outlook on life is roughly divided into two aspects. One is to face the defects of life and grasp the fundamental problems of life, to take bitterness and hardship as a teacher of life , to cultivate a supra–mundane–mind so as to be honest with oneself and know what the fundamental problems of life are. The other aspect is to cherish life, give play to the characteristics of human nature, keep self–awareness and develop Bodhicitta, so as to create the full merit and free life.

The Buddhist outlook on life is expressed in the cognition of life, the representative views include The "Four Truths". (1) duhkha–satya: that the world is a place of suffering; (2) samudaya–satya: that karma and troubles are the root of suffering; (3) nirodha–sacca: the nature of extrication and enlightenment; (4) marga–satya: the way out of suffering."The Twelve Nidanas " (1) avidya: a general term for all troubles; (2) mitzvah: all acts; (3) awareness:karmar, which is driven by past karma for good and evil; (4) namarupa: mind and body; (5) the six indriyas:eyes, ears, nose, tongue,body and mind; (6) contact: touch and feeling; (7) vedanā:accept; (8) lusting: greedy heart; (9) gaining:pursuit of acquisition; (10) samsara: cause and effect; (11) consequence:future recompense; (12) aging: old age and death."Eight Sufferings of Life": (1) suffering of birth; (2) suffering of old age; (3) suffering of sickness; (4) suffering of death; (5) suffering of being apart from the loved; (6) suffering of meeting the resentment and hatred (7) suffering of not–getting what one want; (8) suffering of five sorts of bewilderment."Skandha": (1) rupa–skandha: all kinds of tangible things that can be felt; (2) vedana–skandha:the mood generated by the environment; (3) samjnana–skandha:accumulated thoughts; (4) Sankhara: good and evil in act, parole and minds; (5) vijnana–skandha: the discriminative cognition of the world. Buddhists first face up to the suffering of life, and then search for a fundamental solution. As far as Buddhism is concerned, all the sufferings in life are precious and can be conquered as long as we change our attitude towards a positive awareness. Even sufferings can be regarded as active experiences for the sake of relieving all sentient beings of suffering, because of witnessing the emptiness of suffering, one can achieve the happiness, with the sense of comfort and ease. Secondly, what Buddha affirms is the superiority of humanity, the nature of human being includes:

being smart and thoughtful, rich in creativity; being self–controlled, courage to reshaping; benevolent consciousness, the quality of buddhahood.

The Buddhist outlook on life is expressed in the code of conduct of life, which is representative of The "Five Precepts": (1) abstain from killing; (2) abstain from stealing; (3) abstain from adultery; (4) abstain from delusions; (5) abstinence from wine."Ten Positive Virtues" : (1) no killing; (2) no stealing; (3) no sexual desire; (4) no lying; (5) no stiring up enmity; (6) no obloquy; (7) no blandishments; (8) no covetousness; (9) no kruddhi; (10) no evil opinion."Catuh–samgraha–vastu" (four approaches to help people): (1) alms giving: be willing to give alms and gifts and Dharma; (2) kind language: comfort with gentle, loving words of kindness; (3) acts of benefiting: Do all kinds of good deeds by devoting oneself and benefiting all beings; (4) sharing and joining: be close to sentient beings by sharing and guiding accordingly. To follow the four approaches, one must take"catvāri n apramānāni"(four spiritual states of mind) as the foundation to achieve the integration of exterior effect and interior intention. They are: (1) a kind heart: the intention of giving joy; (2) a sense of sympathy: the willingness to eliminate sufferings; (3) the empathy of happiness: the feeling of rejoice to see people doing and enjoying goodness; (4) an attitude of fairness: the standard of behavior that all living beings are treated equally."Sad–paramita" (six ways to practice Buddhist doctrines): (1) keep giving; (2) keep the precepts; (3) endure humiliation; (4) keep progress; (5) keep in meditation; (6) reach for highest wisdom(Prajna).

In the eyes of Buddhists, Buddhas are sentient beings who are already enlightened, and sentient beings are Buddhas who are not yet enlightened. The view of life advocated by the Buddhists is for all living beings, and the profound philosophy of life contained in the Buddhists is extensive and profound, which is often difficult to comprehend thoroughly even after decades of study. Nevertheless, the tenet of Buddhist life view is obvious, which is to stop and prevent evil deeds and thoughts, to actively present kindness and beneficence, and to purify and improve oneself. Buddhist culture is an important part of Chinese traditional culture and has positive guiding significance for building a harmonious socialist society. The contemporary educational value of the basic concept of Buddhist culture is reflected in: (1) Its emphasis on"harmony" is conducive to social stability and harmony. (2) The wealth view of Buddhist culture is helpful for people's social view to develop from one–sided to scientific one. (3) Understanding the contemporary value of traditional Buddhist culture is helpful to strictly distinguish the essential difference between excellent culture and cult, and to promote humanistic quality. (4) In Buddhist culture, the concept of self–discipline and unselfishness is conducive for improving people's moral standard.

III. The Evolution of Sense of Values

As a stable system of concepts , sense of values is the standard and viewpoint to judge all kinds of relations, good and evil, true and false, beauty and ugliness, it is internalized in the self-awareness of consciousness about an individual or nation, and is reflected through people's social practice. Sense of values often changes with different times and nations, therefore, a value system contains the diversified features depending on different times, nationalities, and variability. China is an ancient civilization with a long history and complete cultural system and structure, Confucianism, Buddhism and Taoism are all important parts of this system. Although Confucianism, as a mainstream value system, has shown a relatively stable state in China, it has different forms of expression in different historical stages. Chinese values have their own vicissitudes, especially in the different period of historical stage, the evolution of values is more significant. From ancient to modern times, the profound roots of Chinese traditional culture are like the rich nutrition and source for contemporary socialist core values, and still continue unfolding strong vitality and influence.

3.1 Traditional Sense of Values

The realistic foundation of the Chinese sense of traditional values is Chinese traditional farming civilization, the premise of traditional values is "Tao" and "virtue", the core content of traditional values is "benevolence and love", the fundamental spirit of traditional values is "unremitting self-improvement" and "commitment to moral values", the standard system of traditional values is patriarchal law and ritual system. Chinese value system has a long history. It is born in the time of "Three Emperors and Five Sovereigns in ancient China", conceived in The "three generations" of Xia, Shang and Western Zhou Dynasties, and formed completely in the Spring and Autumn period and the Warring States period. The dominant ideas have also experienced the process of changing, but the mainstream system of values has gradually accumulated and has lasted through the whole traditional society.

In the vast range of Chinese traditional values, the typical ideas are integrated in different schools and cultural philosophies. They include: (1) searching for the intrinsic meaning of life: Chinese philosophers did not attribute value only to the desire and demand of the people as the subject, but to the inherent attribute of each object, believing that there was a world of values above the physical world, in which each individual was a microcosm, all of which upheld universal values and Tao, the realization of value cannot be separated from individual self-cultivation and inner transcendence, thus the meaning of life can be constantly embodied and pursued; (2) focusing on the relationship of "individual and group" as well as "justice and interests": the pursuit of an ideal society of overall harmony and coordinated development of social groups is also a long lasting ideal of value system. To realize this ideal, while dealing with the relationship between different levels of society, the government should depend on benevolence,loyalty and filial piety, moral governance and discipline, etiquette and enlightenment in theory. In practice, the government should depend on harmony without distinction, clearly distinguishing social groups, teaching people to value justice over profit, cherishing the law of nature over human desires as the realm of a gentleman, advocating self-righteousness and convincing others with virtue; (3) concerning the family, the country and the world: Traditional values concentrate a lot on governance and relations between nations, this is reflected on view of harmony over dispute, universal love and peace, all nations in perfect harmony, prosperous country and powerful army, people being the fundamental of the state, and the social ideal of great harmony. The world of peace and harmony is regarded as the best state of human society and the embodiment of the traditional values that deal with social and peace issues. (4) following the law of nature. Traditional Chinese sense of values has long recognized that man is not the master of nature, to survive and develop, we must follow the laws of nature and live in harmony with them. Such thoughts are embodied in the concept of Tao to nature, rational understanding of everything, the knowledge that everything has its own advantages, the concept of moderation, the truth of endless life, and the attitude of understanding thoroughly the truth of world and handling with it accordingly. Such concepts contain the respect for nature and the vision of sustainable development of human society.

In brief, there are different ways to realize traditional Chinese values, Confucianism is concerned with the realm of life and the dignity of sages, the realization of personal life value is integrated with the pursuit of "benevolence" and "justice" together; Taoism stresses the natural inaction of Tao, and believes that the civilization construction of human society should be in harmony with the law of nature, emphasizing passive inaction and develop a kind of ideal personality that follows the trend of time and situation. Secondly, Chinese traditional values are not limited to the value of society and the people themselves, but to the height of the value of heaven and earth and the universe. In addition, Chinese traditional values emphasize moral spirit and its value while highlighting the central position of human beings in the universe, and this confirms the people–oriented sense of values. It can be seen that Chinese traditional values put forward the issues of ideal personality, ideal interpersonal relationship, and ideal country and society, it is to standardize and guide the individual and the society with an ideal cultural value, so as to maintain the harmonious and healthy development of the country, society and individuals.This provides important inspiration and referetial significance for the construction of values in contemporary society.

3.2 Modern Sense of Values

Chinese modern values are the unification of the transformation and inheritance of traditional values, it is therefore an integral part of China's value system. On the one hand, Chinese modern values criticized the superstitious autocratic ideas in traditional philosophy, on the other hand, they propagated the new culture and new ideas of the western bourgeoisie, it shows essential differences with traditional values in terms of ontology, epistemology, human nature and social theory, and it holds distinct enlightening character in opposition to feudal traditional culture. The character of enlightening has become the historical mission and basic feature of modern Chinese values.

The enlightenment of modern Chinese values is reflected in all aspects of modern thoughts: (1) In the view of nature, atheism was used to outlaw the theory of the mandate of heaven. Man is said to be the master of his own fate based on modern psychology which advocates subject consciousness; (2) In ontology, the new discoveries of natural sciences from west was absorbed such as atomism, elementalism and aether to drive out the natural theory of vitality, and occupied and replaced the educational world of nature and the mind theory with the rich and colorful inner world; (3) In epistemology, the empiricism principle of "actual measurement of objects" has replaced the intuitionism of conjecture and insight. Epistemology is no longer entangled with moral cultivation, and has become a completely independent field; (4) In dialectics, the interaction of Yin and Yang is cleared up by concepts of force and reaction force, attraction and repulsion force, which then sublimated into a universal law of the world, rather than an individual phenomenon and temporary state; (5) In terms of ethics, it criticizes the traditional obscurantism and the three principles and five virtues, asserting that human beings have flesh and blood, emotions and desires, and their value and significance lies in the pursuit of happiness, which can be the source of human behavior and the motive force of social progress; (6) In view of politics, the social contract theory, natural human rights theory is greatly praised, eulogizing the idea of freedom, equality and fraternity. The influence of enlightenment on Chinese modern values is extensive, which is concentrated in the distinct characteristics of modern values, including: (1) pay attention to the individual and subjective will, emotional likes and dislikes; (2) attach importance to sense and perceptual experience, and believe that sense plays a decisive role in understanding, transforming and dominating the world; (3) concern people's material desires and physiological needs, there is no good and evil about human nature , in the acquired human behavior, pain and pleasure is the standard to measure; (4) talents with personalities and capacity are the masters of social history, they are the embodiment of personal value. From the historical perspective, this enlightenment and subjectivity is never away from the value seeking for national salvation. From the idea of "learning from the barbarian to control the barbarian" to the strategy of "taking the group as the one and taking the advantages of changes into practical use", to the cognition of "civil rights, human rights and national rights", and then to the awakening of "national character" and patriotic consciousness, all of these thoughts are oriented by global view and national survival.

On the surface, it is the historical changes and capitalist industry that impacted Chinese traditional values in modern times, but more fundamentally, it is the system of values of western liberalism that played an important role. It can be said that the values of modern China are based on natural science, while striving to call for the subject value, trying to use the dual attributes of nature and society to recognize human nature, people were trying to objectively examine the value system. Because of its enlightening and subjectivity, modern Chinese values have played a role in paving the way for the awakening of national consciousness and the sublimation of patriotism in the historical change.

3.3 Contemporary Sense of Values

Since the 1920s, socialism has become a social trend of thoughts that has deeply influenced the course of modern Chinese history, during the New Culture Movement ,Chinese New culture intellectuals transformed the individualistic identity into the class identity and socialist identity after the May Fourth Movement. Since the founding of New China in the mid–20th century, the socialist spirit, as the distinctive banner of modern Chinese values, has gradually been implemented into social morals, systems, policies and activities, from independence and self–reliance, to serving the people wholeheartedly, to exploring the path of national rejuvenation, and to gathering consensus on core socialist values, these values are gradually implemented into the social morality, system, policies and activities, so that they are turned realistically into social culture, into people's inner beliefs and codes of conduct, thus forming the values of contemporary China.

From the view of significance and function, contemporary Chinese values are the value system that embodies the spiritual value of China's current times, it fully displays China's national image and reflects the soul of China's national soft power. From the perspective of practical basis and theoretical origin, contemporary Chinese values are the overall understanding of value relations formed by the Chinese people in the course of their participation in the great practice of socialism with Chinese characteristics. They fulfill the requirements of the times, practical requirements and their own demands, the value system is formed by integrating the essence of socialist core values, Chinese traditional cultural values and western modern cultural values, it has the attributes of socialism and contemporary China. In view of the essence and function, as an important part of the ideology of socialism with Chinese characteristics, contemporary Chinese values are not only the source of social theories, but also the driving force to promote economic and social development, they are also beneficial to highlight the discourse power of socialism with Chinese characteristics. Core values as the core content of Contemporary Chinese values are also systematic. It is clear from the Chinese Communist Party's speech and propaganda spirit, the core value is the ultimate goal and basic principle of the organic unity of the system. The ultimate goal of the value system put forward by the Party is "the great rejuvenation of the Chinese nation", its basic meaning is "national prosperity, national rejuvenation and people's happiness", among which the happiness of the people holds a more profound ultimate meaning.

The "24 Chinese Characters" advocated by the core value concept: The values of prosperity, democracy, civilization, harmony, freedom, equality, justice, rule of law, patriotism, dedication, integrity, and kindness"have inherited the genes of China's fine traditional culture while carrying the ideals and beliefs established by the Chinese people through painstaking efforts since modern times, and thus present the beautiful vision of individual citizens. China's fine traditional culture is the gene and source of the socialist core values, however, contemporary values are not the copy of traditional culture, but the sublimation of traditional culture, making it adapt to the needs of socialism and the development of the value spirit of the times in terms of integration, reconstruction and innovation. Each of the core values in the three aspects is based on the socialist system, and reflects the socialist nature with a distinct and advanced value orientation in the new era of socialism, this is the soul reason why the traditional culture is full of vitality and values of the times.

In short, to understand the values of contemporary China, one needs to explore the cultural root in social life and practice of contemporary Chinese people. The exploration and practice of socialism with Chinese characteristics has rejuvenated a poor and weak ancient civilization, and has exerted a profound influence on contemporary Chinese values. Socialism aims at establishing a social value concept of fairness and justice based on public ownership of the means of production that enables everyone to get free and all–round development. Up to today, the fine culture of the Chinese nation has been deeply embedded in the great national spirit of unity, peace–loving, industrious and courageous, and unremitting self–improvement with patriotism at its core, it has given birth to a system of values with the unique consciousness, character and temperament of the Chinese nation, this is also an important social and cultural premise for the modernization of Chinese traditional educational concepts.

Section Three Virtue Orientation in Life Stories

In Chinese educational culture, traditional system of virtues is not only the social code of morality condensed by thousands of years of history and culture, but also the core soul of the Chinese nation's humanistic spirit to be inherited. These traditional virtues have been spread and carried forward from generation to generation in the field of education through the life stories of historical celebrities. The life stories have played a significant role in personal cultivation, family ethics and even state governance, and have had a wide and far–reaching impact on social development and civilization progress.

I. Loyalty and Patriotism

Loyalty and patriotism originates from the political ideas advocated by Confucianism. The first book that recorded and promoted "Loyalty and Patriotism" was the *Biography of Yue Fei* in the Song Dynasty. It is reported that the back of Yue Fei is engraved with "be loyal and patriotic" deep in the skin. Later, it was called "serving the country with loyalty", referring to the purest loyalty to serve the motherland. As a matter of fact,"serving the country with loyalty", as a spirit of patriotism, has long been a basic virtue in the history of the Chinese nation. It appears in the life stories of patriots of all generations, deeply enlightened people in mind and education field.

1.1 The Total Dedication of Zhuge Liang

Zhuge Liang was the most famous statesman and strategist in the Three Kingdoms Period. He was a knowledgeable and resourceful advisor to Liu Bei, the founding emperor of Shu Han political power. Due to his outstanding achievements in the establishment and consolidation of the Shu Han regime, he is known as the embodiment of wisdom. In order to repay Liu Bei's appreciation and support, Zhuge Liang planned the "Converstion and Countermeasure in Long Zhong" for Liu Bei to establish the state. Later, according to this political strategy, Liu Bei allied Wu against Wei, established Shu Han regime in Chengdu, and made Zhuge Liang Prime minister. After the death of Liu Bei, the state of Shu was in turmoil, with internal and external troubles. However, Zhuge Liang worked hard and did his duty with all his heart. He was in charge of every single aspect of state affairs personally. In order to achieve the goal of the national unity, Zhuge Liang led his troops to attack Wei six times, but all of them failed because of the strong military power of Wei. In the winter of 228 AD, Zhuge Liang once again gathered his army and launched a northern expedition. He led his men to actively organize attacks, but they were not able to achieve complete victory. Finally Zhuge Liang fell to sickness with fatigue, unfortunately died of illness in the barrack. Zhuge Liang left to the world the famous articles through the dynasties like *Memorial on Sending Out the Troops*, *Letter of Admonition*, *Post Memorial on Sending Out the Troops* and other ancient articles all have a profound influence in Chinese history. Among which *Post Memorial on Sending Out the Troops* analyzed the situation of the war at that time, expressed Zhuge Liang's own ambition, at the end, he wrote down the words "I exert all my efforts, until my death", which is also the summary of his life's hard work and loyalty to the country. Zhuge Liang was buried in Dingjun Mountain, with the posthumous title "Loyal Marquis ".

The evaluation of "dedication" is a high recognition of Zhuge Liang's personal image and spiritual symbol. His service was premised on his devotion to his country, which was chiefly manifested by the great feats of leadership and command, from governing the country to running the army, he often calculated his strategies thoroughly and defeated the enemy. The principles of identifying, cultivating, encouraging and employing people proposed by him all coincide with the art of leadership in modern times and are still instructive to the modern organizational leaders. At the same time, as the embodiment of wisdom, he once compared himself with Guan Zhong and Yue Yi, such a theme has attracted attention of later generations and has become an important content of remembering, inheriting, innovating and spreading the excellent traditional Chinese culture. Zhuge Liang has also been a model for later generations to learn, as he is respected as "the Number One among Famous Prime Ministers in China for All Time".

1.2 The Frontier Marriage of Wang Zhaojun

Wang Zhaojun was a maid in the imperial palace of Emperor Yuan in Western Han Dynasty, and is regarded together with Diao Chan, Xi Shi, Yang Yvhuan as one of the four great beauties of ancient China. She was originally a palace maid in the Yuan Emperor period of Han Dynasty, and later married the Huns. Wang Zhaojun maintained the stable relationship between Xiongnu and Han Dynasty of Han–Hungarian relations for half a century, and the story of "Zhaojun going out of the frontier fortress" has been passed down through the ages.

Wang Zhaojun was born in 52 BC in what is now Xingshan County, Hubei Province, into a common family, and was later elected to the palace as a folk girl. Because she refused to bribe the court painter Mao Yanshou, her portrait was not painted beautifully, she was therefore not elected to Emperor Yuan's harem. In the first month of 33 BC, Xiongnu came to the court and asked for a Han woman to be his wife. The Yuan Emperor then gave the Zhaojun to chief of the Xiongnu, who was very happy and submit a written statement that he was willing to keep the border safe for long. After arriving at the land of huns, Wang Zhaojun is called NingHu Yanzhi. Zhao Jun and Huhan Xie the chief lived together for three years and gave birth to a son. After the death of her first husband, Zhaojun wrote to Han Court asking for return, Emperor Cheng of Han Dynasty decreed to "follow the Hu Custom" in accordance with the nomad system of succession marriage and made Zhaojun remarry the eldest son of Hu Hanxie called Chief Fu ZhuLei, they lived together for 11 years and had two daughters. In 20 BC, Fu Zhu Lei passed away, less than two years later, Wang Zhaojun died of illness. She was buried in the southern suburb of Hohhot City, near the Yellow River and the Great Green Mountains. Later generations called it "Qingzhong". Because Zhaojun is known as The "messenger of national friendship" in the history of ethnic relations, even the burial place of Zhaojun "Qingzhong" has been given a unique symbolic significance, therefore, the image of Wang Zhaojun has become a kind of literary image rooted in historical memory, casting a cultural model beyond time and space.

As an ordinary palace lady, she was willing to bear the heavy responsibility entrusted by the Han Empire and lived in Xiongnu for many years, integrating with the Xiongnu tribe. With her extraordinary spirit of sacrifice, she not only effectively safeguarded the good situation of peace created by the joint efforts of the Han and Hun people, but also greatly promoted the economic prosperity and development of all ethnic groups. What is more, she proved to the world that women can serve their country with loyalty. Therefore, in the history of Chinese virtue education, Wang Zhaojun has long been not only a simple girl for political marriage in Western Han Dynasty, but also a permanent memory in the mind of the world, a cultural symbol with rich connotations shared by many ethnic groups. People of all ethnic groups and the intellectual circle regard Zhaojun's marriage as a symbol of national friendship and unity.

1.3 Lin Zexu's Vision of the World

Lin Zexu was a famous statesman and thinker in the late Qing Dynasty. In 1785, Lin Zexu was born in a poor family of teachers in Fujian. His grandfather and uncle had both been private school teachers, and his father also made a living by teaching. Lin Zexu entered the private school at the age of 4, under the careful guidance of his father, he set a lofty ambition from a young age. He became a successful candidate in the imperial examinations at the provincial level at 19 and became a Jinshi in the highest imperial examinations at 26. He served successively as an official, an inspector of Jiangsu, Governor of Shaanxi and Gansu, Governor of Huguang, etc. In 1838, Lin Zexu was appointed imperial inspector and went to Guangzhou to ban opium trading. For thousands of years, the world view of "China" and "Yidi" (barbaric tribes) had dominated the scholars' cognition of international affairs, and the westerners and their civilization were classified as "Yidi". In this context, Lin Zexu was able to resist the secular pressure, tried to acquire foreign knowledge with a pragmatic attitude of seeking knowledge, and took the initiative to recognize the west world. As soon as he arrived in Guangzhou, he recruited talents regardless of their background. In order to obtain foreign information in a timely manner, Lin Zexu began the official history of translating foreign books. In addition to presiding over the translation of western newspapers and books, the *Four Continents Annals* under his facilitating, was the first world geography work translated by modern Chinese people, which greatly expanded people's international vision at that time. Due to the importance attached to western civilization and international relations, such knowledge as references played an important role in the struggle against colonial aggression. He then issued a tough decree in Guangzhou and gave British dealers a deadline to hand over all their opium. While the opium dealer tried to bribe him with money, Lin Zexu severely reprimanded them with the comment: as long as a single civilian was poisoned by opium, I could not sleep or eat well. In June 1839, Lin Zexu publicly destroyed nearly 20,000 cases of opium confiscated in Humen, which dealt a heavy blow to the arrogance of British opium dealers, and demonstrated to the world the determination of the Chinese people to resist opium while safeguarding the dignity and interests of the nation.

As a leader in Humen opium fighting, he led the army and the people to fight resolutely against the British invaders, and was praised as a "national hero". The famous statement in his poem,"To seek for the benefit of the country, not for the fate of myself," has inspired generations of Chinese to strive for national prosperity. He also advocated learning western science and culture, enlightening future generations that the premise of "know oneself and know the enemy" is to open our own horizons, and the way to serve the country with loyalty can also be to "learn from enemy". Therefore, Lin Zexu is known as the first person in China who"opened the eyes to the world". Lin Zexu's set a good example for his children with his whole life. Under the influence of good family tradition, his three sons have grown into the pillars of the country, and the descendants of the Lin family are mostly capable and have made contributions to the country.

II. Filial Piety and Courtesy

Filial piety is the core and essence of Chinese traditional culture education. In short, filial piety means showing respect for elders and keeping harmonious relation with brothers. The traditional filial piety includes two virtuous aspects:"filial piety for parents" and "respect for elder brothers" , they are mutually fit and complement each other in terms of connotation, and share the common cultural meaning, it is respecting and obeying. Filial piety requires respect and obedience from the son to the father, and brotherly respect and obedience is from the young to the elder. And courtesy is the embodiment of Confucian advocation of establishing a nation by virtue. The "three rites" in traditional education, namely the *Rites of Zhou*, the *Rites of Yi* and the *Records of Rites,* have formed a complete system of Chinese etiquette culture. Etiquette, as a constraint on people's behavior, is the norm of shaping the individual personality, the harmony of social relations and the stability of national rules. After the baptism of the spirit of freedom and equality in modern times, the basic content of Confucian ethics can still be used as the basic principle in Chinese modern society to guide people's life.

2.1 The Resignation of Li Mi for Filial Piety

Li Mi was a scholar in the Western Jin Dynasty, his father died when he was young, and his mother remarried when he was four years old. As a young boy he was weak with frail health, and was brought up by his grandmother Liu. Li Mi was very studious and well–read *the Five Classics*, especially the *Biography of Zuo Shi in the Spring and Autumn Period*. He was good at literature and was once a young ministry in Shu Han. After Wei defeated Shu, Deng Ai, a general Who Subdues the West admired his talent and asked him to serve as his chief secretary. Li Mi declined Deng Ai's offer on the grounds of supporting her elderly grandmother. In 267 AD, Sima Yan, Emperor Wudi of the Jin Dynasty, appointed a crown prince, and ordered Li Mi to assist the prince for appreciating his talent.The imperial edict was issued several times, and the counties kept urging him. By this time, Li Mi's grandmother was 96 years old and was troubled by sickness and old age. So he submitted a written statement to Emperor Wudi of Jin, stating the situation of the family to explain why he could not answer the order. This is the famous "*A Letter to His Majesty*", words in which were sincere and touching, so that the Emperor was moved by Li Mi's filial piety to his grandmother, he not only allowed him not to take the position temporarily, but also rewarded him for the filial piety to the elders. Li Mi became an officer after the ending of the mourning period for her grandmother. When he served as the county magistrate of Wen County, Henan Province, he gave strict orders, made remarkable achievements and was known for his integrity. Li Mi originally hoped to take a position in the imperial court and display his intelligence and wisdom, but no one in the court recommended him because the dignitaries in the court feared his integrity. Later, he only served as governor of Hanzhong and returned to the hometown after a year. He died of illness at the age of sixty–four.

Li Mi left for the world "*A Letter to His Majesty*" which is honest and vivid, all from the reality without vanity, highlighting both his filial piety and his wisdom. During the period of Wei and Jin Dynasties, the society was in turmoil and metaphysical and Buddhist were prevalent. In a background that the concept of loyalty was marginalized,"filial piety" was raised to a supreme position and was unprecedentedly strengthened. In the etiquette tradition of governing the world with "loyalty and filial piety" , filial piety came first ahead of loyalty. Li Mi's growing environment determines his filial piety, and "filial piety" is the living foundation of Li Mi. Li Mi wanted to refuse the appointment of an official, and it was very difficult to make Emperor Wu of Jin not blame him. However, Li Mi succeeded in writing the article. He stated the obvious contradictions between his filial piety for his grandmother and the loyalty to the emperor and solved these problems one by one, because ruling the nation with the virtue of "filial piety" is a program of governance, filial piety for grandmother is reasonable and legal, this gave a theoretical basis for "allow me to fulfill the filial piety to the end". Li Mi's story of resignation for filial piety has left the later generations with the affection of Chinese etiquette and the spirit of filial piety, and his style of writing and behavior has become the model of traditional education of loyalty and filial piety.

2.2 The Respectful Waiting of Yang Shi in Snow

Yang Shi was a famous philosopher, litterateur and official in the Northern Song Dynasty. Yang Shi was very clever when he was young. He could compose poems at the age of eight and write articles in traditional style at the age of nine. People who knew him at that time called him a "prodigy". He studied Buddhism as a child and began to study Confucianism as a teenager. In 1076, he won the title of a scholar (a successful candidate in the highest imperial examinations) but did not take up his post, he devoted himself to the study of Neo–Confucianism and wrote down the famous *Li Zi Jie.* After Yang Shi became a judicial officer in Xuzhou, he became Cheng Hao's student to study Neo–Confucianism. Together with You Zuo who is mentioned in the story of waiting in snow, Yi Rong and Xie Liangzuo, he became one of the four disciples of Cheng School. In 1085, when Yang Shi heard that his respected teacher Cheng Hao passed away, he was very sad. He could not leave his position at will while he was in office, so he set up a mourning hall at his living place and wrote a lament while crying plaintively. At the age of forty, although he had made great achievements in Neo–Confucianism, he still chose to join his mentor's brother Cheng Yi, when the story of waiting in snow happened. Once, Yang Shi and his classmate You Zuo went to the teacher's house for consultation. That day, it happened to be snowing heavily, the sky was cloudy and the ground was like freezing. When they reached the teacher's door, they knew that their teacher was taking a nap. They stood respectfully outside the door, so as not to disturb the teacher. After waiting for a long time, Yang Shi's feet were almost frozen and he was shaking with cold, but he still stood respectfully without a hint and expression of fatigue or impatience. When Cheng Yi woke up and saw from the window that Yang and You were standing in the snow, they were then almost draped in snow, the snow around their feet was more than a foot deep. Moved by their sincere passion of learning, Cheng Yi answered their questions patiently and carefully. From then on, Cheng Yi taught them with more concentrated attention. Yang Shi served successively as the governor of Liuyang and Yuhang. He was loved by the people and however also witnessed the corruption of the dynasty. In 1130, he retired from official circles to the countryside and continued to teach his children and grandchildren filial piety until his death at the age of 83.

Through Yang Shi's whole life, he was adhering to the gentleman's virtue. As a connecting scholar between the preceding and the following, he was a transitional figure between the

Cheng school and Zhu Xi especially in Neo-Confucianism research. The experience of waiting respectfully in snow has become a model of respecting teachers and teaching etiquette in China, Zhu Xi also praised him as "a loyal inheritor of Confucius and his disciple Yan Yuan, the model of Cheng school's proverbs and disciplines, and the virtue of Yang Shi as a teacher should be learned and carried forward forever". Later generations often use the story of "waiting in snow" as a metaphor for the eagerness to learn and respect for teachers. China has long been known as a land of rites. In 2011, the legend of "The Respectful Waiting in Snow in the Front Door of Cheng" was successfully selected in the third batch of Luoyang Intangible Cultural Heritage List in the form of folk literature. The core content of the legend is the embodiment of The "Cheng School" culture; it is also a Chinese typical textbook of respecting teachers and valuing education , which is the essence of the excellent virtue tradition of Chinese nation.

2.3 The Effort of Ti Ying to Save Her Father

Ti Ying, surnamed Chunyu, was born in Linzi during the Western Han Dynasty. Her father, Chunyu Yi, liked reading and medicine. He was originally a local official, but because of his upright character and dislike of the striving for fame and fortune, he soon resigned and returned home to become a professional doctor. Chun Yuyi was famous for his excellent skills. But because he refused to flatter the feudal nobility by declining to pay a visit to some wealthy and powerful families, the rich and powerful family then charged him with some accusations, and he was escorted to Chang'an for corporal punishment. At that time, Chun Yu Yi once exclaimed indignantly:"There is no one to help in an emergency if one doesn't have a son". This reflects the typical idea at that time when the absence of a son was seen as a family misfortune. Ti Ying was impressed by his father's words, she wanted to do what a man can do, she went to the capital with his father resolutely, submitted a written statement to the emperor, thoroughly stated his father's honest and innocent. The gist of the statement was like "My name is Ti Ying, little daughter of Chunyu Yi. When my father was an official, the local people said he was an honest upright official. This time he committed the crime and was sentenced to corporal punishment.I feel sorry and sad not only for my father, but also for all those who have to be tortured. A man whose feet were cut off is forever crippled; if the nose is cut off, it can't be put back on, even if one wants to turn over a new leaf, he surely can't. She also said in the statement that she was willing to become a servant and maidservant to be tortured on behalf of her father. The emperor Wen Di was moved, he had the case checked and bestowed forgiveness to Chunyu Yi, furthermore, the corporal punishment was then abolished. As a weak little girl, Ti Ying moved the emperor with extraordinary courage and sincere filial piety, she not only made the father free from physical disability, but also changed the law of the Han Dynasty, the benefit was to the whole nation, this is bound to cause a social sensation, she was warmly praised and admired by people. Early in the late Western Han Dynasty, her story was painted on the folding screen and she thus became a role model for people to respect and learn from.

The story was also recorded into the *Biographies of Heroic Females*

As a historical event involving many people, Ti Ying's effort of saving his father contains many cultural implications. People in the later generations can understand and interpret it from different angles in view of the inheritance and education of traditional virtues. The reason why Ti Ying could move the emperor Wen, and successfully rescued her old father, was her sincere filial piety which is highly recognized in Chinese traditional society, as well as her wisdom and outstanding ability to argue. Although she did not become a bright and vivid literary image like Wang Zhaojun and others, her sincere piety, wit, and brave quality, has long been praised by people, thus adding a wonderful story for virtual education.

III. Honesty and Trustworthiness

Honesty and trustworthiness is the core content of traditional Chinese educational culture, which has long been regarded as the basic moral code of life."Xin" generally refers to credit, reputation and good faith. It requires a firm and honest attitude towards individuals, organizations and societies. As the saying goes,"No surviving without loyalty", it means that if you don't have loyalty and credibility, you can't sustain in society. Therefore, honesty and trustworthiness is an important prerequisite for promoting mutual trust between people and stressing credibility in the society, as well as a moral quality that has always been revered in the course of education of the Chinese nation.

3.1 The Sword Hanging Story of Ji Zha

Ji Zha, also known as Prince Zha, was the fourth son of the King of Wu during the Spring and Autumn Period. He was a sage who could be mentioned together with Confucius and was honored as "South Ji Zha and North Confucious". The evaluation of him in history is "bright and wise, modesty and clear minded, sincere and honesty , and the benevolent thought of the people." According to the Records of the Grand Historian: Once, Ji Zha was visiting various vassal states, when he was in the state of Xu, he paid a visit on Monarch Xu. At the very beginning of the meeting, Monarch Xu was very interested in Ji Bu's sword, but he was too embarrassed to ask Ji Bu for it. After Ji Zha sensed his intention, he wanted to give the sword to Xu. However, due to the need to wear swords and other accessories when visiting countries, Ji Zha planned to give the sword to Xu Jun when he returned to that country.Unexpectedly, when Ji Zha came back from his travels around the world, Xu Jun suddenly fell ill and passed away. Ji Bu was very sad. He went to Xu's tomb and took off the sword to tie it to the branch beside the tomb.The guards of him did not understand Ji Zha's behavior, so they asked,"Since Xu is dead, Why are you still hanging your sword here?" Ji Zha replied,"You don't get it. When I first met him, I decided to give him the sword as a gift. How can I go against my promise just because he is dead?" Hearing this, the guards were moved by the virtue of keeping the word. Later, the story of Ji Zha's keeping the commitment of giving the sword widely spread. After Jizha's death, Confucius himself wrote an inscription for him.

After thousands of years, this story is still celebrated by future generations, and the commitment to honor the original intention behind it is the essence of the traditional Chinese culture. Attaching importance to credibility and commitment is not only the basic virtue of individuals for social living but also the precondition of workplace competition. The enlightenment value of this story for modern social education is also worthy of attention.

3.2 The Fair Honest of Yan Shu

Yan Shu was a statesman and litterateur in the Northern Song Dynasty and also a famous poet with graceful and euphemistic poetic genre. He was intelligent from an early age and took the imperial examination as a prodigy at the age of 14.

He once served as an imperial scholar and later as a prime minister, he is famous and respected for his poetry writing, setting up schools and cultivating talents. An anecdote from Yan Shu's youth time has been praised to this day for demonstrating his honesty and fairness. At the age of 15, Yan Shu was not only called a "prodigy" but also recommended by the county magistrate. On the day he was recommended, more than 3,000 people came to take the exam. When Yan Shu saw the test paper and found that he had answered it a few days before, he was excited and then felt that it was unfair and could be suspected of concealing. So he reported to the examiner truthfully and said,"Your excellency, I have answered this test question before, please test me with another one." He then stressed that without changing the topic even if he passed the exam, it would not be enough to prove a true talent. And if he did not do the new test well with the topic changed, the reason could be his knowledge is not enough, there would be no complaints. The invigilator thought this was reasonable, so he changed the test paper for Yan Shu. When Yan Shu got the new question, he read it several times and thought about it for a moment, then picked up the pen and start the writing. This amazed the invigilator, and the news soon spread. When the emperor heard of this, he spoke highly of Yan Shu's decision. He considered Yan Shu to be honest and trustworthy, and bestowed upon him the honor of being a "fellow scholar" (a successful candidate in the highest imperial examinations).

Yan Shu is not an uncontroversial celebrity because of his history of ups and downs in official circles; but his life story of honest competition and his character of upright and fairplay became the premise of his fame. He made a great achievement in literature following the great style of the Tang and Five Dynasties and exploring the new charm of Song in poem writing, this also laid the foundation for him to select and cultivate talents , revitalize the school, and revive the educational cause.. Yan Shu's honesty and fairness helped him to promote education for the country and cultivate talents with strategic vision and practical spirit.

3.3 The Trust Winning Pillar of Shang Yang

Shang Yang was a statesman, a reformer, a thinker and a representative figure of legalism in the Warring States period. Through the reform of the law, he helped Oin to implement severe punishment and laws, advocate agriculture labor and suppress commerce, and thus made Qin become a powerful country at that time through reforming the land system and the tax system. After the death of Duke Xiao of Qin, Shang Yang was falsely accused of rebellion by Childe Qian and was defeated and killed. The main reason for Shang Yang's successful reform under the support of Duke Xiao of Qin was to establish the prestige of "everything depends on the law". The prestige of this kind of law came from making the public be aware of the integrity and the power of the law. In order to establish his authority and promote reform, Shang Yang ordered to erect a log about seven meters long outside the south gate of the capital, and publicly promised that anyone who could move the log to the north gate would receive a reward of ten liang (a Chinese unit of measurement) of gold. The onlookers could not believe that such an easy thing could be so highly rewarded, and no one would give it a try. So Shang Yang raised the bounty to 50 liang of gold. Generous rewards rouse one to heroism, at last, someone stood up and carried the wood to the north gate. And the 50 liang of gold were immediately rewarded by Shang Yang to show that they are not deceiving the people. When everyone saw this, their eyes widened in surprise. At this time, Shang Yang was heard standing on the gate tower saying to everyone,"As you can see, laws are laws that count. From now on, those who abide by the law will be rewarded; anyone who disobeys the law will be punished." And with these words, he ordered the new law to be proclaimed. This action built up the prestige in the hearts of the people, and then everyone knew Shang Yang's integrity and the prestige of the decrees. The state of Qin slowly grew stronger, and there was a peaceful scene where the properties of passers–by were not stolen and the doors of houses didn't have to be closed at night. The new law made State of Qin increasingly stronger and eventually unified China.

The reason why Shang Yang's success in the reform was a good beginning was that he demonstrated the integrity of laws and regulations through this concrete example, thus establishing the authority of law enforcers. Shang Yang's fate also inspired later rulers and educators:"Only good virtue is not enough to administer a country, only laws can not make governors effective". Only when law is supported by morality can it have a strong social foundation and become a good law to maintain good governance. On the other hand, Shang Yang's thought of ruling by law covered every aspect of law formulation, execution and popularization, forming a logic system with strong theoretical basis. This not only influenced the ancient Chinese society, but also had a profound influence on the educational culture and management of China which stresses the respected teachers and regulations for thousands of years.

IV. Diligence and Great Efforts

The belief that heaven rewards the diligent is the essence of Chinese education and culture. It is written in the records of *Zhou Yi*, which says,"The world moves vigorously, the gentleman should keep self–improvement" and in the *Book of Shang*, which says,"The heaven rewards the diligent", showing the true meaning that hard work reversing hard life. The

Chinese view of the universe believes that heaven and earth form the whole universe, the sky is high and vigorous, and the earth is vast and heavy loaded. Chinese education often further extends the philosophy of life from the explanation of the universe images, that is, ideal of life should be lofty, resolute and with unremitting self–improvement like the sky, and ways of living should be heavy, broad and virtuous like the earth. As an educational concept,"Heaven rewards the diligent", together with" The earth rewards the kindness, business rewards the integrity, vocation rewards the excellence", have become the classic expressions of traditional Chinese philosophy, leading generations of Chinese people to either live rightly alone or contribute to the world.

4.1 The Effort of Lu Ban for Perfection

Lu Ban was born in the State of Lu during the Spring and Autumn Period. He was a famous craftsman and was respected as the grandmaster and ancestor of Chinese craftsman. Born into a carpenter's family, Lu Ban had worked with his family since childhood. He was serious in learning and careful in doing things, which was appreciated by his employers. At the age of twenty, he was already a minor celebrity but was not satisfied with his status and determined to continue improving his skills. He heard that there was an old master in Zhongnan Mountain who was skilled in crafts, so Lu Ban left home to search for the master. After experiencing many hardships, he reached Zhongnan Mountain. When he climbed to the top of the mountain, he found a shabby house with axes and tools scattered about. An old man with white hair was resting in bed. Lu Ban carefully packed his tools and waited patiently for his master to wake up. At sunsct time, the old man woke up. After some tests and an interview, Lu Ban became an apprentice to the old master. At the master's command, he polished the rusty tools until they shone like new ones. Then after cutting huge trees, chiseling thousands of holes in planks, disassembling and installing different models in intensive and diligent training, he made the master feel very satisfied. Lu Ban practiced day and night for three years and learned all the skills from his master. The master then tested him for the last time, he destroyed all the models, and asked him to rebuild them. He restored the model piece by piece with his own memory. The old master proposed many new models for him to build. He thought it over and made it. The result was that everything was done according to the master's instructions. Until one day, the master called Lu Ban to his sight, told him that he shoud be ready to go down the mountain and gave him the tools he had polished. Although Lu Ban could not bear to leave his master, he could only obey him and leave the mountain with tears in his eyes. He bared in mind his master's words: never lose the face or ruin the reputation of his master. From then on, Lu Ban built many machines and utensils for people with the tools his master gave him. He also taught many apprentices, leaving lots of stories of hard work and dedication.

Legends abound in China about Lu Ban's contributions to industries such as construction and carpentry, and many of the tools and construction principles attributed to him are still used today. The reason why Lu Ban's name has become a symbol of the wisdom of the ancient Chinese working people is that his character contains the spirit of diligent learning and unremitting efforts. The connotation of Luban's spirit includes pioneering and innovation, quality first, diligence and eagerness to learn, benefiting one's homeland, etc. Exploring and inheriting the spirit of Luban's intensive learning has always been of value beyond the time and this has profound practical significance in Chinese educational culture.

4.2 The Infatuation of Wang Mian in Learning

Wang Mian with the pseudonym Zhu Shi farmer; was a famous painter, poet and seal cutter of the Yuan Dynasty. He was born in a poor family, without a rich background and many social relations, his talent and skills are accumulated by hard work. Wang Mian had been obsessed with learning since childhood. When he was seven or eight years old, his father asked him to go herding the cattle. However, he secretly sneaked into the school and listened to the students read poetry books. After listening, he wrote them down silently. When he got home in the dark, the cattle was forgotten in the field. Fellow villages often came to his father to complain, accusing Wang Mian of leaving the cattle to trample their fields. His father was very angry and whipped Wang Mian, but he still kept listening to the teaching and forgetting about the cattle. Seeing that Wang Mian was so obsessed with his studies, her mother said to her husband,"In this case, it is better to obey the child's wishes and let him follow his way." So Wang Mian left home and took up residence near a temple. He continued to herd cattle during the day and painted lotus flowers by the pond in his spare time. At night, he quietly entered the temple, sat on the knee of the Buddha, holding the scroll under the lamp to read, often until dawn. Little Wang Mian had a peaceful mind, as if unaffected by distractions. Han Xing, a great Confucianist and neo-confucianist in eastern Zhejiang, was surprised to hear that Wang Mian was so crazy about learning. He believed that Wang Mian had a gift for a thorough understanding of Buddhism and accepted him as a student. Later Wang Mian inherited the knowledge of Han Xing, also became a famous scholar of his time. After Han Xing died, his disciples treated Wang Mian with the same respect as Han Xing. Although Wang Mian was full of knowledge and outstanding talent, because of his nature of lonely proud, his neglect of the bigwigs, he failed repeatedly in imperial competitive examinations. Therefore, he burned all the papers he had taken part in the examination and decided to break from fame and fortune, and devoted himself to the knowledge of painting and calligraphy in a way of seclusion and cultivation. Later, someone recommended him to the official circle, but he refused firmly, and returned south back to his hometown, lived in seclusion in Kuaiji Jiuli Mountain, while selling paintings for a living, and spent the rest of his life there.

Wang Mian was obsessed with poetry and painting all his life. In addition to his profound attainments in painting and poetry, he also learned profound skills in the seal cutting. Wang Mian's life was also accompanied by plum blossoms, which were his spiritual sustenance and artistic embodiment. Plum blossoms spread widely in the world and to later generations with the spirit of keeping pure and lofty. The cultural achievement created by Wang Mian's diligent learning enables him to maintain a strong civilian style, an independent personality pursuit, a dissocial but pure attitude toward life, so that he has not only become the model of Chinese ideal literati, but also achieved a beautiful view in the educational culture.

4.3 The Hard Study Thoughts of Zeng Guofan

Zeng Guofan, whose original name was Zicheng, was a famous minister in the Qing Dynasty. He was a theoretician and writer with rigorous study habits and extensive reading. He was born in Xiangxiang County, Hunan Province, he grew in an intellectual and farming family in a poor mountain and solitary valley. He was diligent and studious all his life, he used two words "diligent","constant" to motivate himself, and educate his sons and nephews by saying that "all kinds of diseases are born from laziness, laziness causes inefficiency". He seized every opportunity to read and did not stop until the day before he died. Zeng Guofan loved reading and was diligent in reading since childhood. He would choose appropriate books according to the changes of the environment and times, and apply the knowledge he had learned to real life, which was beyond ordinary people's ability. Zeng Guofan divided readings into two categories:"extensive scanning" and "intensive reading", and set twelve rules for himself for everyday reading. They are: self–restraint and pursuit, meditation, early rising, one book at a time, history reading, discreet talk, self–cultivation, self–protection, learn something new everyday and not forget the old knowledge every month, writing staying indoors at night. The first three of Zeng Guofan's twelve rules for reading are for reading. Fourth, five, nine, ten, eleven are the methods of reading; while the rest seem to have little to do with reading books, essentially they are stressing oneself to concentrate on reading good books, therefore, the seemingly insignificant rules are important approaches to ensure the quality of reading.

Zeng Guofan lived a full life of official circle and battlefield, worthy of the title of "three immortal achievements on virtue, contribution and writing, and a perfect model of teacher, general and minister". This is closely related to his lifelong dedication to reading and perseverance. To encourage his younger brother Zeng Guoquan to study hard after the war, in order to rise and develop based on accumulated knowledge, Zeng Guofan sent him a pair of couplets that says:"Thousands of years has passed and I am still here, hundreds of battles have ended and I am again reading". This fully reflects his thought of hard study, which has not only played an important role in his lifetime achievement, but also has become the highest realm of learners in every era, and an indispensable nutrient of traditional culture in quality education of contemporary society.

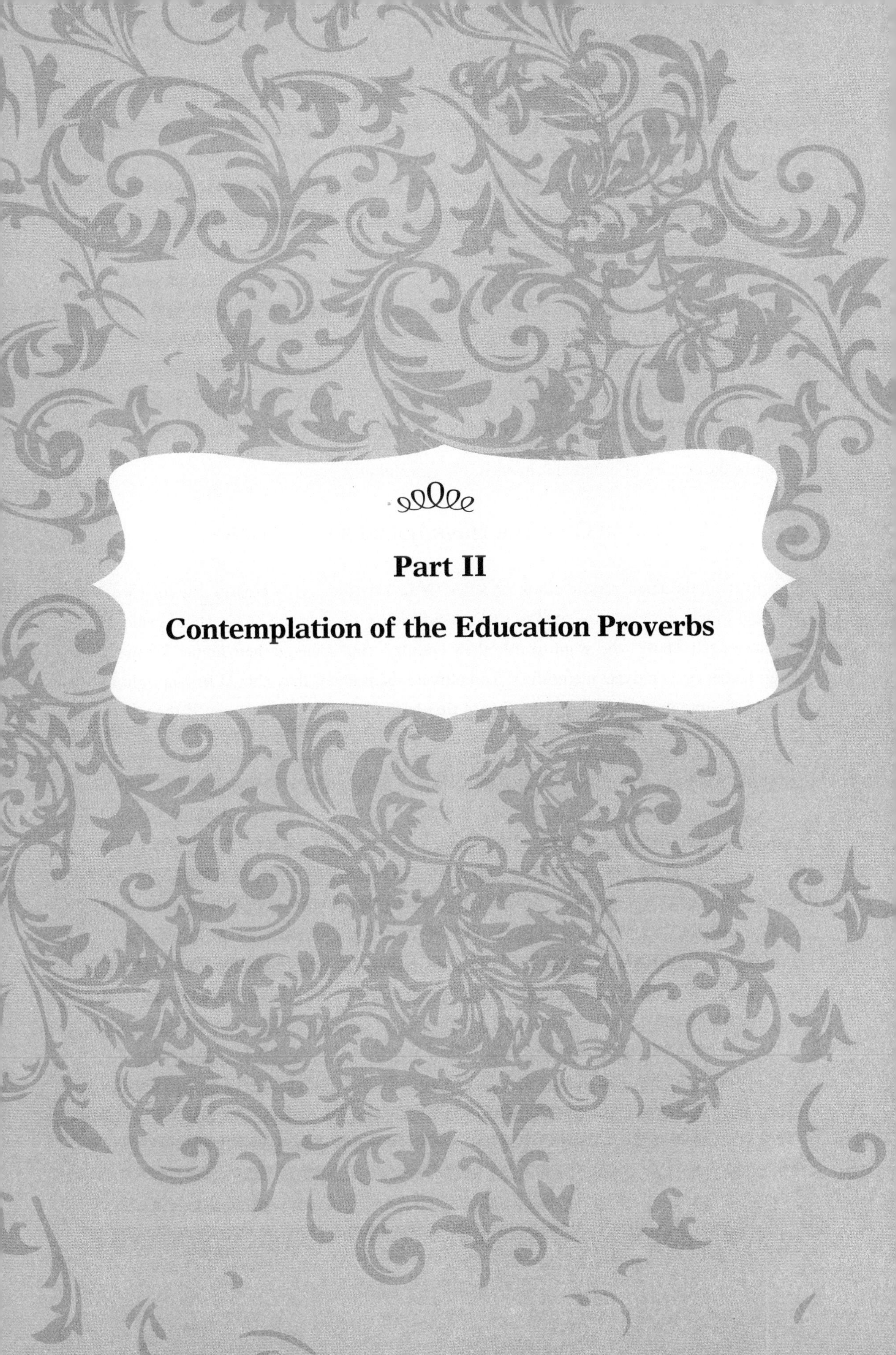

Part II

Contemplation of the Education Proverbs

Chapter Five The Selected Readings of Schools and Thoughts

With the understanding of traditional ideas in the previous part, we have learned that Chinese traditional educational ideas not only boast a long history, profound accumulation and rich resources, but also have changed with time and have been full of vitality. More importantly, these traditional thoughts, inherited by different schools of thought and accumulated over thousands of years of history, have achieved remarkable results and are of great theoretical value and practical significance to education today. This chapter intends to select the representative schools of thought from the past dynasties to present, trying to form a more comprehensive picture to show the essence of different schools of thought full of wisdom.

Section One The Governance and Cultivation

In the Confucian classic *Book of Rites.Great Learning,* it is clearly put forward:"In ancient times, those who wanted to make clear their virtues in the world should rule their country first; Those who want to rule their country, first manage their home; To manage their home, first cultivate themselves; To cultivate themselves, they should first upright their hearts; To upright their hearts, they should first hold the sincere motivation; If they want to be sincere, they should acquire knowledge first, and before that, investigation of the nature of theworld things should be the first step". It can be seen that the essence of Chinese education is to be knowledgeable, sincere and honest, to cultivate one's self and family, and finally be able to help govern the country and the world. And contributing to the ruling of the country is the highest ideal of all generations of scholars. Similarly, under the guidance of the traditional ideas like *Mencius · Heart and Soul Part I*, which put forward the idea of "benefit others when in success, cultivate oneself when in poverty" and the Buddhist Tiantai School, which put forward the idea of "to refrain from doing all evil, to practice all good, and to purify one's own heart, these are Buddhists doctrines", teach to become Buddha, and practice to become immortal has become the highest level of education and enlightenment. The contents of traditional Chinese educational thought schools, whether they are focused on social construction or transcending worldliness, all eventually rise to the level of country governance and self cultivation.

I. The Hundred Schools before Qin Dynasty

In the pre–Qin period, with the development of social production and social progress in ancient China, there also appeared a transition from "learning from the government" to "learning from private organizations", and a situation of hundreds of schools of thought contending appeared. Each school of thought represented by Confucianism, Taoism, Legalism, Mohism and Eclectics school put forward their own ideological system in terms of governing the country, which had a profound influence on the training mode and educational thinking of China's ruling class for thousands of years.

1.1 Confucianism

"Indoctrination over Punishment". The relationship between indoctrination and punishment is a problem that the ruling classes of all dynasties have to encounter. As for the Confucian school, it especially advocates indoctrination before punishment, that is, teaching is more important than punishment, believing virtue is superior to the law. In *The Analects of Confucius–Wei Zheng*, Confucius said: If the country is governed by decrees and people bound by criminal law, for a while the people were free from sin, but they did not feel ashamed of disobedience to rule; If morality is used to rule the people and etiquette is used to restrain them, they will not only have a sense of integrity, but also correct their mistakes. In other words: Guided by decrees and regulated by punishment, the common people simply did not violate the decree and avoided punishment without any sense of shame. If virtue is used as a guide and courtesy is used as the demand, the people will know what disgrace is and what glory is, and they will do right. Confucius also stated that:"To govern a country by moral principles is like the North Star in a certain position, and all the stars will revolve around it". It means with moral administration, one'll get the support of the people, like the north star, stable with stars around.

"Teaching to Benefit the People". Confucianism also advocates that rulers benefit and help the people. *The Analects of Confucius–Yongye* records: Zi Gong asked Confucius: Can bestowing liberally for relieving the people be called benevolence? Confucius replied: This is more than benevolence, it has reached the realm of holiness. Even Yao and Shun did not achieve it completely. To benefit and help people from troubles and bestow widely is the highest political goal stipulated by Confucianism. In *The Analects of Confucius*, we can see the idea of benefiting the people everywhere. Confucius once commented on Zi Chan: there are four ways in which one qualifies as a gentleman, being humble in his manner of life, being responsible and conscientious in serving the king, being gracious in serving the people, being reasonable in administrating the people. In a word, it is the way of a gentleman to be humble, diligent, kind to people and to cherish the labor of people.

"Respect Teachers and Professional Instructors". Confucianism believes that the state cannot afford not to respect teachers. If a country is to prosper, it must respect teachers and value those who impart expertise. When teachers are respected, the country's legal system can be preserved. If a country tends to decline, it will despise teachers, when teachers are not respected, people will indulge their temperament wantonly, and the country's legal system will be destroyed. In *Xunzi– Dalue* it records in Xunzi's view: speaking without mentioning the teacher is a betrayal, teaching without greeting the teacher is like treason, a wise emperor will not accept the traitor, the court officials will not greet a traitor on the road and talk with him.

"Governing by Protecting the People". In the view of Confucianism, it is far from enough to "love the people" just because the people's power cannot be underestimated, but also must use"benevolent government" and good policies to warm the people's hearts, so that they can accept the ruling with sincerity, and achieve the political goal of "ruling as a king" . Confucius pointed out that "the superior is with dignity and danger, people are humble but crucial, protecting the people means survival, opposing the people means perishing and the long lived governors must understand this." Mencius further put forward the concrete measures of "Governing by Protecting the People": The first is to respect the survival rights of the people and improve their economic life; Secondly, in view of the common problem of "warmongering" in great powers, he put forward the idea that those who are good at war should be punished to achieve the purpose of eliminating unjust wars. Thirdly the king should care about the people's suffering and share their joy.

1.2 Mohism

"Govern as the Sages; Encourage Good by Forbidding Evil". It is the core of Mohism's political thought and also its educational thought to rule the world by banning evil and encouraging love. In *Universal Love–Part I* it reads: How can a sage, who has made it his duty to govern the world, not forbid men to hate each other without exhorting them to love each other. It also argues that the sage"can not make it without persuading the people love each other in this way". Mozi regarded it as the main duty of the sage to persuade people to love, that is, to take educating the people of the world to love and benefit each other as the main task of the sage to rule the world.

"The Ancient Wise Emperors Cultivated People by Self–thrift and Setting Good Examples". Thus the people of the world are well governed, and their wealth is sufficient. It is the characteristic of the Mohist school to advocate economizing, simple funeral and non–music and luxury, and it is also the characteristic of its education ideas. Mozi believed that as long as the palace houses could be sheltered from wind and rain, frost and snow, men and women could live conveniently and decently, it should be practically built rather than being extravagant after spending much money. As long as the foods can meet the physical and health needs, they don't have to be very tasty with the extraordinarily precious items. Clothes should be functional in winter and summer, rather than luxurious.

"Respect the Heaven and Ghosts to Benefit More People". Mozi stated that: Heaven has will and feelings, it can reward the good and punish the evil, it can curse and bless people. Mohism believed that heaven was very generous to the people. It created the sun, the moon and the stars, defined the spring, summer, autumn and winter, it sent down frost, snow, rain and dew, and grew grain, mulberry and cotton so that the people could have food and clothing. Besides, heaven can control emperors as Heaven's sons,"The son of heaven can be appreciated if he is good, he can also be punished if he is violent and evil. If the son of heaven, is afflicted by disease, he should fast and bathe, present the heaven and ghosts with all respect the clean wines and grains so that the plague and disease will go away". (*Mozi–Tianzhi Zhong*) Therefore, the will of heaven can not be violated, following the will of heaven, and love each other for mutual benefit is the rule the emperors need to follow.

"Righteousness Helps the Good Governance". Mohism holds that moral spirit should be a valuable concept that is universally pursued from the state to the individual. As far as individuals are concerned, one should protect the interests of others and society with a moral spirit of selflessness and benefiting people and society or even"doing good deeds at the expense of one's own interests". As far as the country is concerned, the moral spirit should be taken as the requirement for the official selection of talents, requiring the them to "uphold justice over private preference". Mohism takes morality as the belief value of national governance, and believes that it can realize the unity of the value pursuit of both the government and the people from the spiritual level, and provide the inner guarantee for this pursuit.

1.3 Taoism

"All Things Respect the Tao and Honor the Virtue". Lao Tzu teaches people to respect the Tao and honor the virtue. Lao Tzu said:"Tao generates all things in the world, and virtue nurtures all things". All things take on various forms, behind all forms, there is a"potential" in control. Therefore, all things do respect the Tao, and cherish the virtue. The reason why the Tao is revered and the virtue is precious is because the Tao grows everything without interfering with it, and the virtue feeds everything without dominating it. Everything happens naturally. (*Lao Tzu–Chapter 51*). That is to say, Tao produces all things, virtue nourishes all things, and potential helps to form all things. Moral dignity is not given by anyone, but naturally formed. Therefore, Lao Tzu pointed out that morality is very noble, so sages who are governing the country, scholars who are cultivating themselves, should learn from the Tao and the nature. Therefore, the sage should do things with the attitude of inaction and teach the people with"no words".(*Lao Tzu–Chapter* 2) and "seemingly do nothing for living, make nothing for career, and take tranquility for taste." (*Lao Tzu–Chapter 63*). Heaven and earth naturally produce and nourish all things, without deliberately cherish all things, saints should also naturally govern people, without deliberately act for achievement. (*Lao Tzu–Chapter 5*)

"Governing with Nature; Letting Things Take Their Own Course". This is not only the goal but also the method of Lao Tzu's ideological education. He said: I do not serve the ordinary people and they will serve themselves; I prefer tranquility and the people will cultivate themselves; I do nothing and the people are getting rich, I have no desire and the people are simple and honest. (*Lao Tzu–Chapter 57*) Just as advocating inactive governance, Lao Tzu also advocated inactive self–cultivation, and natural enlightenment. It means when the emperor does not interfere with the people's behavior, people are free to do their own work. The point is to follow the objective laws that are governed by Tao in political governance while conforming to the naturalness shown by the realization of Tao into the individual. It advocates that the formulation of law on the basis of following and making use of the characteristics of human nature is essential in giving the people a space for autonomy and self–management, and the completion of this process is also carried out under the principle of Taoism.

"A Gentleman Sees the World without Prejudice". Taoism holds a very typical relativism thought, teaching people the homogeneous theory of unifying things. That is, to regard different things as the same and different theories as the same. In *On Leveling All Things*, Zhuangzi stated that: the stem and the pillar, the ugly and the beautiful, the honest and the cunning, the weird and the strange, all are both different and the same. Since everything is the product of the Tao, the birth and success of anything is also doomed to be destroyed. Therefore, the so–called concepts of nobility and lowness, power and weakness, there is no simple standard and fixed quality. In other words, the world cannot be differentiated by judgment, the truth cannot be argued by language. Taoism believes that all things are the product of Tao. In front of Tao, all things are different from each other, but in the end, they are the same. This thought also has a certain influence on the governing ideas of some monarchs.

1.4 Legalism

"Teach and Make Obey". Shang Yang put forward the idea that the sages should govern the country by unified reward, unified punishment, and unified education. By implementing a uniform reward and the army will be invincible, with uniform punishment, then the monarch's order can be carried out, with unification and indoctrination, the people would follow the king's orders. Fair and wise rewards do not waste money; Severe punishment does not kill; Wise education does not change customs. Fair good reward to a certain degree, there is no need to reward, to some extent, strict criminal law will make punishment unnecessary, to a certain degree, honest and enlightened education will cultivate a kind of normality. (*The Book of Lord Shang–Reward and Punishment*) That is to say, the sage governance of the country needs to achieve a unified reward, unified law system, unified education. If the reward is unified, the people will know the standard of reward, the country will be invincible, if the criminal law is unified, the people can be ruled in orderly way, and if the education is unified, the people will follow the laws and rules, and the country will unify the common customs. In this way, the country will gradually reach a situation where there is no necessity for rewarding, punishment and education.

"Law as the Teaching, and Officials as the Teachers". Han Feizi proposed that: A country ruled by a wise ruler should abolish the classics of ancient books, and use laws as teaching materials, no rules from previous kings, and should let officials be teachers; the chivalrous activities of the knights should be stopped, one should take killing the enemy as a brave act. In this way, the people of the country, those who are good at talking, will naturally obey the laws, those who work will devote themselves to farming, and those who are brave and aggressive will do their best in military combat. Thus the country will be rich in time of peace, be strong in time of war. This is the core way of ruling (*Wu Du–The Five Types of People*). In Han Feizi's opinion, what the wise rulers did was to educate their subjects in law rather than in literature and poetry. If the law is to be taught, it is relying on the officials who are familiar with the law, not the poets or scholars. If all the people within the territory take the law as the norm, take practical function as the goal, then a rich country with strong army that is invincible can be achieved.

"Justice without Preference." In *Guanzi* it is stated that the abolition of the private sector is a guarantee of law enforcement. In *Renfa* he stated that "In the governance of the world, the monarch does not know close and distant relationships, noble and common backgrounds, the beauty and ugly appearance, all are judged by law, kill people and people do not complain, reward people and people are not grateful, for everything is the result of the lawful judgement. Officials have no arguments, scholars have no debates, the people have no personal views, all humbly listen to the monarch and behave lawfully. And the monarch, on the other hand, should govern with justice and the rule of law, so it is not a heavy job to administer the state." This means that when the wise rulers govern the state, they should start from the public law instead of the individual preference.

"Weak People Strengthens the Government; People Are Easy to Rule When Ignorant". In the Warring States period, in order to strengthen the monarchical power to the maximum extent, legalists not only committed to weaken the power of nobles and ministers, but also urged to take"weak people" measures, believing"weak people strengthens the government. Therefore, a country with good principles should focus on weakening the people." Legalists also argued that the ignorant people are easy to rule. Although Shang Yang's reform abolished the Well Field System in law and protected the rights of the people to a certain extent, in the view of legalists, the people were not the masters of the country, they were only the tools of the monarch to achieve hegemony. From the historical perspective, the ignorance and backwardness of the people is the soil from which the monarchy, theocracy and idol worship can be produced. Although this "can do the trick of the moment" (*The Record of the Grand Historian · Taishi Gong's Preface*), in the long run, it stifles people's thinking and hinders the real progress of the society.

II. Cultivation Thoughts from Wei to Tang Dynasties

The evolution of spiritual cultivation in Chinese education is related to the concept of nature and human, showing a trend of alternating between worship of nature and worship of personification, and also influenced by the interaction of Confucianism, Buddhism and Taoism: Confucianism puts forward"belief of gods and ghosts is actually the application of forms with spirit", According to Taoism,"one should cultivate both spirit and life" ;

Buddhism holds that "Dharma has no self nature, and everything is the result of Karmic Justice". Confucianism teaches people to become holy, Buddhism teaches people to become Buddhas, Taoism teaches people to become immortal. Being Buddha;immortal and holy is the basic goal of the three kinds of traditional education. From Wei Jin to Sui and Tang dynasties, the rulers increasingly saw the educational and social functions of Buddhism and Taoism. Therefore, after the change of the exclusive status of Confucianism, the localization of Buddhism and the spread of Taoism jointly formed and influenced the cultivation and educational thoughts of this period.

2.1 The Buddhism

The Thoughts of Dao An. As a Buddhist Chinese educator, Dao An attaches great importance to the cultivation of Buddhism. He held that the Tathagata founded Buddhism on the basis of emptiness. People are burdened and stuck in the tangible things, if their hearts realize the truth of the empty, then all the material burden will be gone. It means one should pay attention to the main essence of the universe. Similar records can also be seen in *Jizang's Madhyamika–sastra* of Tang Dynasty. In fact, the so–called nothingness of Dao An is the emptiness of Mahayana Prajna. That is to say, all dharma has no self nature, but are formed by principal and subsidiary causes, so they are empty, unreal and silent."There are three ways to teach Buddhism" he stated in *Preface to the Great Precepts of the Bhikkhu*: The first is discipline, the second is meditation, and the third is wisdom. These three teachings are the gateways to our practice and achievement. Abstinence is to break away from those who fall into the three evils; Zen is a powerful tool for breaking confused and disorganized thoughts. Wisdom is the fundamental prescription for the cure of disease, in other words, the above three ways are the gateway to the truth and the key to becoming a Buddha, by doing so, one can probably attain Buddhahood.

The Thoughts of Hui Yuan. As the originator of Pure Land Buddhism, Master Huiyuan put forward that the relationship of form and spirit is an important issue in Chinese religious thought."The mortal form and the immortal spirit" means our spirits never die, this concept is the carrier of the Buddha's six realms of samsara and the causes and effects of three lives . Hui Yuan argued in *On Buddhist Monk Beyond the Etiquette of Monarch Worshiping* that: if form and spirit is born and die at the same time, then it is difficult to explain people's wisdom and foolishness. Because if this is determined by form, then everyone has a form, why is there the difference between wisdom and foolishness? In addition, the idea that "virtue is rewarded, vice is punished" is the core content of the theory of karma after Buddhism was introduced into China. Hui Yuan also argued in *On the Theory of Retribution* that: Good and evil in the world have retribution, this is because people have the root of obsession and greed, which causes endless yearning for property and life. In this way, the gains and losses, good and bad alternate each other. Thus good and evil continuously causes the respective result, and therefore karmic retribution is natural.

The Thoughts of Zhu Daosheng. When Zhu Daosheng, a famous Buddhist scholar and eminent monk, gave a lecture on *Nirvana Sutra* in Jinling, he put forward the view that people who do not believe in cause and effect and have no root of wisdom can also practice Buddhism. As the saying goes: even laics can become Buddha, in the view of Tao Sheng,"all living beings are Buddhas, and all are to face Parinirvana" (*The Interpretation of Saddharmapundarika Sutra*). It means All living beings have Buddha nature and can enter the world of Nirvana, that is, they can become Buddhas. In the history of Buddhist thought, the question of whether lay people can become Buddhas involves whether everyone has Buddha–nature and whether all living beings can become Buddhas. According to Zhu Daosheng's thought, all sentient beings are born with Buddha nature, this has expanded position of Buddhist enlightenment and directly influenced the Buddhist circle in China since then, especially for the development of Zen Buddhism in Tang Dynasty.

The Thoughts of Tendai Hokke. As the earliest indigenous Buddhism in China, the core concept of Tendai Hokke is summarized in these words:"There are three thousand characteristics in one thought, and one hundred realms are like the Buddhist realm." Three thousand means that the mind of all living beings contains three thousand kinds of worlds. The minds are the essence of the world, and one hundred realms is one hundred Dharma realms, which is the total of the ten Dharma realms multiplied by themselves. This means that every Dharma realm is true. In other words, one's mind can go anywhere and see through any chance. This is also the reason of the enlightenment of Bodhi."The Initial Approach of View and Deep Meditation" is also an important thought of Tendai Hokke, the exposition of it is teaching method and practice method. The so–called meditation means concentrating on one's heart and eliminating delusions. The so–called view is wisdom, which means to increase the Buddha's wisdom and understand the Buddhist principles. In short, only by focusing on the double cultivation, with practice and principles in parallel, can one reach the Buddhist realm.

The Thoughts of Vinaptimātratā School.Vijnaptimātratā School is also called dharma–laksana or dharma–laksana Vijnaptimātratā, the founder was Xuan Zang, Special attention is paid to the analysis of the phases of the dharma, the result of analysis is that all Buddha dharma cannot be separated from mental awareness. In the thought of its religious education, it shows the concept of "updating one's mind and cultivating as Buddha" and regards turning awareness towards Buddha as a way to cultivate oneself. It teaches human beings to break through the obsessiveness, return to Buddhist doctrines, thus entering the Buddhist gate, to the realm of heaven. *In Cittamatra* it says: All the forms of "I""Dharma""All kinds of phenomena" are the manifestation of the mind. They do not seem to exist. Therefore, these three characteristics are not separated from mind. The goal of the religious thought is to make people realize the meaning of changing the worldly awareness, abandon the paranoid view that the world is real, and return to the realm of knowing the nature of illusion and emptiness.

The Thoughts of Huayan School. As an important achievement of the Sinicization of

Buddhism in Sui and Tang Dynasties, the basic idea of Huayan School is "the origin of Dharma boundary". The so–called Dharma realm refers to everything; The boundary refers to the category, the integration of everything is called"Dharma boundary". Huayan School usually uses the term Dharma realm in the sense of the original, noumenon and Buddha–nature of all living beings. Huayan School got its name because it regarded Huayan Sutra as its classic doctrine. The thought of the ten–fold metaphysical gate is the basic theory of the Huayan School to teach people to practice and become Buddhas. With this basic view, one may have the wisdom of Buddha and can reach the realm of heaven. The core of this idea is that although things are different, they are interdependent, overlapping, mutually compatible and harmonious. This theory of Dharma involves many categories, but the basic one is the mutual inclusion and penetration of all Dharma, but the degree of penetration depends on the ability of ingesting other things. In short, Huayan School believes that things are in harmony with each other, and the differences are clear, and there are endless relations of origin and unity. Therefore viewing a speck can help see the Dharma boundary and receive it completely. This mysterious and incomprehensible truth, is called ten–fold metaphysical gate theory.

The Thoughts of Zen. Zen believes that "in–self nature, all dharma can be seen; All Dharma in itself is called pure Dharmakaya.""All Prajna wisdom arises from self nature, not from outside in. A word of enlightenment might help to see the true Buddha nature" . The view of Zen puts forward the idea of "sudden enlightenment" to become a Buddha. As a representative of Zen Buddhism, *The Sixth Patriarch Altar Sutra* advocates that "the mind nature is pure, the Buddha nature is original, the consciousness is not from external pursuit, and the meaning of the truth is beyond the interpretation of written language, and the enlightenment is straight to the mind and heart." *The Sixth Patriarch Huineng said*:"If you start to observe the true prajna, in a flash, all the paranoia is gone, if you know your true nature;one enlightenment can lead one to the realm of Buddha" (*Altar Sutra–Prajna*). In contrast to Huineng, Shenxiu of the North School of Zen advocated"do not do any evil things","pursue all good practice","purify oneself from the worldly", and advocated gradual cultivation. Of course, Huineng does not entirely deny the gradual cultivation. He said,"There is one Dharma, and people have different perspectives; there is one truth, and enlightenment comes in different speeds."

2.2 The Taoism

The Thoughts of *Taiping Sutra. The Taiping Sutra* is extensive in content, involving heaven and earth, Yin and Yang, five elements, ten branches, disasters and differences, gods and so on. It reconstructs the thought of "unity of nature and man" in early Taoism. At the religious level, the main idea is "promoting good and eliminating evil". *The Taiping Sutra* argues,"If good deeds do not stop, blessings will make people happy. God knows what one has done, good or evil.""Now before the man of righteousness, the peace is upon us, and those who wish to be virtuous will flourish, while those who are evil will wither away." According to the *Taiping Sutra*, the reasons why people living in the world should promote goodness and stop evil, are because for the good and the evil, there is always retribution. The good and evil retribution in the *Taiping Sutra*, just like the Buddha's three retribution, is not necessarily self–retribution."Sometimes a man does good and get the bad results, and someone does evil with good rewards, it is because there is the retribution from the ancestors and previous lives." The meaning of good and evil in the *Taiping Sutra* is, abstractly speaking, whether it conforms to the way of nature or human justice. *The Taiping Sutra* also distinguishes good and bad Taoist priests, believing that priests are the embodiment of the way of heaven, and the way of heaven has ups and downs as well as peace and chaos. Therefore, there are also differences between good and bad Taoist priests in the world, with good ones reflecting the flourishing age and bad priests reflecting the age of decadence.

The Thoughts of Tao Hongjing. It is a core and important content of Tao Hongjing Taoism to teach people to be good and keep healthy and become immortal. Tao Hongjing believes that life and death are both congenital and acquired. He stated that the reason why he collected the predecessors' health theory was to nourish the masses of people in order to maintain the health and prolong the life. Tao Hongjing advocates many ways to keep healthy. But the most important thing is to practice qi, nourish the spirit and preserve the essence. He cited from *The Health Keeping with Qi* that: the way to keep healthy lies in the Qi, breathing spirit of energy. To preserve Qi is to gain the Tao, and the Tao will help last longer. The essence of life is from the energy, to preserve essence is to be refreshed, and keeping refreshed means long living. The theory of health preservation is the most important content of Tao Hongjing Taoism, and the infinite extension of life means immortal in his thoughts. Therefore, when the teaching of health preservation is pushed to the extreme, it becomes the teaching of becoming immortal.Tao Hongjing believed that the celestial world existed. He described the Kunlun celestial realm in this way:"There are nine houses on the Kunlun mountains, which are the nine palaces, and Tai Chi is the Supreme Palace. All the immortals are the officials of the nine palaces." In the examples given by Tao Hongjing, some became immortal after taking medicine, some after reading the Tao for thousands of times, and some became immortal after passed the test of gods. The way to become immortal may be different, but the result of becoming immortal is the same.

The Thoughts of Kou Qianzhi. Kou Qianzhi was a famous figure of Taoism in the Northern Dynasty. In the process of carrying out Taoist education, setting up Taoism in way of god was his basic idea, which is from the book *YI Guan*: "The sages teach by the way of God, and the whole world convinced." This way is the way of ghosts, gods and spirits."Guan Gua" means that the sage uses the ways of ghosts and gods to educate the ordinary people in order to convince the people of the world. The so–called"sages of the law of God, the spirit of God, teach the Tao to the people without relying on words and threat, all on the divine view of nature" means the same. Ideological education to the Taoist people is the main way to spread Taoism. The essence of Kou Qianzhi's thought is to cultivate good and absolve of evil. In this respect, he is no different from Confucianism. Kou Qianzhi said,"If the minister is loyal, the son is filial, the husband and the wife is faithful, the elder brother is respectful, the younger brother is obedient, and heart is loving and faithful , then one can be good and become a real person."(*Teaching discipline sutras of Zheng YiFaWen Taoist Master*)He regards moral cultivation as an important condition for the cultivation of Taoism and the exhortation of goodness as the basic content of Taoism. KouQianzhi's Taoist education thought is rich and he revolutionized education in both content and style, thus he established his position in the Taoist education realm of Northern and Southern Dynasties.

Section Two The Neo–Confucianism and The Utility Thoughts

Confucianism, with the ethics of Confucius and Mencius as its core, was constantly reformed after a long period of impact, and developed into a new system of ideology: Neo–Confucianism (or Neo–Confucianism) starting from the Song Dynasty. It integrates the idealist speculation of Zen Buddhism and the cosmology of the *Book of Changes*, Lao Tzu and Chuangzi. It conforms to the historical demand of reforming the moral code at that time, and boils the origin of everything into a concept of "Li" (Neo–Confucianism). From this core idea, the neo–Confucianists explained the order of etiquette, interpreted the relationship between"reason" and "ritual", making"rites" belong to the highest category of "reason". At the same time, the utilitarian trend of education does not have an obvious inheritance system like the Neo–Confucianism in history of China, however, if we objectively restore the educational thoughts in ancient time and the living world, we will find that the influence of utilitarianism in the society can not be ignored, and its evolution process also brings abundant enlightenment to the educational circle.

I. The Neo–Confucianism from Song to Qing Dynasty

Neo–confucianism is the Confucianism of Song, Yuan, Ming and Qing dynasties, the establishment of Neo–Confucianism was marked by the rise of Zhou Dunyi's learning, the Two Cheng's learning and Zhang Zai's learning. From the middle of the Northern Song Dynasty through the Southern Song Dynasty to the Yuan Dynasty, Neo–Confucianism continuously evolved and was divided internally. Later, there was a trend of integration among different schools, among which the educational ideas are widely followed today.

1.1 Sima Guang

"Reward virtue and abstain from evil while taking history as a mirror." This is the Neo–Confucianism thought of Sima Guang, a statesman and historian in the Northern Song Dynasty. It is also a feature of traditional Chinese education. Sima Guang said in his book *Tongjian · Records of Wei*:"The debate of orthodoxy and unorthodoxy, from ancient times to modern times, people have not been able to reach a consensus, what I state today is only the desire to describe the rise and fall of the country and the solidarity of the people's lives so as to make people choose their own views according to the historical records. It is not like *Spring and Autumn Annals* that has established the law of reward and punishment, and helped govern a turbulent society, after bringing it back to the right path. It is not the historian's task to distinguish between the orthodoxy and the unorthodoxy of a dynasty. He explained that he wrote *Tongjian* only to describe the rise and fall of the country and the solidarity of the living people, so that the readers of history can take the good as an example and the evil as a lesson, so as to improve the political and moral quality of the rulers and take history as a mirror, which is beneficial to governance. Sima Guang's intention to take history as a mirror is repeatedly mentioned in his book.

"The key to civilizing the people and purifying the customs lies in the system of selecting officials". The so–called civilization, also known as custom, fashion, education, refers to the social education and influence, from generation to generation of fashion and social popular atmosphere and customs, it is adhered to by the majority of society. The civilization of a society is closely related to the quality of social education and the rise and fall of social politics. In *Zi Zhi Tong Jian Volume 68*, he stated that "education is the urgent business of the country, and the mediocre officials feel annoyed, customs as the world's significant events are ignored by fatuous and self–indulgent rulers. Only the wise monarch, with sensible foresight knows its long–term great interests". He regarded social education and the formation of a good social atmosphere or customs as the first task of governing the country.

"Teaching with belief of Frugality Nourishes Virtue". Focusing on family education is also the core content of Sima Guang's educational thought. In *Educating Kang with Honesty and Frugality* he admonished that:"We are actually from a poor family, the family tradition of innocence and frugality is passed down from generations, extravagance is not in my nature. While Everyone is proud of extravagance, my heart alone long to frugality, people sneer at me for being stubborn and simple, I do not think it a demerit." Here, Sima Guang professed that frugality and innocence were his family tradition, called frugality and innocence. Sima Guang thought it as the ancient virtue, advocated by Confucius, as a person with lofty ideals, he should regard frugality as virtue, and should not be proud of extravagance, Sima Guang also cited the history stories of family prospered with frugality and ruined by extravagance as examples. As a famous prime minister of the Song Dynasty, he taught his children with frugality, which had a wide influence on later generations.

1.2 The Cheng Brothers

"The way of governing people is based on education". Like traditional Confucianism, The Cheng Brothers (Cheng Ying and Cheng Yi), as the originator of Neo–Confucianism in the Song and Ming dynasties, advocated governing the country based on moral education. They held"Since ancient times, there has been a mechanism of education from parties to state governance, when subjects are eight years old, they enter primary school, so there is no one without the experience of education, common people cultivate themselves, gentlemen know virtue and the right way, so the wise men gathered in the court, good deeds prevail among the people, Propriety and righteousness are universal, and folk customs are fine. Although the judicial branch was established and no one commits crime,the generations of prosperity is the result of education". In Brother Cheng's opinion, this is the tradition of Chinese politics and should be carried forward, rather than only concentrating on punishment without understanding the value of virtue education, that is not the way to achieve the good custom and governance. Why is education necessary for good governance? The Cheng Brothers believed that good governance depended on talents, and talents are cultivated by education.

"Preserve heavenly principles and eliminate human desire". Although Zhang Zai first advocated the theory, it has not yet formed a systematic theory. It is the Cheng Brothers that constituted a systematic moral cultivation education theory based on it. The so–called heavenly principles referred to the ethics of the three cardinal guides and the five constant virtues, because it was derived from heaven and nature. The Cheng Brothers held that "heavenly principles of nature is an objective existence, not subject to people's subjective wishes". (*Posthumous Papers–Vol. 2*) They believed that the so–called human desire referred to the excessive pursuit of material and spiritual life and the selfishness of human behavior. They contrasted nature against human desire; arguing that all behaviors and speech and motivation should be based on heavenly principles which also include rites, anything away from the principles are selfish desires. As for the way to preserve heavenly principles and eliminate human desire, the Cheng brothers put forward"Preventing evil thoughts while keeping honest". It is the content of moral cultivation education to preserve heavenly principles and eliminate human desire, and preventing evil thoughts while keeping honest is the methodology, both of the statements are organic parts of the Cheng brother's moral theory.

1.3 Chu Hsi

"A sage teaches with set principles." Chu Hsi, as the master of Confucianism and a famous neo–Confucianism in the Song Dynasty, he repeatedly emphasized the so–called set principles. It means that education has fixed principles. Such principles are called by Chu Hsi as "Great Mind". He said:"To see the truth, one must have a strong mind. Under which there are many different reasons and sub–disciplines."(*Quotations of Chu Hsi's Remarks– Vol. 9*) In Zhu Xi's view, the sage taught with right principles and minds, that is the basic standard. What is the underlying principle? It is human ethics. *The School Mottos of Bai Ludong Academy* by Chu Hsi are actually the set principles of teaching. Among which the basic principle is: there should be affection between fathers and sons, affiliation between monarchs and courtiers, distinction between husbands and wives, order between seniors and juniors, and trust among friends. While learning, questioning, thinking and differentiation are the basic principles of the research, faithfulness, respect, punishing resentment and stifling desire, repenting for the good, are the set principles of the cultivation. A man of benevolence keeps his righteousness without seeking his own profit, and clarifies the meaning of Tao without considering his own merit. The principle that:"Do not impose on others what you yourself do not desire" is the way of treating people. The above principles are the promotion of Five Ethical Norms in education.

"Primary education is based on practice; High education is based on theories" Chu Hsi divided education into two levels: Primary education and high education. The difference between them is that primary education is preliminary and belongs to children's education, while high education, on the other hand, is on a higher level. He held that "Elementary schools are all about doing; College education is mainly about the reasons of doing (*Quotations of Chu Hsi's Remarks– Vol. 7*). Chu Hsi believed that practice should be taught in primary school, this is adapted for the age characteristics of the child. Compared with primary schools, higher education referred to the study of recondite knowledge. Academies after the Song Dynasty were also known as universities, where education is to probe extensive knowledge and truth. As Chu Hsi once said:"The great learning is for a lofty person and scholar with virtue; Highlighting means to carry forward the learning. The people get virtue from the nature with a peaceful state of mind, and a clear understanding of everything in the world, with the knowledge of the principles of nature, one can deal with all different things. What Chu Hsi explained as virtue in *Great Learning* is in fact the benevolence of Confucianism, it prevails between heaven and earth, fills the universe, and is omnipresent.

1.4 Xu Heng

"To educate is to teach human relations of ethics". As a famous educationist in Yuan Dynasty, Xu Heng put forward the theory of teaching human relations of ethics as the educational goal. He said: to teach is to make understand; human relations are the foundation of ethics. God has the mission for each person and each has his own job. Like there is affection of father and son, the righteousness of the monarch and minister, the difference between husband and wife, the order of the old and the young, the faith of friends, is the so–called the natural bonds and ethical relationships. Three generations of the holy kings, set up the libraries, the orders, the schools to teach people, just because they know this principle of truth. If people do not understand the principle of human relations, the upper and lower ranks, the order of the society could fall in confusion, and people cannot be ruled. (*The Collection of Xu Heng–The Gist of Elementary Education*)Human relations can be the basic relationship in the world, which is from nature and to the people, so it is also called the natural–bond relationships. Therefore, Xu Heng regarded it as the main content and goal of teaching and learning. It is believed that although heaven bestowed people with the bound–relationship, people are still born with worldly atmosphere, if the atmosphere is turbid it will hinder the bound relationships , then education is needed.

"The way to teach is to practice first". Xu Heng believes that in knowing and doing, doing is more important than knowing. He advocates combining learning with practice. He said: the way to learning, must be practicing step by step, not just the reading and writing from books". (*The Collection of Xu Heng–Quotations Part I*). Xu Heng believes that in the process of reading, we should combine our own thoughts with reality. People should be encouraged to practice the skills they have failed to master; Where there is an unreasonable method, it must be corrected with warning. The benefit of real learning is in its practice. The reason why the former king set up schools to teach people was to benefit the whole world. If we could not guide people by deeds and only teach them by subjects, we would have lost the original intention of setting up schools. It can be said that it is Xu Heng's consistent teaching style to teach people by doing and to read the *Six Classics, The Analects of Confucius, MengZi* and other classics according to one's own reflection and reality.

1.5 Wang Fuzhi

"Teach to the nature and teach with differentiation". As a great thinker in the late Ming and early Qing dynasties, Wang Fuzhi had a relatively complete philosophical system of ideological theory in education. Wang Fuzhi believes that the human body is condensed by heaven, the earth, the Yin, the Yang and the five elements, and its nature is condensed by the Qi, which is called talent in terms of temperament and character in terms of the Qi theory. He argued that long–term habits will form a character. The habits meant by him consist the teaching style and social customs, which may help people become gentlemen. The difference is that customs affect people unconsciously, while teaching styles influence people consciously. And good customs and teaching styles can make humanity in a similar way. He argued that "Therefore the wicked will not come to the door of the gentleman, and the gentleman will not choose the wicked people to teach". (*On the Four Books*) In view of Wang Fuzhi, teachers must distinguish between good and evil, and only the goodness shall be taught, but not the wicked. This is the same reason why god gives wisdom only to man, but not to birds and beasts. Wang Fuzhi believes that Confucius'"teaching without classification" does not mean teaching without distinction between goodness and evil, but educators should be consistent in teaching, otherwise they will fall into the indiscriminate view of education.

"Heavenly principles are hidden in human desire". The distinction between heavenly principles and human desire is a fundamental issue in the moral cultivation theory and ideological education in the Song and Ming Dynasties. In the Song and Ming dynasties, the orthodox neo–Confucianists all took preserving the principle of nature and eliminating human desire as their teaching content. Contrary to orthodox neo–Confucianism, Wang Fuzhi believed that heavenly principles and human desire were not opposites. He stated in *On the Four Books– Advanced Part that*: havenly principles and human desire are not the opposites, and heavenly principes is embodied in human desire. All sensuality is the carrier of nature. If human desire is destroyed and nature prevails, wouldn't all utilitarian things such as military and agricultural rites and music be regarded as obstacles to nature? If these obstacles are to be removed, wouldn't it be Buddha's heresy of "all things in the void" ? Of course, Wang Fuzhi does not believe that one can be indulged in human desire, it can only be reasonably realized in The "production of heaven and earth", he was against both abstinence and indulgence. This concept of rationality is more acceptable to the public.

II. The Utility Thoughts in Song Dynasty

The thought of utility in Song Dynasty mainly refers to the school of thought that opposes the teaching about life and nature in vain, it advocates practical and factual work. While opposing viewpoints of Neo–Confucianism of nature and human desire, justice and profit, this school emphasized the function and profit, and believed that governing a country should be based on the running of finance. This thought elevates"profit" to the status equivalent to "justice" and argued that one should not talk about moral benevolence and justice in vain without awareness of utility.

2.1 Li Jin

"To build a country and rule the people, education is the first foundation". Li Jin, a famous thinker in the Song Dynasty, attached great importance to education, believing that education was the first important thing for the country and people. In *Policy of Governing and comforting People* he said: The so–called comforting people is not only to solve the livelihood problems for the people and give orders, but also to give priority to education. What is education? The worldly views are attaching importance to criminal law and neglecting moral principles. However, Li Jin advocated morality before punishment. The reason why there are evil crimes in society is that people do not attach importance to education, and education is a good tradition of our country. He also offered proposals to education: The feasible way is to expand the scale of the schools, recruit excellent students widely, select the talents as teachers, divide the different professions, extend the length of schooling, strictly implement the examination system, and conduct long lasting inspections, only in this way can the state cultivate excellent talents.

"Virtue as the core of talent, education as the way to achieve". Li Jin believed that "human nature can be built, the key is teaching". He stressed that "if the school is not established, the teaching is not conducted, people don't know who can be a teacher and what to learn, then justice and virtue is nowhere to be known and practiced". He believed that the so–called teaching was actually the adjustment of human's natural desire. The natural desire of man is not said to be unreasonable, which is the difference between him and traditional Confucians, therefore teaching in his view is not against human nature, on the other hand, the natural desire of human beings can not develop infinitely, it must be tempered. Li also stressed that saints should not choose people to teach, and he was not approved with geographical determinism. He cited many historical stories to prove that: heroes are not determined by north and south, but that talents can be cultivated through education.

"Rites are the Lord of the world, the foundation of teaching is the teacher". In the content of education, Li Jin highlighted the rites and stated that: Rites are the key of governing people.

The reason why the monarch owns the country, the princes govern their states, and the reason why the ordinary people can maintain their livelihood is all because of the rites and order. Throughout the universe and eternity, rites and orders are indispensable.(*On Rites–Part Six*) He regarded rites as the highest standard of humanity, the basic means of the sage to govern the world, the main principle of moral cultivation and the main content of social education. He also paid full attention to the role of teachers in ethics. He said: In moral and ideological education, teachers play a leading role, so the choice of teachers can not be arbitrary; In Li's opinion, the decay and confusion of thoughts was due to the poor choice of teachers. (*Fifteen Articles in Guang Qian Shu*). Li Jian also put forward the requirements of strengthening the construction of teachers' ethics:"Take education as the job and virtue as the priority. It is pointed out that teachers should not only teach, but also educate people, and students should not only read, but also should cultivate morality.

2.2 Wang Anshi

"The aim of education is to contribute to the country" . Wang Anshi, a reformer in the Northern Song Dynasty, emphasized the cultivation of usable talents and put forward the aim of education, he said: What is the way of education? Since the ancient dynasties, from court officials to fellow villagers all have education experience, the officials of education are widely organized and strictly selected. The ritual, music and judicial institutions of the court all depend on learning and education. The content of teaching is in line with the former monarch's intention of governing the country, which is useful for the country. (*Collection of Wang Wengong–Lengthy Statement to Emperor Renzong*) Wang Anshi's way of teaching, at the institutional level, is to set up schools; At the level of content, it is teaching for the useful talents for the country. In addition to school, Wang also emphasizes the influence of social customs on education of talents. He said: Saint on the will of God, as the people's lord, the key way is to benefit and comfort people. And the key factor is the right customs, which is affecting the motivation and willingness of people, and is connected with ups and downs of the country, therefore it is worth careful exploring. What is related with the above thoughts is the way of selection, appointment, and cultivation, all reflecting the utilitarian thought of governing and education. Wang Anshi takes the application of the knowledge as the purpose of academic research, and believes that the complementarity of Confucianism and Buddhism is conducive in promoting social development and the talent cultivation.

"The way of reform lies in the concentration of doctrine itself". For the malpractices of the school at that time, Wang Anshi had a deep understanding. He stated in *Collection of Wang Wengong–Lengthy Statement to Emperor Renzong* that: The schools in counties only function as the walls and teaching facilities, the qualified teachers and effective teaching are insufficient, the teachers in imperial college are not strictly selected and the ritual, music and judicial knowledge of the court are not well learned. Wang Anshi pointed out that in schools, the teaching is completely divorced from reality. All useful knowledge such as court rites and politics were excluded from school teaching. Schools only taught lessons for test articles. Even if people learned it well, it was not enough for the running of the country. Such a wasting of time was actually destroying talents. So he put forward ideas for improving school education, and suggested in his *On the Reform of Imperial Examination Decree*: it is advisable to remove the disease of testing antithetical parallelism text so that scholars can concentrate on the meaning of the classic doctrine, schools are to be built by the court. the three–generation education election act should be reinstated and implemented. Wang Anshi's memorial to the throne put forward the targets and tasks of the reformation of education: to build schools and recovery of three generations of education election, and to reform the current exam–oriented education system of selecting scholars based on poetry and Fu (a type of classical Chinese writing) memorization, so that talents can put their knowledge into practice.

"The way of being a teacher is the heartfelt teaching". Wang Anshi values the role of teachers. He said,"Without a teacher, a king doesn't know why he is a king, a minister does not know how to be a minister, that is the significance of a teacher." He believed that the ruling of world needed the education of saints, but the way of saints needed to be carried forward, so teachers were not dispensable. For social education, Wang Anshi stressed the issue of virtual education. The so–called virtue education refers to the influence of monarchs on the public, which should be persuading rather than suppressing. According to Wang Anshi, those who are qualified to educate the people and become teachers should adopt the former method rather than the latter. Wang Anshi's education method of persuasion rather than oppression, influence instead of enforcement is the so called heartfelt teaching," it is conducive to social order and useful to practical education.

2.3 Chen Liang

"Keep the humanity and develop the ability and morale". Chen Liang, a thinker in the Southern Song Dynasty, believed that the role of schools was to cultivate talents and boost their morale. He said:"The emperor set up schools in the capital, so that the scholars can gather and communicate from time to time while tolerating the opinions of hundreds of schools and criticizing current problems, thus the humanity is kept and the ability and morale is developed". He argued that the state should set up schools to teach the children of officials, so that there would be no shortage of talents available to the court. In order to produce useful talents, Chen Liang arguesd that education should not go against human nature. He said in the *Collection of Chen Liang–Volume 4*: The common nature of human beings can be fully satisfied with wealth and honor, and vice versa is danger, distress and disgrace. However, whether people's desires can be satisfied is not determined by themselves, but by the regulation of ritual, music and punishment, and the so–called rituals, music and punishments are based on human nature. Therefore, the teaching of ritual, music and punishment should not only be the temperance of human nature, but also should conform to human's natural life desire. In Chen Liang's opinion, the moralists' study of life and the teaching of keeping reason and discarding desire is totally against human nature and the correct talent cultivation, constrained with these thoughts, the people will not be upright, customs cannot be simple, and talents must be scarce. He suggested that education should make clear about qualified teachers, spread benevolence and justice, and use talents in an eclectic way. In this way, the country can prosper and the world can be peaceful.

"Teach in the way of manhood, instead of self–discipline in Confucian ethics". Chen Liang argued that education should be aimed at helping people growing, rather than being restricted to making people pure Confucians. He stated frankly: Liang believes scholars should learn to be adults, and Confucian is also a portal in the great learning, without teaching in the way of manhood, pure Confucianism and self–discipline is far from enough and will leave eternal regret in education. (*The Collection of Chen Liang–Vol. 20*) In Chen Liang's opinion, the teaching approach of adulthood from Chu Hsi is not worth pursuing, he felt that the real"adult" should be the internal cultivation of "benevolence" , and the external attention to practical effects, thus to achieve benevolence, wisdom and courage and virtue, and stand side by side with heaven and earth. Compared with traditional Confucianism, Chen Liang's"way of manhood" has distinct pragmatic and utilitarian features. In his opinion, the personality characteristics of the manhood way are different from traditional Confucianism, but the quality that first integrates justice, interests, reason and desire, and second includes both"benevolence, wisdom, courage" and virtue, as well as a strong sense of social responsibility and moral mission. It is the so–called"the responsibility of the world", which combines individual value with social value, moral value with utilitarian value. The way of manhood in Chen Liang's thought is a kind of ideal personality construction, which has important practical significance to the spiritual civilization of modern education.

2.4 Ye Shi

"What is cultivated depends on what is used". Compared with Cheng–Zhu Neo–Confucianism, Ye Shi has a distinct"utilitarian" nature in terms of governance and education. Ye Shi attaches great importance to the effect of social governance, emphasizes the promotion of commerce and industry, supports merchants and circulates money with the power of the state. The overall view of Ye Shi's thought shows that "utility" is a means to achieve national social governance, its origin is still to serve The "benevolent government". He said:"Those who nourish the world must take from it, those who nourish the mountains must take wood, those who nourish the lake and river must fish, and that is the rule for everything, a long cultivation aims at taking the essence. The purpose of raising and cultivating is for the taking. It means that the use must depend on the former nourishing and support, the rule applies to the nature, especially in human society. If one wants to use talents, you must first raise them, and if you want to take scholars, you must first cultivate scholars. As for the way of nurturing, Ye Shi emphasized the quality of the educational officials themselves. Only when the officials themselves have a good quality can they talk about teaching people to be successful. He said:

Being open and lenient, the officials will reflect and cultivate themselves; being frugal and less desiring, the officials will raise themselves. Therefore, self–cultivation is more urgent than teaching others(*Ryan County Re–study Records*). Ye Shi advocated that teachers should teach people morality, but righteousness and interests are not incompatible.

"What is taught must be useful". Ye Shi argued that if morality repels utility, morality is useless and empty. Then he put forward the idea of the integration of teaching and politics, learning and use. He said: what ever its quality, the articles should be practical and relevant to the reality. The so–called reality is social–political affairs, it must be beneficial to education and related to current affairs. Ye Shi emphasized that the content of the article should be reasonably practical, especially for the imperial examination, it must adhere to a pragmatic orientation. He once criticized that " education and politics are separated as two fields." (*The Collection of Ye Shi–On Miscellaneous Levies*). It means that what we have learned today is the way of the former governance , but once we are official, what we do has nothing to do with what we have learned. Schools are for learning, the work is about politics, if learning and doing are regarded as two different ways, how does this avoid talent decadence, and political decay? Therefore, Ye Shi believed that the imperial examination, the system of policy as well as the study and education must be"pragmatic", practice should be taken as the premise and empty talk must be opposed, this is in line with the idea of governing the country. Based on this, he believes that scholars should first be pragmatic in their study and self–cultivation.

Section Three The Mind Philosophy and Practical Learning

Both mind psychology and practical learning are the important contents in the development of education and philosophy in China. In the *Philosophical Dictionary*,"mind psychology" and "Lu Wang Mind study" are integrated into one, which was founded by Lu Jiuyuan in the Southern Song Dynasty and further developed by Wang Shouren in the Ming Dynasty. This school believes that the heart is the foundation of the world in the philosophical world view. In fact, the concept of practical learning has a long history in China. On the one hand, it is the embodiment of the practical thought of Confucianism of participating into the world affairs that has run through the Confucian education thought; On the other hand, it is also a form of reflection and criticism of Confucian culture generated in a specific historical period, it is The "innovation" factor of the ordinary people's culture as the new trend of social thought dispelling the scholasticism of Confucianism. It is of great help to understand the representative figures of mind philosophy and practical learning and their main thoughts so as to understand Chinese education culture.

I. The Mind Philosophy from Song to Qing Dynasty

The thought of mind learning in the Song, Yuan, Ming and Qing dynasties is a school of Confucianism that emphasizes the heart as the source of value. In Ming Dynasty, Wang Shouren said in *The Complete Collection of Lu Xiangshan–Narration*:"All the Leaning from Saints is about Mind Philosophy". Therefore, later scholars called the thoughts initiated by Lu Jiuyuan and Wang Shouren as school of mind philosophy, as the distinction from the neo–Confucianism school represented by Cheng and Zhu. The basic difference between mind psychology and neo–Confucianism is that the former advocates the mind–ontology, which is different from the rational–ontology of Neo–Confucianism; The second is the characteristic of the educational theory of mind psychology, which emphasizes the subjectivity of the educated ones, believing ideological education only expands and induces the innate conscience nature of human beings, rather than teaching what human nature does not have.

1.1 Lu Jiuyuan

"To keep, cultivate and set free the mind". As a famous philosopher and educator in the Southern Song Dynasty, Lu Jiuywan's thought of mind learning opened the learning approach of Confucianism for civilians in the middle and late Ming Dynasty. In Lu Jiuyuan's view the so–called education, in essence, is to teach people to preserve and cultivate their conscience of mind, when conscience is blinded or lost, it is the mission of education to help people find it. He said: There is no child who does not know how to love his parents and how to respect the senior family members, ethical and moral education is to make them know the gist and keep the nature of human mind. This is also the way of Sant Yao and Shun. This is not a very high and difficult task, how can we ignore ancient customs, and give up on the sages! (*The Collection of Lu Jiuyuan–The Rebuilt Guixi County School Records*) That is to say, the so–called education, is to teach people to keep their own mind without losing the true conscience. Why the key in teaching is to keep, cultivate and set free the mind? It is because mind is reason. Reason is not outside the mind, not filled within heaven and earth, but only in the hearty mind. Benevolence, righteousness, courtesy, wisdom and faith are all different manifestations of the heart. To seek benevolence and righteousness is to seek the principle contained in the mind of people, to know right and wrong is also to know the reason contained in the mind. He also stressed that if a person's conscience is lost, the most important thing is to keep and cultivate the mind, that is to recover the nature of conscience, so what is terrible is not"indulging", but"giving up without seeking". Therefore, apart from teaching to keep and cultivate the mind, we must teach people how to set free the mind for seeking truth.

"Learning with a teacher, teaching with orders". In line with the tradition of confucianisom, Lu Jiuyuan believed that people should not fancy themselves as teachers, they should be guided by teachers. He stated in *To Zhang Fuzhi* that "the serious problems of scholars lies in the self–willed learning, if they fancy themselves as teachers, then they cannot discipline themselves, and cannot listen to instructions, even if they read the books of sages and hear the words of sages, they can only increase the mistakes". He emphasized that the advantage of following a teacher was that the teacher could give orderly instruction in his studies and help the scholar avoid limitless reading of irrelevant texts. The knowledge that is not taught by teachers is only some complicated and unsystematic message, which can not be called knowledge. He also stressed learning with a teacher and teaching with orders. In his view the systemic truth of the universe is unique, which can not be changed by nature and supernatural beings. Although teachers are indispensable for learning, a wise teacher is difficult for learners to find. Scholars should not waste time without the guidance of the master, but should make efforts at all times.

"Perseverance with ambition and virtues as the priority". It's believed that the reason why sages are sages is that they do not fall from their aspirations under difficult conditions. Although Confucius had no success in his career, his lofty ambition and perseverance made him worthy of being a sage. He argued that the biggest problem was lacking of ambition. Where there is a will there is a way. Therefore, to teach people, the first step is to motivate people to be determined (*The Collection of Lu Jiuyuan–Quotations*). This thought of Lu Jiuyuan is in line with that of Mengzi. At the same time, Lu Jiuyuan taught people to "respect virtue" first. He believed that compared with talent and art, virtue was undoubtedly more important than talent. The reason is that virtue is the foundation of a person's life."A commoner has virtue, he can protect his body, an official has virtue, he can protect his family, a vassal has virtue, he can protect his manor, the emperor has virtue, he can protect his world.""being wealth without virtue will increase the evil and aggravate the calamity of the future. Though rich today, how can you keep it long?" (*Miscellaneous Sayings*) Lu Jiuyuan stressed that reading should be based on the premise of an upright heart, otherwise the more one learn, the greater the harm there would be.

"Self–reliance as the principle, burden alleviation as the approach". Self–reliance means to be your own master, not dependent on others. Lu Jiuyuan said to his disciples: From today on, try to be independent, sit straight with cupping hands before chest, clean up your minds and believe everything in control after efforts. then nothing is impossible to achieve (*The Collection of Lu Jiuyuan–Quotations*). It means when people are their own masters, they are to have the spirit of independence and self–mastery , then they do not have to lean against the wall, as long as the heart is clean, even if one is illiterate, it does not prevent him from becoming a gentleman. Therefore, education first is to teach people to be a real human, and then learning knowledge and art is the second. At the same time, Lu Jiuyuan advocated simple and burden alleviation approach in teaching. He once wrote a poem saying:"simple theories will eventually spread, trivial theories will eventually drift away." He did not advocate showing many commentaries to the students, he suggested learning from the ancient wisdom was enough. This teaching approach, is called burden alleviation, he believed only burden alleviation could improve the efficiency, and cultivate a generation of talents.

1.2 Wang Shouren

"Clarify human relationships". As a great thinker, strategist and educator, Wang Shouren inherited the ancient Confucian educational tradition, his "mind learning" system reflects the social landscape of the Ming Dynasty. He said,"The learning of the ancient sages is nothing but clarifying human relationships. The sages like Yao and Shun gave instruction that:"There is no heart without sinister, Tao heart is upright and subtle; Only with continuous progress, the heart of the people can be transferred into the heart of the Tao and achieve harmony in line". (*The Essay of Wansong Academy*) In Wang Shouren's view, the purpose of education is to clarify ethics, that is to say, there is affection between father and son, gratitude between the emperor and the minister, differences between the husband and the wife, and etiquette order between the elder and the younger, faith among friends, education without human relations is paganism, knowledge outside human relations is heresy. To act in line with human relation is the right way to govern the world; to act against human relations is to create troubles. This educational thought for the purpose of clarifying relationship can be seen everywhere in the complete works of Wang Yangming (Wang Shouren). He stressed that: teaching human relationship looks easy, but it is actually very difficult. It is easy in a sense that it is the nature of man to know, and even a child knows to love his cousin and respect his brother. Therefore, to teach it is not to infuse moral principles into the human heart from outside, it is only to inspire what is already in human nature through education. It is difficult in a sense that, to achieve the perfect human relationship is hard even for saints, let alone ordinary people. Wang Shouren stressed that the significance of human relationship education was not the explanation but the practice. This requires teachers to take the lead in setting an example for themselves. Otherwise, he would not make himself trustful, though he can explain it so eloquently.

"Inspire the motivation and open the mind". Wang Shouren emphasized that in education for children, moral education should be the first priority, so that they can develop good moral qualities from an early age, and he also advocated cultivating children with poetry, courtesy and reading. He stated in *The General Idea of Child Education* that "To stimulate their feelings of humanity with poetry, to teach them manner with etiquette , and to develop their intelligence with reading". Of course, the education of poetry and etiquette should be carried out according to the age and psychological characteristics of children, and should not be carried out according to the method of teaching officials. Zhuangzi once put benevolence, righteousness and morality in opposition to human nature, while Wang Shouren carried out moral education according to people's natural temperament, which was more brilliant. Wang Shouren criticized contemporary children's education as totally against the physical and psychological characteristics of children, as a result, children"regard school as a prison and refuse to enter it, and teachers as enemies and refuse to see them", how can children be guided well? Wang Shouren's thought is full of wisdom of teachers and conforms to the law of children's psychological development, and is worthy of attention for future generations.

"Unity of knowledge and practice". It is believed that the knowledge of the truth is inseparable from the practice. Knowledge refers to inner awareness, cognition of things, and practice refers to actual behavior. It is not only the core of Wang Yangming theory, but also the proposition of epistemology and practice in ancient Chinese philosophy. Inspired by this thought, China's traditional educational philosophy holds that people's external behavior is governed by their internal consciousness, and only those who genuinely want to be good ("with knowledge and sense of virtue") can perform external and spontaneous good deeds, so there is a unity of knowledge and practice. Wang Shouren's unity of knowledge and practice includes"There is practice in knowledge and knowledge in practice. Knowledge is the key to practice, and knowledge determines practice". Wang Shouren strongly opposed the disconnection between knowledge and practice in moral education and The "knowing but not doing". He put all morality in the individual's conscious action, which is of positive significance. Besides, he believed that: morality is the guiding ideology of human behavior, to act in accordance with the requirements of morality is the ability to achieve"conscience", the mental activity produced under moral guidance is the beginning of action, the behavior in line with the requirements of the code of ethics is the completion of "conscience". This kind of unity of knowledge and practice is mainly an idealist moral cultivation theory of "checking and controlling". The essence of knowledge and practice, which has not been separated by private will, refers to the conscience of "knowing filial piety when one sees his father, knowing the kinship of brothers when meeting them, and knowing compassion when witnesses the child falling into a well". He believed that "to bring the conscience of my heart to everything in reality" is real practicing. His "conscience" is the unity of knowledge and practice, it is the effort of "eliminating evil for good", and the capacity of "ignoring human desires and preserving nature's principles".

1.3 Huang Zongxi

"Morality and utility as one". As a famous thinker and statesman in the late Ming and early Qing dynasties, the relation between Huang Zongxi's mind and his political thought was first reflected in his Confucian view of "integrating morality and utility". As far as the ideological history is concerned, it reflects the convergence and transformations of the mind nature and the study of utility as the two pillars of modern neo–Confucianism. The educational and political significance of his mind philosophy is also embodied in the dimension of "the way of heaven and man". He said: Since the separation of morality and utility, scholars pursuing for benevolence and righteousness are like submerging in the mud, there is no lofty ambition; What they don't know is that in ancient and modern times, no utility can be achieved exclusive of morality and vice–versa. The essence of Huang Zongxi's theory of "the connection of nature and man" lies in carrying on the principle of heaven with human actions. For the mandate of heaven, a gentleman should take the initiative to undertake and realize it actively apart from keeping it and waiting for it. A gentleman should not only have the morality of "standing by", but also the responsibility of "creating fates". On the one hand, the transcendent spiritual dimension provides important support for political and legal reform; On the other hand, Huang argued that God's will is reflected by public opinions, while opposing fatalism and calamity theory, he encouraged people to actively take the fate by their own practice, thus, his thoughts showed a sense of responsibility and active awareness of education and politics.

"Spirit is based on substance". The basic characteristic of Huang Zongxi's view of Spirit and substance is that he advocates"integrating the two instead of separating them". The relation between Qi(substance) and Li(spirit) is the basic proposition of Neo–Confucianism in Song and Ming dynasties, Huang Zongxi's objection to the dichotomies of Li and Qi" is based on his criticism of the theory of separating"knowledge and practice". He demonstrated the basic viewpoint of "Qi and Li are the principles of each other" from the ontology, and then put forward the new cognition to the issue of Li and Qi. The deep reason for the formation of Huang Zongxi's thought is: after the rise of Yangming School in the middle Ming Dynasty, it had a great social influence. One of its basic claims is "unity of knowledge and practice", it criticized teaching about"knowledge" without practice of moral cultivation. In view of this shortcoming, Huang Zongxi questioned the practice of some Confucian scholars who emphasized only"knowledge" and "understanding" rather than"action" and "effort" in the study of sages. He argued the idea of "unity of knowledge and practice" of Wang Yangming should be inherited. Then from the perspective of ontology, the unity of "knowledge" and "practice" must require the unity of "spirit" and "substance". Huang Zongxi believed that the root cause of the collapse of the Ming Dynasty was the collapse of the ethical order. The root cause of this lied in the loss of the morality of human heart, which is caused by the separation of LI and Qi. The relationship between Li and Qi is two sides of the same matter, which is originally one thing. It is just given different names because of different viewing angles. He said:"The mind has no noumenon, the cultivation of the spirit and substance is its noumenon". This idea emphasizes the true meaning of existence and opposes the withdrawal of reason from real life. In addition, the thought that "Spirit is based on substance" provides a comprehensive demonstration for the distinction between understanding and doing in Neo–Confucianism in Ming Dynasty; turning the direction of the Confucianism from "pursuing simplicity inward" to "combination of history and society outward".

II. Practical Learning in Education of Qing Dynasty

The so–called practical learning is the humanistic pragmatism. This school believes that knowledge must be beneficial to the people of the countries. As an academic trend of thought, practical learning is opposed to cultivation of indifference to fame or gain. School of practical learning in Qing Dynasty advocated hands–on practice and paid attention to practical knowledge. It is believed that the objective existence of objects, is the basis of knowledge, so reading can not be separated from the reality, because only practical knowledge is beneficial to the national economy and people's livelihood, practice ability can be applied in the world.

2.1 Bao Shichen

"The reason of prosperity and decline lies in people". Bao Shichen was a famous practical thinker in the Qing Dynasty. He had a deep understanding of the social situation, the sufferings of the people and various kinds of malpractice at that time. But he believed that "Destiny changes with the actions of people." As long as people work together and take timely reform measures, they can"right the wrongs". How to "set things right"? Bao Shichen believed that the first step was to find out the root cause of social chaos and crisis. He said:"In the world, we must see the root of the problems and the source of the errors, and then we can find the right strategies to solve them". He also put forward a principled policy"make progress gradually, accumulate small to make big", advocating making reform from the grassroots system and implementing good policy to improve the social situation. Bao Shichen also put forward the idea of "creative reform", among which the suggestion of establishing"court of judges" is quite valuable. He called on scholars to consciously take"civil affairs" as their work, so that Confucianism can meet the needs of social groups and solve social problems, what he expressed is the appeal of reforming traditional Confucianism and making it practical. Although Bao Shichen's reform thought had some limitations for the shortcomings like the feudal system in China and the new ideas had not been spread to China, his pragmatic thought that "the reason of prosperity and decline lies in people" had important practical significance for the Chinese education in different periods.

"All civil affairs are jobs for the talents". Bao Shichen believed that educators and intellectuals, no matter they were The "superior ones" who"talked about the life philosophy" or The "inferior ones" who were"arrogant and eloquent", were not true"talents". The real talents should be those devoting ones, with their practical knowledge working for the country and the people. He believed that the scholars ranked first among the four social classes (Scholars, farmers, workers and merchants) because they could understand agriculture, industry and commerce and guide and promote the development of agriculture, industry and commerce with what they had learned. He hoped that intellectuals could consciously realize and assume their social responsibilities and play their due roles in production, circulation and social management. In order to motivate the intellectuals to apply their knowledge to the world, he once suggested that the imperial examination should be reformed,"instead of the test of eight–part essay, two aspects of understanding economic skills and planning current affairs should be the focal content for examinations". (*The Complete Works of Bao Shichen*)Bao Shichen explained the value of Confucianism to be satisfying"human needs" and persuaded scholars into serving the people. Targeting at the situation of old Confucianism failing to meet The "human needs" and officials ignoring The "civil affairs" , his thoughts of reforming have a positive enlightening effect on the educational ideas of later generations.

2.2 Yan Yuan

"Teaching for practicing". Yan Yuan, a thinker in the early Qing Dynasty, as a representative of practical learning was an educator who attached great importance to practical education. All his life, he criticized the reading for meditation, and advocated teaching for practicing. In his work *Editing on Learning* he stated:"The teaching of poetry, classic books and the six arts are not empty talks, it needs practicing, and contextual explanation when learners encounter difficulties". Yan Yuan hammered home that one of the most prominent defects of traditional education was being divorced from reality, so he advocated practical learning as a proxy for Neo–Confucianism. Yan Yuan's so–called practicing means"doing", which has the meaning of exercitation in modern teaching. Why should teaching attach importance to practice? Yan Yuan believes that the objective and actual existence is the actual content of people's knowledge. Only by practicing in person, can knowledge be mastered. Even if we obtain theoretical knowledge, only through practice can we turn theoretical knowledge into our own knowledge. Otherwise,"knowledge remembered in mind , spoken with words, and written on paper without learning from practice are all useless!" (*Editing on Learning –Volume Three*). Moreover, teaching is for application, and people's energy is limited. When it is consumed in speaking and reading, and with paper and ink, then one would be less energetic in practice.

"Teach by motion, not by stillness". In ancient China, most Confucian and Taoist thinkers taught with the concept of tranquility rather than that of excitement, because they believed the nature of morality static, not dynamic. In Yan Yuan's opinion, the momentary ease of Jin and Song dynasties, the emptiness of Buddhists, and the meditation of Neo–Confucianism were the fundamental reasons for the depletion of talents, and the demise of the holy way, as well as the weakness of the country. He was convinced that only with motions and practice, can one strengthen the body, and consolidate the family and the country. It is stressed repetitively that "to keep fit is to be good at exercises , to strive night and day, to keep busy with spirit, keep regular work and then grow stronger. He also stressed that people have leisure when idling around, with leisure, one will crave comfort, the love of ease leads to sloth, and idleness leads to corruption. When there is leisure, ease, idleness, and depravity, selfish desires will arise (A *Record of Words and Actions from Yan Xi Room*). It means if people are idling around with more leisure days, the habit of laziness, and selfish desire will follow. Only by keeping active, can one be full of vigor and spirit, so that selfish desires will not be generated. Yan Yuan's conclusion is:"Since the Song and Yuan Dynasties, Confucianism has appreciated stillness, today it is time to change for active actions!" (*A Record of Words and Actions from Yan Xi Room*) Thus, the active education concept of Wang Fuzhi was further advanced.

"Teach with real practice, not with empty theory". The so–called"real" refers to practical and applied knowledge and moral practice, while the so–called"emptiness" refers to the study of heaven and life."Teach with real practice, not with empty theory" is another basic principle of

Yan Yuan's education thought. It is believed that the real practice is the natural way of heaven, earth and humanity. He said that the way of heaven and earth is reality and not emptiness, just as the world is reality and not emptiness, the Buddhism speaks of emptiness and the Daoism speaks of nothing, but they cannot make the sky without light, the earth without mountains and rivers, and the people without eyes and ears, therefore, in a lifetime, though there are bad career fortunes, it is still worth creating achievements with the practical text, practice, and entity, and learners can not be like the scholars in Song Dynasty who talked about the nature of life without caring about the prosperity of the nation and people, so Yan Yuan's teaching was characterized with practice. When he presided over the Zhangnan Academy, the academy was set up as six departments including four practical subjects like literary affairs, military provisions, history of classics, and skills of art. Although the departments of Neo–Confucianism and text of the imperial examination were also set for they are the mainstream education style of the time, Yan Yuan opened their relevant door to the north to show that it was not important.

"Teach Confucianism, not prose". Confucianism refers to the school founded by Confucius. Teaching Confucianism means teaching the theories and ways of Confucianism. The so–called prose refers to articles, literature and art. Not teaching prose does not mean avoiding teaching writing the articles. Yan Yuan distinguished and even opposed Confucianism and prose. He stated that the real Confucian, is to benefit the fate of people, and the fortune of the country (*A Record of Words and Actions from Yan Xi Room–Volume Two*). It means that Confucians take practical learning as its work and economic career as its contribution, while literati take articles as their learning. There is a world of difference between the two. Yan Yuan was a fierce critic of his society, which prefers literature to Confucianism, he argued: Later generations do not emphasize the study of human relations, the application of knowledge, the virtues of honesty and integrity, the state selects scholars based on literature, and the school also takes literature as its main merit, the communication in family and among friends is relying on words. Then how can the whole kingdom be governed well? These practical thoughts of Yan Yuan are full of his concern for the world and profound consideration on education reform, which is very valuable at that time.

2.3 Li Gong

"No teaching of mysterious nature of heaven". As a successor of Yan Yuan school, Li Gong inherited the tradition of teaching in real practice rather than in empty theories, he believed that sages taught people in practical ways rather than in mysterious concepts of nature and heaven. In his *Preface of Zhouyi Notes* he argued:"The mission of nature is to cultivate lives with humanity, the mission of human is to run the world with knowledge. If nature takes the place of human to run the world, then its mission is neglected, if human beings take the mission of nature, then nothing could be achieved by them". Why didn't the sages teach mysterious nature of heaven and spread practical knowledge of human world instead? Li

Gong believed: nature of heaven is hidden in the knowledge and events of human world, in other words, reason is not a solitary thing, it is just in the human practice. Like Yan Yuan, Li Gong also Sharply criticized scholars in Song Dynasty who just focused on theories instead of practice:"The physical world has its rules. What is the theory to do without the practical world? And the Tao of morality is only superficial, therefore, how can the mysterious teaching without frequent practice and physical objects be regarded as the same authentic Confucian school !" It is stated that there is no higher education without lower practice, there is no knowledge separated from real matters. It is only the Buddhist and the Taoist thought, not the Confucian tradition, to see Tao or reason as an isolated concept. Therefore, like his teacher Yan Yuan, he believed that "reason lies in Qi". He said,"If people practice in order, reason is already there."(*Notes on the Analects of Confucius*) This thought is the embodiment of "No teaching of the mysterious nature of heaven", it is also li Gong's significant contribution to the materialistic thought.

"The knowledge lies in the study of the physical world." Li Gong inherited the tradition from his teacher's"the study of the physical world is significant for morality, human relations and skills" , stressing that although higher education is teaching reasons and theories, it should not be separated from physical world. He saw the *Great Learning* as taking the three qualities in *Rites of Zhou* as the physical skills, and taking practice as studying. The so–called study of the physical world is to learn the art skills and moral ethics. Why is it necessary to learn with practice, and to teach in physical world? Li Gong claimed: the so–called learning is to practice and deal with matters, these are inseparable from real issues in real life. He stated: the so called physical world needs honesty, integrity, cultivation, management, governance, and peace, learning these are connected with each of the above practice, *Rites of Zhou* and other classic works are all about the physical world. Learning from the physical world is always the way of the sages, practice leads to knowledge, and knowledge is from learning. He compared the learning to walking on road, arguing that "without knowing one can not move forward, without practicing there is no true knowledge". He added that "knowing and practicing are two different matters, One must first ask the way, and then try to walk on". It is because of his understanding of The "study the nature of things" and the relationship between"knowing" and "practicing" that he regards"knowing" and "doing" as two parallel aspects, which highlights the dialectical and objective characteristics of his academic ideas.

Chapter Six The Comprehension of Classic Proverbs

From the former chapters, it is not difficult for readers to find that in the long–term development of Chinese traditional education, there are numerous books and profound thoughts in Chinese educational culture. In the long history of education, the incisive words and wisdom are dramatically significant. Some of them have been widely circulated for a long time, and become educational maxims, broad and profound, full of philosophy, all generations of teachers have regarded them as the treasure of education, through constant recording and modification they carried forward these classic proverbs for later generations.

Most of the classic proverbs selected in this chapter are from *A Collection of Chinese Maxims* and *Dictionary of Ancient Chinese Fanoues Sayings*. Although it is impossible to cover all the thought provoking words, and it is inevitable to miss a great deal in this chapter, it still can be an effective way to inherit the essence of wisdom in education culture through tasting the classic sayings from the aspects of self–cultivation and learning inspiration and it is inevitable to miss a great deal in this chapter, it still can be an effective way to inherit the essence of Chinese traditional education culture through tasting the classic sayings from the aspects of studies and self–cultivation , inspiration and worldly philosophy.

Section One Studies and Self–cultivation

In Chinese educational culture, the first essence of Confucian "learning" is "self–cultivation". The concept of so–called "self–cultivation" is not only moral cultivation or moral education; it is based on the premise that "heaven and man","world and me", and "body and mind" are integrated and connected, so as to achieve a full personality of "out from within" in the sense of the harmony of world and self, mind and body. In ancient China, there were abundant ways of Studies and self–cultivation, which aimed at improving the spiritual cultivation of individuals with colorful ideas and methods, and at constantly enriching one's own knowledge, molding a perfect personality with virtue and wisdom, so as to obtain the freedom and perfection that is not driven by material desires.

I. Around Qin and Han Dynasties

1.1 On Learning

Learned and defermined, inquiring and reflecting. (*The Analects of Confucius–Zi Zhang*)

A piece of jade cannot be made into anything useful and precious without being cut and polished; a man cannot know about the principles of morality and justice without being taught.

(*The Book of Rites–The Book of Learning*)

Learn extensively, inquire carefully, think deeply, differentiate clearly, and practice faithfully. (*The Book of Rites–The Doctrine of the Mean*)

Only by learning extensively and by explaining in detail can a man reach the essence. (*Mencius –Lielou Xia*)

He who acquires new knowledge by reviewing old knowledge is qualified to be a teacher of others. (*The Analects of Confucius – On Governance*)

In broadening his learning, the gentleman each day examines himself so that he will be discerning and his actions without fault. (*Xunzi –Encourage Learning*)

Judging by my experience, a whole day's thinking was not so valuable as a moment's study. (*Xunzi –Encourage Learning*)

A lifetime is limited, but knowledge is unlimited. (*Zhuangzi–Master of Health Preservation*)

As for the teachers, they should not concern about power, treasure and noble background, but should pursue the truth and virtue they are to teach. (*Mister Lv's Spring and Autumn Annals–Encourage Learning*)

When a king makes great effort to study, he will widen his knowledge and wisdom. When he endeavors to practice Tao, he will improve his virtue day by day and will achieve great success. (*Strategies for Selecting Virtuous People*)

Although Wuhao (a kind of bow) is of excellent workmanship, it cannot correct itself without a tool for holding the bow in position; although one is gifted with unusual talents, one still cannot score great success without learning. (*Shuo Yuan–Shuo Cong (expostulation for the governors*)

Learning is thus like climbing a mountain: as one moves the higher one ascends. It is also like sleeping: the more time passes the more one is satisfied. (*Treatise on the Middle Way–on Scholarly Research*)

Mountains of precious gems are sure to have well–watered soil and forests. Similarly, men of replete virtue are sure to be widely skilled in the arts. (*Treatise on the Middle Way–on Craft Disciplines*)

Literature is no less noble an issue than the governing of a state; it is also a way to immortality. The years pass and one's life runs out its natural course. Honours and pleasures cease to be with one's body. Against these inexorable facts, literature lives on to eternity. (*Classic Treatises–on Articles*)

Literature serves the purpose of proclaiming the phenomena of Heaven and Earth, of making manifest the order in human relationships, and of determining the right and the appropriacy of all things in the universe. (*Annals of The Three Kingdoms–Annals of Wei–Biography of Wang Su*)

A hundred times of reading makes the gist clear. (*History of the Three Kingdous*)

Wind of thoughts rises in the mind; Stream of words flows through the mouth. (*Ode to Literature*)

I constantly fear that in my conception's not being equal to the things of the world, and my writing's not being equal to my conceptions. (*Ode to Literature–Preface*)

If one is fond of learning, he will be living on in spirit even after death; if one hates learning, he will become a walking corpse though alive. (*The Literature Relics*)

Our youth, once gone, will not come back again, for the selfsame dawn we wait in vain. Grasp the time and work hard as you can, because the time and tide awaits no man. (*The Miscellaneous Poems*)

Articles should be valued for three kinds of simplicity—simplicity of using allusions, simplicity of word recognition, and simplicity of chanting. (*The Collection of Shen Yin Hou*)

Men may have high or low social status, but education should be offered to them without distinction of their classes. Especially those who are of humble birth should not be excluded from education. (*The Annotation of The Analects of Confucius*)

1.2 On Cultivation

I would still feel happy even if I had to eat coarse food, drink cold water, and take my arms as a pillow when asleep. (*The Analects of Confucius*)

When trouble befalls you from Heaven, there is still way of avoidance; but when you ask for it, there is no hope of escape. (*The Book of History–Taijia*)

To be tolerant is to be successful. (*The Book of Historyy–Junchen*)

A kind and benevolent lord distributes his wealth to his people to make the most of his virtues, and the heartless lord casts away his virtue to extort wealth from his people. (*Book of Rites–The Great Learning*)

Sincerity does not mean to promote one's achievement alone, it promotes all things also. (*The Book of Rites–The Mean*)

You must exercise forbearance, which will help you to succeed. (*The Book of History–Junchen*)

If some people have done you favour, you should not forget that. If you have done others a favour, you should forget it. (*The Strategies of the Warring States – Book of Wei IV*)

A tolerant person would not cause damage to others to benefit himself. A benevolent person would not pose a threat to others and gain fame for himself. (*The Strategies of the Warring States – Book of Yan III*)

Good medicine is bitter in the mouth but it cures sickness; faithful words are harsh to hear, but they help us to do right. (*Book of sayings of Confucius–Volumn Six*)

If you are in a hurry, your personality will not come into play; if you let yourself be distracted by petty profits, you can hardly succeed in great ventures. (*The Analects of Confucius–Zi Lu*)

Their wills repress the merely private, and thus they are able to be public-spirited. In their conduct, they repress their emotional inclinations and inborn nature and are thus able to become cultivated. (*Xunzi–Confucian effect*)

Without strengthening one's shoulders, one cannot be charged with a significant duty. (*Remarks of Monarchs–The State of Lu*)

Good virtue comes not from outside, neither can good name be falsified. (*The Nine Chapters–Pondering*)

Where big issues are at stake you cannot trouble about trifles; in matter of consequence you cannot adhere to the minor courtesies. (*Records of the Grand Historian–Primary Chronicle of Xiang Yu*)

One must show proper love for himself, then others love him. One must show self–respect for himself and then others respect him. (*Speech in Accordance with the Law–Men of Noble Character*)

If you do not want people to hear it, you'd better not say it and if you do not want people to know it, you'd better not do it. (*Remonstrating with the King of Wu*)

The dirt cannot be removed from the face without washing it; The evil idea will appear without cultivating the mind daily. (*The Commandments for Women*)

This is a life–style for a man of noble character: to cultivate his mind by keeping a tranquil heart, and nourish his morality by a means of frugality. Only freedom from vanity can show one's lofty aspirations; and only tranquility of mind can help achieving something lasting. (*Collection of Zhuge Liang–the Commandments*)

Do not fail to do a good deed because it is trivial, do not commit a bad deed because it is small. (*The History of the Three Kingdoms*)

The way of behaving oneself is different from the way of writing. While the latter needs free thinking, the former requires prudence. (*Collection of Emperor Liang Jian Wen Di*)

Those who reform themselves thoroughly are sure to wash the dirt of dust off their faces with clear water. (*Baopuzi–on Penalty*)

II. Around Tang and Song Dynasties

2.1 On Studies

If one fails to know that they should study assiduously when he is young, he will definitely regret in vain when grey–headed. (*On Encouraging Learning*)

Having studied over ten thousand volumes, / one can produce fluent writing with godly power. (*Collection of Du Shaoling*)

In mountain climbing of knowledge, diligence is the only way. On the boundless sea of learning, diligence is also one's own vehicle of passage. (*Poetic Couplets on Learning*)

Students learned from teachers since ancient times. For the mission of a teacher is to propagate the doctrine, impart professional knowledge, and resolve doubts. (*On Teaching*)

Two lines of poetry are the achievement of three years' pondering, two drops of tears are the result of chanting them. (*Sentiment after the Poem Inscription*)

Not only is it hard for a literary man to find someone who truly understands him, knowing others is also hard. (*Notes on Classical Poetry*)

The conversation with a sage overnight is worth studying for ten years. (*The Words of Mr. Ikawa*)

A writer in ancient times was capable of cultivating all, while quoting the ancients expressions into his writings, just like a grain of panacea, turning iron into gold by a touching. (*A letter to Hong Jufu*)

Learning should be based on thinking. A man can only obtain knowledge by thinking and reflecting deeply. (*The Notes from Mr. Chao*)

Knowledge gained through mere reading is superficial. The only way to gain real knowledge is in practice. (*Words to Ziyu while Reading at A Winter Night*)

Learn whatever it may be, learn whenever you can, and learn wherever you will. That is the way of success. (*The Notes from Zhuxi*)

How can it be so clear and cool? / For water comes fresh from its source. (*Reading Books with Sense*)

Judgment is the dominant factor in the study of poetry. The beginning direction must be correct, and your mind must be set on highest goals. (*Notes of Poetry in Canglang–Poetry Appreciation*)

Learning is indispensable to man, just as water is indispensable to the fish. But what a pity it is that learning is regarded by many as something superfluous nowadays. (*Collection of Lu Jiuyuan–and Huang Xunzhong*)

Words that come the natural way remain forever fresh; / Sincerity can be seen in poems free of flowery diction. (*On the Quatrains of Poetry*)

Peach blossoms year after year are the same. But the faces of people year after year are changed. (*The Story of Pipa*)

2.2 On Cultivation

Earth sticks together and makes a wall, people unite to each other can build a kingdom. (*The Book of the Northern Qi Dynasty –Biography of Yujing*)

Being ignorant of one's own mistakes is worth worrying, yet while getting aware of them and unable to correct them, he is a man without courage. (*The Preface of the Proverbs*)

Those who are not self–satisfied can acquire great benefit; those who are not opinionated can obtain wide knowledge. (*The Record of Saving the Mind*)

Anything can possibly be accomplished with respectful dedication; On the contrary, one will fail in everything with a lazy attitude. (*History As A Mirror*)

If you make all your effort without distraction, you will be able to succeed finally. (*Dream Pool Essays*)

He who can be impervious to the temptation of wealth and high position, and be happy in impoverishment and humbleness, will surely be a warrior and hero in this world. (*The Accidental Lines*)

To save oneself from suspicion, don't put on your boots in a melon field; nor adjust your hat under a plum tree. (*Yuefu poetry–Manners of Gentleman*)

It is wealth that ordinary people yearn, and it is morality that gentlemen cherish . (*Miscellaneous Sayings*)

To mature you can't do as you please; / If you do as you please, you'll never mature. (*Jade Dews of Crane Forest*)

Correct mistakes if you have committed them and guard against them if you have not. (*The Collected Notes*)

An act of compassion is better than reciting Buddha's name a thousand times; the evildoer can't be helped by burning ten thousand sticks of incense. (*The Story of Pipa*)

It is fundamental for a man to keep faith. One who does not is not worthy of the name of a man. (*Romance of the Western Chamber*)

III. Around Ming and Qing Dynasties

3.1 On studies

Never in the world has there been a superlative essay which has not come from the mind of the child. (*Book Burning– On Childlike Innocence*)

To learn without an ideal is just like planting a rootless tree. There will be nowhere for the tree to get its vitality. (*To Zhang Shiwen*)

One needs to read countless books for true knowledge; and travel a far distance to enrich experience. (*Tenor of Painting*)

A scholar should have illustrious thoughts and elegant tastes. If his freedom of thought and action is constantly restrained by worldly joys and sorrows, then he is in the grip of autumn's decay and is bereft of spring's vigour. How then can he help make the universe flourish? (*Tending the Roots of Wisdom*)

When censuring someone for his faults, do not be too severe; consider his level of tolerance. When teaching a man correct conduct, do not get goals which are too lofty for him to reach; consider what he is capable of accomplishing. (*Tending the Roots of Wisdom*)

With all your effort and devotion, an iron rod can be ground into a needle. (*Annals of the Land of Shu*)

An inch of time is an inch of gold; /an inch of gold cannot buy an inch of time. (*The Story of Eunuch San Bao to the West World*)

Knowledge cannot be accumulated without learning; scholarly attainments cannot be accomplished without the calm mind. (*Popular Collection of Traditional Chinese Wise Sayings*

Farmers and scholars work hard in their respective professions, / great achievements can be build in this way. (*Important Words to Awaken the World*)

In writing a composition, there must not be one sentence or even one word which is brought in at random. (*On Romance of the Western Chamber*)

Any book in the world that wishes to be placed in the Hall of Fame and be handed down to later generations, must possess the quality of exquisiteness and strictness. (*On Water Margin*)

Good articles are valued for exquisiteness rather than celerity. (*Strange Tales of Liao–Zhai–Zhi Cheng*)

The man who is infatuated with something can be much devoted. So whoever obsessed with books can certainly be a good writer, and whoever obsessed with art can certainly be a skillful artist. (*Strange Tales of Liao–Zhai–A Bao*)

The benefit of reading varies directly with one's experience in life. It is like looking at the moon. A young reader may be compared to one seeing the moon through a single crack, a middle–aged reader seems to see it from an enclosed courtyard, and an old man seems to see it from an open terrace, with a complete view of the entire field. (*Dream Shadows*)

A remarkable book is one which says something never said before. (*Dream Shadows*)

A writing can hardly be both sophisticated and excellent. It is like metal–smelting—only when the coarse ore is done away with, and the black and dirty gases are eliminated that the bright and glossy metal can be brought to light. (*To Cheng Ruohan*)

Expecting to obtain knowledge without diligence is just like waiting to reap harvest without cultivating. (*Collection of Bewilderment in Learning*)

In writing an essay, the mind should remain as clear as the human eyes. (*Unofficial History of Officialdom*)

It is not easy to put it in common language, which only comes natural through trying innumerable times. (*On the Twelve Quatrains of Poetry*)

One tends to regret that the knowledge is too limited while it is needed; and it is hard to realize how hard an undertaking is until one has experienced it. (*Stories of Buddha Jih*)

All the world's affairs are genuine knowledge when well understood; all worldly relations are true learning when maturely mastered . (*A Dream in Red Mansions*)

After reading repetitively 300 poems of the Tang Dynasty by heart, one is certainly skillful in chanting even if not in creating poetry. (*Preface of the Three hundred Tang poetry*)

Knowledge is the candle to guide life to the bright and true world. (*Dangerous Ideas and Freedom of Speech*)

Mere reliance and imitation will never produce true art. (*Essays of Demi–Concession*)

3.2 On Cultivation

A man without manner is low, wealth gained without rectitude is valueless. (*Water Margin*)

A man who gains fame shouldn't forget his benefactors. (*Water Margin*)

Horses always neigh in recognition of Bo Le, the supreme judge of horses, and when a man has found his lord he dies for him. (*Romance of the Three Kingdoms*)

Honor brooks no reservation, nor does loyalty respect death. (*Romance of the Three Kingdoms*)

Without a clear mirror, a woman cannot know the state of her own face; without a true friend, a man cannot know the errors of his own acts. (*Treasure of A Wise Mind*)

When living in the world you must be forbearing; Patience is essential when training oneself. (*Journey to the West*)

Do people a good favor whenever you can; If it is possible, treat them with mercy. (*Journey to the West*)

If you do good deeds for a thousand days you still won't have done enough, but if you do ill for one day that will be too much. (*Journey to the West*)

Wealth and honour, glory and fame, are determined by fate: No one should act against conscience to covet any of them. (*Journey to the West*)

Wipe the dust off your mind, Wash out the dirt from your ear. Without the most terrible suffering, you cannot be a great man. (*Journey to the West*)

There is no need to stand in the wind if one really owns musk with the scent spreading automatically. (*Verbiage of a Guest*)

On a narrow path, step aside one pace so that others may pass. When treated to fine food, offer part of it to your fellow diners. (*Tending the Roots of Wisdom*)

The accomplished man must engage in mental strife while unoccupied, and enjoy repose while exerting himself. (*Tending the Roots of Wisdom*)

Snatch leisure from busy affairs, seek tranquility from noise. In this way, you can considerably strengthen your ability. (*Tending the Roots of Wisdom*)

A thousand days might not be sufficient for learning goodness; and less than a day may be long enough to be corrupted . (*The Story of Eunuch San Bao to the West World*)

It is by no means a loss of face to forgive others. And yet it can save much anger about trifles. (*Important Words to Awaken the World*)

One should discipline oneself in the spirit of autumn and live with others in the spirit of spring. (*Dream Shadows*)

From hardship and poverty great virtue is often achieved; out of pride and satisfaction, disastrous failure may be formed. (*Collection of Snow Pine Hall*)

There shouldn't be anybody hating you if you have never done anything shameful all your life. (*Popular Collection of Traditional Chinese Wise Sayings*)

One single slip may cause everlasting sorrow; to go back and correct it, one would have to live a hundred year long. (*Romance of Sui and Tang Dynasties*)

Only the great heroes can show their distinctive character while the genuine celebrated intellectuals always reveal their admirable life–style. (*The Biography of the Heroic Youth*)

Claiming to know the unknown is much stupid; Making trouble out of nothing is extremely unfortunate. (*The Record of the Aphorisms–A Memo Writing*)

Self–renewal consciousness is the mother of progress, while self–deprecation is the source of degradation, so one should keep self–renewal consciousness and keep away from self–imposed humility. (*Self–consciousness and self–deprecation*)

Just like writing an article, behaving oneself in a lifetime contains needs correction and cultivation. (*Non–dream Collection–Black Nightmare*)

Section Two Inspirations and Worldly Philosophy

In the history of Chinese education and culture,"inspirations" and "emotions" are the core concepts handed down from generation to generation. The so–called "inspiration", according to the explanation in *Ci Hai* (a Chinese word dictionary) is "to strive, concentrate on a certain aspect", *The Modern Chinese Dictionary* explains it as "encouraging ambition". The concept of "worldly philosophy" in Chinese culture refers to "ways of the world and people" as well as "the ethos of the time". From the classic sayings of the past dynasties, we can see that the Chinese traditional education on inspiration and the worldly philosophy is not only full of the spirit of the Chinese people's worldly effort, but also implies the great wisdom of treating people and doing things, guided by which countless scholars can study, cultivate one's morality, set up ideals in doing things, adapt to the society, so as to achieve a higher value of life.

I. Around Qin and Han Dynasties

1.1 On Inspiration

Heaven moves constantly, likewise, the gentleman makes untiring efforts to strengthen himself. (*The Book of Changes–Qian*)

The great way sages are pursuing is that the world is for all the people. (*The Book of Rites–Li Yun*)

Pride must be curbed, desires must be restrained, complacency must be guarded against, and pleasures must not be indulged in without restraint. (*The Book of Rites–Qv Li*)

To select one's duty to be kept and performed is wise. Knowing clearly that one faces death and not avoiding it is valor. (*Tso Chuan–the 20th Year of Duke Zhao*)

If I could discover Tao in the morning, let death come to me that very night. (*The Analects of Confucius–Li Ren*)

The commander of the forces of a large state may be carried off, but the will of a common man cannot be taken from him. (*The Analects of Confucius –Zi Han*)

A scholar has to be highly aimed and broad–shouldered for he is burdened with great responsibility and faced with long way ahead. (*The Analects of Confucius–Tabo*r)

When poor, scholars should better their own condition; when advanced to dignity, they should better the condition of the whole empire as well. (*Mencius–Jin Xin*)

He who does not have a strong will can hardly have high intelligence; he who does not keep his promise can hardly act resolutely. (*Mozi –Self–cultivation*)

The great cause for men of virtue is to dedicate themselves for the benefits of the world and to eliminate the harm in the world. That is their mission. (*Mozi • Public Welfare*)

The difficulty of keeping the will lies not in conquerring others, but in conquerring oneself.(*Han Feizi –Yu Lao*)

The way is long, and wrapped in gloom, I will urge on to seek my vanished dream. (*Li Sao*)

A young idler, an old beggar. (*Yuefu–Long Lines of Poems*)

A strong wind came forth, the clouds rose on high. Now that my mighty rules all within the seas, I have returned to my old village. Where will I find brave men, to guard the whole of my land? (*The Gale Song*)

Though death befalls all men alike, it may be weightier than Mount Tai or lighter than a feather. (*A Letter to Ren Shaoqing*)

The bird may not have flown yet, once it does, it will soar to the sky. It may not have cried out yet, but once it does it will startle everyone. (*The Historical Records– Funny Biography*)

Where there is a will, there is a way. (Guangwu Emperor Commending Geng Yan in Linzi)

The old steed though stays in the stable, aspires to race a thousand miles. The hero blessed with senior years never lets droop his lofty ideal. (*Though Turtles Live Long*)

How brave and generous are those heroes. Their only willingness is to overawe the entire world. (*Intone Poem*)

A piece of the finest gold always keeps its purity even though it is melted a hundred times. A hero never loses justice even though subject to peril and hardship. (*Baopuzi –Boyu*)

The headless Xingtian wields its axe and shield, forever full of morale and iron–willed. (*On Reading the Classic Shan Hai Jing*)

1.2 On Worldly Philosophy

The highest good is like that of water. The goodness of water is that it benefits all the creatures; yet itself does not scramble, but is content with the position that others disdain. It is this that makes water so near to the Way. (*Lao Tzu–Chapter Eight*)

It is upon bad fortune that good fortune emerges, upon good fortune that bad fortune rests. (*Lao Tzu–Chapter Fifty–Eight*)

Light assent inspires little trust. And much easiness means many a hard. (*Lao Tzu–Chapter Sixty Three*)

Sincere words are not fine, fine words are not sincere. (*Lao Tzu–Chapter Eighty One*)

The ordinary people will do evil or wicked things when leading an idle life. (*Book of*

Rites–Great Learning)

Just like different faces in the world, people have different minds and thinking. (*Zuo Zhuan–The 31th Year of Xianggong's Reining*)

There is always a teacher in the company of three. I'll find out their merits to learn from and their demerits to avoid from. (*The Analects of Confucius–Shu Er*)

If you want to see what you cannot see, you should watch with care what is neglected by others; if you want to get what is beyond your reach, you must do what others are unwilling to do. (*Lizi–Zhongni*)

The quality of being tough must be kept by the quality of being soft. Sufficient softness helps grow tough. (*Lizi–Huangdi*)

Tides ebb and flow; things help and harm; creatures live and die. (*Han Feizi–Guan Xing*)

Misfortune lies in coveting profits. Harm lies in drawing the mean person near. (*Wei Liaozi–Twelve Tombs*)

The true affection is revealed by life and death ordeal, the real friendship is beyond the gap between the rich and the poor. (*A History of China–Biography of Kidzheng*)

Man scarcely lives more than a hundred years, but tastes a thousand years of cares and fears. (*A lifetime Less Than A Hundred Years*)

It is hard for a man to have four fortunes at the same time: a propitious time, a beautiful scene, a cheerful disposition and an enjoyable experience. (*Poetry Preface to Wei Prince by Ye Zhong*)

If a man attains the Tao (enlightenment and immortality), even his hen and dog become immortal too. (*Biographies of the Deities and Immortals–Liu An*)

II. Around Tang and Song Dynasties

2.1 On Inspirations

A great man would prefer to die in glory rather than live in humiliation. (*Book of the Northern Qi Dynasty–Biography of Yuan Jingan*)

If you want to widen your view beyond for distance, go up one storey higher of stairs. (*Climbing White Stork Tower*)

Old as one is, he gains vigor with age and by no means wavers in his aspiration. Poor as one is, he is all the more determined in adversity and by no means gives up his ambition. (*Preface to Tengwang Pavillion*)

Washed and filtered a thousand times and again, the sand would be flushed off, and the gold remains. (*Lake Waves Washing the Sand*)

Though emerges from the mud, the lotus flower keeps unstained; having purified in the clean water, it doesn't look bewitching. (*Ode to the Lotus Flower*)

It is not people's inability that worth worrying, but one's own laziness that is blushed for. (*Words of Advice to Emperor RenZong*)

Since a long way lies ahead for a gentleman to achieve great success, he must be patient with preparation; since his final aim is grand, he must tolerate trivial insults. (*Comments on Jia Yi*)

To what can the trace of human life be compared? Perhaps to a swan goose's footmarks on snow. (*Nostalgia at MianChi with Zi You*)

Who says that there is no restart of youth period in life? The stream at the temple's foot even flows westward! (*Huan Xisha–At Qingquan Temple*)

The sea's breadth allows the fish to leap; the sky's emptiness lets birds fly. (*On Knowledgeable Comments of Poetry*)

Generals and ministers are not inborn, men of ambition should create out their own career. (*Child Prodigy Poem–Encourage learning*)

Be a man of men while you're alive; Be a soul of souls even if you're dead! (*Wujiang River*)

Without the bone–piercing winter chilliness, where comes the fragrance of the plum blossoms? (*The Story of Pipa*)

To be a success, one must read thousands of books; any moment we have must be used with care. (*The Story of Pipa*)

A gentleman cares about righteousness instead of profit ; and remembers kindness of people without holding grudges. (*Characters and Manners of Gentlemen*)

2.2 On Worldly Philosophy

It is better to walk ten safe steps than to take a risky step. (*The Three Heroes and Five Gallants*)

Don't doubt the one you choose for an important position, and don't rely on any one you don't feel sure of. (*The Book of the Old Tang Dynasty–Biography of Lu Zhi*)

Do not let me hear you talking together about titles and promotions; For a single general's reputation is made of ten thousand corpses. (*On the JiHai Year*)

One is free without official work; One is snug with off spring around.
(*Congratulations to Zi You on His Fourth Grandchild*)

The balcony near a pond enjoys the moonlight first; The flowers and trees facing the sunshine feel spring earlier. (*The Uncompleted Poetry Lines*)

The world unfair, true manhood rare. Dusk melts away in the rain and blooming trees turn bare. (*Chai Tou Feng–the Cold Worldly Affairs*)

A man may have acquaintances all over the world, but very few true friends. (*Vast Record of Varied Matters–Aphorism that Admonish the World*)

Stacks of gold seem to have less real value than a family's carefree joy. (*The Story of Pipa*)

Don't complain that the arguments last all day; For if one turns a deaf ear, the arguments will cease. (*The Story of Pipa*)

A thousand sails pass by the shipwreck, ten thousand saplings shoot up beyond the withered tree. (*A Poem as a First Meeting Gift at a Banquet Table in Yang Zhou*)

No flowing without damming, and no motion without rest. (*The Original Dao*)

Things will develop in the opposite direction when they become extreme, and the luck also changes and increases when it reaches the end. (*On the Foundation of Governing a Country*)

The perfect happiness is so rare—The moon does wax, the moon does wane, just as men meet and say goodbye. (*Shuidiao Ge Tou–The Mid–Autumn Festival of Bing–Chen*)

Man's whispers are heard in heaven as loudly as thunder. Guilty deeds done in the dark can never escape being seen by divine eyes. (*Vast Record of Varied Matters–Aphorism that Admonish the World*)

Causes of goodness will meet with good recompense and evil with evil results; if the effect is not forthcoming, it is because the time has not yet come. (*Debt to the Next Life*)

III. Around Ming and Qing Dynasties

3.1 On Inspirations

He who can not distinguish between gratitude and hatred is not a real hero. He who cannot tell black from white is no genuine stalwart. (*Water Margin*)

We will serve the country with one heart and strive to distinguish ourselves. (*Water Margin*)

Reduce me to dust, to powder, I am fearless. So long as I remain stainless, and pure. (*Ode to Calcareous*)

Only those who take leisurely what the people of the world are busy about can be busy about what the people of the world take leisurely. (*Dream Shadows*)

To start a business is difficult, but to keep it going is no easier mission. (*Popular Collection of Traditional Chinese Wise Sayings*)

Don't boast of being an early starter, for there must be someone who set out earlier than you. (*The Three Heroes and Five Gallants*)

Lend me strength, good wind, to soar up to the azure sky at last. (One should also be good to borrow "external forces" to achieve the career) (*A Dream in Red Mansions*)

Clear from the clear, turbid from turbid. (*The Story of Yi Zhu–The Gift of a Sword*)

To bestow without expecting reward; to be satisfied without greed. (*Ordinary Words to Warn Ordinary People*)

The world produces a limited number of gifted men; it is not good to belittle oneself unreasonably! (*The Travels of Lao Can*)

The fighter for all his blemishes is a fighter, while the most whole and perfect flies are still only flies. (*The Collection of Canopy –Soldiers and Flies*)

When thoughts spread wide to fill the whole of space, amid the silence comes the crash of thunder. (*An Untitled Poetry*)

3.2 On Worldly Philosophy

Endure a moment of anger, lest a hundred days of worry. (*Popular Collection of Traditional Chinese Wise Sayings*)

He who lives near the water knows the disposition of fish, and he who lives near the hill is acquainted with the sound of birds. (*Popular Collection of Traditional Chinese Wise Sayings*)

The empire, long divided, must unite; long united, must divide. (*Romance of the Three Kingdoms*)

It is easy enough to disturb the peace of the world; nothing is harder than preserving it. (*Romance of the Three Kingdoms*)

Mistakes cannot be fully avoided even by a saint, yet it is because of his ability to correct what is wrong that nothing can prevent him from being a great man. (*Improvement and Correction*)

The world is full of heartrending occasions. Parting from dear ones or the beloved dead is the most difficult thing of all. (*The Biography of the Heroic Youth*)

A tree may grow ten thousand feet tall, but its fallen leaves will gather round its roots. (*The Unmasked Officialdom*)

True friendship is like delicious food in a famine year and warm clothes in a freezing winter. (*Theory of the Present Life*)

If all men were disinterested, the Empire would keep peace. If all men schemed for private advantage, then the Empire would be in chaos. (*The Travels of Lao Can*)

When fallacy is taken for truth, truth is fallacy, if non–being turns into being, being becomes non–being. (*A Dream in Red Mansions*)

Old age should be free from want. (*A Dream in Red Mansions*)

The fragrance of flowers comes not from of its quantity, an elegant room doesn't need to be large. (*Zheng Banqiao Couplet*)

Chapter Seven The Essentials of Famous Family Instructions

In the traditional Chinese education concepts, because "every man has his home, and every family has its instruction", the tradition of Chinese family instructions has a long history since ancient times. It is also because of the cultural atmosphere of respecting elders and ancestors that China has always attached importance to family education. Many ancient sages have condensed their wisdom in lifetime into family traditions for their children and grandchildren, and unreservedly taught their children and grandchildren the essence of the thoughts as well as the understanding of the world that they have experienced in their lives. With the development of the society, the educational content contained in Chinese family instruction classics is gradually enriched, including all aspects of family life and life wisdom. It can be seen that the family traditions and instructions of the past dynasties are like the bright light lit by the ancestors for their descendants, and also a mirror reflecting the mainstream of social education in different historical periods in the mode of "the family and the world", which not only carries profound educational concepts, but also carries the unique wisdom and life proverbs of the Chinese civilization. Today, as the descendants of the Chinese nation, full of piety, through the study and inheritance of the classic family constructions, more people can get the teachings of the sages, so as to bath in the light of the sages and help open wisdom, improve education, create a happy life, thus make the learning a beneficial action and great merit. This chapter will show the Chinese ideal family traditions and spiritual wealth condensed with the warm feelings and wisdom of time from two aspects of education, namely: self–cultivation and social living; family management and career achievement.

Section One Self–cultivation and Social Living

Almost without exception, the traditional Chinese family letters and family instructions are all based on teaching self–cultivation. Its most important content is to conduct self–cultivation education to children, educate children to shape the perfect personality of both character and learning, and help them to be a good person with both virtue and ability. The content of self–cultivation includes many aspects, such as being prudent and self–disciplined, faithful and benevolent, virtuous and honest, modest and prudent, upholding the purity and respecting justice, mental cultivation and keeping temperance, prolonging life and so on. In daily life, how to treat people and deal with complex social relationships is also an important content reflected in traditional Chinese family education through family letters and instructions. In general, Chinese family teachings of all dynasties emphasize the basic principles of being cautious in words and deeds, being honest and trustworthy, tolerant and kind to others.

I. Famous Names and Instructions about Self-cultivation

In the family teachings of the past dynasties, teaching the descendants how to cultivate themselves is often placed in the first place of family education. From the Instructions of Qian, Kong, Wang family and *An De Elder Words*, we can all read the importance of self-cultivation in family education.

1.1 Qian Liu *Qian's Family Instructions*

Qian Liu, styled name Ju Mei, from Lin'an in Hangzhou, was the founding ruler of Wuyue. Qian Liu was the garrison commander of local vassal army at the end of the Tang Dynasty and was then crowned King of Wuyue by the Central Plains Dynasty. During the reign of Qian Liu, the state adopted a policy of safeguarding the state and ensuring the security of the people, as a result, the economy was prosperous, the literature and art were well known. In the thirteenth year of the Republic of China (1924), Qian Wenxuan, the 32nd grandson of the King of Wu, summed up the *Qian's Family Instructions* based on the *Eight Precepts* and the *Last Precepts* of his ancestors.

- Be careful and strict with thyself, be incorruptible with prudence in the face of material wealth.
- Only struggle forward the situation will be increasingly narrow, looking back the perspective will be more and more wide.
- Being reformed and the God is no longer angry, keeping one's duty and the ghost has no excuse to hurt.
- By reading classics you can have a deep foundation of knowledge, and by studying history you can talk with extraordinary insight.

1.2 Kong Shangxian *Ancestral Instructions and Counsels of Kong's Family*

Kong Shangxian, styled Xiangzhi and pseudonym Xi'an, was the 63rd grandson of Confucius. He was determined to "live up to the ancestral instruction, to the grace of the country, and to the knowledge of learning". In the eleventh year of Wanli (1583), in order to regulate the words and behaviors of the clansmen, Kong Shangxian promulgated the *Ancestral Instructions and Counsels of Kong's Family* on the basis of his ancestors' teachings and self-reflection, which played a guiding role and became the family rules and disciplines passed down from generation to generation by Kong's family. Kong Shangxian pointed out clearly in *Ancestral Instructions and Counsels of Kong's Family* from the very beginning that:"my ancestral Xuansheng, eternal teacher, with virtue of heaven and earth, ways for ancient and modern, many descendants difficult to count. Some of them taught and studied oversees, some received official degrees and became officials, they have lived and scattered in different directions and guided by the instructions. We now make public to the world and the clansmen the Ancestral Instructions...". This *Ancestral Instructions and Counsels of Kong's Family* includes ten pieces, among which there is a code of conduct for self-cultivation, the Confucian tradition of "respecting Confucianism and respecting Taoism, advocating propriety and upholding morality" is taken as an important part of the family rules. Besides, no matter where descendants of Kong family are or what kind of occupation they are engaged in, they are required to follow such family disciplines as "self-abnegation and impartiality" and "being educated and reasonable". In the long history, Confucius' Eight virtues' and Kong Shangxian's '*Ancestral Instructions and Counsels of Kong's Family*' have cultivated the gentle, upright and selfless character of the Kong family, It also shaped their characters of worshiping virtue and kindness, honesty and comity. The essential contents of it include:

• Teach and discipline children day and night according to the instructions handed down from our ancestors, make sure they are educated and reasonable, gain the fine reputation and honor the ancestors without poor taste and mediocre quality.

• No official in office can act arbitrarily. In case of great events, they should be declared to the court, the small cases still should be managed with the help of the family chief.

• Advocating virtue and kindness, honesty and etiquette, as a descendant of the Kong family, one should not be addicted to profit and forget righteousness, and should not do anything harmful to the virtues of our ancestors.

• If there are officials among the descendants of Kong Family, when they encounter civil litigation, they must make a rational judgment for the case has its turns and twists, with a heart of pity, do not be complacent, and one should be worthy of being a competent official.

1.3 Wang Yangming *Family Letter of Wang Yangming*

Wang Yangming, first name Shouren, styled Bo'an, was a famous thinker, educator and strategist in Ming Dynasty. He was an Official to the Nanjing Department of military Shang Shu, although with a lifetime of ups and downs, he advocated virtue and justice, with great military talents and outstanding achievements. In Wang Yangming's opinion, self-cultivation is integrated with family management, governing the country and making a peaceful world. Such aspects are of the equal importance, ignoring any part and one can not reach the ultimate goodness. If Confucianism neglects governing the world and only values self-cultivation, it will become like the Daoism, which values to be hidden from the world, detached and isolated. If Confucianism ignores self-cultivation and only emphasizes the governance of others, it will become like legalists and political strategists, only emphasizing utility and power. The former, though innocent, is easy to ignore reality; The latter, though realistic, lacks innocence. The letters left by Wang Yangming integrate the little bits and pieces of the righteous education he received since childhood, and also convey his cordial teachings to future generations. The essentials include:

• My children, you should listen to the teachings: study hard, be filial to your parents, love your brothers, learn to be humble and behave with etiquette; keep abstemious diet, idle less, abstain from lying. don't be greedy and capricious, no fighting with others; no blaming on others, learn to control yourself. To be humble to people is real ambitious, to accommodate others is broad–minded; a person is determined by his moral nature, a kind man has a benevolent mind, a vicious man has a malicious heart. Just like the fruit of a tree, it has a seed in its heart. If the seed is corrupted, the fruit will surely fall. This is all that I can teach you now. You should listen well and don't give up easily.

• On learning, nothing is more important than setting ambitious goal. Without ambition is like planting a tree without planting its roots and cultivating the soil and water the tree in vain, and the hard work that leads to nowhere. Ambition, is like the commander of the spirit, life of a man, the root of the tree, and the source of water. If water is not dredged, it will stop flowing, trees will wither without roots, if life does not continue, people will die, without aspirations people will be muddleheaded. Therefore, in learning, a gentleman always takes a lofty goal as a priority.

• At home, you should always follow the instruction. Keep reading and adhere to the family rules and make progress day by day, this is what I expect of you to do. All my life, I have been teaching the principle of "conscience". Benevolence refers to the human heart; Conscience is integrated with sincerity, true love, grief, and sadness is benevolence, without sincere love and compassion, one cannot reach conscience. You should take a deep introspection on this.

• The ancients said:"To stay away from those vulgar people, one should make friends with those wise people." This saying is good enough to serve as a warning, my child you must understand this truth.

1.4 Chen Ji–ru *The Adages from the Elders*

Chen Jiru, style name Zhong chun, pseudonym Mei Gong, was a famous writer and painter in Ming Dynasty. At the age of 29, he abandoned his reputation as a scholar and lived in seclusion with his family in Xiaokunshan, Songjiang. Later, he moved into Dongyu Mountain and devoted himself to literature, painting and calligraphy. Together with Shen Zhou, Wen Zhengming and Dong Qichang, he was called one of The "Four Masters". Chen Jiru, who attached great importance to the family discipline and tradition, wrote family instruction *The Adages from the Elders*, which passed on his perception on surviving and living from his long experience to future generations. The full text appears in the form of aphorisms, with a total of 122 recorded adages, it mainly includes the following contents: practicing good deeds to accumulate good fortune, being cautious of oneself, decreasing one's desires, practicing virtues, forgiving others and so on. This kind of family instruction of concise language style is rare, which can be described as with fresh style and meaningful philosophy, and has had an important influence on time and later generations.

• I don't know what benevolence is, only know what warms people's heart is good; I don't know what evil is, except that what is hateful is evil.

• Only after sitting in meditation did I realize that I was restless in my daily life, only after holding my tongue did I know that I spoke too much, only after inspecting the vulgar issues did I know my time wasted, only after closing the door, did I know that I made too many friends randomly, only after removing worries and desires did I know they hurt the body, only after understanding the human nature did I know I used to be stubborn. Preserving one's integrity and cultivating the moral character is a virtue,

• It is a good character for scholar–officials not to be greedy for official and money, but if one doesn't help others at all, it's not what the sage wants. Helping others and benefiting the society is contribution. Is it enough to accumulate virtues without contributions?

• Reading can not only change people's temperament, but also can refresh people's minds, probably because the moral truth can elevate people's spirit.

• Closing the doors is like being secluded in the mountains, concentrating on reading makes everywhere pure land.

• Only talking about different schools without paying attention to knowledge, only emphasizing face keeping without communicating ideas, these are the superficial forms without substance.

II. Famous Names and Instructions about Social Living

Chinese culture attaches great importance to the relationship between people and society. In the world of life, knowing how to behave in society is not only an important content of Chinese education culture, but also the core goal of family education. Most of the classics of Chinese family education focus on this eternal theme.

2.1 Yuan Huang *The Four Teachings of Liao Fan*

Yuan Huang, styled Qingyuan, later changed to Liao Fan, was born in Jiashan County, Jiaxing Prefecture, Zhejiang Province, and was a thinker in Ming Dynasty. He is very talented, and studied astronomy, mathematics, water conservancy, military politics, medicine and other research fields. His *Four Teachings of Liao Fan* is a combination of his personal experience and lifelong knowledge and accomplishment, in order to educate his children and grandchildren for the family. This book persuades people to accumulate good deeds and reform themselves, emphasizes self–cultivation starting from the treatment of the heart, and clarifies the thought of "establishing one's own destiny and seeking one's own happiness". It makes statements with real examples and while combining Confucianism, Buddhism and Taoism thoughts with his own experience, it clarifies the gist, encourages the self cultivation, cautious and independent personality, and self–seeking for more blessings to keep away from disasters. The book has been popular and influential since the late Ming Dynasty.

• *The Book of Changes* provides advice on how to move towards auspiciousness and avoid danger for virtuous people. If the fate of heaven is fixed, how can we seek good and avoid bad? *The Book of Changes–Kun Gua* says: 'A family that does good deeds will surely have excess blessings to pass on to its children. Can you believe this?

• If individuals can treat people and do things with even sincerity, then it is consistent with the way of heaven. When good blessings are to come, they can be foretold by one's good deeds; And when disaster comes, it can also be predicted by his wickedness. Now if you want to get a good reward and avoid evil, before we talk about good reward, we must start from correcting ourselves.

• In this world, everything is earthly impermanence; the body is vulnerable, as soon as one passes away, there was no way to correct and reform ourselves. Then in the living world one will have to bear a bad reputation for thousands of years and be reviled by others. Although there are filial sons, kindhearted grandchildren, they can not wash away the bad name. As for those in the underworld, they will be tormented in hell for countless years, which even sages, Buddhas and Bodhisattvas cannot help or guide. How can we not be afraid of such kind of evil?

• What does it mean to persuade people to be kind? Who, as a human being, has no conscience? However, in this vast world on the road, people are obsessed in pursuing fame and wealth and this is the most easy way to fall and lost. Therefore, everyone who gets along with the public, whenever the discovery of this phenomenon, we must subtly remind them, and try to help them out of confusion. It's like waking one up in the middle of a long night of dreaming. Or as if to relieve people of their troubles and make them sober and relaxed. Such blessing is the most universal one. Han Yu of the Tang Dynasty once said,"To persuade people with reason can only benefit a few people for a short time. To persuade people permanently and universally, books must be written to spread the ideas.

2.2 Zhang Ying *Words in Cong Xun Bookroom*

Zhang Ying, styled Dunfu, pseudonym Lepu, born in Tongcheng, Anhui Province, was a famous minister in the Qing Dynasty. He served as a chancellor of Hanlin (imperial) Academy, a master of Wenhua Hall and a director of the Board of Rites. He successively served as a compiler of many books, lived a decent life as an official with humble comity,"a lifetime of humility without loss of sense of propriety" is the comment for him as a model of moral conduct. *Words in Cong Xun Bookroom* mainly tells about family management, reading, moral cultivation, choosing of friends, keeping healthy and enjoying life. It is a family tradition handed down from generation to generation with simple sentences and profound thoughts.

• Those who study diligently will be respected by others, those who keep their property will not be threatened by hunger, those who accumulate good deeds will not corrupt, and those who choose their friends carefully will not fail.

• Reading can develop an objective perspective, it is the first thing to nurture the mind and heart.

• When reading one needs to have an environment with bright windows and a clean desk, there is no need of too many books. While reading and writing articles one should be concentrated and peaceful minded, with bright eyes. With notes clearly marked on pages, one will not get lost in bewilderment. Reading a lot of articles without understanding the meaning is just like a general who doesn't drill soldiers, who can not act in battle, and who wastes his energy like a man fighting with air.

- The ancients said: modest people have nothing to lose. Lao Tzu regards tolerance as a treasure, Zuo Qiuming also said:"modesty is the root of morality."
- Be worthy of praise in what you say, worthy of emulation in what you do, neither be conceited, deceitful and false, nor critical and heartless, and keep prudent in your manner.

2.3 Zhang Tingyu *Words in Chenghuai Garden*

Zhang Tingyu, styled Hengchen, pseudonym Yanzhai, was born in Anhui Tongcheng, the second son of Zhang Ying. He successively served as the official of the Ministry of Rites, the Official of the Ministry of Household Affairs, the Official of the Ministry of Civil Affairs, the grand secretary of the Royal Hall of Preserving Harmony and the Chief Military Minister. Zhang Tingyu was educated by his father, Zhang Ying, and benefited a lot from his instructions and manners. He was gentle, elegant, and learned, very cautious in personal relationship and political management, fair and generous in legal judgement , praised widely by the people, later he became the only Han minister in the Qing Dynasty to enjoy the imperial temple. His book *Words in Chenghuai Garden* is a summary of Zhang Tingyu's experience of self–cultivation and family management and governance.

- Those who see everything too simple are too shallow in experience. People who like to blame others, are not in the situation. The word "forgiveness" is the natural expression of virtuous people. Only those with above average qualifications can realize it after they have experienced it.
- One should consider every word, every thing to be beneficial to people, and should be afraid of damaging the interests of others.
- It is better to seek happiness in prudence than in speech.
- It is necessary to be honest and upright. The first and foremost condition of being an official is keeping honest with clean hands . To keep a clean conduct, the most important thing is to endure. If a man can refrain from accepting unappropriated property, then he has already understood most of the way in being an official.
- In the world, a generous person can tolerate many things, and tolerance itself is easy to make people safe and sound, in return they are easy to adapt to the world comfortably.

2.4 Yan Zhitui *The Family Instructions of Yan Clan*

Yan Zhitui, who was born in Jiangling, was a writer and educator in the Southern and Northern Dynasties. Academically, Yan Zhitui was learned and knowledgeable, and he wrote a lot of books in his lifetime, including *The Family Instructions of Yan Clan and the Return of Grievances*. The book The *Family Instructions of Yan Clan* was written after Sui Emperor

Wen destroyed Chen and before Sui Emperor Yang ascended the throne (about the end of the 6th century AD). Yan Zhitui describes his personal experiences, thoughts, and knowledge in this book to warn his descendants, comprising seven volumes and twenty chapters.

- For a man living in the world, it is important to be able to do some beneficial work, it is far from enough just to pay attention to lofty talk, elegant music and books, and waste the salary and position given by the monarch.
- The most honest words, are not easily believed by others; The most noble behavior is often suspected by people, because the reputation of such words and actions is too good for people to believe.
- *The Book of Rites* says:"desire can not be indulged, ambition can not be satisfied. The grant universe is possible to reach its limit, but human nature does not know the end of its desire, only when we are content with little desire can we help ourselves set a limit.
- There is a tendency in the world to value what we hear and not what we see, to value what is far away rather than what is near; to deal with the people around, even if they are wise people, we always tend to give affection or insult, but not respect, but for people and news in other places, a little smell of the wind, we may be yearning with elongation necks and stand on our tiptoes with interests.
- In preventing the quarrels of the laity, the teachings of the sages of Yao and Shun were less useful than the advice of the wife in the family.
- Better being clumsy and honest than being cunning and hypocritical.

Section Two Family Management and Career Achievement

The Chinese nation attaches great importance to family education and the inheritance of family traditions. The formation of family tradition is often reflected in the lifelong education of a family's idea of establishing a family and a career. After generations of the family's descendants abiding by the ancestral mottoes, the prevailing style of the family has formed a distinct moral and aesthetic style in the establishment of a family's culture. The family instruction for the family management and the career achievement is often condensed into a rich life experience as an outstanding representative of the wise elders of a family, and also is condensed into a family style handed down from generation to generation, it is full of profound affection and expectation for children and family, and has extensive and far–reaching educational significance.

I. Famous Names and Instructions about Family Management

In the Chinese educational thinking from "mind correcting and self–cultivation" to "family management and governing the country","harmonious family" is an important premise and guarantee to great ambition of benefiting the world. An adage "Harmonious family is the precondition of all prosperity" highlights the central role of family management in China's educational and cultural life.

1.1 Wang Xizhi *Jin Court Wang Clan Pedigree–Old Preface*

Wang Xizhi, styled Yishao, is a famous calligrapher in the Eastern Jin Dynasty, known as The "holy master of calligraphy". He successively served as a court secretary, General Ningyuan, Governor of Jiangzhou, and later as the internal minister of Kuaiji, served as the right general, known as "Right General Wang". During the reign of Emperor Qianlong in Qing Dynasty, Zhou Zixun, an military instructor of Shengxian County, wrote the family mottoes of Wang's family into the preface of *Wang Clan Pedigree*; in addition, one section of the cases in *Jin Court Wang Clan Pedigree* also contains 26 clan rules; starting from the country running, the relationship between the country and the home , and finally the implementation of how to be a man. The descendants of the Wang family believe that the ancestral family rules and instructions are also a kind of spiritual treasure. As the descendants, while carrying forward the art of writing, they should continue to improve the family rules and use the spiritual connotation of the family rules and instructions to educate and inspire the future generations.

• The country and the family are governed by the same way; filial piety and family harmony are of significance.

• Manage by the law; be discreet and dutiful; keep meritorious duty and make more efforts.

• Sincere concessions for the manner of a gentleman, more good deeds for the benefit of descendants.

• Our family has always been known for its kindness and good manners, if any unworthy descendant commits transgressions, corrupts ethics and morals, humiliates the clan customs, the patriarch should gather the clan and imposes heavy punishment on him in the ancestral hall. If he doesn't repent, the patriarch should work with his neighbors to escort him to the government, he should be given a new treatment according to the law, and he should be expunged from the genealogy and never be allowed to enter the family clan again.

1.2 Sima Guang *The Collected Works of Wen Guowen Zheng Sima Guang*

Sima Guang, styled Junshi, pseudonym Qiansou, was born in Xia County, Shaanxi Province, he was a statesman and historian of literature in the Northern Song Dynasty. As a royal minister he served four emperors and was respected by people, among abundant works in his life, he paid much attention to family education. He believed that "before governing the country, one must first manage the family well". He stressed family education to a political height that affected the country and society. His book *Family Disciplines of Wen Gong* comprehensively and systematically elaborated the methods of family management, the way of self–cultivation and the principles of human behavior, forming an independent and complete theoretical system of family education, which can be regarded as a model in the history of Chinese family instruction and has influenced and educated countless generations.

• *TuanCi* teaches us:"There should be dignified parents in family, the father and mother. The father should be like a father, the son should be like a son, the elder brother should be like a brother, the younger brother should be like a younger brother, the husband should be like a husband, the wife should be like a wife, so the family order is right. The world will be stable if the family has the right morals."

• *The Great Learning* teaches us:"In ancient times, those who wanted to develop great moral character had to govern their own countries well; if one wants to run the country well, he must run his family well. If one wants to manage his family well, he must cultivate his own character. From the emperor to the ordinary people, it is essential to improve their self–cultivation. Ignoring the essential part is like putting the cart before the horse, running the country well will be impossible!" This is the gist of strategy, this is the highest wisdom. If you want to manage your country well, you must first manage your own family. That is to say, it is impossible to govern your country if you cannot manage your family well.

• The necessities of life that people rely on to survive are indispensable, but don't be too greedy, too much will become a burden. If future generations are really capable, how can they not even obtain coarse grain and cloth by themselves, and freeze and starve to death on the roadside? What is the use of a house full of gold if the descendants are incompetent? Therefore, I think it is very foolish for parents to hoard too much property and leave it to their children.

• I am only following my nature by dressing against the cold and eating to fill my stomach, not by deliberately wearing dirty and shabby clothes to show that I am different. Many people are proud of extravagance and waste, but in my heart, frugality and simplicity are virtues.

• Did the ancients care nothing about the poverty of their children? Some people say: Why don't they leave a lot of properties to their descendants? Ancient sages knew how to bequeath to their posterity noble virtues and strict rules of propriety; sages bequeathing to their posterity incorruptible qualities and simple styles of life.

1.3 The Su Family *The Annals and Collections of the Su Clan*

The Su family are the famous family in Sichuan in the southwest of Chengdu Plain during the Northern Song Dynasty. There have been three famous writers who are known as The "Three Su". The father and sons have been highly accomplished in literature, and influenced by good family education, they were all aboveboard, honest and upright, concerned about the fate of the country, sympathetic to the suffering of the people. The family tradition of Su clan is sincere and magnanimous. Su Xun, Su Shi, Su Zhe all left a large number of words and poems about family management.

• If there are young orphans, the adults in the family should take care of them. If there are poor and homeless people, the wealthy members of the family should adopt them. Anyone who does not do so is to be condemned by the whole clan.

• Serve parents with utmost filial piety, treat brothers with mutual care, get along with friends with honesty and trust. Be strict with yourself and magnanimous with others.

• I would not take even a dime if it is not what I should have.

• One should always be eager to learn the way of sages with this inkstone; use it to pursue progress, one should always be alert; when it is used to write fiscal rules, it should always be done in the interest of the public. Use it to write prison articles, one should often think of giving prisoners more opportunities to repent.

1.4 Yang Shen *The Genealogy of the Young Clan*

Yang Shen, styled with Xiu, pseudonym Sheng 'an, was born in Xindu, Sichuan, and his ancestral home was Luling. He was a well–known litterateur in Ming Dynasty, and the first on the list of Three Talents. All his life, he was an honest and upright official. Yang Shen was diligent and studious all his life. He read widely and wrote many books, all of which had a high academic level. The Yang Shen family, with the long history of honesty and decency, still keeps many family disciplines and instructions handed down from generation to generation. For example, in the *The Genealogy of the Young Clan*, apart from the deeds of Yang's ancestors who became officials, Yang's family rules and instructions are also recorded. Under the influence of good family tradition, Yang´s family has cultivated a large number of talented people.

• Future generations should maintain the family and with diligence, they should advocate frugality, live within one's means, only by following the instructions can they inherit the family property.

• The etiquette of family management lies in good relations between people;The propriety of family management lies in attaching importance to education.

• Thatched house is my dwelling, there is no need for the luxuriant. No matter how magnificent the room it won't last forever. Sheltering me from wind and rain is enough. Simple food can satisfy hunger, don't think about eating delicious food. Exquisite and exotic food is rare. Luck of me to have simple food available, no longer want goose paws and pig feet, away from starving is enough.

• My wife does not have to be too beautiful. I just hope she is gentle, kind, modest and thrifty, and filial to her parents and elders. My kids don't have to be too smart, and sometimes being too smart and tough isn't always a good thing. I just hope he can find his own way to make a living, with filial piety is enough.

• In the face of profitable things, I dare not compete with others; in the face of upholding justice, I dare not hide behind others.

1.5 Zhu Bailu *Family Instructions of Master Zhu*

Zhu Bailu, styled Zhiyi, self pseudonym Bailu, was born in Kunshan County, Jiangsu Province in the late Ming and early Qing Dynasties. He was a famous neo–Confucianist and educator. Zhu Bailu devoted himself to study since childhood. He was once admitted as a scholar and later lived in the countryside to teach students. He also devoted himself to neo–

Confucianism, advocating knowledge and practice, and gained a great reputation at that time. *Family Instructions of Master Zhu* also known as the *Family Management Maxim*, is an enlightenment textbook based on family morality. It clarifies the way of self–cultivation and family running splendidly, and is a classic work in family education. Many of the contents inherit the excellent characteristics of traditional Chinese culture, such as simple living, righteous parenting, diligent and thrifty household, neighborliness, etc. It has been revered by scholars in the past and still boasts practical significance today.

• As a parent, the most valuable character, is the benevolent affections; As a child, the most valuable character is filial piety; As an older sibling, the most valuable character is fraternal love; As a younger sibling, the most valuable character is respectful love; As a husband, the most valuable character, is a harmonious attitude; As a wife, the most valuable character, is a gentle temperament.

• When you see old people, respect them. When you see young children, love them.

• Never do evil things though they may be insignificant, never given up good deeds though they may be minor matters.

• When dealing with public affairs, one should not interfere with private enmity. When dealing with family affairs, do not be affected by selfishness.

• You can't fail to read the classics of the ancient sages, you can't fail to understand etiquette and moral rules. You must not fail to educate your children, you must not fail to care for your servants. We must respect the traditional culture, and the literate people, we must also help those who are in trouble.

II. Famous Names and Instructions about Career Achievement

In the long history of China, there is no shortage of outstanding people and inspirational thoughts who take making career achievements as their ideal. This kind of educational concept full of devotion and strength can be found in the family teachings of well–known historical and cultural figures, and some of them have become popular famous sayings.

2.1 Fan Zhongyan *The Words of Commandments*

Fan Zhongyan, styled Xiwen, was born in Bin Zhou, he later moved to Wu County in Suzhou. He was a well–known statesman and litterateur in the Northern Song Dynasty. Fan Zhongyan made achievements in both local governance and border protection, and his literary achievements were outstanding. His spiritual idea of "Be concerned about the affairs of state before others, and enjoy comfort after others", and his moral integrity had a profound influence on later generations. Fan Zhongyan was rigorous in family management. He specially wrote the *Words of Commandments* to teach his descendants and taught his people to cultivate their moral integrity and actively do good deeds. Later, he left to the world the *Anthology of Fan Wenzheng Gong*.

• Read more useful books to cultivate the virtuous mind and righteous behavior , in order to establish a good character. We should pay attention to the noble ethics instead of casually discuss the rights and wrongs of others, a temporary popularity could lead to more trouble and regret in the future.

• To read more books of sages, respect teachers the same way as respecting parents.

• Propriety first, no arrogance, keep modest and good relations with neighbors. Respect the old and love the young, pity the orphan, help the poor.

• Be modest and respectful, honest and self–disciplined, and guard against arrogance and impetuosity. Don't throw away the paper that has been written, and be grateful for the grain that has raised us.

• Be concerned about the affairs of state before others, and enjoy comfort after others.

• Do not say that the kindness and diligence of the official can not be measured by years, just see the mountain of herbs growing with new seedlings has become a lush land.

2.2 Gu Yanwu *Daily Notes* *The Collection of Mr. Tinglin*

Gu Yanwu, styled Zhongqing, was born in Kunshan, Jiangsu Province. Scholars respected him as Mr. Tinglin because of the Tinglin Lake near his former residence. Gu Yanwu was an outstanding thinker, historian and phonologist at the end of the Ming Dynasty and the beginning of Qing Dynasty. Together with Huang Zongxi and Wang Fuzhi, he was called one of "three great scholars". Although Gu Yanwu led a wandering life and was gloried in honest poverty, he was erudite and rigorous in his academic studies. The thought of setting up a career and the patriotism of bearing in mind the world that he left for later generations deeply influenced the scholars of later generations.

• We should first have the ambition to serve the society and the people, so as to have the mood to study the sages and talk about the past and present.

• Every common man has an unshirkable duty to protect his country.

• Today, it is our duty to save the people from suffering and create a peaceful foundation for generations to come.

• He who does concern greatly about the people of the world can be called a Confucian scholar. Only such sages can revitalize traditional culture from decadence.

• Do not curry favour with the rich and powerful, do not set foot on the road of greed.

• Although my knowledge is limited, I have no attempt to ingratiate others .

• Conscientious articles should not disappear from the world, because they explain the truth, describe political affairs, understand the sufferings of the people, and praise the good deeds of others. Articles like this are good for the world and the future, each one is beneficial to the world. As for those full of strangeness, of valour, of rebellion, of ghosts, of nonsense, of plagiarizing, of flattery, such articles do harm to both the writers and others, and every one of them does harm to others.

2.3 The Emperor of KangXi *The Mottoes of the Court*

Aisin Gioro Hyun Ye, the emperor of Qing Dynasty, was the second emperor after

Beijing was established as the capital of Qing Dynasty. Xuanye ascended the throne at the age of eight, reigned for 61 years, and made many achievements. *The Mottoes of the Court* was created by Yin Zhen, in emperor Yongzheng's eighth year, who repeated his father's admonitions to the princes in daily life. It consisted of 246 items, including self–cultivation, governance, establishment of a career, ways of treating others and trivial matters in daily life. Emperor Kangxi cherished the world and the family career very much, and longed to pass it on to generations to come. He was confident that the wisdom and experience in his life would be beneficial to his children and descendants, which made *Mottoes of the Court* concrete, vivid and real.

• When nothing happens, be as cautious as when something is happening, then nothing will happen. When something is wrong, be as calm as when nothing is wrong. The ancients said:"The more careful and cautious, the more bold and courageous one will be." Things should be dealt with in such a state of mind.

• I never look down upon anyone and call them ignorant people. Everyone has his or her own wisdom. I often say to my ministers, if you know anything, you can tell me. As long as it is reasonable, I will accept it.

• Whatever happens, no matter it is big or small, we must be very cautious, carefully observe and study, so that there will be few hidden troubles. Therefore, Confucius said,"To those who do not first ask, 'what shall we do' or 'how to do' , shall I finally say to them, 'what shall we do about this matter?" These are indeed wise words!

• Both *The Great learning* and *The Doctrine of the Mean* take conscientiousness as an important doctrine, which is the first key of becoming a sage. Later, people often say,"Don't be careless in a dark room." There are two aspects of being careful. One is when we are alone, and the other is in the hidden places of our hearts. Both are occasions that only we and no one else can see.

• There are only limited truths and principles recorded in classical books, but issues in the world are varied and endless. Therefore, those who study with books tend to be inflexible, while those who experience a lot of things tend to be tactful . These two kinds of people are both single–faceted. In my opinion, when reading, we must experience a lot of world affairs, and when dealing with practical work, we should study that issue repeatedly according to the book knowledge. Only in this way can we avoid the disadvantages of both of the above.

2.4 Zheng Banqiao *Family Letters of Zheng Banqiao*

Zheng Banqiao, styled Kerou, pseudonym Mr. Banqiao, was born in Xinghua, Jiangsu Province. He was a famous literati painter. He served as governor of Fan County and Tan County. For his official clean and honesty, diligence and his loving for the people, he accomplished quite a lot of achievements. After his resignation, he lived in Yangzhou, selling paintings for a living, and became one of The "eight eccentrics in Yangzhou". As a classic work of "Family Management" culture in ancient China, *Family Letters of Zheng Banqiao* contains rich humanistic thoughts of loving all beings and being moderate and generous, it has been passed down from generation to generation and has been widely praised. In the Qing Dynasty, someone evaluated the letters as " colorful with human emotion, and full of Taoism wisdom", the language is true and heartfelt , vivid like leaping on the paper.

• When a person studies, he does not know whether he will be successful in the future, however, even if one cannot achieve great success in the future, one cannot afford to give up learning. Once you make up your mind, even if you don't pass the imperial examination, you can still gain knowledge. This is a good deal to gain.

• Shen Jinsi was once asked, what is the best way to change the fate of poverty? Shen replied,"Study." This person thought that Shen Lang was pedantic and inappropriate, in fact, Shen was not. Rather than running errands for getting official positions and, wasting time to delay the study, and lose character for nothing, it is better to travel in the history of the book, though ask for nothing, the benefits are present. Learning from Shen's wisdom and you will prosper, otherwise take the fate of poverty. The key is whether a person has the vision and determination to persevere.

• If I have not been admitted as a scholar so far, where can I go to complain? How dare you be arrogant in front of your friends just because you are an official. We need to be kind to our family members, to be on good terms with them, to care about old friends, that's it.

• Isn't a rich family that makes people stupid, and poor family environment is enough to set up aspirations and determination to cultivate wisdom?

2.5 Zeng Guofan *The Family Letters of Zeng Guofan*

Zeng Guofan, styled Bohan and pseudonym Disheng, was a statesman and litterateur in the late Qing Dynasty and a leader of the armed Hunan Army of Han landlords. He promoted the westernization movement and introduced western military and technology, and was known as one of the well–known officials of the late Qing Dynasty. *Family Letters of Zeng Guofan* is a collection of Zeng Guofan's letters, written in the mid–19th century of the Qing Dynasty. It records Zeng Guofan's 30 years of academy and military career, with nearly 1,500 letters. The contents involved are extremely extensive, which is a vivid reflection of Zeng Guofan's main activities and his way of governing the state, family and studies. The writing style of *Family Letters of Zeng Guofan* is calm and fluent, the form is free, the wording is smooth, and the true wisdom and persuasive words are accumulated from ordinary life, which is full of inspiring power.

• For us, there are only two things we can rely on: virtue and cultivation. Advancing virtue is the traditional benevolence, righteousness and filial piety, and the second is poetry and writing. These two things are up to ourselves, no pain and no gain. Improving your virtue today is like accumulating a litre of grain; an effort of study every day is like earning a penny. The family prospers when there is progress in morality and career. As for fame and wealth, it is determined by God, and not controlled by subjective wills.

• If people can set up lofty aspirations, they can be like the sage and hero to accomplish achievements, why rely on the power of others? Confucius said, as long as one is willing to practice benevolence, benevolence can be achieved. As long as I want to become a saint like Confucius and Mencius, then I study day and night tirelessly, who can stop me? But if you have no ambition, even if day and night you live together with many saints, you are all irrelevant, they have no influence on you.

• If you are diligent and inquisitive, why worry about not making great progress every day?

• In the lifetime, one should only live on in accordance with The "self reform and becoming better" , that is to carry forward the right path and constantly correct the mistakes; for a family, it should rely on"cultivating virtues and studying hard" For these principles, If you can achieve a portion, there is a portion of good fortune, if you lack a portion, there is a portion of disaster.

• On all official business, one should think thoughtfully and see far. From ancient times to today, fame and high position is a difficult place to be.

• Without reason and complain about the world, the heaven will not agree. People will not be convinced if they are blamed without reason; The law of heaven–human induction should be followed and obeyed.

• Generals should have four talents, one is to know people well and to discover able people for suitable posts. Second, he is good at inferring the situation of the enemy. The third is the courage and sense on the battlefield. Fourth, the capacity of managing things in order in camps.

• I silently observe the officials, the people, and the governors, and generals of the provinces. There seems to be no sign of stability in the world. I can only use diligence to achieve loyalty, love the subjects to repay parents. Because of my ordinary talent and knowledge, it is difficult for me to make achievements. I can only abide by diligence and hard working all day to alleviate my worries.

• Reading is based on lectures, poetry is based on tones, serving elders is based on pleasant mood, health is based on peace of mind; career is based on careful words, family life is based on early rising, being an official is based on not being corrupt, marching is based on not disturbing the people.

• Among all emperors and generals from ancient times, everyone has prospered from self–reliance. Even sages have their own way of self–improvement, so they can be independent without fear and be strong with perseverance.

Chapter Eight The Scanning of University Mottoes

School motto is a highly summarized philosophy of the school education and learning style, a concentrated reflection of the school–running tradition and educational goals, and one of the fundamental symbols that can best reflect the school's characteristics and value orientation in education. The general definition of the school motto is: For the convenience of discipline, the school selects a number of moral principles printed on horizontal boards and hangs them on the public places in the school for the purpose of carrying forward its ideology and making individuals pay attention to it and practice it at any time. From a narrow sense, the school motto is an important content of campus culture construction, and from a broad sense, it is also the embodiment of the culture and spirit in local education. The university culture conveyed and carried by the school motto is not only an important part of social culture, but also a reflection of the value orientation of a country's education, and the level of educational development.

Section One An Overview of the School Motto Culture

As the embodiment of the school–running philosophy and the spirit of the institution of higher learning, the motto is inseparable from the long–term accumulation of educational ideas, and has been paid more and more attention by education researchers. Since the 1990s, different researchers have studied the relationship between the school motto and the university philosophy, campus culture and moral construction, as well as the educational function of school motto from the perspectives of pedagogy, linguistics and culture. In recognition of the importance of the school motto, institutions of higher learning, while carefully building their own images and improving their cultural tastes, are constantly trying to refine their ideas in the motto, so that it can not only represent the university culture, but also be unique and distinct. Therefore, a comprehensive interpretation of the motto culture is very necessary for us to understand the higher education culture in a region.

I. The Origin of the School Mottoes

Any type of the university is the product of educational culture and environment. As one of the means of school education and the illustration of the educational concepts, the school motto is no exception. It is not simply the result of whimsical ideas, its formation is inseparable from the traditional ideology and educational history that it has always inherited.

1.1 The Ideological Origin

In ancient times, there is no precedent of "school motto" as a word, it is not like "family instruction" in ancient books that has long formed a separate phrase. In the process of the continuous development of educational culture, the formation of school motto is inseparable from the educational thoughts it has always inherited. The ideological source of Chinese school motto is the ethical culture of "family–oriented, human relation based" and the educational ideal of "the world as common community, the world for peace and harmony", and it is manifested in the thoughts of "virtue and kindness" and "harmony and stability". The source of Chinese school motto in modern sense can be traced back, the rudiment of the school motto appeared in ancient times.

Chinese culture does not focus or rarely focuses on wisdom, knowledge and truth that are divorced from ethical doctrines. With emphasis on moral and ethical indoctrination as the main theme, the education emphasizes the ideal personality design of "moral type" and "ethical type", and neglects the cultivation of "intellectual type" and "experimental type" talents. The so–called "knowledge" in ancient China is not a pure understanding of the objective world, but a moral creed and a study of the world on how to settle down and manage the country. The discussions about the objective world in cosmology and epistemology are all based on moral issues. They are based on moral cultivation, with the purpose of unifying the family and ruling the country and surviving in the world. They consciously maintain the social order of upper and lower classes with moral norms. Chinese education emphasizes collectivism and patriotism based on "harmony and stability". Confucian ethics emphasizes the concept that individual social obligations are more important than rights. Under the influence of this concept, the Chinese people have formed a strong sense of responsibility and obligation to the nation and the country, making the whole Chinese nation full of strong vitality and cohesion. The harmonious and stable ethic of collective interests of the country has created a group of heroic figures who are willing to share the country's worries, sacrifice their lives for the country, and devote themselves to justice, and has also cultivated a sense of self–restraining and public service. One concrete embodiment of this idea in the school motto is to emphasize loyalty and patriotism.

1.2 The Historical Origin

The appearance of the school motto in ancient China can be traced back to the early period of classical academy. Early academies mainly undertook the task of collecting, collating and arranging books, and the academy as a new educational system was established in the Song Dynasty. Especially in the Southern Song Dynasty, the conditions of academies were greatly improved and their functions were more complete, forming systematic rules and regulations; therefore, it is possible to finally establish the school motto that reflects its own style, status and school–running characteristics.

In the Southern Song Dynasty, *The Revelation of Bai–Ludong Academy* by Chu Hsi is a guiding document for the construction of academies, which clearly stipulates the objectives and purposes of academy education, the principles for learning, the basic requirements for self–cultivation, dealing with affairs, and social communication. Many school mottoes of later generations are based on this, it can be said that this revelation is a kind of school–running idea, educational purpose or school–running goal, it is the dominant idea of the school mottoes. Later it spread to Korea, Japan, as the school rules and mottoes with its far–reaching influence. *The Revelation of Bai–Ludong Academy* and the motto of "loyalty, filial piety, integrity and frugalness" were presented in the form of an inscription in the lecture halls, set in the walls or hung from the lintel, they are short and to the point and easy for students to memorize. Under their influence, in later generations there also emerged a batch of fine academy mottoes, which is antithesis neat and rich in connotation, and became the prototype of modern school mottoes in China. Although there is no school motto concept in ancient times, the entity of school motto did appear, the word "school motto" is a new term imported from Japan. When the entity of "school motto" was introduced into China, the problem it faced was that there was no fixed and unified Chinese name. After the Sino–Japanese War, the term "school motto" was introduced from Japan, which was a "Japanese loanword returning to Chinese characters". The introduction to this word made the school motto entity in missionary universities and even later in new universities have a clear Chinese title–"school motto". Inspired by the name of school motto and the entity of church university, Chinese ancient school mottoes are transformed into modern school mottoes. In addition, like "school motto " "school spirit" is also a new term introduced from Japan, and appeared earlier than "school motto". After the school motto integrated into the educational system of the school education and was widely adopted and accepted by modern schools in China, a large number of famous school mottoes rich in cultural implications and full of the characteristics of times emerged in China. Since missionary universities appeared earlier than modern universities in China, the motto "Light & Truth" of Shanghai St. John's University and "Unto a Full Grown Man" of Soochow University are the earliest school mottoes among missionary universities in China.

In short, in the history of local education, the cultural and moral information conveyed by the profound and age old school mottoes, which is rich in cultural significance, will surely be integrated into the national spirit as time goes by. The school motto in the modern sense appeared with the beginning of modern education in China, however, modern education began to develop slowly and passively under the forceful penetration of western culture, and there is a top down spreading of the motto culture from higher education to secondary education.

II. The Forms of the School Mottoes

As the product of educational culture, the form of school motto contains certain characteristics and rules. Its form of expression and linguistic features reflect the basic fashion, aesthetic orientation and educational mode of a region or school.

2.1 Forms of Manifestation

The aphorisms in Chinese classics have a great influence on the form of school motto in Chinese schools. For example, in the *Book of Learning*, "To educate people into good customs, education is the way" and other spiritual ideas, with the language expression of "four words and eight characters" have influenced the formal structure of the modern university motto although it was not the school motto in the modern sense. A large number of school mottoes of modern education adopt this form of "four words and eight characters". At the same time, the following three forms have influenced the forms of school motto language in Chinese schools: family motto, couplet and inscription on tablets.

As mentioned in the previous chapter, Chinese society is a "family–oriented" society, and family instructions play a very high position in education. The form of Chinese ancient family instruction has some influence on school mottoes. King Wu of Zhou first used "Ming" to teach his son."Ming" is an ancient style of family instruction, the contents of the admonitions were engraved on the objects for posterity to see, which laid the foundation for the ethical norms of families, schools and society in later generations. The form of "Ming" is more intuitive and easy to understand. It helps teenagers who lack life experience to rise from perceptual understanding to rational understanding and quickly understand the profound truth in it. The family instruction in the Tang Dynasty appeared in the form of poetry, emphasizing neat, antithetical rhyming, so it was called poem instruction. The poem motto is vivid, euphemistic and beautiful, and focuses on educating with emotions and explaining with metaphors. In the course of the development of family instruction in Ming and Qing dynasties, there appeared a kind of family instruction in the form of aphorisms, admonitions, epigrams and song formulas. In the middle and late Ming Dynasty, with the prosperity of popular culture, the new form of family instruction was short and popular, similar to vernacular, and was easy to memorize. Most of the family teachings in the Qing Dynasty were full of profound wisdom and philosophic words, they are concise and comprehensive, but the meaning was far beyond the words. The development of family mottoes from inscriptions to poems and to aphorisms has great enlightening significance to the forming of school mottoes and provides a model for reference. In the same way, the Chinese ancient writing tradition of antithetical couplet has made it necessary to write orderly with rhyme, especially some maxims couplets have a high generalization for aspiration, learning, self–discipline, and philosophical reasons, which is very enlightening to the form of school motto. Especially the couplets in ancient academy of classical learning with a special form, concise and comprehensive, have provided a kind of refined style and writing art, which has played a role that long lecture and classroom activities can not do. In addition, the inscription of classical sentences on stone is also a unique form of Chinese educational dissemination. In China, there are not only stone inscriptions on rocks of famous mountains and rivers, but also on the gates of local government schools, which may have a certain relationship with the appearance of school mottoes in the form of inscriptions. Hanging or posting the plaque granted by the emperor in the form of tablet engraving and other forms, has a significant inspiration for later generations to post the school mottoes and hang it in a prominent place in the school. These forms inherent in our country have great influence on the development of the school motto culture, which can be regarded as the best prototype of ancient school mottoes.

It can be seen that the main form of expression of Chinese school motto is based on the educational content of Chinese traditional classics and traditional culture. It is expressed in the form of family instruction, couplets and tablet inscriptions, and in the beautiful and concise language emphasizing the neat and orderly antithesis, which has become the most vivid symbol to express the spirit and educational concept of the education institutions.

2.2 Language Features

In general, the language features of Chinese school mottoes are as follows: The sound is clear, the rhyme is harmonious, although the majority of the rhymes do not accord with the rules of poetic composition, the whole reading is still catchy with cadence; The vocabulary is exquisite, mostly are commendatory terms, concise and rich in connotation. In terms of sentence patterns and rhetoric, most school mottoes have no punctuation, no subject, no conjunction, but complete in meaning and sentence structure. This is a unique language phenomenon in the school mottoes, which reflects The "triple" thinking characteristics of the Han nationality, which emphasizes simplicity, compositionality and comprehension. Most of the sentence patterns in the school motto are balanced and symmetrical, and beautiful words emerge one after another, which reflects the psychological characteristics of the Han nation in pursuit of harmony and beauty.

In terms of sentence patterns, the sentence patterns of the school mottoes before the founding of the People's Republic of China were basically equal in proportion, keeping the balance and coordination of proportion, except for the large proportion of one word, four words and eight words. Before the founding of New China, sentence patterns and types of school mottoes are varied. The one–phrase school mottoes gradually decreased over time, and were replaced by the two–phrase and four–phrase school mottoes. This is the most obvious in the school motto culture after the founding of New China and before the reform and opening up. After the reform and opening up, the two–word and eight–character school mottoes have decreased significantly, followed by the form of "four–word and eight–character" school mottoes, other sentence patterns of various kinds also emerged, as well as new ones that did not exist before. Such as three words, seven words, eight words, ten words, and even one sentence form with more varieties. Chinese school motto is very rich in terms of wording, it can be said that the wording of the school motto reflects the thinking modes of Chinese people.The tendency of "verb thinking" in Chinese philosophy is also evident in the school mottoes. For example, the school mottoes of "uniting" "innovating" "loving the nation" "truth seeking" "persevering" "striving" "pioneering" and so on all use verbs in Chinese characters. Four–phrase school mottoes, such as "respect work, enjoy the group" "to learn and practice". The five–phrase school mottoes, such as "nourishing the righteous integrity; following the sages in ancient and modern times" "Establishing first–class character, seeking first–class knowledge, and creating the first class career", are all patterns of verbs. Of course, in different period of time, one–word school mottoes are basically composed of adjectives and nouns, such as adjectives like "honest" "simple" "loyal" "diligent" "cautious" and "respectful" and nouns like "wisdom" "courtesy" "justice" "public" and so on. After the reform and opening up, some modern words have gradually become the source of the school mottoes, forming complex language features, with both classical words and modern words. In addition, most metaphors in Chinese university mottoes are inspired from water, land, tool, stone, road , travelling, and planting oriented, which reflects a certain educational cultural cognitive tradition.

In short, the language features of Chinese school mottoes not only reflect the traditional way of thinking and educational cognition of the Chinese people, but also represent the beauty of Chinese phonology, structure and rhetoric. These language features make the school motto culture a special calling card and carrier for Chinese universities to spread educational culture abroad.

III. The Connotation of the School Mottoes

The connotation of the university motto reflects not only the model and ideal of education, but also the epitome of the history of running a school and the spirit of the time. The university motto combined with the connotation of the time can become an inexhaustible driving force for the continuous development and progress of the university. The connotation of school mottoes can be interpreted from its essence and value.

3.1 The Essence of School Mottoes

Since the concept of "school motto " was introduced from Japan, the discussion about the essence of school mottoes has emerged increasingly. Some scholars first ascribe the school motto to discipline and make school motto the target of school discipline. With the deepening of the research, some scholars hold that the essence of the school motto cannot be separated from the national educational policy, so famous sayings, aphorisms or sentences in the national educational policy should be selected as the school mottoes. The further clarification of the essence of the school motto shows that some schools start from their own school–running characteristics, let the school motto reflect the spirit and goal of the school education while making the school motto an important content of educating, and generally emphasize that the school is the subject of formulating the school motto.

In modern times, the concepts of "discipline" and "lecture" appeared in the history of Chinese education. Later, with the development of society, these concepts were replaced by "moral education", especially "discipline" and "lecture" have rarely been seen. With the change of times, the definition of school motto has changed. It is no longer limited to the content of discipline, famous sayings, aphorisms or sentences in the national education policy appear as the motto according to the specific characteristics of the school. In this way, the school motto not only plays the guiding role of the spiritual core, but also pays attention to the influence of external forms. The definition of the motto that elevates the motto as an educational policy is represented by the essence of the motto listed in the *World Dictionary of Education*: School motto is a specific educational guideline formulated according to the legal educational objectives of the national and local education committees, while taking into account the history, tradition, region, the actual situation of students and other conditions of each school and giving full play to the autonomy of the school. It refers to the educational concept involving the formation of moral personality. So far, the essence of the school motto has been further developed and changed, based on the characteristics of the school itself, it focuses on carrying out moral education to the students, reflecting the spirit and goal of the school, emphasizing that the school is the subject of formulating the school motto. Up to now, the academic circle generally regards the school motto as a standard, a code of conduct and a goal of struggle, and believes that the school motto is an ideal state to be achieved by the construction of the school culture, the soul of the school culture, and the reflection of the school–running philosophy and spirit. In short, the essence of school motto is a kind of education proverb which is formulated on the basis of school running principle and according to certain social goals. It is highly condensed to represent the traditional spirit and characteristics of school running, and has guiding, normative and encouraging effect on teachers and students' behavior. In other words, the school motto is the guidance of the school spirit and culture, which has the characteristics of syntactic consistency, literary beauty, motivational inspiration, long–term influence and epochal character.

3.2 The Value of School Mottoes

The value of school mottoes in educational culture is reflected in its relationship with various elements of school culture and its guidance to school culture."School culture" lies not only in the guidance of spirit, but also in the guarantee of a unique system. It does not exist in isolation, it constitutes social culture with other subcultures together, while leading other subcultures, it plays a guiding role to social culture. School culture, as a high–level culture with the highest research level, forms a special structure in the process of cultural inheritance and innovation, which integrates school spirit and individual expression. It is divided into four kinds: material, ideology, system and behavior culture. The ideology culture, such as the school motto, the school philosophy, school spirit, teaching style, learning style, is the spiritual guidance of the visible form of the school culture. The cultivation and promotion of school ideology is the core of the construction of school culture and the premise of the existence of school culture, and the school motto is a way and means of school education, which can be initiated through the school mottoes.

The relationship between the school motto and the school spirit, teaching styles as well as learning styles is like the relationship between course and voyage. School motto is the concentrated embodiment of school running ideology and the soul of school running. It should take the leading position in school work and be reflected through the school spirit, teaching spirit and learning style. In the course of running schools for a long time, many schools have formed school mottoes with characteristics of their own and contemporaneity based on the requirements of the time, school traditions and disciplines. Once the school motto is accepted by teachers and students in the long–term practice of school culture, it will naturally be consciously carried forward by them, so as to evolve and sublimate into the school spirit representing the pursuit of the whole value of the school, form the highest level of the whole school culture, and become the main melody of school culture including the school spirit, confrontation and learning style. The motto of the school is like the lighthouse on the sea and the stars in the sky. It can highlight the characteristics of a school. When you step into the campus, what you see is often the eye–catching school motto. The motto has become the soul of school culture with its unique expression and profound cultural connotation. It plays its unique and great role in the construction of school culture with its invisible impact, appeal and cohesion.

In summary, the value of the school motto lies in that it constructs the soul of the school culture with its unique expression and profound cultural connotation, it inherits the school culture, holds the school–running direction, fosters the styles of teachers and students, carries forward the school spirit, and embodies the high sense of social responsibility and a strong sense of the historical mission of those who run the school. It can be seen as the sublimation of educator's unique value inheritance and eternal personality charm, and it is a kind of epitome of educational culture and a pursuit of human dignity.

Section Two Some Characteristic School Mottoes

In today's world where science and education is strongly advocated, whenever people read a school motto, their spirits will be aroused, and they are all impressed by its precise wording, proper expression and profound meaning. The motto of the school is so impressive and beneficial that it can never be forgotten. Because after several years of accumulation, many schools have formed a reflection of their own culture and regional characteristics of the school spirit, this spirit after tempering has become the school brand and has been deep in the spirit of the school. This section will take representative universities with different characteristics in China as examples and enumerate the mottoes from different regions, so as to show the orientation of Chinese educational culture.

I. Universities in Eastern China

1.1 Shanghai

- Fudan University
  Rich in Knowledge and Tenacious of Purpose; Inquiring with Earnestness and Reflecting with Self–practice
- Tongji University
  Discipline; Practicality; Unity and Creativity
- Shanghai Jiao Tong University
  Gratitude to the Alma Mater and Responsibility for the Country
- East China Normal University
  Truthful Innovation; Model of Virtue
- Shanghai University
  Self–improvement in Whole Life; Contribution to All World
- Donghua University
  Encouragement of Virtue and Knowledge; Inspiration of Motivation and Truth
- Shanghai Institute of Technology
  Virtue; Intelligence; Knowledge

1.2 Jiangsu Province

- Nanjing University
  Unremitting Self–improvement; Virtue Based Social Commitment
- Dongnan University
  Aiming at Absolute Perfection
- Soochow University
  Unto A Full Grown Man
- China University of Mining and Technology
  Virtue and Knowledge
- Jiangsu University
  Knowledge; Truth; Virtue
- Yangzhou University
  Struggle and be Independent
- Hehai University
  Hardship and simplicity; Truth and Facts; Exact Demands; Brave Exploration

1.3 Zhejiang Province

- Zhejiang University
  Truth and Innovation
- Zhejiang University of Technology
  Virtue and Practice
- China Academy of Art

Diligence; Reverence; Comprehension; Perspective

- Ningbo University
  Truth from Facts; Pragmatism in Society
- Zhejiang Normal University
  Learning and Practice; Truth and Innovation
- China Jiliang University
  Careful Consideration about the Country; Meticulous Measurement for the People
- Zhejiang Chinese Medical University
  Truth Seeking and Lofty Aspiration

1.4 Anhui Province

- University of Science and Technology of China
  Virtue and Proficiency; Theory and Practice
- Hefei University of Technology
  Virtue; Knowledge; Truth; Innovation
- Anhui University
  Sincerity and Tenacity; Knowledge and Diligence
- Anhui Agricultural University
  Unity; Diligence; Truth; Innovation
- Anhui University of Finance and Economics
  Integrity and Erudition, Knowledge and Practice
- Anhui Jianzhu University
  Fine Virtue; Lofty Motivation; Learned Mind; Excellent Construction
- Anhui Medical University
  Being Studious and Diligent; Cultivating Qualitied Doctors

II. Universities in Northern China

2.1 Beijing

- Tsinghua University
  Self–improvement; Moral Commitment
- Central University of Finance and Economics
  Loyalty; Unity; Truth–seeking; Innovation
- Beijing Foreign Studies University
  Inclusive and Open– minded; Knowledgeable and Diligent
- Bei Hang University
  Virtue with Ability; Knowledge and Practice
- Beijing Institute of Technology
  Virtue for True Wisdom; Knowledge for Fine Workmanship
- China Agricultural University

Knowing the Hardship of Livelihood; Nurturing the Talents of the Nation.

- Beijing Normal University

  Learn to Be an Excellent Teacher; Behave as a Good Example

- The Central University of Nationalities

  Share Beauty and Value ; Combine Knowledge and Practice

2.2 Tianjin

- Nan Kai University

  We Serve Them and Serve You; the Sun Shines Each Day New

- Tianjin University

  Seek Truth from Facts

- Hebei University of Technology

  Diligence and Prudence; and Justice and Loyalty

- Tianjin University of Traditional Chinese Medicine

  Learning with Virtues; Inheritance with Innovation

- Civil Aviation University of China

  Virtue Helps Build Perfection; Inspiration Leads to Prosperity

- Tianjin Foreign Studies University

  East and West We Explore; For Virtue Worth and More

- Tianjin University of Commerce

  Eradication; Inspiration; Morality; Utility

2.3 Liaoning

- Dalian University of Technology

  Unity; Perseverance; Truth; Innovation

- Northeastern University

  Strive to Be Stronger, Study to Become Pragmatic

- China Medical University

  Firm in Direction and Excellent in Profession

- Dongbei University of Finance and Economics

  Rich Knowledge for the Social Wealth

- Liaoning University

  Virtue with Knowledge; Practice for Strength

- Shenyang Agricultural University

  Unity; Diligence; Truth; Innovation

2.4 Jiling

- Jilin University

  Innovative for Truth; Inspirational for Prosperity

- Northeast Normal University

  With Diligence and Innovation; We Perform as the Model.

- Changchun University of Science and Technology
  Virtue; Knowledge; Truth; Innovation
- Yanbian University
  Truth Seeking; Excellence Pursuing; Knowledge Embracing
- Northeast Electric Power University
  Diligence; Preciseness; Truth; Innovation
- Changchun University
  The Unity of Knowledge and Practice; The Pursuit of Sincerity and Perfection
- Beihua University
  Virtue with Knowledge; Action with Strength

2.5 Heilongjiang

- Harbin Institute of Technology
  Strict Specification; Supreme Skills
- Northeast Forestry University
  Knowledge from the World; Virtues to the Nature
- Heilongjiang University
  Learn Widely and Think Carefully; Explore the Universe and Study the World
- Harbin Normal University
  Stress Virtue and Knowledge; Encourage Willpower and Inspiration
- Northeast Petroleum University
  Work Hard for Career; Study Hard for Knowledge
- Harbin University of Commerce
  Strive for Truth and Virtue; Cultivate for Morality and Ability

2.6 Shandong

- Shandong University
  Knowledge is Infinite; Integrity is Magnificent
- Ocean University of China
  All Rivers Run into Sea; All Dreams Cost Long Journey
- Shandong Normal University
  Great Virtue and Lofty Ambition; Wise Mind and Earnest Practice
- Qingdao University
  Morality; Erudition; Integrity; Excellence
- Shandong University of Science and Technology
  Truth and Novelty
- University of Jinan
  Perseverance; Knowledge; Truth; Virtue
- Yantai University
  Trustworthy and Realistic; Studious and Practical

III. Universities in Western China

3.1 Sichuan Province

- Sichuan University
  The Sea Embraces All Rivers; There Is Room for Greatness
- Southwest Jiaotong University
  Hard Learning; Lofty Ambition; Decisive Action; Faithful Practice
- Chengdu University of Technology
  Seeking Truth; Seeking Triumph
- Sichuan Normal University
  Morality; Learning; Practicality; and Beauty
- Sichuan Fine Arts Institute
  Set Your Heart on the Truth;and Seek the Enjoyment in the Arts.
- Southwest Minzu University
  Cooperation with Harmony; Self–improvement with Confidence

3.2 Shaanxi

- Northwestern Polytechnical University
  Patriotism ; Honesty; Courage; Perseverance
- Northwest University
  Patriotism ; Honesty; Diligence; Artlessness
- Shaanxi Normal University
  Virtue; Knowledge; Motivation; Practice
- Chang'an University
  Perseverance and Virtue; Knowledge and Innovation
- Yan'an University
  Life in the Service of Nation; Knowledge for the Service of Society
- Xi'an International Studies University
  Patriotism; Diligence; Erudition; Innovation

3.3 Chongqing

- Chongqing University
  Hard–working; Simplicity; Diligence; Patriotism
- Southwest University
  Embracing and Promoting; Inheriting and Developing
- Chongqing Medical University
  Preciseness; Practicality; Assiduousness; Aggressiveness
- Chongqing University of Posts and Telecommunications
  Virtue; Erudition; Truth; Innovation
- Southwest University of Political Science & Law
  Knowledge and Practice; Virtue and Law

- Chongqing Normal University
  Virtue; knowledge; Ambition; Innovation
- Chongqing Technology and Business University
  Virtue and Erudition; Truth and Innovation

3.4 Gansu

- Lanzhou University
  Insist on Self-renewal; Aim for Distinction
- Northwest Normal University
  Comprehensive and Extensive Knowledge; Correct and Upright Behavior
- Lanzhou University of Technology
  Strive for Progress; Strive for Truth
- Gansu Agricultural University
  Encouragement of Virtue and Knowledge; Progress in Motivation and Capacity
- Northwest Minzu University
  Diligence; Devotion; Unity; Innovation
- Lanzhou University of Finance and Economics
  Erudition and Cultivation; Trade and Morality

Ⅳ. Universities in Southern China

4.1 Guangdong

- Sun Yat-sen University
  Erudition; Examination; Reflection; Discrimination; Investigation
- Southern University of Science and Technology
  Virtue and Truth; Daily-Renewal and Self-improvement
- Jinan University
  Loyalty; Faith; Sincerity; Respect
- Southern Medical University
  Comprehensive Knowledge; Faithful Practice
- Shenzhen University
  Self-reliance; Self-discipline; Self-improvement
- South China Normal University
  Thrifty Perseverance; Rigorous Scholarship; Practical Innovation; Model of Virtue
- Guangzhou University
  Practice with Knowledge; Update with Time

4.2 Fujian

- Xiamen University
  Self-improvement towards perfection
- Fuzhou University

Virtue and Sincerity; Erudition and Ambition

- Fujian Normal University

  Wise Learning and Hard Practice; Sincere Character and High Achievement

- Huaqiao University

  Knowledge of Eastern and Western; Education for Virtue and Talent

- Jimei University

  Sincerity and Perseverance

- Fujian Agriculture and Forestry University

  Virtue; Wisdom; Erudition; Innovation

- Fujian Medical University

  Diligence; Preciseness; Practicality; Innovation

4.3 Yunnan

- Yunnan University

  Dignity; Knowledge; Justice; Action

- Kunming University of Science and Technology

  Virtue and Responsibility; Knowledge and Practice

- Yunnan Normal University

  Firm and Resolute; Strong and Excellent

- Dali University

  Erudition for Truth; Virtue for Reason

- Yunnan Minzu University

  Knowledge and Virtue; Wisdom for Benevolence

- Yunnan University of Finance and Economics

  Studious and Diligent; Virtuous and Sustainable

- Yunnan University of Chinese Medicine

  Virtue and Harmony; Erudition and Practice

4.4 Hong Kong, Macao and Taiwan

- The University of Hong Kong

  Virtue and Wisdom

- The Chinese University of Hong Kong

  Knowledge and Etiquette

- City University of Hong Kong

  Devoted and Sociable

- Hong Kong Baptist University

  Belief and Behavior

- University of Macao

  Benevolence; Righteousness; Propriety; Knowledge; Fidelity

- Macao University of Science and Technology

Sincere in Motivation; Assiduous for Knowledge

- National Taiwan University

  Righteousness; Diligence; Patriotism; Benevolence

V. Universities in Central China

5.1 Hubei Province

- Wuhan University

  Self-improvement; Strong Mind; Truth-seeking; Pioneering Spirit
- Huazhong University of Science and Technology

  Virtue and Knowledge; Truth and Innovation
- Central China Normal University

  Be Realistic and Innovative; Cultivate Morality and Talents
- Wuhan University of Technology

  Virtue with Erudition; Pursuit of Excellence
- Huazhong Agricultural University

  Study Hard and Cultivate Hard; Help Self and Help Others
- Hubei University

  Ponder with Wisdom Day by Day; Practice with Ambition Faithfully

5.2 Hunan

- Hunan University

  Seek Truth from Facts; Dare to be the First
- Central South University

  Knowledge with Practice; Integration for Application
- Hunan Normal University

  Benevolence and Diligence
- Xiangtan University

  Erudition and Practice; Virtue and Progress
- University of South China

  Morality; Erudition; Truth; Sustainability
- Jishou University

  Honor the University with Schoolfellows; Serve the Country with Career

5.3 Henan

- Zhengzhou University

  Truth and Responsibility
- Henan University

  Virtue Demonstration; Human Centered; and Excellence
- Henan Normal University

  Virtue and Erudition; Highest Excellence

- Henan Polytechnic University
  Understand Virtues and Take Responsibilities
- Henan Agricultural University
  Virtue Demonstration and Self Improvement; Truth Seeking and Hard Practicing
- Henan University of Chinese Medicine
  Virtue and Erudition; Inheritance and Innovation

5.4 Jiangxi Province

- Nanchang University
  Knowledge for Self Renewal; Virtue for Social Benefits
- Jiangxi Normal University
  Meditation and Investigation; Justice and Righteousness
- Jiangxi University of Finance and Economics
  Sincerity; Wisdom; Honest; Perseverance
- Jiangxi Agricultural University
  Unity; Diligence; Truth; Innovation
- Nanchang Hangkong University
  Daily-renewal and Self-improvement; Knowledge and Practice
- Jingdezhen Ceramic University
  Sincerity; Simplicity; Generosity; Consistency

Section Three The Comparison of Chinese and Western School Mottoes

The school motto is not only the soul of a school representing the campus culture; but also the embodiment of a cultural and educational ideology. There is an indissoluble original relation between the school motto culture and the country's traditional culture; which is closely related to its social foundation; religious belief and cultural trend of thought; and is essentially in line with its historical background; historical evolution; value orientation and national consciousness. Due to the differences in history; culture and social environment, the culture of Chinese and western school mottoes keeps its own characteristics respectively, and the value orientations of Chinese and western education are also reflected in the school mottoes. Therefore, comparing Chinese and western school motto culture is of great significance in understanding the differences between Chinese and western educational values and discovering the characteristics of traditional educational culture as well as constructing campus culture in the new era.

I. The Comparison of Cultural Sources

Behind the differences of any cultural phenomenon, there are differences in thinking modes and forms of cultural products. The origin of the difference between Chinese and western school mottoes lies in the difference of educational ideas and the different forms of expression in language and culture.

1.1 The Source of Ideology

• The Ideology Source of Chinese School Mottoes

The ideological source of Chinese school mottoes, is first the moral thought of "virtue oriented" and "kindness seeking". Chinese culture is a moral culture of keeping kindness, namely "virtue culture", with Confucian culture as the main ideology. The so–called "knowledge" is not the pure understanding of the objective world, but the moral creed and the study of the world on how to settle down and govern the country. The discussion about cosmology and epistemology all attaches to or based on the topics of morality. Such "moral culture" determines the Chinese school motto to always put virtue first and serve it with wisdom. The content of the school motto is established around "virtue", such as "diligence" "honesty" "respect" "public" and other words all reflecting moral education, and there are many synonyms of them. Mottoes of this type can be found everywhere. The second is the holistic thought of "emphasizing stability" and "stressing harmony". Confucianism regards heaven, earth and human as a unified whole, and regards "the unity of nature and human" as the highest state. It believes that harmony is the eternal law of the world. One of the manifestations of stability, harmony and holistic thinking is to emphasize the love of the country and loyalty to the motherland, to do "state affairs as one's own, to take the rights of the state as one's own rights, to regard the shame of the state as one's own shame, and to see the honor of the state as one's own glory", thus showing the deep feeling of sharing the country's worries and the determination to serve the country. The supremacy of patriotism is highlighted in the campaign of "education saves the country" before the founding of the People's Republic and The "education revitalizes the country" after the founding of the People's Republic. The third is the innovative thinking of "self–improvement" and "keeping vigorous and capable", which promotes a positive and optimistic attitude towards life that emphasizes the constant pursuit of physical, intellectual, technical and moral perfection.

• The Ideology Source of Western School Mottoes

The Source of western school mottoes is firstly, The "knowledge oriented" and "truth seeking" scientific thought. Western culture distinguishes knowledge from moralism, with morality giving way to truth, everyone is equal before truth. Wisdom, as the highest virtue in Greek traditional morality, has always been concerned by philosophers. Their "knowledge oriented" thought has an enduring influence on the development of western culture and education, and can also be seen as the spiritual origin of the school motto stressing "knowledge" and "truth". The "knowledge oriented" thought laid the foundation for the formation of the later ideas of the universities. The British Cardinal Newman pointed out in his book *The Idea of the University* that "the university is a place to explore all kinds of knowledge". Imparting knowledge and exploring truth are essential features differentiated universities from other places. The second is the religious thought that concentrates God. Western culture can be described as "religious culture". Especially in the Middle Ages, religion was so powerful that everything had to be done under the banner of God. All activities of the university had to reflect the will of religion, even the formulation of the school motto. The most representative one is the motto of the University of Oxford in Britain,"The Lord is my light", which highlights the influence of religions on universities in the Middle Ages and emphasizes "revelation" as the source of knowledge and truth. The third is the thought of "autonomy" and "freedom". For western universities in modern times, university autonomy is not only their ideal, but also the lifeline to ensure academic independence. From the autonomy of medieval universities, we can see the germination of the modern university autonomy tradition. This autonomy and academic freedom have a profound influence on the education ideology in universities.

1.2 The Source of Form

- The Form Source of Chinese School Mottoes

As mentioned in the previous overview, the form of Chinese ancient family instructions has some influence on the school mottoes. The earliest family instructions were inscribed on objects for their descendants to see. In the Tang Dynasty, The "poem instruction" that emphasized order and antithetical rhyming appeared. In the Ming and Qing dynasties, family instruction was mainly in the form of aphorisms, admonitions, epigrams and song formulas. These family instructions are characteristic of fresh, concise and comprehensive language style that is full of wisdom, profound and intriguing. Chinese ancient couplets also have some influence on the form of school mottoes. Couplets emphasize antithetical order and rhyming, in a subtle way to convey serious philosophical and cultural implications. In particular, some aphoristic couplets have a high degree of summary of perseverance, learning, moral cultivation, friendship, social issues, and family management, and rationality, which have a profound impact on the form and content of the school mottoes.

- The Form Source of Western School Mottoes

Christianity is the matrix of modern western culture, and the *Bible* has become a part of western traditional culture, so the western school motto is influenced by the *Bible*. Due to the limited materials available, most people can only speculate that the form of the motto of western universities may be inspired by The "Ten Commandments" in the *Bible*. According to the *Bible*, the omnipotent God issued the Ten Commandments to the Hebrews and wrote ten commandments on two stone tablets. This gives inspiration to the prototype of the western school mottoes, so that the university motto is also formulated in such form of physical objects.

II. The Comparison of School Motto Characteristics

Although there are many commonalities between Chinese and western school mottoes, there are some differences in terms of their language features and content features, due to the differences in ways of thinking and forms of expression.

2.1 Features of Language

The differences between Chinese and western ways of thinking affect the features of the school motto language, which is reflected in the features of vocabulary, syntax and rhetoric respectively.

- Lexical Features

Generally speaking, the common points of Chinese and western school mottoes are: simple, popular, concise and stable in language. The most significant difference is that Chinese mottoes are antithesis and concise in phrases, while western mottoes are free in forms and objective in expressions. Chinese school mottoes are mainly phrasal verbs, most in the form of one phrase with two words, or four phrases with four words, or two phrases with eight words, among which the form of two phrases with eight words is the most popular one. On the other hand, western school mottoes mostly adopt the form of sentence and noun structure, which is free and easy, and pays little attention to rhyme and antithesis, reflecting the western idea of pursuing freedom. Chinese school mottoes predominated by verbs reflect the strong spirit of pragmatism. The western school mottoes, which are more demonstrated by nouns, show more speculative style; Chinese school mottoes emphasize subjectivity and cover more content while western school mottoes focus on objectivity, and its content is relatively concentrated, often involving only one or two aspects of meaning. For example, the motto of Harvard University: Let truth be your friend; Yale's motto: Light and Truth.

- The Syntactic Features

The syntactic features of Chinese university mottoes are relatively simple, mainly in verbal parallel structure and nominal parallel structure. Western university motto structure is diversified, mainly in the following four structures: One is the noun parallel structure. This structure is straightforward, simple and impressive, which is the same as that of the motto of Chinese universities. West Point's motto: Duty, Honor, Country is an example. The second is a sentence that begins with a preposition. Such sentences aim at stating the purpose to be achieved under a particular condition, thus highlighting the uniqueness of the school motto. As the motto of the University of Cambridge says,"From here, light and sacred draughts". The third is the declarative sentences. This structure adopts The "A is B" format, with simple structure, and is easy to remember. For example, the motto of University of Oxford, UK says that :The lord is my light. The fourth is the imperative sentences. This structure takes the form of imperative sentences to call on and encourage people, making people feel friendly and urging them to progress. The motto of the University of California, Berkeley is a typical example: Let there be light.

- Rhetorical Features

In the long process of evolution, the motto language of Chinese universities has been deeply imprinted with traditional culture, integrating the language and form of poetry, couplets and tablet inscriptions. It has the features of being concise and comprehensive, with orderly form and rhyming beauty. Firstly, the motto of both Chinese and western universities tend to be expressed through metaphor, which is the most obvious similarity. For example, the motto of Stanford University is "The wind of freedom blows". The motto of Beijing Forestry University is "Cultivate upright quality of green pine and learn from the character of bamboo and plum". Secondly, antithetical parallelism is the most used rhetorical device in the school motto of Chinese universities, which is closely related to the character of Chinese people who like to be even and stable. Of course, such antithetical parallelism includes not only strict pattern, that is, the number of words, parts of speech, tonality are strictly relative. It can also be a loose pattern, that is, the same or similar number of words, structure, etc. The mottoes are generally in loose pattern. Third, much of the school motto of Chinese and western universities is not often expressed in simile, but it is also reflected sometimes. For example, the motto of the University of Toronto is "As a tree with the passage of time". The motto of Fuyang Vocational and Technical College is "The Highest Good is Like Water". Generally speaking, the rhetorical devices of the motto in western universities are more diversified than those in China. Besides the above–mentioned similes and metaphors, there are also personification and metonymy in the expression of mottoes like University of Washington (Seattle) :"Knowledge brings us together", and Massachusetts Institute of Technology:"Mind and Hand". The use of these rhetorical means reflects the aesthetic law of the school motto language and gives people the enjoyment of beauty.

2.2 Features of Content

There are many similarities in the content of the mottoes of western and Chinese universities. For example, both cultures emphasize virtue, knowledge, truth, innovation, patriotism and so on. Both cultures like to use "big words"."Big words" is a kind of popular saying, generally refers to the language of long words, difficult words, rare words, etc., its degree of formality and register is higher than the general vocabulary. However, the different features in the content of Chinese and western school mottoes also reflect the different cultural traditions in education.

- Content of China's School Mottoes

Most Chinese university mottoes quote classics, such as the *Analects of Confucius, The Great Learning, The Doctrine of the Mean, Book of Changes, History of the Han Dynasty, Mencius* and the *Book of Rites*, and interpret these traditional cultures in a modern way, making the mottoes reflect the light of ancient classical culture in the new era. Therefore, it is reasonable to believe that university mottoes of China have well inherited and developed the cultural traditions of ancient China. Due to the influence of traditional culture, especially Confucian culture, the content of Chinese school mottoes has a strong moralistic tendency of "pursuing goodness and virtue"; the holism orientation of "valuing collectivism and harmony"; the school tradition of "advocating intuitive meditation" and the value orientation of "focusing on the cultivation of the will." When these orientations are expressed in many school mottoes of Chinese schools, the phrases like "virtue" "quality" "unity" "meditation" and "perseverance" then become the most frequent keywords. For example, the motto of Nankai University"The Fair Virtue, The Daily Changes"; the motto of Dalian University of Technology:"Unity, Progress; Truth seeking; Innovation"; the motto of Jiangxi Normal University:"Meditation and Practice, Balance and Fairness"; the motto "Self–improvement, Perseverance, Truth and innovation" of Wuhan University all reflect such cultural traditions of moral education.

• Content of Western School Mottoes

In terms of the source, the content of western school mottoes is mostly influenced by the *Bible*. Christianity is the cornerstone of western culture, and the *Bible* has become an indispensable part of western traditional culture. It is no exaggeration to say that mottoes of western universities have been deeply imprinted with the *Bible* to some extent. Therefore, the mottoes of many western universities are religious, deeply influenced by God and the *Bible*.

These school mottoes demonstrate the historical trace of "pursuing knowledge and believing in religion"; the cultural atmosphere of "individualism and freedom" and the humanistic characteristics of "equality consciousness and self–consciousness". This can be seen in the content of the famous representative school mottoes, like the motto of Duke University "Knowledge and Religion"; Caltech's motto "The truth shall make you free"; and the motto of Harvard University," Make friends with Plato, with Aristotle, and more importantly, with truth", all of which reflect the commonality of western education and culture in the pursuit of freedom and understanding.

III. The Implication of School Motto Culture

The study of Chinese and western school mottoes reveals the general law of cultural contrast: behind cultural products are cultural ideology, behind cultural phenomena are the educational results formed by long–term accumulation of local educational climate, and comparison and reference is always an effective way for the symbiotic development of education and culture.

3.1 The Educational Culture behind the School Mottoes

By comparing the cultural origins and content features of the Chinese and western school mottoes, it can be seen that they have inherited and carried forward their traditional culture respectively, and have been infected and influenced by their respective national cultures, and reflected their educational and cultural backgrounds with different styles. Through the comparison of the sources of the forms of the mottoes of Chinese and western universities, we can see the similarities between the motto forms of Chinese and western universities: All of them are embodied in the form of objects and presenting the content by quoting classics. The school motto culture is promoted by hanging proverbs, maxims, moral instructions, instruction and other language forms in the conspicuous place of the school, reflecting the society needs of local education, cultural roots, education concepts, value orientations and school visions. However, due to the differences between Chinese and western thinking modes and language habits, the school motto culture also reflects the main differences between Chinese and western educational culture: The west "values knowledge" and China "values morality"; The west "seeks truth" and China "seeks goodness"; The west "values God" and China "values relations"; The west values freedom and China values stability. The western stresses "self", and China stresses "holistic intuition"; The West advocates The "opposition analysis" and China advocates "practical application"; while the Chinese school mottoes include a large part of verbs, which reflects the strong sense of normative education and the spirit of the society. The western nominal–based school mottoes have more speculative style, paying more attention to the exploration and internal guidance of knowledge. The reason is that the value orientations of Chinese and western educational spirit are different. The value orientation of Chinese education culture focuses on the realm of mind while the west attaches great importance to religious spirit; China advocates the personality of sages while the West values the search for truth. China advocates community relation cultivation while the West respects individual development; the collectivist virtue culture in China that attaches more importance to "seeking public authority" is derived from the aesthetic realm beyond life, while the intellectual culture of individualism in the west that prefers "seeking truth" is derived from the cultural characteristics of binary opposition. In the Chinese education culture, the value orientation of serving the society and pursuing the realm is obvious. The Chinese realm of mine originated from the philosophy of changing and valued the universality and publicity of the aesthetic value in Mencius' thoughts of common enjoyment. Comparatively speaking, due to the influence of Platonic idealism, Aristotelian deduction, Bacon induction and Cartesian intuitive reasons, education culture in western countries obviously has the characteristic of extremely distinct binary opposition. Duality includes subject and object, or mind and matter. Although "duality" is often separated and opposed because of its interdependence and transformation relationship is ignored, it is the value orientation of western universities and the driving force of science and technology.

3.2 The Educational Enlightenment of School Motto Culture

The Chinese and western school mottoes demonstrate respectively their own characteristics of educational culture, reflecting the school–running philosophy and spiritual outlook. The school motto culture is long–term and inheritable, representing the educational ideal of a country. Analyzing and comparing different educational cultures behind Chinese and western school mottoes can help to understand the differences between Chinese and western educational cultures from a cross–cultural perspective, learn from the essence of the world's first class universities and reflect on the deficiency of our education cognition, which has practical significance in enriching our future construction of school mottoes and connotation of educational culture.

The analysis of the mottoes of representative universities in China helps to find that Chinese educational culture, under the guidance of Confucian traditional ideas, attaches great importance to the harmony of individual knowledge and practice as well as the harmony between individuals and society. This culture even stresses the unremitting self-improvement type of enterprising in order to pursue personal physical and mental harmony, and emphasizes self-sacrifice for the social harmony, this goal reflects the essence of Chinese gentleman's traditional education of following sages and pursuing perfection and the unique Confucian cultural value of public morality. Through the analysis of the attributes and origins of the motto culture of western first-class universities, it can be found that there are mainly four types:"oracle" (religious orientation),"truth-seeking" (knowledge and academic orientation),"service" (social orientation),"personalizing" (innovation orientation), etc., which reflect value goals of development, academy, public welfare and novelty pursuing. Through the comparison of Chinese and western school motto culture, education researchers have seen the cultural heritage and value of each other, and also put forward the aspects of Chinese school motto concept yet to be improved: The similarity of different school mottoes is obvious. The expressions of "truth seeking, innovation, unity and preciseness" are relatively common. The universal presentation of the goal of moral education weakens the personality in the specific goal of education. Therefore, some scholars put forward the direction of improving the school motto culture: First of all, more attention should be paid to human personality and all-round development. Due to the historical conditions of modern times and the influence of Chinese traditional culture, the emphasis is placed on human's social attributes and responsibilities instead of human's natural attributes and personality, therefore the overall development of individual body and mind needs to be strengthened. The second is to attach importance to the educational and cultural status of aesthetic education. Since modern times, the mottoes of the universities directly stress the realistic, utilitarian and meaning of the world, full of "truth" and "kindness" requirements, but lack of "beauty" content. This is not only because"aesthetics" is a foreign word, but also because the traditional Chinese thought of "virtue" puts more emphasis on the beauty of the soul."Beauty" is over summarized by"virtue". The third is to return to the traditional concept of natural harmony. Since ancient times, Chinese philosophy has placed great emphasis on the harmonious relationship between man and nature, believing that man and the universe are born of the same Qi and depend on each other. However, since problems in mordern China are mainly social and human problems, under its influence, the mottoes of modern Chinese schools reveal the practical concept of elite saving the world with science and technology, and the traditional concept of harmonious coexistence with nature is relatively weakened, and there is a phenomenon of "absence of nature". Under the background of the new era, the Chinese humanistic spirit, the value of green mountains and clear water, and the consciousness of sustainable development all have become the important contents of contemporary Chinese education and culture.

Therefore the concepts of : all–round development of people, the humanistic spirit of beauty and the concept of sustainable development of the environment are very important to carry forward in the contemporary school motto culture.

Taking a comprehensive look at the motto culture of Chinese universities, one can see the traditional essence of Chinese educational culture and the development process of modern social civilization. Moreover, it can be seen that Chinese university education is influenced by the real world, in addition to inheriting the classical Confucian sayings in language, the educational goal is more oriented to the world of meaning. With the rapid development of economy and the improvement of material level, with the appeal of "soul keeping with foot pace", the humanistic nature of education has been placed in a prominent position again. Since modern times, universities have replaced traditional religious or cultural spiritual institutions and become the main field for a country to carry out science, humanities and the education cause and to promote the search for truth. However, confronted with the inherent syndrome of modern civilization, many universities are facing the dilemma of becoming higher vocational training institutes. The book *Excellence Without Soul* by former dean of the Harvard College reflects on how schools forget the purpose of education in the utilitarian mechanism. If the educational culture is only concerned with the inheritance of professional knowledge and skills, and the goal of running schools is only to provide professionals for society, then education will lose its original spirit and only produce professionals who are good at integrating themselves into the social system as exquisite egoists. On the contrary, the original spirit of education is to preserve, spread and enrich the cultural spirit of a nation, which requires the vitality of young people and the freedom and courage to pursue the truth. Therefore, while absorbing the advanced technology of the contemporary society, we should not forget to protect the essence of the humanistic spirit of education culture, and it has become the need and call of contemporary education to construct the modern motto culture with Chinese characteristics. In this process, the mottoes of the universities, as the spirit and essence of the university culture, will play an crucial role.